DEMOGRAPHY AND RETIREMENT

DEMOGRAPHY AND RETIREMENT: THE TWENTY-FIRST CENTURY

Edited by
Anna M. Rappaport
and
Sylvester J. Schieber

Published in cooperation with the
Pension Research Council of the
Wharton School, University of Pennsylvania

PRAEGER

Westport, Connecticut
London

Library of Congress Cataloging-in-Publication Data

Demography and retirement : the twenty-first century / edited by Anna M.
    Rappaport and Sylvester J. Schieber.
        p.   cm.
    "Published in cooperation with the Pension Research Council of the
Wharton School, University of Pennsylvania."
    Includes bibliographical references (p.   ) and index.
    ISBN 0-275-94248-1 (alk. paper)
    1. Old age pensions—United States—Finance—Forecasting—
Congresses. 2. Pension trusts—United States—Finance—
Forecasting—Congresses. 3. Social security—United States—
Finance—Forecasting—Congresses. 4. Retirement income—United
States—Forecasting—Congresses. 5. Medicare—Forecasting—
Congresses. 6. Aged—United States—Forecasting—Congresses.
7. Population forecasting—United States—Congresses. 8. Twenty-
first century—Forecasts—Congresses.   I. Rappaport, Anna M.
II. Schieber, Sylvester J.   III. Wharton School. Pension Research
Council.
HD7105.35.U6D46   1993
331.25'2'0973—dc20   92-46552

British Library Cataloguing in Publication Data is available.

First published in 1993

Praeger Publishers, 88 Post Road West, Westport, CT 06881
An imprint of Greenwood Publishing Group, Inc.

Printed in the United States of America

The paper used in this book complies with the
Permanent Paper Standard issued by the National
Information Standards Organization (Z39.48-1984).

10 9 8 7 6 5 4 3 2 1

Purpose of the Council

Founded in 1952, the Pension Research Council is one of several research organizations within the Wharton School of the University of Pennsylvania. As part of the nation's first school of business, the Coucil functions in a bracing environment of academic freedom and objectivity. The basic purpose of the Council is to undertake research that will have the effect of strengthening those arrangements designed to provide the financial resources needed for a secure and dignified old age. It seeks to broaden public understanding of these complex arrangements through basic research into their social, economic, legal, actuarial, and financial foundations. Although geared to the long view of the pension institution, projects undertaken by the Council are always relevant to real world concerns and frequently focus on issues under current debate. The Council does not speak with one voice and espouses no particular point of view. The members do share a general desire to encourage and strengthen private sector approaches to old age economic security, while recognizing the essential role of Social Security and other income maintenance programs in the public sector.

Contents

DEMOGRAPHY AND RETIREMENT

1

Overview

Anna M. Rappaport, F.S.A.
and
Sylvester J. Schieber

INTRODUCTION

Demographers, economists, and other social policy analysts are increasingly focusing their attention on the period after the turn of the century when the segment of the population born between 1946 and 1964 pass into their retirement years. This segment of the population, known as the baby boom, is extremely important because it is larger than any other segment of the population born during a comparable period. The sheer size of the baby boom suggests that it may pose special challenges to our national economy and retirement programs when its members retire.

As we anticipate the retirement of the baby boomers, it is important to prepare ourselves to accommodate the changes that their retirements will pose. We must determine ways so that the workers who will have to support the increased burden posed by the retired baby boomers will be sufficiently productive to meet this burden, while simultaneously meeting the workers' own consumption and investment needs. In order to be successful, we must pursue policies that will enhance the productivity of future workers to the maximum extent possible. This need to improve productivity implies that we must now be investing in new and more efficient ways of operating our economy. This implies that we should look carefully at our current national savings behavior and the role that federal fiscal policy plays in this area generally, and the specific role that it has on public and private programs aimed at providing retirement income security. If we do not begin to address these issues now, the baby boomers' retirement burden will be upon us before we are prepared.

This book presents the papers and comments from the Pension Research Council's Spring 1991 Symposium. It focuses on those issues related to the age structure of the population and patterns of retirement as well as our ability to anticipate how these might change in the future.

The purposes of the symposium and this book are to:
- provide a broad-based and in-depth exploration of demographic and related issues that our society faces as we begin to anticipate the retirement of the baby boomers;
- provide a critical examination of the population and labor force projections most commonly used in discussions of retirement in the next century;
- look at issues relating to the health and age structure of the population;
- look at these issues in the context of the support mechanisms that provide retirement income security in our society;
- consider what potential lessons we might learn from the experiences of other major industrialized economies and societies; and
- provide an opportunity for those with different perspectives to discuss these issues and exchange views.

The participants in the symposium included academicians from a variety of disciplines including economics, gerontology, demography, etc.; government representatives; plan sponsors; and advisors to plan sponsors. The perspectives of both labor and management have been represented. This combination of practical, research, and policy experience brings together a rich diversity of perspectives on the issues considered.

The symposium focused on demographics, the work behavior of older people, retirement, and the benefits provided for retirement. The scope of the benefits covered encompassed both social insurance and private benefits, including pension plans of all types and retiree health programs. Long-term care was identified several times as a potentially important issue, but was not discussed in depth. The international perspective was presented by comparing the United States with five other countries.

BACKGROUND

Between 1946 and 1964 the birth rate in the United States significantly exceeded the rate expected based on trends dating back over the prior century. After 1964, birth rates declined significantly from the levels that had persisted over this "baby boom" period. As a result of the baby boom, our society has a disproportionately large group of people in the same age group. During 1991, the oldest of the "baby boomers" will turn 45 years of age, and the youngest will turn 27. The aging of the baby boom is extremely important from a retirement policy perspective. During their working lives, baby boomers will comprise an abnormally large group of workers, who can help sustain the living standards of a relatively small existing retiree population. During their own retirement, the boomers will comprise an abnormally large group of retirees who must be sustained by a relatively small working population.

A great deal has been written about the aging of the baby boom and the resulting implications for the work force and for retirement issues. Much of this work has been built on forecasts made by various government agencies and by individual research and policy analysts. These forecasts are based on a variety of models and assumptions about future developments in the size and health status of the native population, immigration and emigration, the evolution of the U.S. economy, and the effectiveness of various programs related to work and retirement. Often the analysis that surrounds a particular set of forecasts will probe at some of the modeling concepts and assumptions behind the forecasts, often without a critical and deeper analysis of other inherent perspectives on the future embedded in the forecasts.

There have been significant developments over the last few years and more are projected into the twenty-first century that will affect the composition of our population in the future:

- U.S. birth rates continued to fall throughout the latter half of the 1960s, up through the end of the 1980s. Over the last couple of years birth rates have risen somewhat, but it is too soon to suggest that this might be a reversal in the longer-term trend.

- In addition to birth rates, the overall size and composition of the population will also be determined by net immigration. Future immigration and emigration will be affected largely by a combination of political and economic decisions. The political decisions will be made at the national level in the U.S., and by political events beyond our control throughout the rest of the world. The economic factors affecting the demand for immigrant workers will likewise depend on the evolution of our own economy as well as the economies of other countries that might be a potential source of future workers.

- Changes in the health status and life expectancy of the population will also affect the future composition of our society. Recent advances in health care have significantly extended life expectancy, particularly improvements in mortality at older ages. Further advances are possible, if not likely, in this area.

The future of our economy is extremely important, determining what effect the aging of the baby boom will have on our ability to sustain our existing retirement institutions. Policies that encourage the growth of the economy during the remaining working lives of the baby boomers will lighten the load that future workers will have to bear during the baby boomers' retirement years. To a certain extent, the size of the national economy of the future will depend on our national savings rate, which itself is partially dependent on the structure and operations of organized public and employer-sponsored retirement plans. But not only the size of the economy is important. As the generations behind the baby boom begin their careers, the labor force's growth rate is projected to stabilize because there will be a smaller pool of potential workers to draw from. The smaller population of younger people available to staff the work force may be augmented by increased numbers of immigrant workers, by greater percentages of women in the work force, and by extended working careers of increased numbers of older workers. These changes are not forecasted to solve the problem, however.

The extent to which older workers might help ameliorate the pressures of the baby boomers' retirement on the U.S. retirement system will depend on their physical abilities and willingness to remain in the work force longer than older people do today. The health of older people and its effects on their ability to extend their working lives is a complicated issue. The extension of life expectancy that can be gained from new medical technologies or better application of existing ones does not always translate into an extension of the period when an individual is able to work. And given the social acceptability of older people not working, the availability of formal retirement programs may exacerbate the incentives to retire that nagging physical aches and pains provide to older workers. The extent to which Social Security and pensions will be a factor in the retirement patterns of the baby boom will depend on the extent to which existing incentives in these programs persist as the baby boomers join the ranks of elderly Americans.

DEMOGRAPHIC PROJECTIONS AND UNCERTAINTY

Looking into the future generally yields uncertain results. In a world where we cannot precisely predict tomorrow's weather, or next year's economic performance, we should not expect to predict the exact size, composition, and structure of our population 20 or 50 years into the future. The problem is not one of inability to construct reasonable models that precisely project past experiences into the future. Demographers are able to develop fairly detailed mathematical models that are extremely precise, from a computational perspective. The problem with these models is that they can only extend our past experiences or project our future based on uncertain prognostications about how the future will be different from our past. Still, demographic projections give us a glimpse of the way we will be in the future.

For the casual observer, the projections of what our population will look like halfway through the next century, or even after the first decade of it, must seem somewhat mystical. On reflection, though, it is relatively easy to understand that the majority of people who will be around in 2010 are already here. A baby born this year will turn 19 years old in 2010 if it survives, and most will. A person who is 60 years old today, on average, will have a remaining life expectancy of 20 years; i.e., on average he or she can expect to live through 2010. Today, roughly 83 percent of the population is under age 60. In 2010, current expectations are that about 75 percent of the population will be 20 or older. In other words, the majority of the population that we expect to be around in 2010 is already here. Indeed, they comprise the majority of our current population. So we already know much about the population that will be here for some time into the future. But there are also some things that we do not know.

While the majority of people who will be around 20 or 30 years from now are already here, there is a great deal of change in the population occurring continuously at the margins. New members of society are added by births and immigration. Other members of society depart through death or emigration. If our future birth rates, death rates, and immigration and emigration rates mirrored those we are currently experiencing, our demographic projections would prove to be extremely reliable previews of the future. The science of demographic calculation is sufficiently well developed that the models give us reliable answers. But we know that medical science, environment, and social attitudes and behaviors vary over time, each affecting birth rates, death rates, and immigration and emigration.

Our ability to predict the rate of change at the margins of our populations is limited. We can develop mathematical models that project recent trends in birth rates, improvements in life expectancy into the future, etc. But these projections may be far off the mark if social patterns change or if medical science achieves major breakthroughs in treatments of illnesses such as cancer and heart disease. It is possible that in a short period of time we could add significantly to life expectancy. On the other hand, the potential of AIDS to reduce life expectancy among the general population is not yet fully understood. If this horrible disease (or some other disease) spreads at epidemic rates through the population, life expectancies may show little improvement over the coming decades. The same kind of uncertainty applies to our ability to predict future birth rates. Certainly, birth rates have declined significantly from the rates that prevailed for nearly 20 years after the end of World War II. But over the last couple of years, we have had a somewhat unexpected upturn in birth rates. It is certainly too early to tell if this trend is of any long-term significance, but it may be. And immigration and emigration are both driven by a wide array of political, economic, and cultural phenomena that themselves are not subject to any precise projection.

Our ability to predict the ebb and tide of population change at the margins is more art than science, and shall continue to be so for the foreseeable future. And the artisans who participate in the process of developing population projections do not share a single vision of the directions in which some of the important marginal variables are going. A number of the papers in this volume, and the comments on them, describe the variations in opinion about future birth rates, expectancy, etc. Professor Preston's paper highlights the variation in perceptions about the marginal factors that will affect the composition of our population in the coming decades. His paper also documents the implications of these varying opinions on population projections.

Certainly, the projections done by the U.S. Bureau of the Census and the Social Security Administration have to rank among the most important demographic projections done in this country. The Census projections serve as the basis for a wide variety of policy initiatives at all levels of government and in the private sector as well. The Social Security projections, on the other hand, are used more narrowly for the development of national retirement policy, at least as it affects the largest program in the U.S. retirement system. Professor Preston documents some of the variations between Census and Social Security estimates, and the reasons for believing that either set of estimates might be called into question.

While it is highly desirable that public policy is made with the best possible perceptions, it is also important that it not get bogged down in methodological discussions that cannot be resolved, or that would have little impact on the public policy issues for which they are being used. In regard to the expected increase in the elderly population after the turn of the century, the actual projections themselves are not as important as the burden they imply for the future economic infrastructure. That infrastructure will be woven from the combination of the capital base that exists at that time and the work force that can utilize it. The size of the work force itself will be partially determined by our demographic evolution, but also by health factors determining whether older people can work, to any great extent, longer than they do today, and the socio-political factors which will affect their decisions to do so. The size of the capital base will be determined, in large part, by the extent to which our level of national economic production exceeds our level of national economic consumption in coming years.

Steven Gauss and Francisco Bayo's comments on Professor Preston's paper generally agree with Preston that the best estimate demographic projections made by various interested parties do give different glimpses of the size and composition of our future population. But they also point out that the variation in the elderly dependency ratio is substantially different from one set of projections to the next. It is this dependency ratio that is the most important variable to focus on from the perspective of national retirement policy planners. It would seem that the demographic projections are providing reasonable input for policy makers as they focus on the implications of the demographic shifts we face in the next century. Having said this, it is clear that it is critically important that demographers and retirement policy analysts keep their eye on the changing social and scientific factors that drive the changes at the margins of our demographic evolution.

It is equally important that policy makers keep their eyes keenly attuned to the changing socio-economic factors that will affect long-term dependency ratios. If we are to be faced with an increasing portion of our population living to older and older ages, it is critically important that we attempt to structure our society and economy to accommodate the changes. Similarly, the potential of a larger elderly dependency ratio spells the need for improving worker productivity. To accomplish this, we must take better advantage of the labor force we will have after the turn of the century, which means we should now be investing in new capital and more efficient ways of operating our economy.

RETIREMENT AGES

One of the key issues and unanswered questions for the twenty-first century is what will happen to the age pattern of people withdrawing from their working careers and moving into retirement. How will retirement be defined? Are we talking about a level of work activity, attachment to the paid labor force, or eligibility for receipt of a specific benefit? From the point of view of employers who are pension plan sponsors, it appears that the key issue may be eligibility for receipt of a benefit, rather than complete withdrawal from the labor force, since a former employee may go on to other activity elsewhere. From a Social Security and public policy perspective, activity level as well as eligibility for benefits are important. The interrelationship between the two is also important.

Several of the papers provide perspectives which are helpful in exploring retirement age patterns. In Preston's paper, the issue of the age structure of the population is explored, and there is a critical examination of the Census Bureau and Social Security administration projections. Evidence is presented that the improvements in life expectancy may be greater than projected by these agencies. This evidence implies a further lengthening of retirement periods if current retirement age patterns continue.

The Department of Labor forecasts a continuation of the current early retirement patterns, but the most recent projections to 2000 show less early retirement than the earlier projections. Mitchell and Levine review the performance of earlier forecasts at times when trends changed direction. Generally, the forecasts provided for continuation of the trends, and the forecasts were incorrect where there was a change in direction. Mitchell and Levine suggest that the trend toward early retirement will slow and perhaps reverse in the next decade.

Schieber looks at the social insurance systems and the strains on it created by the demographics. He suggests that the strains of the baby boomers' retirements will pose a much bigger threat because of the growth in potential Medicare costs than because of the increased cash benefits they will claim from Social Security. Biggs suggests that pension policy should move away from a structure of tax incentives encouraging employer-based plans to one that encourages individual retirement accumulations. He advocates more freedom of choice allowing a greater dispersion of retirement ages. He suggests that future pension plan designs will facilitate that end, but Rappaport challenges his conclusions in her comments on his paper. Clark notes that there are parallel issues in Japan and other Western industrialized countries. He shows that the demographic and retirement issues, to which we are only now awakening, are already being addressed because other nations are now experiencing the aging of their populations that the U.S. will not experience until after the turn of the century. Crimmins and Ingegneri look at the health status of the population, and conclude that it is most likely that while people are living longer, their health status is not improving; rather, there is a longer period of limited activity or illness toward the end of our lives.

The various analyses of retirement programs and their effects on retirement ages can be synthesized into a small number of arguments for and against policy changes that will affect retirement patterns in the future.

There are powerful macroeconomic and governmental policy arguments for encouraging later retirement:

- the changing demographics may result in future labor shortages and we may need workers to stay on longer than they do today simply so we can sustain economic growth; and
- it is desirable to reduce the burden on our organized retirement programs, especially those that provide health benefits to the retired population.

There are also powerful social and economic arguments for continuing current retirement patterns:

- people with adequate retirement income security prefer earlier retirement as exhibited in long-term historical trends not only in the United States, but in many other Western nations;
- employers need to be able to use the economic incentives in their retirement plans to manage their personnel needs which do not always correspond with the goals of national policy; and

• the issue of whether or not increased life expectancy will allow longer working careers, on average, has not been clearly resolved. It is clear that treatment of many chronic illnesses might prolong life, but such medical expenditures may not be an effective means of extending the working lives of most of those affected.

ELDERLY DEPENDENCY AND ECONOMIC ISSUES

A concept central to any discussion of the relative burden that retirement programs pose is the ratio of workers in a society to retirees. In an economic sense, the total goods and services that a society has at its disposal at a given time depend on the effort of the workers in that society. While it is possible to borrow from other economies for a time, and to use those borrowings to buy imports, ultimately such borrowings have to be paid back. Thus, over time it is the ratio of nonworkers to workers that defines the concept of dependency within a society. Because younger nonworkers pose a different type and level of burden on a society than old nonworkers, a concept used to define the burden posed by retirees is defined as the ratio of retirees to workers.

The net effect of mortality, fertility, immigration, and the definition of who is dependent will determine dependency ratios. There is general agreement that aged dependency ratios will rise markedly during the next century. In the papers presented here, the discussion focuses on both the potential increase in aged dependency ratios and future uncertainties with regard to these ratios. Bayo points out that the growth in the dependency ratio will be relatively slow to 2010. Table 3 in Robert Clark's paper shows that in the United States, the ratio of the population age 65 and over to the age 20 to 64 population has increased from 14.1 percent in 1950 to 21.3 percent in 1990, and this ratio is projected to grow to 35.1 percent by 2025. For West Germany, the corresponding ratios are 15.7 percent in 1950, 24.1 percent in 1990, and 42.2 percent in 2025. Clark's paper also shows a projected ratio of 42.9 percent for Japan in 2025. Shigeo Wakamatsu's discussion of Clark's paper indicates that population aging will probably occur more rapidly than indicated by Clark.

This prospect of having a much larger retiree population relative to the work force than we currently have is primarily important because of its economic implications for future workers. With fewer workers per retiree, higher levels of worker productivity are going to be required if we expect to maintain or increase living standards over current levels. Professors Alan Auerbach and Laurence Kotlikoff focus on the impact of demographic changes on capital formation. Capital formation in the national economy is financed by private savings, government savings, and net inflows of capital from foreign investors. The rate of national savings and capital formation are extremely important issues within the context of national retirement policy because an expanding capital base ties directly to the productivity of future workers. Generally, economic theories of savings are based on the assumption that individuals or households save during their working years so they can ensure consumption over the years when they are not working. In the context of retirement policy and changing demographics, these theories suggest that the prevalence of baby boomers in their working years should be boosting national savings rates.

Auerbach and Kotlikoff observe that none of the models of savings that they have tested do very well in explaining U.S. savings rates. Indeed their own projection models estimate savings rates should have been rising during the 1980s, while they document that the opposite actually happened. They conclude that the savings decline cannot be accounted for by recent demographic changes in our population structure. While they concede that economists have only a limited understanding of U.S. savings behavior, they argue that their projections are informative for demonstrating the potential of demographic change on national wealth and productivity.

The authors' results suggest that our national savings rate will decline steadily for several decades after the 1980s, and that this will have a detrimental effect on capital formation. With less capital, future workers will have fewer resources to offset the increased burden of the added retiree population inherent in the baby boom generation. Auerbach and Kotlikoff argue that current fiscal policy is causing an illusion of wealth, because accumulating Social Security trust funds are counted as current income without recognizing that they are accumulating to pay an even larger accumulating liability. They suggest that the wealth illusion inherent in current accounting procedures may be leading government, and possibly even private savers, to lower their savings from levels that would otherwise prevail if the accumulating trust funds were being accounted for on a present value versus a flow basis. They argue that the trust fund income should be offset by the accumulating liability in current accounting.

Dr. Alicia Munnell's comments on this paper observe that there are practical as well as potential political problems in adopting the proposed solution to federal fiscal budgeting. The limited ability of economic theory to explain savings behavior leads Munnell to conclude that any effort focusing on demographics as a major determinant of future savings should be viewed cautiously.

While economists may not be able to fully explain savings behavior, they can prescribe various ways to improve our national savings rates. Even the slightest potential that U.S. savings rates might continue at their recent low levels, or worse, that they may decline, deserves immediate policy attention. It is time that we address the fundamental imbalances in current federal fiscal policy and implement policies to encourage additional private savings as well. If we do not address this issue soon, the size of our future economy will be smaller in real and per capita terms than if we do raise our savings rates. A smaller economy will ultimately mean lower consumption levels for either retirees, workers, or both.

AGING AND HEALTH

Health is a recurring theme throughout the discussion and appears in several different contexts. Crimmins and Ingegneri present data and discuss various theories about the health and age status of the elderly. They conclude that there has been no discernible trend in the health of the middle-aged and older population in recent years. The incidence of reported ill-health has been stable while the period of limitation has continued to increase. They indicate that while the decline in mortality has resulted in people with health limitations living longer, people with severe impairments do not appear to be living longer. They also indicate that until it is possible to prevent diseases, there is no reason to expect an improvement in the health status of the population.

Twinney's discussion of Crimmins and Ingegneri's paper focuses on important issues regarding health. He documents the magnitude of the burden of health care costs on large employers and how the change in accounting treatment affects employers, raising questions about how they will manage retiree health plans and the level of commitment they will make in the future. He also points out the need to reconsider what we consider appropriate care, and to reduce ineffective and inappropriate care.

Schieber, in his discussion of social insurance, relates the long-term issues and concerns to bigger picture issues related to medical care. He points out that the U.S. is spending more on medical care than other countries—in 1989, 11.8 percent of Gross Domestic Product compared to a 7.6 percent mean for all OECD countries. He points out the inadequacies in health care coverage, and the fact that long-term care benefits are not provided on a universal basis. The greatest needs for these services are for the over age 85 population, which will be the fastest growing age group.

Biggs points out the relationship between health and retirement benefits in a total retirement package. The Rappaport discussion picks up this theme. In dealing with health in the future, issues related to values and ethics will grow increasingly important and difficult to deal with. As the age-mix of the population changes and as technology creates ever increasing opportunities to extend life, it will be increasingly important to deal with questions like: "When should life be prolonged?" "How should resources be allocated?" Competing pressures from social insurance, employee benefits, and other social needs will not let us avoid these issues.

AN AGING SOCIETY AND AN EVOLVING ECONOMY

Demographic change has a major impact on labor markets. Mitchell and Levine examine labor force trends and projections. The structure of the labor market today is greatly influenced by the declining number of young people who are potential entrants into the labor force. This has led to substantial controversy over whether there will be shortages of workers. Mitchell and Levine carefully investigate this issue and provide perspective for the discussion. They examine several points in the past when there were turns in labor force participation and they look at the projections made prior to and at the time of such turning points. They find that generally the projections missed the mark and the graphs in their paper illustrate times when this occurred. They point out that the techniques used are inadequate to deal with turning points. This leaves us with unanswered questions and the need for further thoughtful exploration to understand the labor force issues of the next decade. The areas where there appears to be a lot of uncertainty today include:

- What are the likely changes in the labor force participation of women at different ages?

- What are the likely changes in labor force participation at the ages where people are likely to retire?
- What might immigration do to the overall picture?

Mitchell and Levine discuss the issue of retirement and predict that retirement ages are likely to increase.

Andrews, in her comments on the Biggs paper, discusses the changing labor force and the implications for pension plan design. She points out that the percentage of women and minorities in the labor force has increased and that these groups have lower earnings. She indicates that employers believe that these groups have different expectations about mobility and retirement, and that some employers will want to establish different types of employee benefits as their work forces become more diverse. She also points out the shift from the manufacturing to the service sector, and the fact that service firms are less likely than manufacturers to sponsor pension plans.

DEMOGRAPHIC CHANGE AND RETIREMENT INCOME SECURITY

The financial security of most Americans comes from a variety of different sources. Social Security and Medicare are the largest sources of income security for most retirees in our society. Employer-sponsored pensions and retiree health benefits also provide significant income security to a growing number of the elderly. Finally, personal savings and asset holdings provide retirees with a significant claim on goods and services available in the national economy.

The aging of the population may take on its greatest significance in the context of retirement income security policy. One of the long-term goals of public policy has been to provide a retirement system in this country that allows people to maintain an adequate level of living during their elderly years. Virtually from the inception of the federal income tax system in this country, pension saving has been encouraged through the deferral of taxes from the period when pension rights are earned to the period when benefits are actually paid. Looking back through the history of retirement policy in the United States and the federal government, one of the first major discussions about national retirement policy took place in 1935 when the Committee on Economic Security developed the Social Security proposals submitted to Congress by the Roosevelt administration. The committee's studies and reports clearly convey that Social Security was to be a base for retirement income security, but there was also a clear expectation that individual workers also would participate in the accrual of income rights for their own retirement. The expectation was that somehow workers should save to provide some retirement income for their own retirement security as a supplement to their federal benefits. There was an indication that the committee felt that employer-sponsored pension plans were one viable option for the added retirement savings that Social Security anticipated. This basic tenet of Social Security policy has been repeatedly reaffirmed by policy makers and policy analysts over the years.

The implications of our pending demographic changes on various facets of our retirement system vary from element to element. Dr. Sylvester Schieber points out in his paper on our social insurance system that the Social Security cash benefits programs will undergo some strains as baby boomers pass from their working lives into retirement. But his analysis suggests that the extra claims on our national resources that these benefits will claim is not so large that they cannot be sustained. In order to sustain them, however, there will have to be some modifications to the Social Security Act as it now stands. The benefits that are currently promised by the program cannot be provided under the funding legislation now in place. But there is ample time to deal with the changes that will be needed to maintain the program, although it would be worthwhile to begin considering some appropriate changes now. Schieber also points out that the current fiscal polices being pursued by the federal government, namely the extremely large deficits, are going to complicate the process of dealing with the Social Security funding situation in the long term.

The prognosis for Medicare is far bleaker than for the Social Security cash benefits programs. Medicare is currently projected to be inadequately funded shortly after the turn of the century, fully a decade before the first members of the baby boom become eligible for benefits under the program. Schieber suggests that the problems with Medicare are part of a larger systemic problem with the delivery and payment mechanisms that exist in the medical provider sector of our economy. Current projections suggest that as the baby boom moves fully into retirement, Medicare claims on the general economy may actually exceed those of the Social Security cash benefits program unless there are fundamental changes in the whole medical delivery system. But, as Dr. Barry Edmonston asks in his comments to Professor Preston's paper, "Can a system that is organized to 'cure' the sick, at considerable expense, change to 'care' for the aged, at a reasonable cost?" To be sure, the changes that will be required will provide a tremendous challenge to our society as we address the issues. But address them, we must.

Some policy analysts suggest that the funding questions related to Social Security and Medicare are not separable. Over 90 percent of Social Security cash benefits are funded through the payroll tax and nearly half of Medicare benefits are funded that way. The projections of the future cost that Medicare would pose if it continues to grow as it has in recent years and is not modified substantially by the time the baby boom begins to receive benefits suggest that the combined payroll tax levels needed to sustain both systems may be beyond the level of political sustainability. In other words, if the level of benefits provided through Medicare is not somehow brought under control, the medical benefits portion of our national retirement program could begin to crowd out the cash benefits portion of the program. This potential raises the stakes for dealing with the underlying dysfunction that appears to have stricken the health delivery sector of our economy. Once again pointing to Dr. Edmonston's question posed above, we need to move toward a system that provides care to the aged, as well as other members of society, at a reasonable cost.

The other major element of our national retirement system is the employer-based and sponsored pension system. In his paper on the future of employer-based pensions, Dr. John Biggs takes a decidedly pointed view that the future of these plans will be predominantly in the direction of defined contribution plans. Neither of the authors of this overview chapter share his perspective. We believe that the future structure of plans will change the balance between defined benefit or defined contribution plans, but that both will persist as important elements of the employer-based system for a variety of reasons that Anna Rappaport, FSA, presents in her comments on the Biggs' paper. Given the tilt in public policy against defined benefit plans over the last decade, it is not surprising that there has been a shift toward defined contribution plans in recent years. But public policy could again change direction in the future vis à vis defined benefit versus defined contribution plans, especially since Congress has never discussed the implications of the shift in direction it has taken in recent years.

It is also clear that many of the personnel management elements that are inherent in defined benefit plans will continue to provide significant value to employers. At the same time, the aging of the baby boom will undoubtedly make defined benefit plans more attractive to this "aging majority" of the U.S. work force during the last half of their working lives than they were during the first half of their careers.

Prognostications over the future tilt of plans toward defined benefit or defined contribution may be missing the more important implications of the current evolution of private pensions as it relates to the aging of the baby boom. Much of the legislation affecting pensions that has been passed over the last decade has the practical effect of reducing the contributions that employers have been making to their plans. The Bureau of Economic Analysis in the U.S. Department of Commerce tracks the level of employer contributions to pension and profit sharing trusts. Adjusting these estimates to account for inflation, contributions in 1990 are roughly equivalent to those in 1972, two years prior to the passage of the Employee Retirement Income Security Act, which was largely aimed at increasing the funding of employers' pension obligations. In 1972, there were approximately 27 million workers participating in pension plans in the United States. In 1990, there were approximately 49 million workers participating in plans. On an inflation-adjusted basis, employers' pension contributions declined every year throughout the 1980s. Today, annual contributions per worker are only about half what they were immediately prior to the passage of ERISA.

The decline in pension contributions during the 1980s is not coincidental. Throughout the decade, repeated legislative measures reduced the amounts that employers could contribute to plans. In measures such as the Tax Equity and Fiscal Responsibility Act of 1972, the contributions were limited through reductions in benefits that plans could provide higher-income workers. Similar provisions were included in the Deficit Reduction Act of 1984 and the Tax Reform Act of 1986. It was thought such measures would wring excesses out of the system without threatening benefits for rank and file workers. But after a while, it is possible that reductions at the more generous levels of plans result in somewhat proportional reductions further down the economic ladder.

The Omnibus Budget Reconciliation Act of 1986 (OBRA86) may have been the most important in a whole series of new laws enacted over the decade. OBRA86 changed the way that maximum funding limits are computed for defined benefit plans, and had the practical effect of moving part of the funding of the baby boomers' pension benefits from the first part of their career to the latter part. There is considerable risk in this approach to retirement policy: employers may not be able or willing to bear the extra funding load that will be put upon them because they have had to delay the funding of these pension obligations. If OBRA86 results in a cumulative underfunding of pension benefits, it will ultimately result in lower levels of benefits being provided by these plans. In other words, the baby boom may actually be facing the prospect of receiving lower levels of benefits from their pension plans than they currently expect to receive. This is a policy not widely understood by the majority of people who will ultimately be affected by it.

The pension funding provisions in OBRA86 were put there because the federal government wanted to raise additional tax revenues without raising tax rates. In large measure, this approach to pension policy is consistent with the handling of the Social Security trust fund accumulations that Schieber describes in his paper. While the growth in these trust funds was supposed to be saved to help pay a portion of the baby boomers' claim on Social Security, in effect they are being "lent and spent", to use the words of the late Senator John Heinz of Pennsylvania, to cover the deficit in the general accounts of the federal budget. The federal deficit is a common thread that links pension policy and Social Security policy. And the ultimate result of the deficit is the underfunding of the baby boom generation's retirement benefits. That is a serious policy issue that few among the baby boom realize, and one on which policy makers are not focusing.

THE INTERNATIONAL PERSPECTIVE

Professor Robert Clark looks at the demographic and retirement issues considered throughout this volume from an international perspective. The same trends regarding population aging and birth rates which are present in the United States are present to a great degree in other Western industrialized nations and in Japan. In some cases, their populations are aging faster and birth rates are lower than ours.

Table 1 in Clark's paper shows that of the countries compared, the United States spends 7.0 percent of GNP on Old Age, Survivors, and Disability Insurance compared to a maximum of 14.0 percent for the Netherlands. Table 2 shows the growth of the age 65 and over population by country; the United States has one of the lowest percentages of the six countries today and this will still be true by 2025, but all will experience substantial growth in that percentage. Clark concludes that "Population aging will necessitate major changes in social security systems in all developed countries." He states that "The likely reduction of replacement rates from social security will increase the need for additional retirement income." He points out the tension between past trends and a likely need to increase social security retirement ages. The challenges in the United States are paralleled by challenges in other countries, Clark says, and the uncertainties are parallel to similar uncertainties. In some cases, the issues are worse in other countries.

Clark then examines five questions related to employer pensions:
- How will pensions respond to changes in Social Security?
- How will pensions respond to higher retirement ages?
- How will pensions respond to further governmental regulation?
- How will pensions respond to the aging of the labor force?
- How will the public and private retirement programs of Europe develop during the 1990s with the continuation of economic unification?

GENERAL OBSERVATIONS AND CONCLUSIONS

As the Pension Research Council was considering the organization of this symposium nearly a year before it was actually held, we hoped to organize a program that would cover the policy spectrum of issues pertinent to retirement policy during the next century within the context of the changing demographics that we face. It was not until the eve of the symposium that we realized we had not commissioned a paper on the politics of our changing demographics and the implications they have for the future evolution of retirement policy. While this oversight was significant, we felt that it was not a fatal flaw in the conference because of the roles that various participants in the conference had taken in retirement policy analysis and development over the years.

Professors Auerbach's and Kotlikoff's paper rings a somewhat pessimistic note on the potential political effects of the demographic shifts that we are facing. They seem to believe that as the population ages, it will be increasingly difficult to amend policies that would restrain our national retirement system. At any time over the next 75 years, we face the likelihood of there being an ever-increasing share of the population over the age of 65. Modifying retirement policy now would minimize the political liabilities of doing so on two counts: Fewer people would be immediately affected than at any time in the future, and it would give the baby boomers more time to adjust to the changes than any future adjustments would give them.

While retirement policy changes now might be optimal from a long-term perspective, our policy-making perspective often is decidedly based on short-term considerations. It is unlikely that we will see immediate changes in fiscal policy that will result in the true saving of the Social Security trust funds now being accumulated. It is even more unlikely that Congress will reverse direction and implement new policies to accelerate the funding of pension plans. Congress also does not seem disposed to take further action on retirement ages at this time. In other words, we may be stuck with dealing with necessary retirement program adjustments only when there is a greater sense of crisis.

As society becomes increasingly aware that its retirement promises are underfunded and underfinanced, there will be a growing clamor to modify our policies. The older members of society will undoubtedly maintain that benefit promises have to be met. But the burden of meeting unfunded promises falls largely on the backs of workers and they will resist the pressure to make up for past promises. In a political context, current policy is weighted heavily against generations of future workers, especially those behind the baby boomers.

While it is easy to be pessimistic about the future prospects of the U.S. retirement system, the paper by Professor Clark indicates that other democratic industrialized countries recently have been able to modify their retirement systems even though they are 10 to 15 years ahead of us on the demographic curve. In certain regards, necessity is a great motivator to enact change. It is almost certain that sometime during the next 10 to 15 years the health elements of our retirement systems will have to be modified fundamentally. Within 30 to 40 years, the cash elements of the retirement system will also require certain modifications. The longer we wait to make these changes, the more radical they will have to be when they are finally made.

One lesson that might be learned from the modifications to Social Security enacted in 1983 is that the burden of the changes was shared among workers and retirees. It may seem that future policy changes will tilt more in favor of retirees and against workers, but that is not a foregone conclusion. Even in 2030 when the last of the baby boomers has passed the age of 65, there will be approximately 2.7 potential voters under age 65 for every one over age 65. Today there is a pattern of the elderly voting in political elections in much greater percentages than younger voters. But we also know that when taxes are central to public elections, all voters tend to turn out in greater numbers than when taxes are not an issue. If the burden of solving our retirement problems in the future falls almost totally on workers, it is going to require significant increases in tax rates. The discussion surrounding the tax increases required to sustain current benefits promised by Social Security and Medicare will be of such magnitude that it is inconceivable that it will not become a heated political issue. Furthermore, it is likely that some of the program adjustments that are in store for the future will entail benefit modifications. In this context, sound retirement policy calls for the changes to be made as soon as possible.

Each year Social Security and Medicare actuaries develop detailed projections of the expected future operations of their respective programs. These are then reported to Congress and serve as a good road map for the planning of programmatic operations. Employer-sponsored retirement programs are also subject to disclosure and reporting requirements, but these are not aggregated in a fashion that keeps Congress abreast of the evolving potential of this element of the retirement system. As we move toward the twenty-first century, it is imperative that we begin to look more carefully at federal policy affecting the employer-sponsored tier of the national retirement system to make sure that adequate accumulation of benefits is possible through employer plans, and that adequate funds are being laid aside to assure that the promised benefits due them will be paid to all future generations.

The collection of papers and comments presented at this symposium suggest that the baby boom will pose a serious challenge to our economic and social institutions. When this group of our citizens is completely retired, it will place the largest retirement-support burden on the working age population in the history of our country and its retirement institutions. The burden on our cash-oriented retirement programs, Social Security and pensions, will grow significantly over current levels, but is somewhat predictable. The burden on our medical-oriented programs, Medicare and employer-sponsored retiree health plans, will almost certainly exceed that on the cash benefits programs, but the magnitude may be unpredictable. As we look at the experience of other societies that are ahead of ours in the aging of their populations, we find that they have found the political capital to adjust their systems to tolerable levels. It is likely that our retirement income security systems also will have to be modified as we move forward if they are to remain viable as the baby boom moves into retirement.

2

Demographic Change in the United States, 1970-2050

Samuel H. Preston

This paper focuses on the future size and age composition of the population of the United States. The impending changes are viewed through the prism of population projections made by two federal agencies: the Bureau of the Census and the Social Security Administration. The successes and failures of the projection programs of these agencies is briefly evaluated, and we consider at greater length the plausibility of their most recent intermediate projection series. Our conclusion is that mortality is very likely to improve at a faster pace than they have projected. Exaggerating the impact of this factor on population size, but partially offsetting its impact on age structure, we anticipate that future fertility rates will be higher and immigration flows faster than projected by these agencies. These conclusions are based upon analyses of recent demographic change in light of broader social and economic trends.

BACKGROUND

Population projection is a mechanical exercise that demonstrates the implications of particular sets of fertility, mortality, and migration rates, combined with an initial population age structure, for future population size and composition. Age-specific mortality rates are applied in order to survive the population forward in time; age-specific fertility rates are then applied in order to project births. Immigrants and emigrants are typically added at the last stage. The procedures are logical and algebraically coherent. They have the virtue of making endogenous one of the most important determinants of demographic change, a population's age structure. Populations with larger proportions over age 50, for example, will have higher death rates and lower birth rates and growth rates, ceteris paribus.

The initial population size and age distribution are usually known with a high degree of accuracy, and vital rates used in the early years of a projection period are typically mild extrapolations of recent levels and trends in reliable indicators. Since changes in vital rates have been relatively slow in the past several decades, short-term projections have performed reasonably well during this period. Of course, uncertainty grows as the length of the projection period increases, and the performance of long-range projections has been less satisfactory when measured by the ratio of actual to expected population size.

The U.S. Bureau of the Census issues new population projections every five years. The latest projections were published in 1989 with a baseline of 1988 (U.S. Bureau of the Census, 1989). The Bureau now makes 27 different projections combining high, medium, and low assumptions about the future of fertility, mortality, and net immigration. The Bureau's latest projections extend to 2080.

The Social Security Administration (SSA) produces a new set of projections annually, each of which extends 75 years beyond the baseline year. The most recent projections were done in 1990 (Trustees of OASDI, 1990). Demographically, three scenarios are distinguished, designated Alternative I ("optimistic"), Alternative II, and Alternative III ("pessimistic"). These labels are chosen to reflect the impact of demographic assumptions on the financial balances of the Social Security system (OASDI), which are closely related to the ratio of persons aged 65 and above to those aged 20-64. Thus, the "optimistic" scenario includes high mortality along with high fertility and migration, while the "pessimistic" one has low mortality, fertility, and migration.

Before describing and evaluating the most recent projections of these agencies, let us briefly consider their track record in making projections. Performance in the past is hardly a perfect guide to performance in the future, but it may point to some enduring organizational characteristics that affect future performance. It has been said that "each generation thinks that its demographic conditions are permanent," and that is a useful short summary of projection successes and failures. When conditions have changed little, projection has been most successful. But the major shifts in rates of childbearing from the low-fertility 1930's and early 40's to the high fertility 50's and 60's and then to the baby bust of the 70's and 80's were not anticipated. According to medium series Census projections in the 1940's, the U.S. population would now number 164.5 million and would be declining (Whelpton, 1947). According to projections in the late 1950's, we would have reached our present size sometime in the 1970's (U.S. Bureau of the Census, 1957). The large errors even in short term projections that were committed on the eve of these demographic turnarounds should interject a heavy dose of caution into these discussions.

Fertility has stabilized since 1974 at a total fertility rate of about 1.8-1.9 births per woman. Consequently, the performance of short-term projections has improved. In a useful review, Grummer-Strawn and Espenshade (1991) show that five-year population projections by the Social Security Administration in 1955 and 1965 had absolute errors in projected population growth rates of 0.25 percent and 0.11 percent, compared to only 0.05 percent for projections made in the early 1980's. The Census Bureau showed similar improvements. Interestingly, the authors show that, apart from projections made in the late 1950's and 1960's, all projections for all projection periods for both agencies since the 1940's have underestimated the size of future populations.

Table 1.   Main Demographic Parameters Assumed in "Medium" Population Projections of the U.S. Census Bureau and Social Security Administration

	U.S. Census Bureau	Social Security Administration
Total fertility rate in 1990	1.85	1.93
Ultimate total fertility rate (births per woman)	1.80	1.90
Year ultimate total fertility rate attained	Begins with cohorts born in 1985, continues thereafter	2015
Life expectancy at birth in 2050 (Mean, males and females)	79.8 years	79.7 years
Life expectancy at age 65 in 2050 (Mean, males and females)	20.2 years	19.6 years
Ultimate annual net immigration	500,000	600,000
Year ultimate annual net immigration attained	1998	1990

Sources: U.S. Bureau of Census (1989); Trustees, OASDI (1990)

The agencies can hardly be faulted for failing to anticipate changes in fertility that almost no one else anticipated either. Their record on mortality projections seems, in retrospect, less satisfactory. During the 1960's and 1970's, both agencies projected mortality improvements that were much too slow (Crimmins, 1984). For example, the Census Bureau's 1971 projection anticipated a life expectancy of 72.2 years in the year 2000. But by 1982 life expectancy had already reached 74.5 years, having increased twice as much in 10 years as it was expected to increase in 30. This projection, and others over a course of 15 years, reflected a slowdown of mortality gains in the 1960's, especially for males. To some analysts, this slowdown reflected the fact that the more malleable infec-

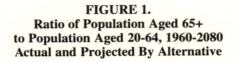

FIGURE 1.
Ratio of Population Aged 65+
to Population Aged 20-64, 1960-2080
Actual and Projected By Alternative

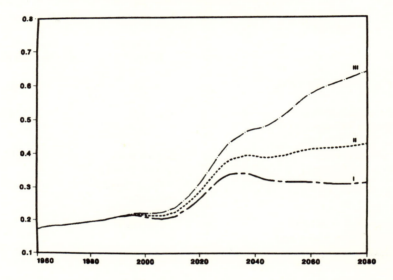

Source: Social Security Administration (1989)

tious diseases were no longer major causes of death and progress against degenerative causes would be much slower. But this reasoning ignored demonstrations that the slowdown for males was primarily a reflection of <u>increasing</u> mortality from degenerative causes associated with deleterious life style changes, especially increased cigarette smoking (Enterline, 1961; Preston, 1970). These changes were, of course, reversible, as the Surgeon-General's anti-smoking campaign demonstrated. Underlying the slow gains in mortality that have been projected during the postwar period appears to be a deepseated biological determinism about the maximum life span. As discussed below, there is little evidence that this concept has been useful in forecasting the future.

MOST RECENT CENSUS AND SOCIAL SECURITY PROJECTIONS

Most analysts use the medium series projections as the agencies' best guesses about future population prospects, and the agencies appear resigned to having these series treated as forecasts. Table 1 presents the main parameters of their most recent medium series population projections.

The demographic assumptions in the medium series of each agency are very similar, which is not surprising since there is evidently extensive communication between them[1]. The slight differences all show the SSA to be more "optimistic" from the point of view of the ratio of persons 65+ to persons 20-64: fertility is higher, immigration is faster, and life expectancy at age 65 is lower. The fertility difference is not a reflection of SSA's having an additional year to observe the recent small increases in actual fertility, since its 1989 projections also included an ultimate total fertility rate of 1.90 (Trustees of OASDI, 1989). Table 2 shows that the difference in the old age dependency ratios between the two agencies' medium series is 6.1% by the year 2050.

Table 2.   Old Age Dependency Ratio in 2050 According to the Medium P opulation Projections of the Social Security Administration and Census Bureau

Projected Population Aged (in 1000's)	Source of Projection		Ratio
	SSA	Census	
All ages	324,790	299,849	.923
65+	70,454	68,532	.973
20-65	179,624	164,592	.916
Old Age Dependency Ratio	.392	.416	1.016

Source: U.S. Census Bureau (1989:99) Trustees of OASDI (1990:88)

In either series, of course, the old age dependency burden increases dramatically. Figure 1 shows the actual and projected ratio in SSA projections done in 1989 (Social Security Administration, 1989)[2]. In this Figure, the medium projection series is that identified as Alternative II. The old age dependency burden grows very slowly from .173 in 1960 to .209 in 1990 and .220 in 2010, whereafter it rises dramatically to .390 in 2030 (Trustees of OASDI, 1990:88). In the space of two decades, the old age dependency ratio is projected to rise by 77%. The nation has two decades to prepare for this massive increase, during which time the relative small birth cohorts from 1925 to 1945 will be reaching age 65.

It is difficult to imagine a figure that is more important than Figure 1 to imprint in the minds of domestic policy-makers. How the nation adapts to these impending demographic changes - which obviously have profound implications for medical systems as well as retirement systems - will affect the well being not only of people over age 65 in several decades of the next century but of all age groups over a much wider time span. Indeed, the preparations already in place, in the form of a rapid build-up of social security reserves, are already affecting in a

FIGURE 2
Age Distribution of the U.S. Population: 1987, 2000, 2010, and 2030.

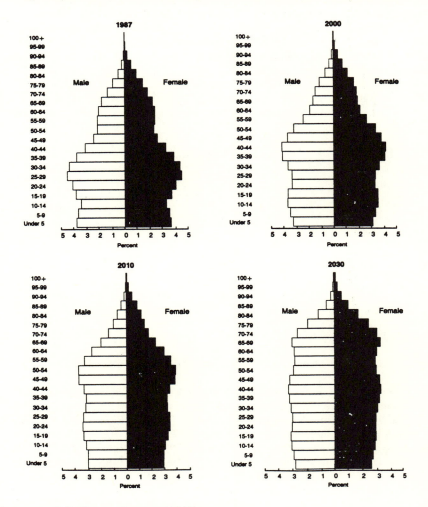

Source: U.S. Census Bureau (1989)

major way the tax rates of lower and middle class persons and the post-tax distribution of income (Congressional Budget Office, 1987). Clearly, the adaptations will also affect the viability of private defined benefit pension plans that are tied to the level of OASDI benefits.

Alternatives I (''optimistic'') and III (''pessimistic'') are also shown in Figure I. The demographic assumptions underlying these alternatives are shown in Table 3.

Table 3.   Demographic Assumptions Underlying Various Projection Series of the Social Security Administration and Bureau of the Census

Social Security Administration
I = Optimistic
II = Medium
III = Pessimistic

Year	Total Fertility Rate			Life Expectancy at Birth (Mean, Male and Female)			Life Expectancy at age 65 (Mean, Male and Female)			Annual Net Immigration (in 1000's)		
	I	II	III	I	II	III	I	II	III	I	II	III
1990	1.94	1.93	1.92	75.2	75.1	75.2	16.9	16.9	17.0	750	600	450
2010	2.16	1.91	1.65	76.2	77.4	78.4	17.0	17.9	18.9	750	600	450
2030	2.20	1.90	1.60	76.9	78.6	80.8	17.3	18.8	20.6	750	600	450
2050	2.20	1.90	1.60	77.4	79.7	82.8	17.7	19.6	22.2	750	600	450

U.S. Bureau of the Census
H = High
M = Medium
L = Low

Year	H	M	L	H	M	L	H	M	L	H	M	L
1990	1.96	1.85	1.76	75.1	75.5	76.7	17.0	17.2	17.5	800	575	300
2010	2.23	1.85	1.56	75.5	77.8	80.7	17.5	18.6	20.3	800	500	300
2030	2.26	1.83	1.53	76.2	78.8	82.8	17.9	19.4	22.2	800	500	300
2050	2.20	1.80	1.50	76.9	79.8	85.0	18.2	20.2	24.2	800	500	300

Sources: Trustees of OASDI (1990) U.S. Bureau of the Census (1989)

The pessimistic scenario has fertility falling to 1.60, life expectancy at birth reaching 82.8 years by 2050, and net immigration falling to 450,000 annually. None of these assumptions is as pessimistic as the equivalent assumptions in the Census Bureau's tripartite series, where fertility falls to 1.50, life expectancy rises to 85.0 years by 2050, and net immigration declines to 300,000. Life expectancy at age 65 is 1.4 years higher in the "pessimistic" Census series by the year 2010 and 2.0 years higher by 2050.

Differences between the agencies on the optimistic side of the ledger are smaller. Both foresee a plausible future maximum fertility of 2.20; immigration is 750,000 annually for SSA and 800,000 for the Census Bureau; and life expectancy increases only to 77.4 by 2050 for SSA and to 76.9 for the Census Bureau. In other words, if we were to replace the SSA series in Figure 1 with the equivalent Census series, the optimistic series would be quite similar, the medium series somewhat more pessimistic, and the pessimistic series much more pessimistic. In 2050, the Census Bureau's equivalent to SSA's pessimistic series has an old age dependency burden of .593, compared to SSA's .506 (U.S. Bureau of Census, 1989:106). The prospect of having one person above age 65 for every two people 20-64 is daunting enough; having two for every three is a pension actuary's nightmare. Under the Census Bureau's pessimistic scenario, the old age dependency ratio of .209 in 1990 would be achieved only if the age at which it were calibrated were raised from 65.0 to 79.0.

In order to provide a clearer sense of how the full age distribution of the population is projected to change, Figure 2 presents the Census Bureau's medium series age distributions from 1987 to 2030, by which time the old age dependency burden has experienced the large majority of the increase projected to occur over the next century. In this configuration, there will be fewer children 0-4 than persons in any 5-year wide age group below 75-79.

There have many efforts to translate the procedures of population projection into the language of statistics. None of these efforts is very convincing because the error structures in projection are exceedingly complex and random error, which the discipline of statistics is best equipped to model, is a negligible factor in populations as large as the U.S. However, several useful attempts have been made to evaluate and model the extent of error in past projections (Grummer-Strawn and Espenshade, 1991). Stoto (1983) reviews medium projections for developed countries and calculates a standard deviation of Δr (the difference between actual and projected growth rates) of 0.28. On this basis, one should expect projected growth rates to be within 0.3 percentage points of actual growth rates about two-thirds of the time. There is little evidence that the standard deviation varies systematically with the length of the projection period. The difference in growth rates between the high and low Census projections to 2030 is .0084, or three standard deviations by this reckoning. This range is much broader than that contained in the Bureau's 1977 projections (Stoto, 1983).

SENSITIVITY OF PROJECTED SSA FINANCES TO DEMOGRAPHIC ASSUMPTIONS

Nearly all projection results of the Social Security Administration are based upon a combination of demographic and economic assumptions. It is not possible to isolate the unique contribution of demographic assumptions to financial balances in these instances. However, the results are much more sensitive to demographic than to economic assumptions because "average benefits rise at about the same rate as average earnings [so that] the pattern of

FIGURE 3
Estimated OASDI Income Rates and Cost Rates By
Alternative, Calendar Years 1989-2065

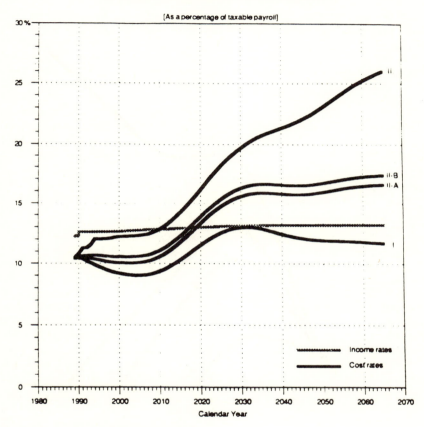

Source: Trustees of OASDI (1990)

annual cost rates is similar to that of the annual ratios of beneficiaries to workers.'' (Trustees of OASDI, 1990:77). In turn, the Report notes, the ratio of beneficiaries to workers is very closely related to the age structure of the population.

Figure 3 presents the time series of annual cost rates and income rates that are scheduled in law under the optimistic, medium, and pessimistic scenarios. The income rate is defined as the combined OASDI employer-employee contribution rate scheduled in the law, plus the income from taxation of benefits, expressed as a percentage of taxable payroll. The annual cost rate is simply the annual outgo

FIGURE 4
Estimated Contingency Fund Ratios, For OASI and DI
Trust Funds Combined, Calendar Years 1989-2065

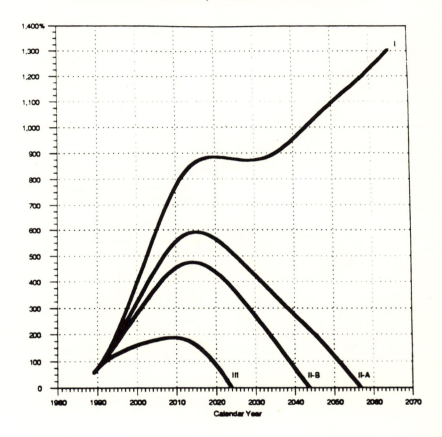

Source: Trustees of OASDI (1990)

expressed as a percentage of taxable payroll. Since the income rate differs very little among the scenarios, only one rate is presented on the Figure (Scenario II B). Note that income from interest is not included in the income rate. Alternatives II A and II B are based upon the medium demographic projections and differ only in economic assumptions.

Because of their close connection, the general configuration of the time series of annual cost rates is clearly very similar to that of the time series of old age dependency rates shown in Figure 2. Under the medium series (II B), the annual deficit (the difference between income rate and cost rate) is 3.16% by 2030 and

3.54% by 2050. Under the pessimistic scenario, the deficits are 6.42% and 9.61% in these years and under the optimistic one, .01 and -1.03% (i.e., a surplus) (Trustees of OASDI, 1990:67-8). These results suggest very considerable uncertainty in the future financial balances of the social security system, an uncertainty that is largely tied to the nation's unpredictable demography.

Figure 4 shows the level of the Trust Fund balance under these three scenarios at different points in time.

Which of the three demographic elements contributes most to this uncertainty? If we accept as reasonable the ranges for the three variables provided in Social Security projections, then future mortality is the greatest source of uncertainty, followed by fertility; variation in immigration levels appears to have little effect on future social security balances.

Table 4 presents the impact of substituting the pessimistic for the optimistic levels of a demographic variable on the actuarial balance of OASDI over three projection periods. These figures include the full effect of interest payments earned by the trust fund. In evaluating the effects of changing one demographic variable, the other two demographic variables are always set at their medium values and economic variables at their level in projection II-B.

Table 4.   Effect of Varying Demographic Assumptions on the Actuarial Balance* of OASDI in Different Projection Periods from 1990

Variable for Which Pessistic Assumption Is Substituted for Optimistic	Projection Period		
	25 Years	50 Years	75 Years
Mortality	-0.32	-0.85	-1.45
Fertility	0.05	-0.22	-0.99
Immigration	-0.08	-0.16	-0.19

Source: Trustees of OASDI (1990:103-06)
*Actuarial balance is the difference between OASDI income and cost rates over the period shown. The initial trust fund balance is included in income, as well as interest payments derived from the trust fund. The balance is expressed as a percentage of taxable payroll.

According to Table 4, financial balances are most strongly influenced by the assumed level of mortality, whether the projection period is 25, 50, or 75 years. For the first fifty years, mortality variation has at least four times the impact of variation in either of the other series. Fertility change is slow to affect balances because there is an average lag of about 20 years before a change in the number of births affects the size of the labor force. Within the longer projection horizon, however, fertility differences have a very sizable impact (1% of the entire 75-year payroll) on actuarial balances. More than three-quarters of this long-term effect is expressed in the period between 50 and 75 years from baseline.

Changes in immigration have slightly larger impacts than changes in fertility in the short term, but their long-term impact is minor. The more advantageous long-term effect of high fertility than of high immigration on the actuarial balance reflects in part the fact that additional births have a lifetime to contribute to social security before drawing benefits, whereas most immigrants enter part of the way through their working lives. The ages of immigrants was not an important factor in the discussions surrounding the two recent revisions of immigration laws and probably deserves more consideration than it has received.

Simulations of differing economic scenarios show that, over the 75-year projection period, none of the economic variables has as large an impact on the actuarial balance of OASDI as mortality. These variables include rates of growth in real wages (0.8% vs. 2.2%), the rate of inflation (2.0% vs. 6.0%), real interest rates (1.0% vs. 3.0%), and disability rates. Obviously, the outcome of these sensitivity analyses depends on the range of variables that is chosen for simulation purposes. There is no guarantee that these ranges are equivalent from variable to variable (e.g., represent similar confidence intervals). In this connection, however, it is worth noting that the SSA's range in making mortality projections is much narrower than that of the Census Bureau. By 2050, life expectancies at birth in the high and low Census projections differ by 8.1 years, compared to a difference of only 5.4 years in SSA projections (Table 3). The ranges of life expectancy at age 65 are somewhat more similar at 6.0 years (Census) and 4.5 years (SSA).

These results suggest that long-term social security balances are more sensitive to uncertainty about the future course of mortality than to that involving any other demographic or economic variable. This result applies even though range of uncertainty in mortality used in these calculations by the Social Security Administration is substantially less than that assumed by the Census Bureau. In the next sections, we review research and data on each of the three demographic variables in order to assess the plausibility of their projected levels, as well as of the uncertainty attached to those levels. Rather than attempting to be a one-man band in competition with two orchestras, I will try to play the role of an independent critic reviewing particular performances. I will take variables in the order of their effects on social security balances: mortality, fertility, and immigration.

THE FUTURE COURSE OF MORTALITY

Life expectancy at birth has risen to 74.9 years in 1988 from a level of 68.2 in 1950, 69.7 in 1960, 70.8 in 1970, and 73.7 in 1980 (U.S. National Center for Health Statistics 1991a). Trends in life expectancy at age 65 are much less certain because of problems of age misstatement at older ages in a country where the Birth Registration Area was not national in scope until 1933. "Official" life tables constructed by the National Center for Health Statistics show life expectancies at age 65 of 13.8, 14.4, 15.0, 16.5, and 16.9 years for 1950, 1960, 1970,

1980, and 1988. Because 79.1% of births survive to age 65 under the 1988 life tables, any substantial improvements in life expectancy in the future will have to result principally from declining mortality above age 65.

It is clear from the figures cited above that mortality in the postwar period fell most rapidly during the 1970's. Reasons for the exceptional performance during this period are not firmly established. Perhaps the most plausible explanation is the expanded use of drugs to treat hypertension, although many other factors undoubtedly contributed. One of these is the introduction of Medicare in the late 1960's. Interestingly, there is no visible notch in age-specific rates of mortality decline during this period at age 65, although use of model life tables to provide a ''standard'' against which to gauge progress does reveal a notch at ages 65-69 for women (Preston, 1984). In any event, the very rapid declines in the late 60's and 1970's have not continued into the 1980's.

Does this slower progress mean that we are finally approaching a genetically-endowed life span that has been hypothesized for millennia? A variety of evidence suggests that the answer is negative, or at least calls into question the utility of the life span concept.

A. International evidence

Himes, Preston, and Condran (1990) reviewed mortality trends by single year of age for persons aged 40 and above in 16 developed countries over the period 1950-85. They applied a rigorous data quality filter to age-specific death rates, requiring that cohort size match very closely from one census to the next after allowance for intercensal deaths (Condran, Himes, and Preston, 1991). They found that the array of filtered data (which did not include any from the United States) could be efficiently represented through the following formula:

$$\log \frac{{}_1M^i_x}{1-{}_1M^i_x} = A_i + B_i \log \frac{{}_1M^s_x}{1-{}_1M^s_x} ,$$

where ${}_1M^i_x$ = death rate at age x to x+1 in country-period combination i

${}_1M^i_x$ = death rate at age x to x+1 in the standard mortality function estimated on the entire data set

A_i, B_i = parameters representing, respectively, the level and slope of mortality in country-period combination i

If mortality rates were approaching their biological minimum at very old ages, one would expect that the slope term, B, would rise for a particular country over time, reflecting larger mortality declines at younger ages. Perhaps surprisingly, the B term has actually fallen systematically in 10 of 15 countries for females and in 9 of 15 for males (Himes, Preston, and Condran, 1990). It was essentially unchanged in 3 other countries for women and one other country for men.

A more straightforward demonstration of old age mortality declines is supplied by James Vaupel (1991). Using the excellent vital registration data for Sweden, he simply plots the registered death rates at age 90 for each calendar year between 1895 and 1985. Results are presented in Figure 5. Lines fit to these data have a slope of - .0046 from 1895 to 1987 and of -.0109 for the subperiod 1946-87. Over the past four decades, mortality at age 90 has declined at a rate of about 1% per year. Similar trends are exhibited at other very high ages in Sweden. One of the factors undoubtedly at work in the Swedish data is that more recent cohorts of 90-year olds were exposed to a lower burden of infectious disease in childhood. Tuberculosis was a particularly important cause of disease and death in Sweden (and the U.S.) at the turn of the century and left its imprint on a cohort's entire mortality history (Hobcraft et al., 1982). Today's 90-year olds were born in 1900, when the U.S. had a life expectancy of about 49 years and an exceptionally heavy burden of infectious diseases (Preston and Haines, 1991). As macro and micro disease environments improved, children developed better physiques and were less scarred by the sequelae of infection. These improvements were more or less continuous through 1950; children born that year will not reach age 90 for another half-century.

B. Mortality Trends in the United States

There is a vast literature on the subject indicated by this heading. We will focus on a single recent study that is most pertinent to mortality forecasting. Lee and Carter (1990) examine age specific mortality changes in the United States from 1900 to 1989. After experimenting with alternative models, they find one exceptionally parsimonious model that fits the data remarkably well:

$$\ln M(x,t) \quad = \quad a_x + k(t)\, b_x, \text{ where}$$

$$M(x,t) \quad = \quad \text{death rate at age x in period t}$$

a_x, b_x =   parameters representing, respectively, the shape of the age pattern of mortality and shape of the age pattern of mortality change

$k(t)$ =   level of mortality in period t

This model accounts for 92.7% of the within age-group variance in death rates from 1900 to 1989. The age-pattern of a_x's is, of course, U-shaped and the age-pattern of b_x's is declining from age 1 to 60, whereafter it is approximately constant. Remarkably, the time pattern of $k(t)$ has been highly linear during the entire course of the twentieth century, as shown in Figure 6. During the entire period 1900-1989, $k(t)$ fell at a rate of .365 per year; from 1980 to 1989, the rate of decline was .363.

Lee and Carter show that forecasts of life expectancy at birth in 1989 that are based on a linear extrapolation of $k(t)$ from its values during 1900-44, or during

FIGURE 5
Trends in Natural Log of Death Rate at Age 90 in Sweden

Source: Vaupel (1991)

1933 to 1962, were accurate to within one-fifth of a year of life expectancy. They also show that forecasts of life expectancy based upon k(t) have less than half as wide a confidence interval as those based directly upon the life expectancy series (using auto-regressive moving average methods).

Having found a level of mortality parameter whose behavior has been highly stable and predictable over nine decades (apart from the influenza epidemic of 1918-19), Lee and Carter then use this parameter to forecast future age-specific death rates and life expectancy. Their estimates for selected dates and ages are:

Year	Life Expectancy at Birth		Life Expectancy at age 65	
	Lee and Carter	SSA Medium	Lee and Carter	SSA Medium
2010	79.04	77.4	18.89	16.9
2030	81.84	78.6	20.61	17.9
2050	84.34	79.7	22.31	18.8

They do not provide a complete series of confidence intervals but note that the 95% confidence interval for life expectancy at birth in 2038 is 6.4 years and in 2065, 6.8 years. Thus, the Social Security Administration's medium life expectancy estimate by 2050 falls outside Lee and Carter's 95% confidence interval. SSA's "high" life expectancy series is within the 95% confidence interval but, at 82.8 years in 2050, is still 1.5 years below Lee and Carter's forecast. The Census Bureau's high life expectancy series exceeds Lee and Carter's forecasts by 0.7 to 1.7 years over this projection period.

FIGURE 6
Comparison of Mortality Forecasts to 2065, from 1900-1989
(dots) and from 1933-1989 (solid), with 95% confidence band.

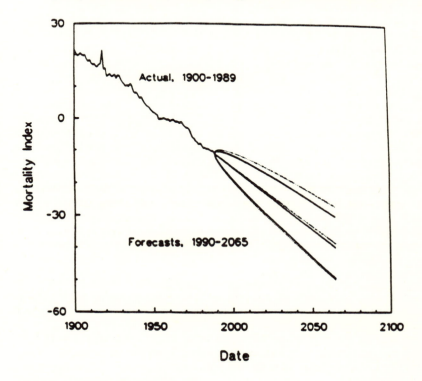

Source: Lee and Carter (1990)

A weakness of Lee and Carter's analysis is that it does not distinguish between male and female mortality. Nevertheless, it is the most sophisticated and convincing statistical model for mortality forecasting that has been developed to date. Alho (forthcoming) concludes that statistical time series models have outperformed forecasts based upon "expert opinion" in the past, and SSA's forecasts are partly based upon such opinions.

C. Attempts to infer biological limits to the life span

Several analysts have proposed that individuals are genetically endowed with a maximum life span that would be realized in an optimal environment. The research of Hayflick (1965), which suggest that the number times a human cell can divide is strictly limited, provides an intuitive basis for this hypothesis. So does the accretion of morbid conditions with age in most elderly people. Fries (1980, forthcoming) has been the most outspoken proponent of the limited life span hypothesis, placing the mean of genetically endowed life spans at 85 years with a standard deviation (in his most recent estimate) of 7 years. The rate of mortality improvement is expected to slow down sharply as this biological limit is approached. Recently, Olshansky et al. (1990) published a well- publicized article in <u>Science</u> that appeared to endorse the 85-year limit. The only justification for this limit in the article is that, without a medical breakthrough that slowed the rate of aging (which they considered likely to occur), the changes in age - or cause - specific mortality that are required for life expectancy to exceed 85 years are "implausible".

The "compression" of ages at death predicted by Fries as the U.S. population approaches its genetically endowed life span has not been observed empirically (Manton, et al., forthcoming; Olshansky et al., 1990). Manton (1990) notes that Hayflick's experiments, combined with the rate of cell division in humans, are consistent with a life span of 200-300 years. In a series of papers, Manton (1990, 1991, forthcoming) has attempted to predict what life expectancies would be if people changed their health behaviors in optimal ways. These efforts rely upon data for participants in the Framingham study, Alameda County members of an HMO whose health habits have been carefully tracked, Mormon high priests, Seventh Day Adventists, and Harvard alumni. The effort requires some estimate of how relative mortality rates would change at the very old ages as a result of the adoption of healthy habits, since there are typically very few observations at these ages. Using either quite simple assumptions or complex stochastic models, Manton typically finds life expectancies in the 90's or even low 100's for both men and women if optimal life styles are adopted.

These are, of course, not projections. They are indications of what could be accomplished using existing medical techniques and epidemiologic knowledge. To convert them into projections, they would have to be combined with assumptions about how rapidly health habits will change. Recent changes have certainly been in a healthy direction. Since the 1950's, per capita tobacco consumption has declined by 40%, saturated fat consumption has declined by more than a third, seat-belt use is increasing, and at least 30 million Americans regularly practice aerobic exercise (Fries, forthcoming). Yet there is also potential for considerable additional improvement; for example, the U.S. still ranks high on cigarette and saturated fat consumption by European standards.

The calculations of Manton and others call into question whether 85 years is in any way a useful estimate of the maximum average life span. Nor has a biological theory of aging or life span emerged that has gained much currency among specialists. The editor of a recent volume where many of these issues are considered comments that there appear to be as many theories of aging as there are gerontologists (Johansson, forthcoming). Undoubtedly, the risks of death rise (roughly) exponentially with age and will continue to do so; but that statement alone tells us absolutely nothing about future life expectancies. Such a pattern could also be observed in a population with a life expectancy of 150. The rate of aging parameter in Gompertz' exponential model has declined in recent cohorts in Sweden and the United States (Manton, 1990). Many of the processes that once appeared to be an inevitable part of senescence (e.g., Alzheimer's) now appear to be specific disease entities whose incidence or fatality is potentially alterable. According to some analysts, a surprising number of these processes may be a result of earlier viral infections (Rose, forthcoming).

The most explicit test of the utility of the genetically-endowed life span hypothesis has been conducted by Vaupel (1991). Using data on Danish twins, he asks whether their mortality risks at the very high ages are more similar to one another's than those of randomly-chosen pairs of individuals from different sibships. The answer is negative. Twins do share common mortality risks throughout life, but there is no indication that the similarity is greater at very high ages in a way that would suggest that they shared a common genetically-endowed life span.

We conclude that the hypothesis of a genetically endowed life span has weak theoretical and empirical support in the present state of knowledge and lacks utility for mortality forecasting. In the absence of such a hypothesis, the best guide to future mortality prospects is what has happened in the recent past, and whether it is reasonable to suppose that similar influences will be operative in the future. Lee and Carter (1990) have provided the most convincing statistical summary of trends in American mortality. As to the future, we expect that research on risk factors in disease and death will continue to bear fruit and that individuals will continue to take advantage of this information in their daily practices. It also seems likely that medical technologies will continue to advance in ways that keep individuals with a certain level of morbid pathology alive for longer periods. This latter expectation could prove incorrect if society decides that the accumulation of morbid conditions in the population that it implies is too heavy a price to pay for the extension of individual lives. Even in the absence of additional life extending technologies, however, there is evidently ample scope for additional preventative measures to increase life expectancy.

The diffusion of preventative measures seems likely to affect sex differences in mortality. Ingrid Waldron (1986) reviewed twelve epidemiologic studies and concluded that about one-half of the difference in age-specific death rates between males and females over the age interval 40-80 in the United States was attributable to the higher prevalence of smoking among men. Recent surveys suggest that men are abandoning the habit more rapidly than women. It is noteworthy that, for the first time in the twentieth century, sex differences in life expectancy at birth have narrowed in the 1980's. Between 1979-81 and 1988, official NCHS life tables show that males gained 1.4 years in life expectancy at birth, compared to 0.7 years for females (U.S. National Center for Health Statistics, 1991a:13). At age 50, males gained 1.0 years of life expectancy and females 0.3. It seems reasonable to expect that this narrowing will continue as men and women approach greater equality in the distribution of risk factors. Certainly, there is greater potential for behavioral changes to improve the mortality of men. In this regard, it is surprising that the sex difference in life expectancy at birth in 1988 of 6.8 years is expected to increase to 6.9 years by 2050 in the Census medium series and to decline only to 6.5 years in the Social Security Administration's.

The AIDS epidemic will undoubtedly slow the progress of life expectancy through the 1990's. The epidemic has not progressed as rapidly as had been feared, largely, it appears, because of rapid behavioral changes (National Research Council, 1989:132). In any event, the age distribution of deaths from the disease is such that it has relatively little long-term impact on the ratio of population aged 65+ to that aged 20-64[3]. Therefore, the epidemic does not appear to have major implications for social security balances. It is, however, clearly on its way to becoming one of the many disease processes that are highly concentrated among the black population (McDaniel, 1990).

In short, it appears that the Census Bureau has adopted a more plausible range of future life expectancies than the Social Security Administration. The medium series for both agencies are very similar and project less than half of the improvement in life expectancy at birth by 2050 than do Lee and Carter (1990). This latter study provides an excellent representation of the past and a sound basis for projecting into the future. Of course, structural differences may render the past a poor guide to the future. The most plausible such difference would be genetically-endowed limit to the life span that is rapidly being approached by population averages. Despite its intuitive appeal, this concept has not proven useful in interpreting data on old age mortality. Furthermore, epidemiologic studies suggest that, if such a limit exists, its average value is probably 10- 20 years beyond the current life expectancy at birth.

THE FUTURE COURSE OF FERTILITY

The most unpredictable component of population projection is fertility. Period total fertility rates (representing the average number of children who would be born to a hypothetical cohort of women subject to the age-specific fertility rates of a particular time period) have been highly volatile in the United States during the 20th century about a slowly declining trend. The completed fertility levels of actual cohorts of women have been substantially less volatile.

Following Norman Ryder, it is customary to divide period fertility levels into a timing component (reflecting when cohorts bear their children) and a volume component (reflecting how many children cohorts will actually bear). Because timing shifts have exaggerated the variability in period total fertility rates, cohort fertility rates provide a firmer basis for long-term population projection than do period fertility rates. Table 5 presents a series of cohort fertility rates prepared by Ryder for cohorts born in the 20th century. The series begins at a level of 2.44, meanders up to a peak of 3.20, and declines to a level of 1.92. In contrast, the period total fertility rate peaked at 3.68 in 1957 and was below 1.85 for all years from 1974 to 1986 (Preston, 1986; U.S. National Center for Health Statistics, 1990). The latest available period total fertility rate is 1.93 for 1988 (NCHS, 1990). However, the number of births increased from 3,909,000 in 1988 to 4,179,000 in 1990 (NCHS, 1991b). The increase of 6.9% in births was accompanied by an increase in the number of women of reproductive age of 2.6%, so it appears that fertility rates rose by about 4.2% between 1988 and 1990. If so, the period total fertility rate for 1990 was 2.01. This rate exceeds that for 1990 in any of the projection series of SSA or the Census Bureau.

The very low period total fertility rates of 1974-1986 were partly a product of delays in childbearing, especially of the first birth. The percentage of women aged 25-29 who were childless grew from 30.8 in 1976 to 39.3 in 1987 (U.S. Bureau of the Census, 1988). Yet birth expectations were quite stable over this period at about 2.1 births per woman, and expected childlessness was constant at 10% for women aged 18-34 (Ibid.: 9).

Table 5.   Mean Number of Children Born to Cohorts of American Women During the Twentieth Century

Year of Birth	Cohort Total Fertility Rate	Percentage of Marital Births That Were Unintended
1901-05	2.442	16.3
1906-10	2.286	12.9
1911-15	2.354	12.6
1916-20	2.574	12.1
1921-25	2.857	14.3
1926-30	3.079	18.9
1931-35	3.201	17.2
1936-40	2.950	15.2
1941-45	2.470	11.9
1946-50	2.108*	10.7
1951-55	1.920*	8.5

*Partial projection
Source: Ryder (1986)

In periods when successive cohorts of women are moving to later ages of childbearing, as has occurred in the past 15 years, period total fertility rates will be artificially depressed relative to cohort rates. To understand this more clearly, imagine that all cohorts of women have two births and all of their births occur at one particular age. If cohorts born prior to 1950 had all of their births at age 28 and cohorts born in 1950 and beyond had all of their births at age 30, then the period total fertility rate would be 2.0 for all years except 1978 and 1979, when they would be 0.0. In order for period fertility levels to rise, it is not necessary for successive cohorts to have their births at younger ages (though this would have the expected effect), only that the ages of childbearing stop increasing.

The period total fertility rates from the mid-70's to the late-80's were artificially depressed by delays in childbearing, delays that cannot continue indefinitely and may have already ceased. They are a quite imperfect guide to the future. Nevertheless, the cohort fertility level of 1.92 for the cohort born in 1950-55 is the lowest in American history, and if birth expectations are realized the fertility level would rise only to 2.1 children.[4]

Is the decline in cohort fertility that has occurred over the preceding 25 years likely to continue? Most analysts of fertility conclude that it is (Westoff, 1990; Bumpass, 1990; Bennett and Bloom, 1990). Among the most important influences on long term fertility levels that are expected to continue exerting downward pressure on fertility are increasing wages for women, which have raised the opportunity costs of childbearing, and improvements in methods of contraception, which have reduced the number of unwanted births. Ryder (1986) estimates that unintended marital births fell from .565 per woman in the peak fertility cohort of 1931-35 to .177 in the low fertility cohort of 1951-55, accounting for 33% of the decline in marital fertility over these cohorts. The level of .177, however, leaves relatively little scope for further declines from this source. The 1989 Supreme Court decision (Webster vs Reproductive Health Services) permitting states to restrict women's access to abortion may eventually even act in the opposite direction, reducing the availability of birth control. In 1985, there were 425 abortions for every 1000 live births.

How much of the cohort fertility decline over the past 30 years represents trend as opposed to fluctuation? Without being very precise, I would argue following Easterlin (1980) that a substantial amount of the decline reflects the economic difficulties faced by baby boom cohorts. The question of the affordability of children has always ranked first in salience when potential parents are asked about factors influencing their childbearing decisions. The size of the baby boom cohorts impaired their labor market prospects; they entered the labor force at a time when national economic growth came to a near halt; and they faced a grim housing market whose inflation was largely a product of their own size (Mankiw and Weil, 1988). Furthermore, their social origins, and hence aspirations for living standards, were far more upscale than those of preceding generations because of the disappearance of historic social class differences in fertility among parents of the baby boom generation.

Apart from national economic growth, whose prospects are uncertain, all of these fertility depressants should be converted into stimulants for the baby bust generation when it reaches the ages of parenthood in the next 10-20 years. (The number of births reached its nadir in 1975 at 3.14 million.) It seems highly plausible that fertility will rise above trend for the baby-bust cohorts to a level of, say, 2.3 births per woman. It was, of course, their baby bust predecessors, the Depression babies of 1931-35, who set the twentieth century childbearing record of 3.2 per woman.

Relative earnings for women should continue to rise as service-sector jobs replace manufacturing jobs. These earnings still have a long way to go before they reach equality with men's. The female-male median earning ratio for full-time workers in 1990 was .72 (U.S. Bureau of Labor Statistics, 1991). Because women continue to bear the large majority of the time costs of childraising, a rise in their relative earnings should increase the relative costs of children and put downward pressure on fertility.

Yet such a trend is not an insurmountable barrier to higher fertility, as recent experience in Sweden has demonstrated. Sweden has enjoyed the highest ratio of female to male earnings in the world. In 1982, the ratio of men's to women's hourly earnings in manufacturing was .903 in Sweden, compared to .710 in the U.S. (Blau and Ferber, 1986:326). Sweden shares many other features of family statistics with the U.S.: late marriage, a high divorce rate, and a very high fraction of births born out of wedlock. But the Swedish period total fertility rate has risen from 1.6 in 1978-83 to 2.13 in the first 10 months of 1990 (Hoem, 1990). Hoem attributes rising fertility in Sweden to liberalized government policies regarding maternity leaves, as well as to generous day care provisions and child allowances. Whether the rise in fertility reflects changing patterns of timing or volume remains to be seen. Period fertility rates have also risen in the late 1980's by 0.2-0.3 children in Norway and Denmark, countries that rank second and third out of 16 western countries in relative female earnings (Blau and Ferber, 1986).

American women do not enjoy the same child-raising benefits as Swedish women, nor are they likely to do so in the near future. But more and more of them are finding ways to combine motherhood and work. For example, 61.7% of married women with two year old children were in the labor force in 1988, compared to 37.1% in 1975 (U.S. Bureau of the Census, 1990a:385). Many of these women were paying a heavy penalty for their dual responsibilities. The fact that as many as 1.9-2.0 children are being born to the cohorts for whom childraising has been most arduous is some indication that having children continues to rank high on the private agendas of many American women. Their position on men's agendas is less secure; 26% of births in 1988 were out of wedlock (NCHS, 1990) and the recent increase in fertility is largely confined to unmarried women. Furthermore, approximately half of children born in wedlock will not live with their fathers throughout childhood.

Rather than following northern Europe into higher ground, American fertility could certainly follow central and southern Europe onto lower ground. Recent levels of period total fertility rates in West Germany and Italy are in the range of 1.3-1.4, and recent cohorts in West Germany will finish with levels of 1.5-1.6 (Bourgeois-Pichat, 1986). Japan also has a period fertility rate of about 1.5 children, indicating (like Germany) that rapid economic growth is no guarantee of high or rising fertility. But international comparisons are less helpful in the case of fertility than mortality, where they help to reveal what is possible with existing knowledge and techniques. We already know that a fertility rate of 0.0 is biologically possible; it is culture, institutions, history, and economy that determine where fertility levels come to rest. In these respects, it is Australia, New Zealand, and Canada - frontier societies with abundant land, cheap housing, democratic traditions and predominantly Anglo-Saxon heritage - that are most similar to the United States. It is no surprise that time series of fertility in these countries are relatively similar to one another and to the U.S. (Coale and Zelnick, 1963: Chs 3-4; Preston, 1986a). Unfortunately, this similarity prevents any one of them from serving as a leading indicator for the others.

Although economic factors play a major role in micro and macro fertility outcomes, twentieth century changes in aggregate fertility levels have typically been much faster than would have resulted from stable micro-level relations between fertility and economic variables (Coale and Watkins, 1986; Mincer, 1984). It is obvious that other factors of an interpersonal nature are at work. People take their childbearing cues in part from what other people are doing and from the cultural constructs that reflect that behavior and interpret it in the context of deeper value systems. There is no question that these constructs changed from 1965 to 1980 in a way that depreciated the role of spouse or parent (Preston, 1986b; Popenoe, 1990).

Some see the cultural realm, the ideational climate affecting family and fertility, as having a great deal of autonomy in these developments (Lesthaeghe, 1983; Popenoe, 1990). In this view, the steady march of individualism - the notion that individuals should be free to pursue their own gratifications minimally encumbered by social restrictions and expectations - began during the Reformation and has finally eroded the last bastion of authoritarianism and encrusted convention, the nuclear family.

Undoubtedly, the concepts of individualism and egalitarianism have served as convenient rationales for dismantling the traditional homemaker-breadwinner family during the 1965-1980 period, when dramatic change occurred in all indexes of family performance. But why these ideas, which have been around for centuries, suddenly proved so appealing during this period remains to be explained by this theory. In my view, the social construction of marriage and parenthood changed so rapidly during this period for several reasons: the contraceptive revolution, which reduced the social value of confining sex to marriage; the pervasive notion that the country was overpopulating and that childbearing was a socially damaging act; and the greater financial sacrifices required to raise children, which induced people to search for cultural rationales for self- interested behavior (Preston 1986b).

If this view is correct, the social depreciation of marriage and parenthood is partially reversible. Reverses are likely to occur when conditions for childbearing are more favorable, and they will exaggerate the rise in fertility that would result from individual cost-benefit calculations alone. The cohorts most likely to be in the vanguard of these changes are the baby busters born in the 1970's and early 80's and those who follow immediately on their heels. That some such change may be afoot is suggested by a New York Times poll reported in the Times on March 14, 1991. For several years, young adults have placed "to be true to yourself" at the top of the list of goals for their lives. In 1991, this goal was replaced by "to be a good spouse and parent."

In short, the upper limit of 2.2 in period total fertility rates in the "high" series of SSA and the Census Bureau appears to be a bit on the low side, at least if the bounds are to represent something like 75% confidence intervals. It has proven very difficult to predict fertility, in part because interpersonal processes have added volatility to aggregate behavior. Wider projection bands seem prudent. The value of 1.9 in the SSA medium series seems far more defensible than Census' 1.8. I suspect that medium values will be raised in both projection series sometime in the next five years. But SSA has ample time to observe events and adjust expectations, since social security balances are affected by fertility only after a long lag. The Census Bureau, whose major task is to project the future size of population and its distribution at all ages, needs to be very attentive to the possibility of a substantial increase in fertility.

THE FUTURE OF IMMIGRATION

The long term future of immigration is difficult to predict because it depends on political decisions made in the United States. There is virtually unlimited demand for places in the United States among the rapidly growing populations of poor countries. How many immigrants we decide to accommodate is the outcome of a delicate political balancing act. Motives for expansion are perceptions of a looming labor shortage (or shortage of skilled workers), humanitarian concerns to unite families and provide a haven for refugees, and pressure from existing ethnic groups. Opposed to expansion are groups who fear that rapid immigration drives down wage levels, that a society with more immigrants will be less cohesive, and that population growth is contributing to environmental degradation.

The expansionists have won the last two rounds of the continuing debate. The Immigration Control and Reform Act of 1986 legalized the status of approximately 2 million undocumented aliens. Although the Act increased sanctions against employers hiring illegal aliens (sanctions which appear to be somewhat effective in the short run), there are questions about whether they are severe enough to have much long-term impact (Todaro and Maruszko, 1987). More important is the Immigration Act of 1990, which became effective in November, 1991. This Act increases legal immigration to 700,000 per year from 1992 to 1994 and 675,000 per year thereafter. During fiscal year 1989, 498,000 legal immigrants were admitted (Population Reference Bureau, 1990). Refugees, who have numbered approximately 60,000-70,000 per year during the 1980's (and about 131,000 in 1991) are included in neither figure. The 1990 Act also allows the ceiling in various quotas to be "pierced" under certain circumstances.

Legal emigration is poorly documented in the American statistical system but appears to have been running at about 150,000 per year recently (Trustees, OASDI, 1989). This figure also appears to be a reasonable guess about the recent volume of net illegal immigration, so these two elements may roughly offset one another. Therefore, the balance of in and out movements (including refugees) over the next decade should be in the range of 700,000-850,000. The "high" net immigration series of the Census Bureau is 800,000 annually and of SSA, 750,000. Both appear to be reasonable medium projections. (SSA's actual "medium" projection of 600,000/year is much more defensible than Census' 500,000).

Table 6.   Features of the Census Bureau's Projection Series with High Life
              Expectancy, High Fertility, and High Immigration

	Date			
	1990	2010	2030	2050
Total Size (in 1000's)	251,897	305,882	362,327	413,580
Birth Rate per 1000	15.7	14.5	13.8	13.7
Death Rate per 1000	8.3	7.7	8.8	9.5
Growth Rate (percent)	1.06	0.94	0.72	0.62
Population 20-64 (in 1000's)	147,974	180,089	189,584	216,459
Population 65+ (in 1000's)	31,666	42,527	75,451	87,435
Ratio, 65+/20-64	.214	.236	.399	.404
Percent Black	12.4	13.7	14.8	15.6

Source: U.S. Bureau of the Census (1989)

Putting these different elements together, I would conclude that the projection
series most likely to prevail over the next decade or two combines high fertility,
high life expectancy, and high immigration. SSA's projections do not contain
this combination, but the Census Bureau's projection series does (parameters are
shown in Table 3). Note that Ahlberg and Vaupel (1990) have recently concluded that the Census Bureau's "high" series (high on all these parameters) is
far too conservative as a reasonable upper bound on future population size.
Because this series appears to me likely to come closer to the mark than any
other, I have presented some of its central features in Table 6. Note that the crude
birth rate will continue to fall even though period age-specific fertility rates rise;
and that the crude death rate will rise even though age-specific death rates fall.
The reason is that the population will continue to age, so that fewer will be in
their childbearing years and more in the ages of peak mortality. The population
continues to age because, even at a fertility rate of 2.2, women in the future will
be having fewer children than women have borne, on average, in the past.

Eventually, with fertility, mortality, and migration rates constant, the population age structure stabilizes and growth rates become constant from year to year. In the meantime, the population growth rate will decline, even in the face of "high" fertility, life expectancy, and immigration, from 1.06% in 1990 to 0.62% in 2050.

The growth rate of the population aged 20-64, along with changes in labor force participation rates, is the dominant factor in the growth of the labor force. Table 7 shows the changes that are projected in the average annual growth rate of the population aged 20-64. This rate is on a downward trajectory over a 60-year time span even under the high/high/high scenario. During the 2020-2030 decade, when the 65+ population is growing at a rate of 2.6%/yr, the population aged 20-64 will be virtually constant. The basic reason for the rapid growth at 65+ and the very slow growth at 20-64 is the same: the very large cohorts of people born between 1955 and 1964 will be reaching age 65 during this decade.

Table 7.   Actual and Projected Growth Rate of the Population Aged 20-64

Decade	Average Annual Growth Rate (Percent)	
	Census Bureau "High"	SSA "Medium"
1970-80	1.71	
1980-90	1.28	
1990-2000	0.98	0.85
2000-2010	0.98	0.82
2010-2020	0.37	0.08
2020-2030	0.15	-0.27
2030-2040	0.66	0.12
2040-2050	0.66	0.03

Source: U.S. Bureau of the Census (1989); Trustees of OASDI (1990)

As shown in Table 7, during the next two decades there is relatively little difference in the growth rate of the population of labor force age between the high and medium projections. What difference exists is undoubtedly mainly a reflection of immigration differences. Beyond that point, the series diverge systematically as fertility differences begin to manifest themselves.

The old age dependency burden of .404 in 2050 in our preferred series is halfway between the medium series of SSA (.392) and of the Census Bureau (.416) in that year (Table 2). Thus, for this critical parameter there is nothing very startling in the high/high/high projection. The reason, of course, is that higher fertility and immigration are offsetting the age structural consequences of higher life expectancy. The effect of adopting this variant is much greater on population size; by 2050 there would be 413.6 million Americans, compared to 299.8 (Census medium) and 324.8 (SSA medium).

POPULATION COMPOSITION

A population is more than a number and an age structure. Unfortunately, we must summarize other changes in the composition of the population very briefly.

Racial and ethnic composition.

The Census Bureau projects the population by race, using separate fertility, mortality, and migration assumptions for each racial group. As shown in Table 6, the percentage of the population that is black is projected to rise from 12.4% to 15.6% by 2050. This very slow increase is at variance with many popular impressions, whose origins probably lie more in xenophobia than in demography. The population of Hispanic origin was 8.3% of the total population in 1989 (U.S. Bureau of the Census, 1990b) and is projected by the Census Bureau to increase to 10.9% by 2010, the latest time to which such projections are made (U.S. Bureau of the Census, 1990a). The basic reason why the Hispanic population is growing more rapidly than the remainder of the population is, of course, immigration. From 1981 to 1987, Mexico, Central America, and South America accounted for 925,00 immigrants, or about 23% of the total (U.S. Bureau of the Census, 1990a:10).

The slowly increasing percentage of these minority groups has raised fears that labor force quality will decline. To some, the association is axiomatic. It does appear likely that the skill level of new entrants to the labor force will decline, but the basic reason is a decline in the preparedness of native non-Hispanic whites. Scores on standardized tests of educational performance among random samples of U.S. school children show large, persistent gains for blacks, especially in the South, and level or declining trends for whites (Select Committee on Children, Youth, and Families, 1989:146-50). The Immigration Act of 1990, which places a heavier premium on skill levels than previously regulations, should also result in a higher level of educational preparedness for immigrants.

Geographic distribution.

The Census Bureau makes projections by state to 2010. These take account of a state's age structure, fertility and mortality levels, and recent patterns of migration, including international migration. The result tends to be a recapitulation of recent population trends, with a continuing shift away from the Northeast and Midwest and towards the South and West. Results of the most recent

FIGURE 7
Projected Percent Change in State Populations: 1990 to 2000

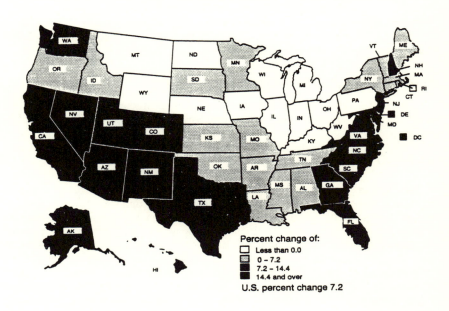

projections are shown in Table 8. A map of changes projected between 1990 and 2000, by state, is presented as Figure 7.

Within regions, populations continue to concentrate in metropolitan areas. The relatively faster growth of non-metropolitan areas of the 1970's has not continued into the 1980's. A factor in the continued metropolitanization of the population is international migration. 94% of immigrants go to metropolitan areas (Long and DeAre, 1988). Nevertheless, smaller cities appear to be growing more rapidly than the largest cities; the growth rate of the densest 10% of American countries was below average over the period 1980-86 (Ibid.). Residential preferences continue to favor smaller places. In 1988, only 30% of the population expressed a preference to live in cities of 50,000 or more and more than half of the population would live in a smaller place even if it meant giving up 10% of their income (Fuguitt and Brown, 1990). It seems likely that economies of agglomeration will diminish with continued advances in informational technology and transportation systems. If so, larger fractions of the population will be able to act on their residential preferences. The diffusion to smaller places (often within or near metropolitan areas) should be especially rapid when the baby boomers retire.

Table 8.   Projections of Population Change by Region, 1990-2010

Region	Population (in 1000's)		Percentage Change
	1990	2010	
Northeast	50,707	50,763	0.1
New England	13,073	13,674	4.6
Middle Atlantic	37,634	37,089	-1.4
Midwest	60,205	61,997	3.0
E.N. Central	42,285	42,916	1.5
W.N. Central	17,920	19,081	6.5
South	86,644	102,577	18.4
South Atlantic	43,427	51,233	18.0
E.S. Central	15,577	17,447	12.0
W.S. Central	27,640	33,898	22.6
West	52,336	66,719	27.5
Mountain	13,808	17,670	28.0
Pacific	38,527	49,049	27.3

Source: U.S. Bureau of Census, 1990c (Series B)

ENDNOTES

1. The projections cover slightly different populations. SSA projections pertain to the Social Security Area, which includes residents of the 50 states and armed forces overseas, Puerto Rico, Guam, American Samoa, the Virgin Islands, and certain other categories of U.S. citizens abroad (SSA, 1989). The Census projections pertain to the resident population of the 50 states plus Washington D.C. and includes Armed Forces overseas. SSA projections adjust the total population for census undercount, whereas the Census Bureau's do not. Both series include illegal immigrants. Census projections distinguish race while SSA's distinguish marital status. Source: SSA (1989), Bureau of the Census (1989).

2. The SSA's medium series demographic assumptions in 1989 were different slightly from those in 1990. The same ultimate total fertility rate was used, as noted earlier, but fertility was slightly higher in the first 25 years in the 1990 medium series. A slightly faster mortality improvement was assumed in 1990, with a mean of male and female life expectancies in 2050 of 79.2 used in 1989 and 79.7 in 1990 (SSA, 1989:13; Trustees of OASDI, 1990:38). More detail is supplied in the actuarial study for 1989 than in the Trustees report for 1990, so we will occasionally rely upon 1989 projections.

3. Projections done at Penn with and without projected increases in AIDS deaths show that, for the white population, the population percentage above age 65 by 2012 is 14.72 without the increase and 14.76 with it. The percentages aged 15-64 are 68.27 and 68.13 (McDaniel, 1990).

4. Birth expectations have historically predicted cohort fertility in the aggregate quite well for married women, but there is much more uncertainty about their predictive power for single women (O'Connell and Rogers, 1983).

Discussions

Francisco R. Bayo

INTRODUCTION

I would like to congratulate Dr. Preston for his informative and well-written paper. It was a pleasure to read it. I will comment on it, and I will use this opportunity to convey some of my views on the subject.

My views are neither unique or singular, but they seem somewhat different. To a large extent, they have been molded by the perspective of the position I hold in Social Security and also by the more than thirty years of accumulation of knowledge or bias.

PERSPECTIVE

I find, for example, that technicians (like most of us are) devote significant attention to the methods being used. I believe, however, that methods have no meaning unless they are part of a strategy to obtain a goal. Before I can effectively pass judgement on the value of a method, I need to have an idea of the goal that is being pursued and of the strategy that has been selected for obtaining that goal.

We feel flattered when much attention is given to the Social Security population projections; particularly when they are brought to the level of comparisons with those prepared at the Census Bureau for open discussions at symposiums. I recommend, nevertheless, that in the analysis and in the comparisons, the purposed followed in the preparation and publication of those populations projections be remembered.

Social Security projections are not intended for general usage. We publish them because (1) we believe that those affected by the Social Security system should be well informed about the actuarial foundations of the system, and (2) it is one of the steps that we follow to obtain helpful comments. For example, the comments that Dr. Preston has included in his paper, which are based on our published projections, will be taken into consideration for future projections.

The population projections that we prepare are one of the principal ingredients in the development of indicators used to judge the financial stability of the Social Security system and of the financial effect of the proposed modifications to it. They are, therefore, just one element in a total set of methods and assumptions. The totality of the set needs to be studied as a unit, although attention could also be given separately to some of its parts. Last year we had a Technical Panel of Experts, that did just that for the Social Security Advisory Council, that is, analyze the totality of the assumptions and methods being used. That Panel performed very well, in general, because of the quality of the experts on its, and in particular, because of the discipline that the panelists exercised in applying the proper perspective about the task that they had been assigned.

GENERAL COMMENTS

It is now generally accepted that there will be a significant and rapid shift in the age structure of the population of the United States. It is also generally accepted that the shift could provoke financial strains on the Social Security system some time around the second quarter of the next century. Although there is agreement about the reality of the shift, there is a lack of agreement about the size of the shift and about what should be done to more properly channel its effects on Social Security.

Regarding the size of the shift, as measured by the old age dependency ratio, it is of interest to notice the highness degree of closeness exhibited in the projections prepared by the Social Security actuaries, Dr. Preston, and the Census Bureau. This ration was 0.209 in 1990 and is being projected to increase, by the year 2050, to 0.392 by the actuaries, to 0.404 by Dr. Preston, and to 0.416 by the Census Bureau. These "best-guess" projections represent increases, over the 60-year period, of 88 percent, 93 percent, and 99 percent, respectively. Given the large size of the increase and the length of time involved, the differences in the results among the projectors is minor. On a relative basis, Dr. Preston projects an old age dependency ratio for the year 2050 that is 3.0 percent higher than the actuaries and 3.0 percent lower than the Census Bureau. On an annualized growth basis, each difference amounts to around 5 hundredth of one percent.

I must confess that I do not believe anyone can claim that degree of accuracy in the Social Security projections. So many different events can occur between now and then that the claim would be either foolish or arrogant. Because I do not believe we can know with precision the size of the shift, I hold that no solution to the consequent effects should be implemented now. As indicated before, there are no doubts about the reality of the shift. Many analysts have no doubts either, that some of the consequences will not be to our liking. But I wonder whether or not preventive or corrective medicines many be truly needed, or whether or not we can truly prescribe, at this time, a remedy that will not turn out to be worse than the sickness. I suggest that the best course is to continue with watchful eyes on the shift for a few more years without jumping into "solutions" for Social Security. After all, the next 20-25 years will be a period of relatively stable aged dependency ratio and of relatively stable Social Security costs.

I believe that most technicians are currently acting correctly be making policy-makers and the Congress aware of the shift and its possible cost implications for Social Security, and particularly, by not requiring that "solutions" be immediately implemented.

Part of the problem may be due to the fact that many of us, when looking into the future, become pessimists instead of futurists. A shift in the age structure of the population is not an entirely new event in our nation. In the 25-year period, 1940-65, the aged dependency ration increased from 0.115 to 0.181, which represents a total increase of 57 percent and an annualized growth rate of 1.83 percent. It was a relatively high growth rate. In the 45-year period that follows, 1965-2010, the ratio is expected to increase to 0.219 for a total of 21 percent and an annualized growth rate of 2.71. Thereafter, the dependency ration is projected to increase relatively slowly. It is correct to categorize the shift expected to occur in the 2010-2030 period as fast and significant, but we should also recognize that the 1940-65 was a period of high growth in the dependency ratio.

I envision the Social Security population projections not as end products by themselves, but as instruments or tools used to assist us in affecting the decision making process about Social Security and its financing. At this moment, the best decision is not to do anything about the shift, beside studying its possible size and effects. This should be done in the most objective manner, without undue fear and pessimism.

SPECIFIC COMMENTS

Long-range projections of population must be approached with a deep sense of modesty. Although their usefulness cannot be denied, they should not be embraced as accurate predictions. In general, they are mostly the product of assumptions that have been adopted and much less the result of methods. Once the assumptions have been adopted, most methods produce essentially the same results. But it is in the nature of assumptions to be uncertain and to be the subject of irresolution. The best a projector can hope for is an understanding from others of the reasonableness of his assumptions and an acceptance of the differences that may emerge. Occasionally he may savor a full agreement, but this could be due more to coincidence than a unity of visions. It is within this sense of restraint that the following specific comments are made about Dr. Preston's preferred assumptions.

MORTALITY

It is axiomatic that those causes of death that have already been conquered cannot be conquered again. Improvements in future mortality will need to come from those causes that we have been unable to conquer in the past. This leads me to believe that new conquests will become more difficult and more expensive. It also leads me to believe that an analysis of the past is useful to the extent that it guides the projector and restrains his imagination. Any direct mathematical extrapolation of past experiences, regardless of the beauty and appeal of formulas, is destined to show its exact nature: a series of beautiful and appealing formulas that have as much accuracy in predicting the future as simpler procedures. I find, though, that these formulas are very good for predicting the past. Although, as a mathematician, I significantly enjoy beauty and appeal in formulas, as well as feelings of having discovered some basic truth; as an actuary, I prefer Social Security projections that are simple and authoritative, that is, that have an author who stands behind them.

I share with Dr. Preston a lack of interest in the squaring of the survival curve and on the hypothesis of a maximum life span. These concepts are useful tools for starting the education of the uninformed, but they should not be regarded as being part of the fundamentals of human mortality.

FERTILITY

As Dr. Preston indicated, fertility is the most unpredictable component of population projections. It is also the most controversial assumption, because of the intensity of feelings among "experts." Those who "know" about this subject display a wide gamma of "best-guess" values. This is another example of the fact that the less truly known about a specific subject, the larger the number of "experts" operating within it. Most of these "experts" truly believe that they are approaching the subject in a most scientific manner: cohort analysis, birth expectations, spacing of pregnancies, etc.. I see most of these techniques as assistance to the projector in the development of his preferred judgement about future fertility, but I truly do not know how much accuracy would be added to the results by incorporating these techniques in the projection model. They do, however, make the model more impressive to the uneducated and the to semi-educated.

MIGRATION

Migration has been, up to now, a relatively unimportant element in the projections of the population of the United States. Its effects have been minor and its variability considered relatively narrow. Lately, Social Security has been paying more attention to this element and has been incorporating an "other-than-legal" component. In the past, we recognized this component only after it was enumerated in a decennial census. Now, we are adopting a specific assumption regarding the annual level of projected net "other-than-legal" migration.

The overall level of net migration that Social Security is currently assuming is similar to the one suggested by Dr. Preston. In its latest projections Social Security could not include the effect of the Immigration Act of 1990, because those projections preceded the Act; but once that effect is included, which will be done in the new projections to be released in the near future, the assumed level will be around the middle range preferred by Dr. Preston. I would like to add, however, that Social Security needs to be cautious in its migration assumption. A proper financing policy may not be generated if it is assumed that, to a large extent, immigrants (legal or otherwise) will come to bail out Social Security.

CONCLUSIONS

The above discussion suggests the following conclusions. It is generally accepted that there will be a significant shift in the age structure of the population of the United States. This shift is expected to start showing its effects within the next 20 to 25 years; in the meantime, the aged dependency ratio is expected to increase very slowly. It is too early to accurately predict the size of the shift, although most "best-guess" estimates fall within a narrow band. The possible effects of the shift should be studied objectively in the coming years, but no immediate "solution" should be adopted or implemented now.

Stephen C. Goss

Sam Preston's paper provides an excellent and insightful analysis of past demographic experience and his expectations for the future. Frank Bayo's discussion covers many of the reactions we share, both working at the Office of the Actuary, Social Security Administration. The comments below provide a few additional insights that I hope will be useful.

MORTALITY

In his paper, Dr. Preston suggests that future declines in mortality rates may be greater than those projected by the Social Security Administration (SSA). An extrapolation of long-term past rates of decline would support his position. However, a more careful look at past trends, and the reasons behind them, lead us at the SSA to believe that declines will not average as large in the future as in the past several decades.

Between 1900 and 1990, the age-sex-adjusted death rate in the United States population declined at an average annual rate of 1.2 percent. However, it is interesting to note that this period has been made up of several distinct periods with very different experience. From 1900 to 1936, mortality rates declined by only 0.8 percent per year. From 1936 to 1954, they declined by 2.3 percent per year. Little decline was experienced from 1954 to 1968, only 0.2 percent per year, followed by rapid decline from 1968 to 1982, at 2.0 percent per year. Since 1982, mortality rates have again been declining slowly, only 0.4 percent per year.

Precise explanation of this seemingly cyclic pattern of mortality is elusive. The rapid improvement between 1968 and 1982 would seem to be related to the introduction of Medicare, bringing more health care to those with the greatest probabilities of death. Slower declines since 1982 might be assumed to be associated with some of the Medicare reforms that decreased service. However, for these periods, the first rapid and then slow decline in mortality was experienced for all age groups, not just the elderly served by Medicare.

Frank Bayo suggests that future improvement will be harder because we have, in effect, already found the easiest cures and further medical cures will be more difficult. Two additional factors will also contribute to ultimately slower mortality improvement than experienced so far this century. Certainly much of the past improvement is due to our ability to make adequate nutrition and health care available to virtually the whole population. These changes can only be made once. They have contributed greatly to the health and thus the life expectancy of the population this century.

While we will continue to see declines in mortality from these changes, and from trends toward better eating habits by some and a reduction in smoking, for many years into the future, ultimate future gains will require new medical interventions and changes in life style that may be difficult to develop and harder to provide the population at large. Our ability as a nation to afford the new medical technologies for all the people is increasingly in question. Economics will likely restrict our ability to make them available. In fact, the level of current health costs suggests that we cannot even afford the current level of health service that is provided. With the upsurge in consumption of fast-food and the rise in pollution levels, future gains in mortality may not be as great as we would hope.

The SSA projections for future mortality improvement range from 1.1 percent per year for the high cost alternative III projection to 0.3 percent per year for the low cost alternative I projection. The intermediate alternative II projection assumes ultimate annual decline at 0.6 percent. Each of these projections is based on separate projections by age and cause of death. Significantly, the recent increases in death rates due to cancer are assumed to reverse and become declines in the future.

Dr. Preston cited the results of the Manton study which found a high average age at death for Harvard faculty. It would be inappropriate to assume that this experience could practically be expanded to the total population. Most obviously, Harvard faculty all survived their infancy and youth, thus making them a select group within the population. Moreover, their attainment is indicative of an above average level of health and wealth that cannot be achieved for the total population.

FERTILITY

We believe the fertility rate to be the most volatile and least easily predicted demographic parameter. Unlike mortality, fertility is a matter of choice and the desirability of children can change from year to year and from generation to generation. Dr. Preston suggests that the ultimate total fertility rates projected by the SSA (1.9 births per woman) and by the Bureau of the Census (1.8 births per woman) are too low. For us at the SSA this is refreshing! For years we have been criticized for assuming that future fertility rate will be too high. Only with recent increases in birth rates have we begun to be criticized for being too low.

We believe that long-range ultimate assumptions should react to experience trends slowly. A 75-year projection should not swing back and forth reflecting short term fluctuations. Declines in the total fertility rate in the 1960's and 1970's culminated in an all time low of 1.7 births per woman for 1976. Since then the total fertility rate has been rising slowly but steadily. The SSA intermediate fertility assumption was not lowered to 1.9 until the 1988 Trustees Report. Although the total fertility rate has actually now reached the 2.0 level for 1989 and 1990, we believe it is too early to tell whether this higher level will persist.

An analysis of birth rates by age group is very interesting. Since 1976, the low point for fertility, birth rates for women under age 30 have been virtually constant. The total fertility rate has risen only because of rising birth rates from women in their 30's. The increase at this age is regarded as evidence of women having delayed births in order to establish careers while in their 20's and early 30's. At this time it is not at all clear whether rates will continue to increase or stabilize for women in their 30's. On the other hand, some argue persuasively that birth rates will continue to decline in the future. We at SSA believe that anything in the range of 1.8 to 2.0 constitutes a reasonable assumption for the ultimate total fertility rate.

IMMIGRATION

The immigration rates cited by Dr. Preston are from the 1990 Trustees Report, for which assumptions were set prior to enactment of the Immigration Act of 1990. This legislation increases the numerical limits on legal immigration. We estimate that net legal immigration will increase by about 150,000 per year as a result. Assumptions thus adjusted for the 1991 Trustees Report will be consistent with levels suggested by Dr. Preston.

RANGE OF ASSUMPTIONS

It is important to remember the context in which the SSA population projections are produced. They are but one component in financial projections intended to help policymakers determine the shape of the Social Security program for the future. The optimistic alternative I and pessimistic alternative III projections are developed in order to show examples of how variation in the assumptions affect the cost of the program. For alternative I, each of the assumptions is selected at a plausible level in the direction that would tend to improve the financing of the program. The reverse is done for alternative III. It should be noted that no confidence limits are assigned to the range of assumptions presented in the report. They are only intended to represent a plausible range.

The effects of altering one assumption at a time are illustrated in the sensitivity analysis found in an appendix of the Trustees Report.

CONCLUSION

Dr. Preston concludes that the government projections include too little improvement in mortality and too low a fertility rate, but such changes tend to offset each other yielding little difference in the aged dependency ratio. We all agree that this ratio will rise significantly and rapidly after the turn of the century.

The implications of this increasing aged dependency ratio are, however, less clear. Increased cost for Social Security benefits will certainly result, but the bigger question is our ability to pay these costs. Relatively more aged persons may result in capital deepening, i.e., more capital invested for each of the relatively smaller number of workers. Then productivity will increase, yielding more goods and services for us all to share. But the possibility of investments of the future elderly flowing abroad, with possibly greater returns through investing in less developed economies, may work in the opposite direction. We must also ask whether the elderly of the next century will have accrued savings or debt for their old age.

The 1983 Social Security Amendments raised the normal retirement age for persons reaching age 62 after the year 2000. Ultimately the normal retirement age is scheduled to rise to 67 from its current level of 65. Further increase in the normal retirement age may be needed in the future, along with higher taxes and/or other reductions in benefits. The uncertainty associated with long-range cost estimates suggests that it may be too early to make further changes that will not be needed until 30 to 50 years from now. On the other hand such changes must be made with considerable advance notice so that people can plan appropriately.

Barry Edmonston

ABSTRACT

The United States is on the eve of sunstantial shifts in the racial/ethnic composition of the population. These changes will occur as a response to new patterns of immigration that have evolved during the last thirty years. Current immigrants are predominantly Asian and Hispanic, with some Black imigrants from Caribbean and Africa and some White immigrants from Canada, Europe, and Oceania. Present immigrants are different from the overwhelmingly European movements of the nineteenth and early twentieth centuries.

This paper assesses assumptions for official U.S. population projections. The paper also presents overall results for a population projection of the racial/ethnic groups of the United States for 1990 to 2090. With annual net immigration of 900,000 to 950,000, the total U.S. population of 249 million in 1990 will top 400 million in 2070 and reach about 432 million in 2090. Thus, the current level of net immigration assumed in these projections suggests considerable population growth for the next hundred years.

The racial/ethnic composition will shift markedly during the next century. Assuming the population conditions of the projection, the White non-Hispanic population will increase its numbers from 187 million in 1990 to a peak 212 million in 2030 before falling slowing to about 209 million by 2090. This group will become less numerous and drom from 75 percent of the total population to less than 50 percent in 2090.

Over the next century, the Black population will increase from 30 million to 54 million, but will remain virtually unchanged proportionately, increasing from 12 percent in 1990 to 13 percent in 2090.

Asians and Hispanics will experience substantial growth during the next century. The Asians population will grow from 7 million in 1990 to 60 million in 2090, increasing its proportionate share from 3 percent in 1990 to 14 percent in 2090. Hispanics will increase from 22 million in 1990 to 108 million in 2090, a gain from 9 to 25 percent in the period. Both Asians and Hispanics would be larger groups than Blacks by 2090, although the Hispanic population will be a larger numerical group than Blacks by about 2010.

INTRODUCTION

The convergence of several demographic forces -- lowered birth rates, increased life expectancy, the aging of the post-war baby boom generation, and changing immigration -- has been producing a marked shift in the growth rates, age characteristics, and racial/ethnic composition of the U.S. population in recent decades. These demographic developments are an important source of change for social programs, including our nation's social welfare and pension programs. Greater number of elderly beneficiaries and reduced numbers of working age contributors will cause an imbalance in our public pension programs in the next 20 to 30 years, when the baby boom cohorts reach retirement age. Such demographic problems, however, are quite separate from shortfalls in public pension trust funds that stem from economic conditions. Demographic arithmetic points up the need to develop solutions to long-range problems, which require considerable lead time to implement, but provides no basis for precipitous changes in taxes or benefits.

Generally, a better understanding of demographic forces should help policy-makers to anticipate future needs in social programs with greater accuracy. Demographers, then, share an interest in lengthening the time horizon for considering public policy debate. Looking to the future adds a difficult time dimension to the context of a shaky economy, stringent budgets, and shifting political currents. Yet, there are some forces acting on society that are predictable and, when studied scientifically, provide a solid basis for anticipating future change. One of the most important solid basis for a look into the future is demographic change.

The following sections describe some aspects of projecting the future population of the United States and the demographic assumptions made for population projections. Next, the paper mentions some highlights about the impact of demographic changes on population aging and the racial and ethnic composition of the population.

FUTURE DEMOGRAPHY

POPULATION PROJECTIONS

When the results of projections made in the past are compared with the population changes that have actually occurred, it is frequently found that the projections have not succeeded in portraying accurately what subsequently occurred. The prospects for success are similar to those of weather forecasting. Like meteorologists, demographers are well aware that they cannot precisely "forecast" or "predict" the future. Demographers therefore tend to avoid the use of these words. Instead, they tend to stress that projections are arithmetic calculations derived from a set of assumptions about population change. Avoiding any miscalculation, the population projection is always accurate, given the assumptions. Users of a population projection therefore need to question carefully the reasonableness of the demographic assumptions inherent in the projection.

Preston's (1991) paper reviews the demographic assumptions made in the two sets of population projections: the U.S. Bureau of the Census and the Social Security Administration projections. The next sections comment on Preston's evaluation for mortality, fertility, international migration, and race and ethnicity assumptions.

MORTALITY ASSUMPTIONS

There are two broad approaches to the task of projecting mortality. One is to examine the experience of past mortality and then to extend them to show the years to come. The other is to consider that mortality may be expected to fall to some "ultimate" level, and then to interpolate values for the death rates during the period between the present and the assumed date of obtaining the ultimate level.

The differences between the two methods is primarily one of emphasis. Whichever approach is taken, the results should also be sensible in light of the alternative approach.

Regarding mortality assumptions for population projections, Preston's (1991) paper provides a succinct and reasonable critique. It evaluates the future course of U.S. mortality in light of international comparisons, recent U.S. trends, and ultimate biological limits. I emphasize next some key conclusions reached in his paper.

First, recent life expectancy improvements were more rapid than researchers had expected about twenty years ago. Mortality declines for selected causes-of-death, especially cardiovascular diseases, have been sizeable. Interpreting recent mortality trends, however, is somewhat confusing. If nothing else, it indicates the importance of including recent mortality data in any projection of population futures.

Second, Preston stresses that future improvements in life expectancy will rely significantly on declining mortality for persons aged 65 years and older (Preston, 1991). His discussion suggests that future mortality improvements are indeed likely for the elderly. In particular, Preston reviews the important study of Lee and Carter (1990) to support his contention that available data provide strong evidence for mortality improvements that are higher than the medium mortality assumptions for the Bureau of the Census's and Social Security Administration's projections. In summary, Preston favors a ''high'' life expectancy series from the current population projections. His argument at this point is reasonable.

Third, Preston notes that the effects of AIDS will slow the rate of mortality improvement. However, he apparently thinks that AIDS-related mortality will not have a marked effect on overall mortality because he relies in general on a high life expectancy projection. The Bureau of the Census (Spencer, 1989) has prepared life tables for 2005 that assume that AIDS remains confined to existing high-risk populations and uses the age-sex- race distribution for AIDS deaths in 1991. These life tables for 2005 indicate virtually no change in life expectancy between 1986 and 2005 for males and only a one year gain for females. My calculations suggest that AIDS-related mortality might reduce the gains in male life expectancy by three years and females by two years, compared to the optimistic forecasts of high life expectancy assumptions. Taking AIDS-related mortality into account suggests that the medium mortality assumptions may be reasonable for males and that an intermediate medium-to-low mortality assumption may be sensible for females. AIDS-related deaths, it should also be noted, are selective by age, sex, and race. Although AIDS may have a minimal impact on the population aged 65 years and older during the next twenty or thirty years, it will have an effect on the younger citizens who contribute to pension funds or who provide health and social care for older family members.

FERTILITY ASSUMPTIONS

The level of fertility today depends on the individual decisions of parents who practice fertility control and who space out the births of their children. In making these decisions, individuals may well be influenced by social and economic conditions (the attractions of alternative roles to parenting, the cost of raising children, and so forth). Social class, ethnic, and generation characteristics may also influence family size decisions.

In these circumstances, there may appear to be little possibility of forecasting births. To assume that current trends continue into the future may seem to have little justification. However, collection and analysis of fertility rates by marriage duration and birth order, coupled with extensive examination of survey data, have improved the basis for fertility projection.

The U.S. population, along with other industrial countries, has made the transition from high to low fertility levels. The population currently display relatively low fertility, but one may expect oscillations in fertility in the future. The norms and social institutions concerning fertility are neither homogeneous nor steady in the U.S. population. Experimentation at the generation level is likely to continue for some time, and one may expect that fertility levels will fluctuate, albeit around low levels, for several generations.

Fertility is unpredictable in an exact fashion. But fertility increased during the 1980s and a higher level of fertility now seems likely for the next decade. A total fertility rate of 1.9 per woman, on average, now seems reasonable.

It should be noted that current official projections assume the instantaneous fertility adaption of immigrants to U.S. levels. This underestimates the childbearing contribution and future growth of newer immigrant populations.

Regarding fertility assumptions, Preston (1991) demonstrates clearly the difference between timing and volume components of fertility. He notes that very recent fertility rates have increased, with the total fertility rate exceeding 2.0 in 1990 for the first time since the early 1970s. Some of the recent increase in period fertility rates represents a ''catching-up'' from past delays in childbearing. Nevertheless, it remains uncertain how much catching-up will occur for older couples in the childbearing years. There are sizeable proportions of women in their late 20s and early 30s who could go on to have more children. However, many of these women have been childless for ten to fifteen years of their reproductive careers and, moreover, many are not now in stable sexual unions (marriage or cohabiting unions). They may not have all the children that they want or say in surveys that the expect to have.

Unless economic conditions improve markedly, along with better housing markets and increased availability of child care programs, I would not expect a significant catching-up of childbearing among potential parents in their late 20s and early 30s. In short, the United States may witness a number of years with the total fertility rate above 2.0, but it is just as likely for the total fertility rate to settle down to a level of 1.8 to 1.9.

INTERNATIONAL MIGRATION ASSUMPTIONS

The effects of migration on population change have the greatest importance for smaller subnational areas and for selected immigrant groups. The treatment of migration depends somewhat on the specific focus of the population projection.

In particular, population projections are improved by detailed assumptions for migrants. Migrants tend to have a particular kind of age distribution and their fertility and mortality may differ from the remainder of the population. There may be reasons for treating them separately from non-migrants.

Immigration has been somewhat higher than current projections assume. Over 2 million aliens were legalized under the general amnesty conditions of the 1986 Immigration Reform and Control Act (IRCA). In addition, about a million and a half aliens sought legalization under the provisions of IRCA concerning special agricultural workers. Our research at the Urban Institute suggests that slightly over one million of those applying as agricultural workers will eventually be granted legal residence. Finally, the recently enacted Immigration Act of 1990 provided legal residence, under special conditions, for about one-half million refugees residing in the United States. Overall, therefore, about 3.6 million individuals were granted legal residence in the United States during the past ten years. This is in addition to the estimated 6.0 million who legally immigrated to the United States during 1980 to 1990, or a total of 9.6 million legal entrants during the decade. An average of 960,000 new entrants exceeds the Bureau of the Census's middle series and is close to the Bureau's high immigration numbers.

Future immigration has an open-ended condition for some immigrant categories. The new Immigration Act of 1990 made several important changes in the number of immigrants: it provided for a three-track immigration system (family-sponsored, employment-based, and diversity-based) and it set a target limit of 700,000 immigrants for the 1992 to 1994 fiscal years. It should be noted that there is, in fact, no numerical limit for the entrance of immediate relatives of U.S. citizens. As past immigrants become naturalized citizens, including the 9.6 million who entered the United States during the 1980s, they become eligible to sponsor the legal entrance of immediate relatives (spouses, children, and parents) into the U.S. without numerical limits under current law. Although the 1990 Act subtracts immediate relative visas from the family-sponsored visas in the following fiscal year, this is a major source of uncertainty about the number of immigrants who will enter the United States in future years. About 220,000 immediate relatives entered the United States in fiscal year 1989, the latest year for which Immigration and Naturalization Service statistics are available.

Evidence is now clearer about the impact of employer sanctions and enhanced Border Patrol activity on illegal immigration. Research by a number of scholars published in a recent Urban Institute volume reports that the IRCA initially reduced the flow of illegal migrants into the United States (Edmonston, Passel, and Bean, 1990). However, a large proportion of the reduced flow stemmed from the effects of the legalization program, which removed individuals from the illegal flow. Initially, strengthened Border Patrol activities appeared to have some deterrent effect on illegal migration. In the last year, however, there appears to be a turnaround in the flow of illegal immigrants and it now appears uncertain whether IRCA will achieve its principal goal of stopping the entry of undocumented immigration. Illegal immigrant flows are apparently back to the levels that were witnessed in the mid-1980s, during the years before the enactment of IRCA.

Immigration is the first component of international migration. Emigration, out-migration from the United States, is the second. Immigration is limited by numeric quotas for entrance to the United States, with population projections setting a number for the assumption of the future annual entrance into the population.

But there is no quota or numeric limit for annual exit from the population. Rather, out-migration is a phenomenon with annual departures developing from a probability of departure from a risk population. In fact, studies of emigration suggest that most departures are recent immigrants who decide to return to their original home country. Rates of emigration vary greatly by country of origin, with higher rates of return migration for Europe and Canada, intermedicate rates for Latin America, and lower rates for Asia.

Official population projections are based on the assumption of an annual number of emigrants. Demographic research, however, suggests that more appropriate model would be to base population projections on rates of out-migration (that vary by country of origin and the recency of immigration).

These assumptions are not trivial for some matters of population projections. Bureau of the Census projections show sizeable emigration from Vermont, for example. But Vermont's foreign-born population includes a high proportion of Canadians, primarily from Quebec, who have resided in the United States for many years. Demographic work suggests that the Canadian-origin population in Vermont are not likely to depart in large numbers. Conversely, the Bureau of the Census projections suggest that fewer people will depart Texas than might be thought, even though Texas includes many recent immigrants from Mexico, a group that is likely to have intermediate levels of emigration in the near future. In summary, the modelling of emigration in official population projections is inadequate and may adversely affect results for regional and racial/ethnic forecasts.

Problems with the international migration assumptions for official population projections, however, have a modest impact on the interpretation of projections for public pension funding. The long-term impact of a steady stream of migration, which may seem counter-intuitive, is to make the population older. This occurs because the immigrants age -- as do residents of the population -- but immigrants enter the population at ages greater than zero. Hence, a constant number of immigrants, with a fixed age and sex distribution, produces an older population in the long-run.

Different international migration assumptions have little impact on the national pension and retirement progams in general. Varying the migration assumptions, however, has special effects for some race and ethnic projections, for population distribution within the United States, and for cultural diversity of the population. Projections of the Asian and Hispanic populations, for example, are sensitive to the migration assumptions that are discussed above.

RACE AND ETHNIC POPULATION PROJECTIONS

The U.S. Bureau of the Census (Spencer, 1986; Spencer, 1989) prepares population projections for the U.S. population by race, including the White, Black, and Other groups. A special population projection is also prepared for the Hispanic population (an Hispanic person may be any one of the main racial groups). In fact, the Hispanic population identifies itself as White about 55 percent, Other about 40 percent, and the Black and Asian for the remaining 5 percent. The fact that the Hispanic population can be any one of the main racial groups is important for interpreting official U.S. population projections: the Hispanic population projection cannot be added or subtracted from the race population projections in an easy manner in order to obtain mutually exclusive population groups.

We have completed race and ethnic population projections at the Urban Institute (Edmonston and Passel, 1991a). We have made several improvements compared to the official population projections, especially for analysis of groups influenced markedly by international migration. First, the Bureau of the Census's projections assume instantaneous adaption of immigrants to the fertility and mortality regime of the U.S. population. Our work distinquishes immigrants from the native-born and permits the assumption of differential fertility by nativity. Second, racial/ethnic groups are likely to experience significant inter-marriage during the next decades and, hence, are unlikely to retain predomi-nantly single ancestry origins. The "fiction" of single ancestry Asian, Black, and Hispanic groups, if not questioned in population projections, provides a false sense of the numbers and intermixture of future racial/ethnic groups. The Urban Institute population projections include various degrees of exogamy for each racial/ethnic group and show the single and mixed ancestry components of future population size.

UNCERTAINTY IN POPULATION PROJECTIONS

Population projections are often taken as endogenous. But one can expect future social and economic changes to affect population dynamics. There are two examples. First, official population projections do not include explicit treatment of marriage, divorce, remarriage (nor cohabitation). Yet marriage patterns are a primary determinant of fertility levels and, hence, future changes are likely to affect fertility in ways that are not explicitely modelled in current projections.

Second, we can anticipate that the U.S. population will experience at least one major refugee flow during the next decade or so. Although one cannot name the country, the United States experienced four or five major refugee flows during the past forty years. It is likely therefore that one major country in the world will witness major civil violence that provokes widespread refugee movements to the United States. This will markedly affect the numbers of immigrants to the United States.

Unfortunately, many problems remain before population projections can include reliable confidence intervals (Stoto, 1983). Current population projec-tions include "low" and "high" assumptions that routinely change as research-ers change their opinions about the likely course of future demographic proc-esses. The formal analysis of error rates for population projections provides some guidelines about the accuracy of past projections, but it is uncertain how helpful these guidelines are for future trends. Nor does the formal analysis of error rates provide a model for selecting the ranges of demographic rates to use for current population projections.

POPULATION IMPACTS

For four centuries, the ethnic and racial composition of the United States has resembled a constantly changing picture of varying sources of immigrants as well as the different fertility and mortality of the native residents and the new immigrants. The population also varied as the immigrants had children and grandchildren, and altered the generational composition of the residents.

The recent thirty years have witnessed a massive shift in the country of origin of U.S. immigrants. A predominantly White society with a Black minority is becoming more heterogeneous. The proportion White is falling, as sizeable numbers of Asian and Hispanic immigrants arrive. There are some new features in the present situation. The fertility of the resident population is so low -- below the long-run replacement level in fact -- that any racial/ethnic group that does not have significant immigration will be reduced in numbers in the next decades. Previous periods of high immigration included large numbers of Europeans, albeit U.S. residents at the time saw these individuals as a ''new'' immigration stream. Current immigrants are Asians, Caribbeans, and Hispanics -- a far cry from the overwhelmingly European movements of the 1800's and early 1900's.

The United States is once again on the eve of large ethnic transformations. In previous instances, major ethnic changes in the pattern of immigration have given rise to social disturbances, followed by periods of adaption and intregration of the immigrants (and adjustments by the U.S. society). The new phase will also likely involve disturbances and raise new questions about the identity of ''American.'' It is for this reason that changes in the ethnic and racial composition of the population warrant objective study of the direction the nation is going.

As part on ongoing research on immigration at the Urban Institute, we have investigated the future immigrant population of the United States (Edmonston and Passel, 1991a and 1991b). We start with the U.S. population in 1990, characterized by age, sex, and race/ethnicity. We project the U.S. population to 2090. Data are used for the White (non-Hispanic), American Indian, Asian and Pacific Islander, Black, and Hispanic groups. We assume that 1990 age-specific fertility levels adjust to a total fertility rate of 1.90 by 2020. We assume a low mortality forecast for our projection and that the sex difference in mortality diminishes: we assume that life expectancy at birth reaches 88.2 years for males and 92.2 years for females in 2090. We assume that Asians and Hispanics have the same mortality at Whites, and that Black mortality decreases in parallel with White trends but does not equal White life expectancy at birth in 2090. Finally, our projections assumes a net immigration of 900,000 in 1990 and that it increases to a net level of 950,000 in 2005, staying constant thereafter.

FUTURE U.S. POPULATION GROWTH

Even without immigration and with the maintenance of currently low fertility levels, the U.S. population would continue to grow over the next twenty years. The current momentum of population growth -- the result of a younger age distribution -- provides a cushion of about thirty million more people in the next decades, even if immigration were to cease. A population projection with no immigration would indicate a U.S. population peaking at about 280 million and then slowly declining.

Table 1.   Total U.S. Population for Racial/Ethnic Groups, 1990-2090 (in millions)

Year	American Indian	Asian	Black	Hispanic	White Non-Hispanic	Total
1990	2.0	7.3	30.0	22.4	187.1	248.8
2000	2.1	11.7	34.1	30.4	196.4	274.7
2010	2.1	16.4	38.4	38.9	203.3	299.1
2020	2.2	21.5	41.8	47.7	209.3	322.5
2030	2.2	26.8	44.6	56.6	211.9	342.1
2040	2.2	32.1	46.7	65.3	210.5	356.8
2050	2.1	37.5	48.3	73.6	208.5	370.0
2060	2.1	43.0	49.8	82.1	208.1	385.1
2070	2.0	48.6	51.1	90.6	208.6	400.9
2080	2.0	54.1	52.5	99.4	208.4	416.0
2090	1.9	59.7	53.8	107.7	208.8	431.9

Source: Edmonston and Passel, 1991a.

The overall total fertility rate of U.S. women hovered around 1.7 to 1.8 for much of the 1970's and 1980's. The total fertility rate has increased in recent years, reaching a level of about 2.0 in 1990. The future trend in fertility is uncertain, although we prefer to use a total fertility rate of 1.9 in our projections, compared to a rate of 1.8 in the Bureau of the Census's middle series.

With an annual net immigration of 900,000 in 1990, Table 1 indicates that the 1990 total U.S. population of 249 million will approach 350 million in the mid-2030's and top 400 million in 2070. Thus, the level of immigration and emigration assumed in these projections avoids any population

Even with continued immigration, the rate of population growth of the United States will slacken. Table 2 shows that the U.S. population will grow an an average annual rate of 1.0 percent from 1990 to 2000. But this rate will gradually diminish, reaching and continuing at a level of .4 percent within the next fifty years.

From this brief review, it is clear that continuation of current immigration levels would contribute to a larger population size. And although the population will continue to growth for several decades even without immigration, these results suggest the prospect for moderate growth for the next century.

POPULATION AGING

Not only has life expectancy changed dramatically since 1900 -- from about 47 years at the turn of the century to about 76 years in 1990, but there has also occurred a dramatic change in the concentrations of deaths among persons 65 years and older. Today, about three-fourths of the deaths occur among persons 65 years and older. In 1900, those under 15 accounted for about 45 percent of all deaths and those 65 and older for only about 17 percent.

Table 2.   Rate of Population Growth for Racial/Ethnic Groups, by Decades, 1990-2090 (in average annual percent growth)

Year	American Indian	Asian	Black	Hispanic	White Non-Hispanic	Total
1990-00	.5	4.7	1.3	3.1	.5	1.0
2000-10	.3	3.4	1.2	2.5	.3	.9
2010-20	.2	2.7	.8	2.0	.2	.8
2020-30	.0	2.2	.6	1.7	.1	.6
2030-40	-.1	1.8	.5	1.4	-.1	.4
2040-50	-.2	1.6	.3	1.2	-.1	.4
2050-60	-.2	1.4	.3	1.1	.0	.4
2060-70	-.2	1.2	.3	1.0	.0	.4
2070-80	-.2	1.1	.3	.9	.0	.4
2080-90	-.2	1.0	.2	.8	.0	.4

Source: Edmonston and Passel, 1991a.

It is the "graying" of the United States, then, that clearly represents a priority for attention in the areas of health and retirement policy. There are also other demographic forces that will have program consequences for the elderly. These include racial and ethnic composition, changing population distribution, and the composition and organization of the family.

The "aging of the United States" will have direct and dramatic impact on programs for the elderly. There will be an increase in the demand for services that reflect the increase in numbers. But the most important impact of the changing age of our population will take place because of sharp increases in the number of older and much older people -- those 75 ad 85 years of age and older.

By the middle of the next century, it is estimated that those over 75 years will increase from 5 percent at present to about 10 percent of the total population. There will be more people over 75 in the population in 50 years that there are over 65 now.

Females now make up about two-thirds of the older elderly (those over 75 years). The poverty rate for very old women is disproportionately high -- nearly twice that of very old males. The plight of very old women, particularly those living alone, is one of the most serious income and health problems among the elderly. The projected expansion of the very old population will prompt additional calls for program reform and will continue pressure on public income maintenance programs to meet the needs of this relatively impoverished group.

It is the chronic health conditions that represent the by-products of the aging process that represent another major challenge for the U.S. health system in the 1990s and beyond. Can a system that is organized to "cure" the sick, at considerable expense, change to "care" for the aged, at reasonable cost? Some observers of the present system are worried that, as the numbers increase and as the age of the population also increases, so too will the demand for services that today's system provides only at considerable expense.

As the population ages, the future outlook is one of essentially more illness in society. But there are also many unknowns. Progress may be made in reducing prevalence chronic disorders, including advances that improve some long-term impairments, such as diabetes. But additional programs may also mean additional lengthened but impaired lives, and more rather than less sickness as we come to grips with health and retirement in the 21st century.

RACIAL AND ETHNIC COMPOSITION

Preston's (1991) paper cites available official population projections of the racial and ethnic composition of the U.S. population. There are two cautions that should be kept in mind when interpreting the U.S. Bureau of the Census's projections.

1) The fertility of immigrants is assumed to adjust instantaneously to the fertility level of comparable ethnic or racial groups in the United States. This underestimates for many ethnic groups the higher fertility of immigrants that persists for one or two generations after entering the United States. This underestimate of fertility levels is probably strongest for the Mexican-origin population and for selected refugee groups, including those immigrants originating in Southeast Asia. These groups will likely grow at faster rates than estimated by Bureau of the Census forecasts. An improved approach would be to disaggregate ethnic groups by generation after immigration, as is done in the

Edmonston and Passel projection model (Edmonston and Passel, 1991b), with different fertility levels by generation.

2) Bureau of the Census projections make the strong assumption that ethnic population remains single ancestry. The official projections assume perfect within-ethnicity endogamy. The assumptions is that all ethnic groups marry or cohabit strictly within their ethnic group and that, therefore, all births have parents of a single ethnic ancestry.

This assumption of perfect endogamy does not reflect accurately the current patterns of ethnic endogamy. And it is politically treacherous to project population numbers several generations into the future that make it seem that there are distinct White, Black, Other Races, and Hispanic population that are demographically separate. A sizeable proportion of the Hispanic and Asian population already marry outside of their ethnic groups, and rates of exogamy increase with generations of residence in the United States. Assuming current levels of exogamy by generation, our projections suggest that there will be about an equal number of single ancestry and mixed ancestry Asians in 2090. How will these mixed ancestry Asians identify themselves? Even for the Black population, we note that about 4 percent of recorded Black births include a non-Black parent. We should not, it seems, discuss ethnic populations two or three generations from now without including a strong caution that these future populations will include a significant number of mixed ancestry members.

One goal of the Urban Institute's population projections is to observe the implications of population dynamics on the racial/ethnic composition of the population. If immigration were zero, then the future racial/ethnic composition would be determined solely by fertility and mortality differentials in the present population. This implies that, even with no immigration, the racial/ethnic composition would not remain static. It also indicates that the resident population composition provides the fixed component -- the stock -- for the effects of immigration.

The immigrant component plays the central role in determining the future size of the U.S. racial/ethnic population. There are two aspects by which immigration affects population growth. First, the level of immigration matters. The number of immigrants has a direct effect on population growth, with each new immigrant adding one new person to a racial/ethnic group. Second, the reproductive value of the immigrant affects the population by adding descendants. The reproductive value of the immigrant is, in turn, determined by the immigrant's age and their fertility level. A young immigrant with high fertility will add the most descendants, while an old or low fertility immigrant will add few descendants. Hence, the future growth of racial/ethnic groups is the product of several interacting factors.

According to the initial results of the 1990 census, 75 percent of the population are White non-Hispanics, with another 12 percent Black, 9 percent Hispanic, 3 percent Asian, and about 1 percent American Indian. Future trends in immigration and differential fertility and mortality levels will lead to major changes in these proportions.

Looking first at the effects on the numbers of persons in racial/ethnic groups (see Table 1), the White non-Hispanic group will increase its numbers from 187 million to a peak of 212 million in 2030 before falling to about 209 million in 2090. Within the next century (see Table 3), this group will become less numerous and drop from 75 percent of the total population to less than 50 percent in 2090.

Over the next century, the Black population will increase substantially from 30 million to 54 million (again assuming the current level and composition of immigration). But their proportion of the total population will remain virtually unchanged, with an increase from 12 percent in 1990 to 13 percent in 2090.

Table 3.   Total U.S. Population by Percentage Racial/Ethnic Groups, 1990-2090 (in percents)

Year	American Indian	Asian	Black	Hispanic	White Non-Hispanic	Total
1990	.8	2.9	12.1	9.0	75.2	100.0
2000	.8	4.3	12.4	11.1	71.5	100.0
2010	.7	5.5	12.8	13.0	68.0	100.0
2020	.7	6.7	13.0	14.8	64.9	100.0
2030	.6	7.8	13.0	16.5	61.9	100.0
2040	.6	9.0	13.1	18.3	59.0	100.0
2050	.6	10.1	13.1	19.9	56.4	100.0
2060	.5	11.2	12.9	21.3	54.0	100.0
2070	.5	12.1	12.7	22.6	52.0	100.0
2080	.5	13.0	12.6	23.8	50.1	100.0
2090	.4	13.8	12.8	24.9	48.3	100.0

Notes: The percents may not add to exactly 100.0 due to rounding. Each percentage is shown to the nearest 0.1 digit.
Source: Edmonston and Passel, 1991a.

Two groups are likely to experience substantial growth during the next century: Asians and Hispanics. The Asian population will growth at rates exceeding 1 percent for the next century, under the conditions of this projection, increasing from 7 million in 1990 to 60 million in 2090. These gains would increase the Asian's proportion share of the population from 3 percent in 1990 to 14 percent in 2090.

Hispanics are assumed to have a larger share of immigration, partially because of their predominant share of illegal immigration, and grow substantially over the next one hundred years. The Hispanic population would increase from 22 million in 1990 to 30 million in 2000 and growth would continue uninterrupted for one century, at which time they would number 108 million and constitute 25 percent of the population. The Hispanic population would have passed Blacks to become the largest minority group in the nation by 2010.

This description of the future racial/ethnic composition of the U.S. population reflects a continuation of high levels of immigration and the current racial/ethnic composition of that immigration. There are serious questions about the reality of these projections over a 100 year period, and we stress the use of these projections as a simulation representing the long-run implication of plausible current trends.

FUTURE TRENDS

To any causual observer, it should be obvious that the composition of U.S society is undergoing considerable change. Our demographic analysis confirms this trend and present evidence about future trends. However, the statistical evidence tells only part of the story. The White non-Hispanic proportion of the population will decline in future years, that seems certain. Both the Asian and Hispanic populations will grow, both numerically and proportionately. Blacks will increase their numbers but their proportion will increase only slightly. Hispanics will increase to a number exceeding that of Blacks by about 2010 and, indeed, under current trends, the Asian population would out-number the Black population by about 2070.

But how will these new immigrant groups adjust to U.S. society? The contribution of immigration within each racial/ethnic group provides data to alert us to potential difficulties. For example, over one-half of Asian and Hispanic residents will consist of first generation (foreign-born) or second generation (sons and daughters of immigrants) persons for the next century.

Both the size and the relative recency of the movements of people from Asian and Latin American countries suggest that the integration process will take some time to be accomplished if immigration levels remain high in future years. Thus, in considering the impact of immigration on the future population of the United States the issue of the time of entry and what it means for adaption is important to consider.

We do not claim to know what the future will bring to the U.S. population. This is always the danger when interpreting population projection numbers to accept them as a statement of fact. We have expressed caveats about the assumptions made for these projections in several places. We have emphasized that they are simulations based on "what would happen under these stated assumptions." They are not predictions about the future. The future depends, in fact, on future demographic behavior.

However, we can use these projections to give us some idea about the direction in population trends. Under currently low fertility, immigration will need to continue at a substantial level to avoid population decline. With continued immigration, the principal conclusion of this study is that the racial/ ethnic composition of the nation will be substantially altered over the next century.

3

Expected Changes in the Workforce and Implications for Labor Markets

Phillip B. Levine
and
Olivia S. Mitchell

INTRODUCTION

While many have written about possible effects of the baby boom on the U.S. economy, few have recognized that this demographic transition provides analysts with a unique and valuable opportunity to investigate how the labor market works. Specifically, as baby boomers move up the age distribution, they impart a one-time shock to the supply of potential workers in each age bracket. Because this change is exogenous, many of the tools labor economists typically apply can be utilized to predict how the aging of the baby boom will alter key labor market outcomes. Theoretical and empirical models which (either implicitly or explicitly) hold constant structural parameters in order to work through the effects of an exogenous shock are well-suited to address this issue.

The goal of this paper is to use economic tools to analyze the impact of the baby boom on three key labor market outcomes: labor force participation rates, unemployment, and wages. We concentrate mainly on this particular cohort's labor market outcomes, but also consider the implications of this group for the labor market as a whole. Since most of the prime-age population participates in the labor market, we focus analysis on labor market trends between the present and 2020, when the majority of the baby boom generation will confront the retirement decision. Consequently, an important topic of discussion will be retirement patterns of older workers and a consideration of whether the trend towards earlier retirement will continue in the next three decades. In addition, we briefly examine the effects of the aging baby boom on unemployment, and on wages for older workers as well as for workers of other ages.

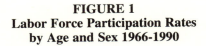

FIGURE 1
Labor Force Participation Rates
by Age and Sex 1966-1990

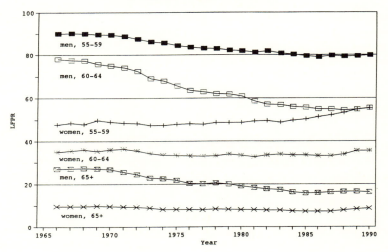

Our review of the evidence leads us to conclude that trends towards earlier retirement will slow and perhaps reverse. New Social Security rules have already been enacted to encourage later retirement. Pension incentives towards early retirement will be curtailed as fewer workers will be available to replace retiring baby boomers. A great deal of evidence indicates that financial incentives have a strong impact on workers' retirement decisions, so these changes in pensions and Social Security should slow the trend toward earlier retirement. Our prediction is further supported by data on projected changes in workforce composition. Since growth will probably not be concentrated in the blue-collar sector where worker's productivity is more likely to decline with age, early retirement may be avoided by more workers in the future.

We also conclude that the aging labor market will bring with it a reduction in unemployment, and will have little impact on relative wages. Both unemployment among older workers and the aggregate full-employment unemployment rate should fall as the baby boom ages. While job displacement of older workers currently leads to substantial hardship, this problem should be somewhat reduced in the future. In future economic expansions, businesses will not be able to rely on a young "reserve army of the unemployed" to fill new positions as in the past; displaced older workers may more often become the new recruits. Steady state aggregate unemployment should also fall as the labor force becomes more heavily weighted with older workers with traditionally lower unemployment rates. The effect of baby boom aging on wages is more difficult to track because employers have the potential to substitute capital for labor, and to hire workers from other demographic groups. However, controlling for all such interactions, there is no support for the conclusion that wages will be substantially depressed either for older workers, or for other demographic groups.

The argument is developed in three parts. A first section reviews recent labor force trends and discusses published predictions regarding retirement patterns as the baby boom ages over the next three decades. The second section identifies determinants of retirement suggested by the labor economics literature of the past decade and offers informed judgement about possible future participation patterns. The third part of the paper briefly examines the effects of an aging baby boom on unemployment and wages. A brief summary concludes the discussion.

LABOR FORCE TRENDS, PAST AND FUTURE

Before examining projections regarding the future labor force, it is useful to briefly review labor force developments to date as well as the explanations for these patterns. Here we sketch past trends in labor force participation, and then go on to discuss previous efforts to project labor force figures into the future.

Looking Backward: Labor Market Trends to 1990

Labor force participation trends for older workers and over have been the subject of intense discussion and debate in recent years. There is general agreement over several key facts:

- *Labor force participation rates for older men have dropped by more than half since 1900.* Among men age 60 and older, 66 percent were in the labor force in 1900, according to archival evidence, while less than half that many, 26 percent, were active by 1990 (Table 1).

- *The trend to earlier retirement among men has not been a steady one.* In fact, men's participation rates were quite stable between 1900 and the mid-'30's, then began falling in 1937, continued falling steadily for fifty years through the late 1980's. (Figure 1). It is possible that the trend to early retirement may actually have reversed over the last two years, inasmuch as participation rates have risen in the 60-64 age range for two years in a row -- a phenomenon almost without precedent in the last quarter century in the United States. (Detailed age breakdowns by age appear in Figure 2 for men age 60-61 and 62-64 since 1960).

- *Labor force trends for women have been more mixed over the century. Since 1900, older women's labor force attachment figures rose, but their rates over the century fell relative to younger women.* Around 1900, older women's (age 55-64) participation rates stood at 21 percent for nonmarried women, and 2 percent for wives. By 1980, participation rates for older nonmarried women rose to 54 percent, and 37 percent for older wives. (Goldin 1990). Older women's participation rates are still about twenty percentage points below those of younger women (USDOL 1991).

- *For older women the trend to earlier retirement may have reversed slightly in the last five years.* As Figure 2 indicates, labor force participation rates of women in their early 60's have risen slightly since about 1986. Nevertheless, older women's participation rates remained at only two thirds those of similar aged male rates by 1990.

Table 1.   Labor Force Participation of Men Age 60 and over, 1870-1990

Year	Percentage
1870	64.2
1880	64.3
1900	66.1
1930	64.5
1937	61.5
1940	54.7
1950	54.5
1960	45.4
1970	40.4
1980	32.2
1990	27.6

Source: 1870-1980: Ransom and Sutch (1988); note 1940 data not strictly comparable. 1990: USDOL (1991).

Overall, the evidence demonstrates a clear and increasing tendency not to work at older ages among men, and a relative decline in participation among older women over time.

Labor market status of older people has also been examined using other variables as well. Some analysts examine whether or not an individual was employed during a short period of time (e.g. work during a single survey week) while others tabulate peoples' affirmative answers to questions like ''are you

FIGURE 2
Labor Force Participation Rates
by Sex and Narrow Age Brackets, 1963-1990

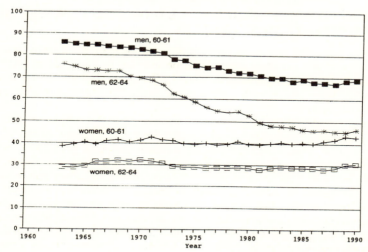

now retired?'' as an indication of retirement status (Fields and Mitchell [1984] and Quinn et al [1990] review various definitions of retirement status). Most of these data are not available over time, so cannot reveal much about trends in labor force attachment.

There is somewhat more research on what has been called "partial" or "phased" retirement, generally viewed as employment subsequent to one's career job with either fewer hours of work per week, or at a lower wage rate, or both. An investigation by Gustman and Steinmeier (1984) showed that almost a quarter of the 64-year old and 38 percent of the 69-year old men examined considered themselves partially retired by this measure during the 1970's. Subsequent analysis of the same data set by Quinn et al. (1990) confirms that most of these individuals spend only a short time in this partial retirement status, moving out of the labor force thereafter rather rapidly. Whether partial or phased retirement is gaining ground among the older workforce of the 1990's cannot be determined yet, since there is no current longitudinal survey of this group. It is anticipated that data necessary to examine these trends in the near future will be provided by the new Health and Retirement Survey, under development by the University of Michigan's Institute for Survey Research and funded by the National Institute on Aging.

Last but not least, there is ample evidence that part time work has become more important in older people's work patterns. As Quinn et al (1990) demonstrate, there is a large jump in the prevalence of part time work at age 65, from 6 to 48 percent for men, and from 20 to almost 60 percent for women. This pattern complements other indicators of the trend toward early retirement in the U.S.

labor market: fewer people are remaining employed at older ages, and when they do they are increasingly likely to work part-time rather than full time.

LOOKING FORWARD: PUBLISHED LABOR FORCE PROJECTIONS FOR THE TWENTY-FIRST CENTURY

Will this powerful trend to earlier retirement in the US labor market continue? Over the past few decades, labor force projections by the U.S. government, combining predicted population trends and LFPR's, have become quite common. This section will consider where these projections come from and what can be learned from them.

There are at least three major sources of labor force projections produced by research and policy organizations and widely discussed in public policy circles. The Bureau of Labor Statistics (BLS) regularly presents projections with a relatively short horizon, typically no longer than 15 years into the future. Two other government agencies have provided labor force projections further into the future. The Bureau of Economic Analysis (BEA) publishes a report every five years with projections that extend 50 years. In addition, the Social Security Administration (SSA) has projected the size of the labor force to the year 2060. This agency's report was not part of a continuing research program, however. It was conducted in the early 1980's to determine whether existing financing methods could generate enough revenue to provide benefits to the anticipated larger cohorts of retired workers.

As noted above, the projected size of the labor force is the product of two elements, the anticipated size of the population and labor force participation rates. Since Preston's paper in this volume extensively analyzes population projections, we focus here on predicted labor force participation rates.

The methodology that is employed in each these projections is quite similar (c.f. Flaim and Fullerton 1978 for a detailed description of the BLS projection method). Typically, past trends are extrapolated to predict future behavior. Ad hoc manipulations are then made to eliminate impossible results (e.g. labor force participation rates greater than 100 percent or less than 0 percent) or results which are "highly implausible" (e.g. women's labor force participation rates higher than men's). Minor adjustments are also made for other factors, such as the level of economic growth (all projections presented here assume moderate growth). Some of the projections are interrelated as well; the BEA's longer term projections start with the predicted rates of the BLS and then extrapolate this series.

Table 2 presents alternative projections of the civilian labor force participation rate for selected years and different demographic groups, in addition to a snapshot of current participation rate patterns. The evident similarity in predicted participation rates for a given demographic group (especially for men) is indicative of the similarity in techniques employed. For instance, the participation rate predicted by the BEA for all men in 2015 is identical to the one predicted by SSA for 2020: both agencies indicate that market attachment among men will fall from the current level of 76.1 percent to 72 percent over the next 25 to 30 years. This prediction is largely a result of the population being more heavily weighted towards older workers who have lower labor market attachment.

There are some differences in projected rates for individual age groups among men, however. Both the BLS and BEA project a continuing small decline in LFPR's among older men (over age 65), while the SSA does not. On the other hand, the SSA's projected growth in teenage labor force participation is considerably greater than in the BEA and BLS.

Projections for women are more variable, as one might expect given dramatic changes in female labor force participation of the recent past. As was the case for the men, market attachment among women as a whole is predicted to decrease after the year 2000 because of the changing age composition of the workforce. Estimates of labor force behavior among individual age groups show marked discrepancies across projections, however. The BLS and BEA project a continued large increase in participation among prime-age women while the SSA predicts virtually no change. Also, SSA projections for older women show virtually no change from current rates, while the BLS and BEA show a slight trend towards earlier retirement.

Table 2a. Current and Projected Labor Force Participation Rates by Sex and Age

	(1)	(2)	(3)	(4)	(5)
	Observed	BLS	SSA	BEA	SSA
	1990	2000	2000	2015	2020
All Men	76.1	75.9	77.5	72.0	72.0
Age group:					
16-24	71.5			74.8	
16-19	55.7	59.0	66.9	63.9	67.7
20-24	84.3	86.5	86.9	84.0	87.4
25-54	93.4			92.4	
25-34	94.2	94.1		92.5	
25-29	93.8		95.0		95.3
30-34	94.6		95.2		95.4

Table 2a.   Continued

	(1)	(2)	(3)	(4)	(5)
	Observed	BLS	SSA	BEA	SSA
	1990	2000	2000	2015	2020
35-44	94.4	94.3		94.9	
35-39	94.9		95.1		95.4
40-44	93.9		94.1		94.4
45-54	90.7	90.5		90.2	
45-49	92.3		92.0		92.0
50-54	88.8		87.7		86.4
55-64	67.7	68.1		62.9	
55-59	79.8		79.5		75.3
60-64	55.5		62.1		57.3
65+	16.4	14.7		13.0	
65-69	26.0		27.0		26.3
70+	10.8		10.6		10.7

Table 2b.   Current and Projected Labor Force Participation Rates by Sex and Age (continued)

	(1)	(2)	(3)	(4)	(5)
	Observed	BLS	SSA	BEA	SSA
	1990	2000	2000	2015	2020
All Women	57.5	62.6	59.0	57.5	54.6
Age group:					
16-24	63.1				
16-19	51.8	59.6	62.4	59.1	63.4
20-24	71.6	77.9	76.9	84.5	76.7
25-54	74.1			79.9	

	(1)	(2)	(3)	(4)	(5)
	Observed	BLS	SSA	BEA	SSA
	1990	2000	2000	2015	2020
25-34	73.6	82.4		84.3	
25-29	73.8		75.1		75.8
30-34	73.4		74.4		75.4
35-44	76.5	84.9		85.6	
35-39	75.5		76.3		77.0
40-44	77.6		78.0		78.4
45-54	71.2	76.5		70.7	
45-49	74.8		76.4		76.3
50-54	66.9		71.6		71.7
55-64	45.3	49.0		43.0	
55-59	55.3		56.5		55.0
60-64	35.5		38.8		36.7
65+	8.7	7.6		7.3	
65-69	17.0		17.6		18.0
70+	4.8		5.4		5.5

Source:
Column 1: USDOL (1991).
Column 2: Fullerton (1989).
Column 3 and 5: US Dept. of HHS (1983).
Column 4: US Dept. of Commerce (1985).

Historically, labor market projections seldom resemble observed behavior. As we will demonstrate, relatively short-term projections by the BLS have not been very reliable for many demographic groups where labor supply patterns have undergone change in the last decades. This calls into even greater question the BEA and SSA projections extending beyond the next 15 years, well into the 21st century.

Table 3 collects three BLS projections for age/sex groups made at three different points in time, along with the observed participation rates in that year for that group. One striking observation is that in some instances, the difference between projected and observed rates is over 50 percent. Groups where projec-

FIGURE 3
Projection Errors using Linear Extrapolation:
LFPR's of 20-24 year old women

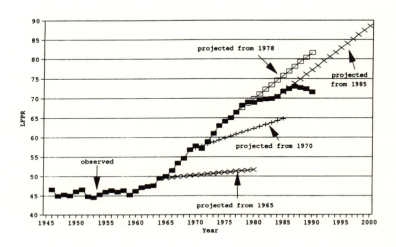

tions are fraught with the largest errors, as one might expect, are women and older workers. For example, the 1985 rate for women aged 25-34 projected as of 1970 was 46.7 percent, but the observed 1985 rate was 70.9 percent. The projections are not always underestimates; thus, for instance, 35.9 percent of men aged 65-69 were projected to participate in the labor force in 1985, but only 24.4 percent actually did.

Table 3.   Comparison of Actual and ''Short Term'' Labor Force Participation
             Rate Projections by Sex and Age

	1980 Actual	1980 Projected*	1985 Actual	1985 Projected*	1990 Actual	1990 Projected*
All Men	76.8	80.3	76.3	80.4	76.1	76.4
Age group:						
16-19	61.2	56.7	56.8	54.3	55.7	64.8
20-24	85.7	87.2	85.0	82.3	84.3	85.0
25-54					93.4	93.1
25-34	94.2	96.2	94.7	97.4		

	1980 Actual	1980 Projected*	1985 Actual	1985 Projected*	1990 Actual	1990 Projected*
35-44	94.6	96.7	95.0	97.4		
45-54	90.3	95.0	91.0	95.3		
55-64	71.4	83.7			67.7	65.0
55-59			79.6	88.2		
60-64			55.6	73.9		
65+	18.3	21.8			16.4	15.0
65-69			24.4	35.9		
70+			10.5	13.2		
All Women	50.9	41.9	54.5	43.7	57.5	57.1
Age group:						
16-19	53.0	46.6	41.2	52.1	51.8	62.8
20-24	69.0	52.6	71.8	57.9	71.6	80.4
25-54					74.1	72.4
25-34	65.3	40.3	70.9	46.7		
35-44	65.2	50.0	71.8	53.6		
45-54	59.6	59.5	64.4	55.6		
55-64	41.1	47.3			45.3	39.8
55-59			50.3	52.3		
60-64			33.4	38.7		
65+	7.6	9.9			8.7	6.2
65-69			13.5	16.3		
70+			4.3	5.1		

Notes:
*All projections assume moderate economic growth. Projections for 1980 were made in 1965, 1985 projections in 1970 and 1990 projections in 1978.
Source:
Columns 1 and 2: Fullerton (1982).
Columns 3 and 4: Fullerton (1988).
Column 5: Flaim and Fullerton (1978).
Column 6: USDOL (1991).

FIGURE 4
Projection Errors using Linear Extrapolation:
LFPR's of 55-64 Year Old Men

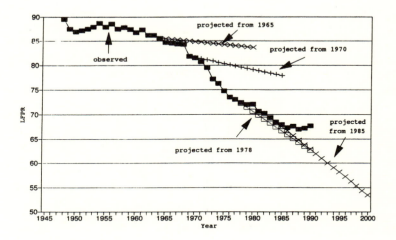

Another observation about these projections is that the pattern of discrepancy has changed over time. Comparing actual data with projections for 1980 and 1985, two patterns were clear: more women were entering the labor market and more men were retiring at younger ages than anticipated. However, in 1990 these patterns appear to have reversed to some extent. Projected participation for younger women, between the ages of 16 and 24, was actually higher than observed. Similarly, more older workers (over age 55, both men and women) remained in the labor market than projections indicated.

This finding highlights an inherent flaw in projection technology which essentially relies on a linear extrapolation with only minor modifications. When behavioral patterns change, projections using the existing methodology will be "too slow" to respond. To illustrate this problem, consider observed and projected participation rates for women aged 20-24, one of the demographic groups undergoing most change in labor market behavior during the last twenty years. (Note that while the focus of this section is clearly on labor force behavior of older workers, this younger group was Cchosen for analysis here because it presents the best example of the patterns we seek to explain).

Figure 3 presents observed participation rates for this group from 1946 through 1990, along with four projections we have made through a simple linear extrapolation technique. To correspond as closely as possible to Table 3, we projected labor force participation rates in 1980 as of 1965, using a linear trend developed from data on observed participation rates during the twenty years immediately preceding 1965. Observed participation rates in the projection year are then incremented by the trend to predict future values from 1980 forward.

The same procedure was followed for projected labor force participation rates in 1985 and 1990, as well as in the year 2000. In each case, the trend was generated from a point fifteen years earlier, and depended on observed participation rates in the twenty years immediately preceding that projection date to establish the linear trend.

As reported in Table 4, rates predicted for 1980, 1985 and 1990 using linear extrapolation are remarkably similar to those projected by the BLS for this demographic group. This suggests that the BLS's judgmental adjustments to extrapolated rates were relatively minimal. Nevertheless, there is a huge difference between the observed and projected rates. Projected figures understate the observed in 1980 and 1985, and overstate them in 1990. This example provides a clear indication of the problems inherent in existing projection methodology. When the rate of change in LFPR's is increasing, linear extrapolation leads to underpredicted values without adjusting extrapolated rates. Similarly, decreasing rates of change lead to overpredicted participation rates. Both of these effects are observed in Figure 3. The fact that extrapolated rates to the year 2000 are significantly different than the BLS projections (as shown in Table 4) indicates that in more recent projections, larger adjustments must have been made.

Table 4. A Comparison of Projection Errors Using Linear Extrapolations and BLS Results, Selected Demographic Groups and Years

	1980	1985	1990	2000
Labor Force Participation Rates of:				
Women Age 20-24				
Observed	69.0	71.8	71.6	----
BLS Projection	52.6	57.9	80.4	77.9
Linear Extrapolation	52.1	65.2	81.6	88.5
	1980	1985	1990	2000
Labor Force Participation Rates of:				
Men Age 55-64				
Observed	71.4	67.9	67.7	----
BLS Projection	83.7	81.3	65.0	68.1
Linear Extrapolation	83.6	77.9	62.7	53.5
Women Age 55-64				
Observed	41.1	42.0	45.3	----
BLS Projection	47.3	45.5	39.8	49.0
Linear Extrapolation	56.6	56.6	43.8	41.1

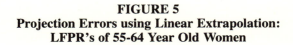

FIGURE 5
Projection Errors using Linear Extrapolation:
LFPR's of 55-64 Year Old Women

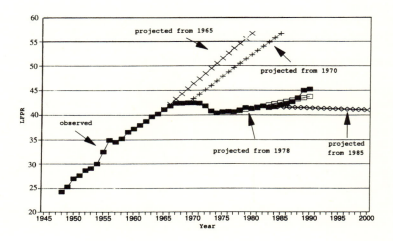

Figures 4 and 5 and the remainder of Table 4 report the results of similar analyses for older male and female workers (age 55-64). For older men, the increasing rate of early withdrawal from the labor force led to overpredictions of the participation rate using the linear trend methodology, until the trend towards early retirement slowed in the mid 1980's. This last effect produced an underestimate of men's participation for 1990 (Figure 4). Note that the similarity in the linear extrapolations and the BLS projections indicates that through 1990, few ad hoc adjustments were made to reported rates. However, the fact that the BLS projections for the year 2000 are considerably higher than those obtained from linear extrapolation indicates that a large ad hoc adjustment must have been made.

For older women, the increasing participation rates prior to 1965 led to substantially overprojected rates for 1980 and 1985 (Figure 5). In contrast, the relatively constant rates from 1965-85 led to projected rates being too low in 1990, after rates began to rise again. The BLS projections for this demographic group, however, have been consistently lower than those obtained by linear extrapolation, indicating ad hoc reductions in projected rates occurred regularly through 1990. For the year 2000, the BLS has now adjusted projections, raising the rate obtained by linear extrapolation.

This section has extensively investigated the limitations of projection methods currently used for "short-term" labor force projections. The problems in this exercise should cast serious doubt on even longer term projections carried out by a variety of agencies and analysts. Our goal has not been to indict current methodology, since under many circumstances it may be the best technique available. Changes in the underlying structural parameters of the labor market are difficult to predict in many cases, implying that a mainly statistical procedure which masks the effects of these economic factors may be the simplest approach. On the other hand, we believe there are economic factors which should also inform a model used to project future labor force outcomes. It is to the development of this model we turn next.

ECONOMIC MODELS OF RETIREMENT TRENDS

To understand how the baby boom will affect labor markets, an economic model of behavior should be constructed. As argued at the outset, models of this sort would be particularly useful in this context because they hold constant structural parameters in order to work through the effects of an exogenous shock such as the one imparted on the labor market by the baby boom. Nevertheless, the task of developing a fully specified economic model to examine the effect of the aging of the baby boom on the labor market is at present not possible. Indeed it probably will require many more years of research. Instead of presenting a clearly inadequate formal model, we instead undertake the job here of describing the building blocks that a fully specified model will certainly need to incorporate. This section employs these building blocks to the question of how retirement trends might be expected to change as we move toward 2020.

THE ECONOMIC DETERMINANTS OF EARLY RETIREMENT

Ten years ago, many researchers in the retirement field believed that most older workers remained employed as long as possible, and retired only when forced to by poor health, mandatory retirement, or other "push" factors. However, this view has been deeply undermined by the last decade of retirement research.

The Role of Poor Health:

It is certainly the case that health problems force some older workers to leave their jobs. When this occurs, it must be agreed that retirement is not a choice but rather a necessity compelled by poor health. The important issue, however, is how numerous are such people and whether the incidence of disabling health problems is increasing among the population experiencing earlier retirement -- that is, workers in their late 50's and early 60's.

After reviewing the evidence, we believe that (1) there is little support for the view that health is a major factor explaining early retirement, and (2) increasingly poor health cannot explain the long-term trend toward earlier retirement in the United States. We focus first on the importance of health as a determinant of early retirement. Here the evidence shows that relatively few give health-related reasons for retirement. For example, only 12 percent of more than one thousand men surveyed by the Social Security Administration gave poor health as the primary reason for leaving their main job (Fields and Mitchell 1984). In addition, many researchers note that these statistics will overstate the role of poor health because retirees' own assessment of their health status is colored by illness/ disability being a socially acceptable rationale for retirement, and because reporting oneself to be in poor health is a prerequisite for various government transfer payments. An excellent review of recent studies can be found in Sammartino (1987). When researchers examine more "objective" health measures from clinical sources, evidence on impairments, and mortality outcomes, they generally conclude that health has some role to play, but by no means is it as important as economic variables in explaining labor market withdrawal (Fields and Mitchell 1984, Quinn et al. 1990). Thus most workers retire for reasons other than poor health.

The weight of the evidence is also not supportive of the claim that the long-term trends toward early retirement was driven primarily by worsening health among workers in their late 50's and early 60's. The evidence is somewhat mixed, because problems arising in self-reported health measures become exacerbated over time. Thus, for instance, Bailey (1987) notes large increases over time in the number of self-reported days of limited activity due to illness or disability among those age 45-64, as well as among the elderly. However the survey questionnaire was changed in the late 1960's, resulting in the same number of people reporting health limitations, but a large increase in the extent to which health limitations were deemed restrictive. Thus the time trend Bailey reports in health limits is less than fully persuasive. Similarly, disability cases seem to be increasing in the older population over time, but changes in eligibility rules for Social Security Disability benefits may explain a large part of this trend. On the one hand, it seems clear that a much older population will have more health problems than will a younger group (Poterba and Summers 1987). On the other hand, there is no strong evidence that the health status of those age 55 to 65 deteriorated sufficiently to explain the strong decline in work among this age group from World War II onward.

Mandatory Retirement:

Prior to 1978, many employers imposed mandatory retirement at age 65. This policy was altered in 1978 with the Federal Age Discrimination in Employment Act, which moved the mandatory retirement age to 70; subsequently the age bar was lifted altogether for most private sector employees.

Even before mandatory retirement was outlawed, however, most firms did not force older workers out using this policy (Fields and Mitchell 1984). Less than half of all private sector workers during the early 1970's were in jobs covered by mandatory retirement provisions, and fewer than 5 percent of retirees appear to have worked long enough to have been forced out by mandatory retirement. Thus it seems safe to conclude that mandatory retirement was not an increasingly powerful force driving workers to early retirement over the last several decades.

Having established that most older workers are not forced to retire, it is necessary to then elaborate other explanations for early retirement. Research on workers reaching retirement age has demonstrated that preeminent among these other explanations are economic factors, including most importantly wages and retirement wealth. Along these lines, an analysis of older men's retirement patterns by Fields and Mitchell (1984) concluded that economic factors such as wages and retirement benefits accounted for three-quarters of the explained variance in retirement ages across people, while poor health was found to account for only one-quarter.

Wealth:

One factor which certainly played a role in inducing earlier retirement over time was an increase in overall wealth. U.S. economic growth since World War II contributed importantly to real wage growth over time, despite periods of inflation and economic slowdown. During most of their productive lifetimes, workers earned more and accumulated more assets than their parents' cohorts. As a consequence, succeeding generations of older persons attained retirement age in better economic conditions than at most any time in the past (Burkhauser and Quinn 1989). Since leisure is a normal good, in economic terms, this increase in older people's wealth permitted additional consumption of retirement years over the decades (Fields and Mitchell 1984).

Long-term asset growth was accompanied by two other developments which also permitted, if not encouraged, earlier retirement: the growth of the U.S. Social Security system, and the maturation of the private pension system.

Social Security:

Several different institutional features of the Social Security system contributed to make early retirement increasingly attractive and feasible over time in the US. First, coverage grew rapidly over the post-WWII period: only about 60 percent of the labor force was covered during the 1950's, whereas over 90 percent of all workers are covered now (Aaron, 1982). Almost all retirees today receive some income from Social Security, compared to only about one-third of all private sector workers receiving a pension (Piascentini and Cerino 1990).

A second institutional change implemented in Social Security over time had to do with the age at which a worker could first become eligible for Social Security retirement benefits. This age, initially set at 65, was dropped for women to age 62 in 1956, and for men in 1961 (Rejda 1982). The fact that retirement payments are payable at 62 has enabled many to afford early retirement that they might not have been able to afford otherwise.

Another way in which Social Security changed making retirement more attractive over time had to do with benefit growth. After taking into account inflation, the average Social Security benefit payable to a newly retired male rose 50 percent in real terms between 1955 and 1985 (Ippolito, 1990). Pre- and post-retirement increases of massive proportions were legislated by a Congress eager to more than protect benefits against inflation, a policy which made retirement more affordable, and thus increasingly prevalent, among older Americans over time.

Two additional features of Social Security have been cited as contributing to earlier retirement. One is that at various points over the years, benefits under the system were structured to subsidize early retirement (Fields and Mitchell 1984). This occurred when the present value of future Social Security benefits payable to a worker who retired early (age 62) were just as high as (or higher than) the present value of benefits payable to someone deferring early retirement. This situation arose somewhat inadvertently, because the rules specified that someone who worked to age 65 paid more tax than if he retired early, yet age-65 benefits were not enough larger to offset this additional tax payment. In addition, the early retiree would enjoy leisure, further weighting the balance in favor of leaving early.

A different way in which Social Security discouraged continued work after eligibility for benefits is via the so called "earnings test". This regulation permits the older benefit recipient to work and earn up to a threshold level, after which point Social Security payments begin to be reduced to offset additional earnings. This Social Security "earnings test" is certainly a labor market deterrent to some older workers, but several studies have also demonstrated that it is not relevant to many others (Leonesio 1990). Part of the reason that the earnings test may not deter work at older ages is that for some people, additional earnings beyond age 60 can have a pronounced positive effect on the Social Security Primary Insurance Amount (this is particularly important when high nominal earnings after age 60 replace low or zero wages earlier in life). While there is still some controversy about the political wisdom of retaining the earnings test, the evidence suggests that removing it would not induce much more work among the older population though it would cost the system a great deal (Gustman and Steinmeier 1991).

While Social Security benefits certainly grew more generous for those retiring since World War II, these benefit increases must be weighed against increases in taxes which accompanied the growth of the system. Taking into account this factor also suggests a damping effect: beneficiaries retiring in 1950 earned an implicit (risk-free) return on their contributions of about 20 percent per year in real terms, far exceeding that which they could have earned in the private market. The rate of return on contributions was about 12 percent for workers retiring only 15 years later (Moffitt 1984), and will probably be even smaller, if not negative, in the future. What this implies is that cohorts retiring forty years ago received relatively greater wealth transfers from the system than do today's older workers, providing those early groups with stronger early retirement incentives than were afforded to later ones. Hence the so-called "start-up" phase of Social Security provided the first several retiring cohorts more wealth than later cohorts got, suggesting a diminution of retirement incentives in recent years. Whether and how retirement trends will respond to future Social Security changes is taken up again in a subsequent section.

Pensions:

A variety of labor market institutions have made early retirement more attractive in the last several decades, particularly the growth and development of employer-sponsored pensions. The growth of the private pension system has been striking: immediately following World War II, only 19 percent of private sector wage and salary workers were covered by pension plans, whereas by 1987 the fraction covered was 46 percent (Turner and Beller 1990) This rapid growth in pension coverage has moderated and perhaps even turned around over the last five to seven years, however, evidently because of changing labor force composition, a shift to smaller firms and a trend away from unionized manufacturing jobs (e.g. Clark and McDermed 1990).

There is ample evidence that employers and their workers enable and often encourage earlier retirement over time, often by means of their pension plan. Recent research has shown that defined benefit plans frequently offer attractive incentives to retire before age 65, and many do not impose an actuarial reduction in benefits among those leaving early (Mitchell, 1991). Retirement supplements and bonuses, early retirement window plans, and a variety of other mechanisms have the effect of offering benefits which are largest if the worker retires as soon as he or she is eligible (Mutschler 1986, Lumsdaine et al 1990). In other words, the present value of the worker's retirement annuity stream from a defined benefit plan will often be maximized if early retirement is accepted, but will gall the longer retirement is delayed (Mitchell and Fields, 1985). Not only do such pensions offer retirement wealth which enables workers to retire earlier, but also they structure benefits in such a way that workers can leave early without suffering large benefit cuts. These patterns have a potent effect on workers' retirement decisions, a finding supported by dozens of econometric studies conducted during the 1980's and carefully reviewed by Quinn et al (1990).

The effect of defined benefit pensions on retirement is indisputable, but in order to account for trends in early retirement it must also be demonstrated that corporate pension policy changed over time in such a way as to increase the appeal of leaving early. Evidence on this point, while difficult to obtain, is beginning to emerge in studies of specific companies tracked over time (Luzadis and Mitchell 1991; Ippolito 1990). Available evidence offers evidence that at least some defined benefit plans changed their retirement incentives between 1960 and 1980 in such a way as to increase the financial attractiveness of early retirement. This was accomplished by increasing benefit payments and tilting pension benefit formulas to lower the age at which pension benefit streams were maximized. Though explanations for these patterns are still only suggestive, it is likely that these early retirement incentives grew more pronounced over time in less profitable firms, and for workers with longer time on the job. It must be concluded that if pension plans could be structured to make early retirement more appealing, it will be possible to reverse this trend should labor shortages develop requiring extending the worklife.

Wages:

Wage patterns by education have diverged substantially over the last two decades, and this subject has been the subject of intense study. In the main, this literature tends to conclude that wages are becoming increasingly unequal over time, with earnings becoming particularly stagnant among the least educated segment of the workforce (c.f. Levy 1987). However few analysts have narrowed their analysis to the older segment of the workforce, and there is little evidence on whether these wage trends are exacerbated among the older age group. In addition, corporate downsizing may have contributed to slower wage growth among older workers. More research is required to determine the extent to which falling wages may have contributed to earlier retirement trends experienced in the last decade.

MODELING THE EFFECTS OF FUTURE DEMOGRAPHIC CHANGE ON EARLY RETIREMENT

Having identified above the most important regulatory and economic factors affecting retirement outcomes, it remains to discuss how these factors might be anticipated to affect retirement patterns as the labor force ages.

Focusing first on the regulatory environment, we suspect that changing incentives will lead to a reduction or reversal in the trend towards early retirement. Many government policies have recently been implemented to encourage continued work both now and in the future. This includes legislation raising and then eliminating the practice of mandatory retirement for most sectors of the labor market, as well as age discrimination legislation and disability regulations providing opportunities for older workers to remain employed in the future should they so wish.

Social Security rules were also altered with reforms legislated in 1983, policies which will be affecting retirement incentives for cohorts of retirees well into the 21st century. In summary form, it is fair to characterize these reforms as raising the normal retirement age under Social Security from age 65 to 67 for baby boomers, and reducing benefits for those retiring prior to age 65. Additionally these reforms subjected a portion of retirees' Social Security benefits to income tax, which in turn reduces the net payoff to retirement and increases the relative attractiveness of remaining employed. Unfortunately, the specific Social Security reforms undertaken will probably have only a tiny effect on retirement patterns over the next thirty five years, according to numerous evaluation studies using a variety of economic models. Instead, what will probably occur at least in the near term is that workers will continue to retire at roughly the same age, but will be more at risk for old-age poverty because benefits are lower (Mitchell, forthcoming).

Other pressures on federal budgets may also affect retirement patterns. For example the nation's health insurance program for people age 65 and over, Medicare, is scheduled to run out of money several years before the baby boom reaches retirement age (Aaron et al 1989). These pressures will certainly strengthen the government's intentions to reverse the early retirement trend, though gradual changes in entitlement programs may not be effective in achieving this end.

The other factor affecting retirement trends, as argued above, is employer-provided pensions. Here too several changes may be anticipated (Andrews and Mitchell 1986). Pensions may become less widespread and/or less generous in the future if, for example, marginal tax rates fall thereby reducing the appeal of pensions as a savings device. If Congress limits or ends the tax-preferred status of pensions in the future, this would seriously decrease pension plans' appeal as a retirement savings devise and diminish the prevalence of corporate pensions. It also is possible that the baby boom generation may receive lower total compensation because of its sheer size (more on this below), implying that pensions may become less prevalent. Other factors also likely to reduce pension coverage are declining firm size and changing industrial mix. Economies of scale make retirement investment more efficient in larger firms, but as the service sector replaces the shrinking manufacturing sector, where smaller firms are more prevalent, demand for pensions will decline relative to the past. Related to this is the fact that union workers have traditionally negotiated pensions more often than their nonunion counterparts; however most labor experts predict continued stasis in the union sector, suggesting that on this count as well pensions will decline in importance in the future.

Government pension policy will also play a role in shaping the environment within which firms structure their pension plans. A host of recent reforms have raised pension costs and reduced the flexibility of compensation arrangements, including provisions limiting integration of pension benefits with Social Security payments, ceilings on the amount of contributions that can be accumulated on a tax-deferred basis, and prohibitions against using age in pension computations. Firms are now required to continue accruing pension benefits after the normal retirement age for older workers, ruling out cuts in benefit accrual and thus inducing early retirement (Mitchell, 1991). Additionally, a very recent reform outlaws the use of age as a criterion in early-out window plans, further limiting firms' ability to reward early retirement. These developments place constraints on the range of policies firms can adopt in the future regarding retirement age policy. If government policy continues to restrict pension practices, this makes providing pensions increasingly costly. Some of these additional costs may be offset by reducing wages or other employee benefits, but in other cases firms may be forced to terminate their pension plans which in turn will reduce the incentives to retire early (Hay Huggins 1990; Mitchell 1991 a, b).

Some nonfinancial factors are also likely to affect retirement patterns. For example, changes in productivity among older workers may also affect the decision to leave the labor force. Mitchell, Levine, and Pozzebon (1988) review evidence indicating that differences in retirement behavior across industries and occupations are correlated with differences in age/productivity profiles. Specifically, workers in blue collar occupations have been shown to retire relatively earlier and to face greater productivity declines with age. However, at a macroeconomic level, the movement away from manufacturing towards the service sector will lead to a smaller share of blue collar jobs in the economy.

Hence, diminished productivity should be less of a problem for older workers and they may be expected to remain in the workforce longer as we move into the 21st century.

The changing health status of older workers may have an impact on future retirement behavior though there is controversy about the direction this will take. Most workers do not retire for health-related reasons, and it may be that the small percentage that does should decline as a result of improving health status in the future. On the other hand increasing longevity does not necessarily translate into better health among older workers; people may simply live longer in a poor state of health (Chapman, LaPlante, and Wilenski 1986; Ycas 1987). Hence offsetting health patterns may not significantly affect future retirement behavior.

In summary: our review of the future paths of the economic determinants of retirement suggests that the trend towards early retirement will slow and perhaps even reverse as the baby boom moves beyond middle age. This conclusion rests on anticipated patterns of financial incentives which have already been legislated (e.g. Social Security) and on others which we have good reason to expect to change (e.g. pensions). In addition, sectoral shifts in the economy away from blue collar work will also lead to reduced early retirement since productivity losses associated with older blue collar workers will be less important as this sector contracts.

OTHER LABOR MARKET IMPLICATIONS OF AN AGING WORKFORCE

Certainly the most direct impact of an aging baby boom will be on retirement behavior. Nevertheless, the demographic change will certainly have other labor market consequences as well. Here we focus on two additional outcomes: unemployment, and wages for both older and younger workers.

While unemployment has been, and will remain, quite volatile over the business cycle, recent evidence indicates that the "natural rate" or what other economists have termed the "full employment-unemployment rate" has varied tremendously over time. For instance, the unemployment rate of 4.1% in 1956 was the lowest rate in the years immediately preceding and following it, indicating the top of the business cycle. The unemployment rate in two other peak years, 1979 and 1989, were considerably higher at 5.8% and 5.0%, respectively.

While different arguments have been advanced to explain changes in the natural unemployment rate over time, one important component of the explanation relies on the changing age structure of the workforce since the baby boom has come of age. In 1956, baby boomers were not yet in the labor force and had no effect on labor force statistics. However by 1979, baby boomers had (for the most part) entered the labor market in full force, twisting the age distribution of the workforce towards younger workers. Younger workers generally have higher unemployment rates even during periods of full employment, because they experience relatively more frictional unemployment. As a result, the aggregate unemployment rate rose, since it is simply the weighted average of each age group's unemployment rate. The weight on younger, higher unemployment workers was therefore higher throughout the 1970's as a result of the numerousness of the baby boom cohort.

This aspect of rising unemployment patterns over time has been analyzed to some extent in the economics literature (Antos, et. al. 1979). For instance, as much as a third of the increase in national unemployment rates between 1957 and 1977 has been attributed to demographic change (Flaim 1979). This change is so massive that some analysts suggest that national unemployment rates "should be computed with a fixed age-distribution of weights" which will reduce the bias in time series observations of a changing age composition of the labor force (Cain 1979).

The good news is that the nation's unemployment rates should begin to fall, in mirror image to what happened during the 1970's, as the baby boom ages. When baby boomers move into the older age group, the heavy weight on a demographic group which experiences relatively little unemployment will again reduce the aggregate unemployment rate. (Taking Cain's perspective, of course, the national unemployment rate will now be "too low", in contrast to the late 1970's.)

As a group, older workers experience less unemployment then their younger counterparts. However those who do lose their job often experience a long spell of unemployment, and older workers may find this more costly than do younger ones because they experience a greater gap between earnings on the old and new job (Podgursky and Swaim 1987, Shapiro and Sandell 1987, Howland and Peterson 1988). Average unemployment duration may also be longer for the older individual than for younger workers. These findings have been interpreted as supportive of the view that firms are reluctant to hire older workers since they will have fewer years remaining on the job over which a firm can recoup investments in firm-specific training (Hutchens 1986, 1988).

We and others suggest that this pattern may change in the next thirty years as the baby boom ages (Johnston and Packer 1987). When boomers flooded the labor market during the 1970's and early 1980's, firms could readily hire younger workers and therefore spread training costs costs over many years. Wages offered to older workers during this time were quite low, if they could find work at all. In contrast, when the baby boom ages, companies may not be able to find enough younger workers. Though costs of hiring an older worker are still high, a shortage of young workers could increase the relative attractiveness of hiring an older worker, a conclusion which agrees with the Workforce 2000 projections (Johnston and Packer 1987). Therefore, looking toward 2020, we predict that displaced older workers will still incur substantial losses upon unemployment, but on the positive side, losses observed during the 1970's and early 1980's may be greatly diminished.

We focus last on the likely effects of labor force aging on wages. One might suspect that baby boomers' relative wages will always be somewhat depressed because of crowding. In economic terms, a simple labor market model might predict that as the quantity of workers in a given age group increases, the wage they are paid will fall (this relies on the own price elasticity of demand being negative). However, this simple analysis ignores the possibilities of substitutes and complements across different labor market groups, and between labor and capital. More complete models which incorporate substitutes and complements have, to date, produced mixed evidence. For example, research on young baby boomers entering the labor market during the 1970's suggests support for the view that the large demographic bulge of workers forced down boomers' wages (Freeman 1979, Welch 1979, Russell 1982). However the reverse pattern does not seem to hold, at least in the one study which has addressed this question to date. Specifically, Levine and Mitchell (1988) found no evidence that wages of older workers would be substantially altered relative to younger workers as the baby boom ages, after estimating own- and cross-price demand elasticities for eight different demographic groups. It seems fair to say that no massive changes in wages can be attributed to demographic aging, on the basis of currently available evidence.

DISCUSSION AND CONCLUSION

This paper examines the likely effects of the aging of the baby boom on labor force attachment, unemployment, and wages. Labor market trends between now and 2020 are the focus of analysis, when the majority of the baby boom generation will confront its retirement decision.

We have demonstrated several inherent flaws in projection methods which make minor modifications to linear extrapolations. When behavioral patterns change, projections using the existing methodology are "too slow" to respond. Therefore we outline the key elements of a more comprehensive economic model to project the consequences of the demographic shock facing the labor market. On the basis of this analysis, we suggest the following conclusions:

1. The trend towards earlier retirement will slow and perhaps reverse in the next few decades.

2. Unemployment should fall among older workers and the aggregate full-employment unemployment rate should also decline as the baby boom ages.

3. The aging of the baby boom will not depress wages substantially, either for older workers or for other demographic groups.

Discussions

Christopher M. Bone, F.S.A.

INTRODUCTION

The authors have provided an instructive paper on potential changes in labor force participation rates as a result of demographic changes early in the next century. The first section of their paper discusses techniques used by the Bureau of Labor Statistics and the Bureau of Economic Analysis to extrapolate future workforce participation rates for specific demographic groups. The authors have performed a service in demonstrating the flaws in using linear extrapolation and similar techniques to estimate future workforce participation rates.

In the second section of the paper, the authors propose replacing these extrapolations with an economic model of retirement, and they draw some preliminary conclusions from application of such a model. The following discussion focuses on this retirement model. Ramifications of the model and additional parameters to be considered in its development are outlined. In particular, the importance of parameters for:

- specific age data
- longevity
- interest rates, and
- employer cost

is suggested. Finally, the authors' conclusions regarding future trends in retirement are reevaluated in light of the additional parameters.

ANALYZING ECONOMIC DETERMINANTS OF RETIREMENT

The authors have outlined a range of factors influencing the retirement decision and have specified the broad terms of a model to be used to further examine retirement behavior. This model must then be applied to the interrelated problem of labor force participation rates among older workers. Although not further discussed by the authors, it would appear that the relationship between retirement and termination from the labor force should also be modeled using the same sort of dynamic model as suggested for retirement. A basic question would be whether the relationship between retirement and termination from the work force is constant, or even predictably varying.

The authors indicate that important roles in modeling retirement behavior should be assigned to wealth, increases in Social Security, and the growth of employer pensions; they cast some doubt on the ability of poor health and changes in mandatory retirement laws to explain changes in early retirement behavior. In addition, certain other factors may profitably be addressed in designing a model to project retirement patterns. However, the most important factor, indeed the measuring scale for determining whether retirement is early or normal, is age. For this reason, any model that is developed should examine both motivations for and results of retirements based on as fine a division by age as possible.

Stratification of Assumptions by Individual Age

The authors' analysis of labor force participation rates is segmented into 5 year age brackets. However, analysis of factors affecting retirement is done in the aggregate, essentially without reference to age categories.

I believe an economic model of retirement trends should be designed to examine incentives and disincentives for retirement at each individual age. A recent study of a California college faculty group shows that motivating factors for retirement vary significantly by age group. The California study used fifteen subjective and objective measures of likelihood of accepting an early retirement incentive offer. For the whole population, discriminant analysis "explained" 87% of retirement decisions. However, when broken into age categories (of ages 55-60, ages 61-66 and age 67 and older), discriminant analysis "explained" 90% to 100% of retirement decisions (Daniels and Daniels, 1991).

While the paper at issue here is concerned with developing an economic, rather than a motivational, model for retirement, it still must be recognized that significant economic factors vary by age. Predictive strength of economic factors, such as general levels of health or asset accumulation may not vary significantly <u>within</u> 5 year age brackets; however, it is likely that significant variation will be seen <u>between</u> 5 year age brackets.

More importantly, social and regulatory constraints generate age-specific discontinuities in retirement rates. For instance, at age 62, first eligibility of a participant for Social Security benefits generates an additional retirement incentive. Eligibility for Medicare and for unreduced Social Security benefits generates another such discontinuity in retirement rates at age 65. Removal of the earnings test may generate another such discontinuity at age 70. The tax code further differentiates in rates of tax on pension distributions based on attainment of specific ages (e.g., 55), which may have some effect on rates of retirement (although not necessarily on labor force participation rates). (1)

Among the advantages that may be obtained from using an age-specific model would be a better clarification of the distinction between accepting early retirement from a career position and withdrawal from the labor force. Lack of data analyzed by age on a particular cause of retirement should not be allowed to stand in the way of setting up such a model. Where data is currently summarized into age brackets, a reasonable distribution of results may be assumed in order to generate an age-specific model. Any question of the reliability of such a distribution only serves to point up the need for stratifying data by age.

Poor Health

The authors' discussion of the relative importance of health as an indicator of early retirement provides a further example of the importance of age differentiation. The authors argue that recent trends to early retirement cannot be explained by deterioration in health status. Even if we grant that health status has not significantly changed in the past few decades, it is still important to quantify the extent to which health affects retirement decisions and so masks other retirement trends. It would appear unlikely that poor health represents a constant proportion of retirements at various ages even if health status is the determining factor for a relatively constant number of retirements at each specific age. In this case, a stratified analysis would indicate the importance of this factor at various ages.

In particular, it would be reasonable to expect health to be of more importance as a determinant of very early retirement. One would also anticipate health-related retirements to be highly correlated with at least temporary termination from the labor force. Results of a recent study by our firm of retiree mortality in the telecommunications industry appear to offer some confirmation of this hypothesis. As in prior studies of that industry, retiree mortality continues to show significantly higher rates of death among the retired population under age 55 when compared to death rate of the active population. If we are willing to assume a high correlation between elevated levels of mortality shortly after retirement and elevated levels of morbidity shortly before retirement, the high mortality rates suggest the continued importance of health as a determinant of very early retirement.

Longevity and Interest Rates

Similarly, measurement of retirement wealth and the value of early retirement provisions in public and private sector pensions may best be studied by use of an age stratified sample. Such an approach would emphasize the importance of interest rates and expected longevity.

From the retiree's point of view, the correlation between wealth and retirement inclination may be viewed as a combination of estate planning and retirement income concerns. For purposes of evaluating the attractiveness of retirement, further economic discriminants would logically appear to be perceived longevity and the perceived real after-tax rate of return which will be earned on wealth accumulations.

If an individual expects to live a long time after retirement, then a greater level of wealth is required, in order to produce the same retirement income. Thus, an increase in expectations for longevity would presumably reduce early retirement inclination. On the other hand, a projected increase in real after-tax rates of return should operate to increase projected retirement income which is derived from wealth accumulations; hence, for a given level of wealth, retirement inclination should increase with rising real rates of return.

Longevity and interest rates are also important considerations in measuring relative corporate subsidy of early retirement. The authors describe recent work and anticipate further work on changes in corporate pension policy which would serve to encourage early retirement. However, it is not necessary for a sponsor consciously to modify a plan in order for real levels of subsidy to change. Instead, changes in cost levels and in real interest rates can easily change the degree of early retirement subsidy in a plan, even though the plan, from the employer's point of view, has not been "improved."

Consider a pension plan which has retained a stable early retirement provision for the past several decades. The rise in real and nominal interest rates over the last two decades would have increased the relative subsidy paid by this plan upon early retirement.

To illustrate the effect of the rise in interest rates, assume that a sponsor installed an early retirement program in the early 70's on the basis that no subsidy of retirement was anticipated. Using an assumed interest rate of 5%, the appropriate nonsubsidized early retirement election factor might be a 10% reduction for each year of early commencement. Fifteen years later, using an assumed rate of return of 8% will generate an early retirement reduction closer to 13% per year. Hence, retention of the 10% factor represents a significant subsidy. However, from the employer perspective, no change has been made in the plan. Indeed a change to the 13% discount would be viewed as a takeaway and, by law, accrued benefits cannot be reduced(2).

The above example assumes a flat dollar pension amount and so calculates subsidies using nominal interest rates. There may be some procedural question as to whether real or nominal rates should be used prior to retirement when the benefit is partially or fully indexed prior to retirement. However, in our example, both real and nominal interest rates have risen since the plan was last amended, thus, in either case, encouraging early retirement.

Changes in Employer Cost

As the authors have pointed out, the increase in the prevalence and generosity of employer provided benefits has likely encouraged the trend toward early retirement. To model future changes in benefit programs, it is necessary to evaluate forces operating on employers to upgrade, maintain or downgrade the benefits provided. Primary among these forces is employer costs.

In the above example, the net effect of an increase in real returns versus increased longevity would probably have been to reduce the cost of pensions to the employer, making offering a pension less expensive. Indeed, as higher rates of return and increased longevity were reflected in the funding of pensions, contributions to single employer defined benefit plans peaked in 1982 (in nominal dollars) and have dropped significantly since that point; while the number of plan participants peaked in 1984 and has declined only slightly since (Turner and Beller, 1990). Evidence of the importance of assumption changes in these cost reductions may be seen in the number of companies making assumption changes in the early 80's. A Greenwich Research Associates 1984 report shows that 70% of the surveyed companies changed assumptions in 1981, 1982 or 1983, of which only 9% changed in 1983. A comparison with the 1980 Greenwich Research Associates Report shows that the mean assumed interest rate rose from 6.0% to 7.3% in the 4 years from 1979 to 1983 (Greenwich Research Associates Inc., 1980, 1984).

The employer is typically much more concerned with total cost of a pension plan than with the relative early retirement subsidy, and is thus less likely to act to restructure early retirement subsidies when overall plan cost is declining. Of course, reductions in real rates of return would have the effect of making pensions more expensive and so would reduce both the attractiveness of retirement to the retiree and the attractiveness of offering retirement on the part of the employer.

With respect to postretirement medical benefits, the increased cost of offering these benefits is already operating to reduce the generosity of benefits under employer-sponsored plans. However, the majority of plans providing these benefits were installed before the enormous increase in medical costs of the last two decades and may still represent, in the plan sponsor's mind, a lower cost than they actually bear. As the true cost of these plans is recognized, employers will attempt to reduce total compensation costs. As discussed below, many employers are reducing compensation by modifying benefit plans, maintaining the cost of the plan closer to the employer's prior estimate of its cost.

Societal, Familial and Cultural Pressures

Finally, a model for early retirement needs to account in some fashion for societal, familial and cultural pressures and preferences regarding the relative appropriateness of work and retirement. Such pressures often contradict stated public policy goals of improving older worker participation in the labor force, such as those embodied in the recent changes to the Age Discrimination in Employment Act and to the Social Security Act. Nevertheless, the pressures are real and have exhibited clear evolution over time. The power of similar pressures to affect labor force participation is amply demonstrated by the changes in female labor force participation discussed by the authors in the first section of the paper.

REGULATORY PLAN ENVIRONMENT

Private Employer Benefit Reductions

Recent developments have forced sponsors to reevaluate the design and cost of benefit plans for retirees. The Tax Reform Act of 1986 and associated regulations under Internal Revenue Code Sections 401(l), 410(b), 401(a)(4), etc., invalidated the pension plans of many employers. In particular, defined benefit pension plans which directly integrate benefits with those provided by Social Security to the maximum extent possible, will need to review early retirement reduction factors to make sure that they reflect reasonable (perhaps nominal) interest rates.(3) Even where the plan does not integrate directly with Social Security it may be anticipated that plans will be redesigned to conform to the new laws and regulations. Due to delays in the issuance of regulations to implement the new law, the redesign process is still under way at many companies. Early retirement subsidies will logically be considered in such redesign.

For postretirement medical plans, new accounting rules must be implemented by 1993 (Financial Accounting Standards Board, 1990). Many plan sponsors, upon evaluating the generosity of benefits provided, have reacted by announcing cutbacks in postretirement medical plans. It is particularly instructive to examine early retirement in a medical plan (i.e. the cost of providing benefits prior to Medicare eligibility at age 65) compared to the early retirement subsidy in a pension plan. These subsidies can be substantial; a recent article demonstrates that for a sample employee, the annual level contribution required to fund benefits for 50 year old retirees ranges up to 12 times the annual level contribution to fund benefits for 65 year old retirees in a medical plan. In a pension plan, the comparable increase in required annual level contribution for early retirees is only a factor of 2 times the contribution for normal retirees (Ranade, 1990).

Given the recent price increases in medical care, and projected, enormous increases in accounting costs for retiree medical plans, many employers are evaluating ways to restructure their health plans. When disparities in plan philosophy, such as those above, have been identified, the employer is likely to reevaluate the generosity of the plan to early retirees. Some plans will be modified to vary benefits based on years of service, further penalizing retirees with shorter service. Other plans will limit the employer contribution towards the cost of medical coverage, vary employer contributions by the employee's age and service at retirement, or introduce dependent cost sharing.

Public Employer Benefit Reductions

Public plans are also reducing early retirement benefits. Recent changes to the military retirement plan reduced benefits available at earliest retirement. Changes have also been made to increase the minimum early retirement ages in the federal employees' pension plan (Schreitmueller, 1988).

THE TREND OF EARLY RETIREMENT

The additional economic factors cited and the trend of plan design changes lend further support to the authors' conclusion that feedback mechanisms will operate to reduce early retirement trends as the baby boom ages. In addition, employer cutbacks in retiree benefits resulting from increased costs for longevity, spiraling medical costs and changes in early retirement pension eligibility and benefits argue for a trend to later retirement.

It would appear that these trends could be turned around, however, by rising real interest rates or by significant environmental changes such as establishment of a national health care system.

Exploration of this last alternative may have important public policy implications for the design of any changes in the provision of health insurance. If a national health system were to be phased in in the same fashion as Old Age Security, the authors' analysis would appear to indicate a return to earlier retirement (or an offset to the trend toward later retirement). Further research into policy alternatives based on the outlined model may provide useful information in public policy debate.

CONCLUSIONS

The authors' proposed model can provide valuable insight into the nature of retirement trends. This discussion has attempted to identify other significant factors potentially affecting retirement. Age at retirement is important, both because of its interaction with government benefit and tax programs and as one endpoint for measuring longevity in retirement. Perceived longevity and real rates of return affect the affordability of retirement and the relative degree of subsidy of early versus normal retirement. These and other factors interact to affect the cost of employer-sponsored benefit plans and hence the employer's willingness to offer such plans.

The authors' use of the model produces valuable insights into the nature of retirement over the next three decades. The additional factors discussed above appear mainly to reinforce the authors' conclusions regarding the future of early retirement trends.

NOTES

1. Internal Revenue Code Section 72(t) contains penalties for receipt of pension benefits before age 55 (or before age 59 and 1/2 in the case of a distribution made prior to termination of employment). However, these penalties apply mainly to the receipt of benefits other than as an annuity, and so serve primarily to restrict the attractiveness of receiving a lump sum distribution of benefits and investing the proceeds outside of an Individual Retirement Account (IRA). Restrictions are also imposed on pensioners receiving benefits before age 55 under Internal Revenue Code Section 402, which denies tax averaging on lump sum distributions. (An exception applies to persons who attained age 50 before January 1, 1986.) Again, the law operates to restrict the recipient of a lump sum from using the money, as opposed to investing it through an IRA or receiving a lifetime annuity. Thus, the primary effect would be anticipated to be on retirement, rather than on termination from the labor force.

2. Internal Revenue Code Section 411(d)(6) and regulations thereunder (1.411(d)-4) forbid increasing the amount charged for early retirement to the extent that benefits are earned as of the date of amendment to increase charges. A company increasing early retirement charges must, at a minimum, freeze the benefit available at any early retirement   age with respect to the accrued benefit at the time of change until the benefit available at   that age with respect to the total accrued benefit, using the new early retirement factors, is   at least as great. More generous methods, which further defer the effect of the change in reduction factors, may also be used.

3. Internal Revenue Code Section 401(l) discusses requirements for plans integrating with Social Security. Since Social Security does not provide early retirement benefits before age 62, pension plans which integrate fully with Social

Security must reduce the amount of offset due to Social Security to the extent that earlier retirement is offered. Proposed regulations under Code Section 401(l) appear, by inspection, to interest rate from Social Security Retirement Age to early retirement at age 55. For early retirement ages below 55, allowable offsets to Social Security benefits must be based on "reasonable interest and mortality assumptions." Arguably, this requires the use of current nominal interest rates.

Joseph F. Quinn

I agree with the general point of Levine and Mitchell's paper. Predictions of future labor force participation rates that are based on extrapolations of past trends are unlikely to be very useful if any interesting changes are underway. Recent research about the determinants of retirement behavior and casual empiricism about likely trends in these determinants suggest what current data already seem to indicate - that the early retirement trend may have already abated or reversed. And accurate predictions about the future require a comprehensive model of retirement behavior that is currently beyond our grasp.

Within this general framework of agreement, I have several comments about the material in the paper, and a criticism about a major focus that is missing - the nature of the jobs that older workers are likely to hold in the future. The latter is the topic of the last section.

I think that the authors shortchange the importance of post-career employment. The extent of it obviously depends on the definition of a career job. Using the Retirement History Study, Rich Burkhauser, Dan Myers and I defined a career job as one held for at least 10 years on which an individual was working full time (35 or more hours per week). We found that during the 1970s, a quarter of the wage and salary workers and half of the self-employed did something other than leave the labor force when they left full time career employment (Quinn, et. al., 1990, pp. 173-178). Wage and salary workers who stayed employed usually found a new job; the self-employed were most likely to move to part-time status on their career jobs. Chris Ruhm (1990b) defined the career job as the longest job held over the life-time, and concluded that fewer than half of the of the RHS workers retired directly from their career jobs. In either case, this seems to be an important phenomenon, and one that may well grow in the future.

Levine and Mitchell quote our research to conclude that "most of these individuals spend only a short time in this partial retirement status." I had used exactly the same table they referenced to conclude that "these transitional jobs were of sufficient duration to represent an important part of the retirement process" (Quinn, et. al., 1990, pp. 189). I am reminded of the scene in Annie Hall in which Woody Allen and Diane Keaton (his wife in the movie) were asked separately about their frequency of sex. "Hardly ever," responds Woody, "about three times per week." "All the time," says she, "about three times per week." In fact, I think partial retirement may well grow in importance in the future, and that it should be a major part of the research agenda.

Concerning the impact of poor health, I fear that the authors' words may be misinterpreted. Although I agree that "increasingly poor health cannot explain the long-term trend toward earlier retirement in the United States," I do not agree that "there is little support for the view that health is a major factor explaining early retirement." Health is especially important in explaining the behavior of very early retirees, and is always a significant explanatory variable in behavioral equations (Kingson, 1982; Sammartino, 1987). A large minority of retirees always name health when asked in questionnaires - 25 percent in the most recent

Social Security survey of new retired-worker beneficiaries, and this excluded those who had first become eligible for disabled worker benefits (Packard and Reno, 1989).

The authors cite research by Fields and Mitchell that suggests that poor health accounts for one-quarter of the explained variances in retirement ages. That strikes me as a lot, not a little. It is true that poor health is less important that it used to be, that it is less important than subjective questionnaires suggest it is, and that it cannot explain the long term trends toward earlier retirement. But it was, is and ever shall be an important factor in many individual retirement decisions. I suspect that we agree on this, but it does not come across in the text.

I have two comments concerning the impact of Social Security. Levine and Mitchell point out that eligibility for benefits at age 62 (since 1956 for women and 1961 for men) ''has enabled many to afford early retirement that they might not have been able to afford otherwise.'' The casual empiricism here is compelling - age 62 is the age of earliest eligibility for Social Security benefits and is the age of the largest drop in participation rates. The problem is that the delayed retirement credit at age 62 is close to actuarially fair. People do not lose much Social Security wealth, and may even gain, if they continue to work to age 65, although they certainly do lose thereafter. With perfect capital markets, mere eligibility would make no difference. The emphasis on the financial incentives imbedded in Social Security is more convincing at age 65 that at 62. Unfortunately, relatively little of the action today is at age 65; most of it has already occurred. To credit Social Security at age 62, one has to turn to liquidity constraints (imperfect capital markets), or to interactions with pension incentives, which often go into effect well before age 65. This is one of the many reasons why I think that pension incentives, about which we know much less, are more important than those in Social Security.

I would have emphasized more the importance of the inter-generational transfer to the cohorts who have retired thus far. As Levine and Mitchell point out, large increases in real Social Security benefits were legislated, primarily in the late 1960s and early 1970s, and benefits were then linked explicitly to the cost of living. The net result was that cohorts of older workers received as benefits significant multiples of what they would have had if the contributions made by them and their employers had been invested at competitive rates of interest (Burkhauser and Warlick, 1981; Moffitt, 1984). For decades, the Social Security system was the world's most successful chain letter, and some authors think that this wealth effect is the primary Social Security contribution to the retirement trend (Hurd and Boskin, 1984). This supports Levine and Mitchell's prediction that early retirement trends will change in the future, since future cohorts will not enjoy this windfall gain. Chain letters work well on triangles, not on rectangles, and Social Security ''returns'' will be much more modest in the future. The effect of Social Security will be more to transfer cohorts' resources over time than to augment them.

I have two comments on future unemployment rates, both of which lead into the next section. Levine and Mitchell concentrate on official measures of unemployment and duration. These exclude discouraged workers - those who would like to work but who are not actively searching. The official statistics also exclude workers who do not want to work given the current terms and conditions offered, but who might under different circumstances. Both of these groups may be substantial among the elderly, implying that the low official elderly unemployment may be partly a definitional artifact.

It is not clear why official unemployment rates are lower among older workers. Seniority may protect them from dismissal, or those who are laid off may be disguised as retired rather than unemployed. But if the importance of part-time post-career employment increases in the future, then the current unemployment situation of the elderly may no longer apply. If many older workers are in post-career jobs with low seniority, the threat of unemployment may increase. If partial retirement becomes a more important part of the landscape, then there may more frictional unemployment as older workers move among these transitional jobs on the way to complete retirement. On the way out, as Chris Ruhm (1990a, 1991) has argued, they may look more like job entrants than stable mid-career employees.

THE NATURE OF LABOR FORCE PARTICIPATION AMONG THE ELDERLY

My major criticism of this very nice paper is that it ignores what is behind labor force participation. A person is defined as employed, and therefore participating in the labor market, regardless of whether s/he is employed full time on a career job, or has left that and is working part-time for much lower wages in an entirely new line of work. The emphasis on labor force participation obscures these differences, and this is precisely where I think many of the interesting labor market changes may come.

The number of Americans aged 65 and over will more than double over the next 40 years, while the number aged 55 to 64 increases by nearly two-thirds. At the same time, the number of Americans under age 18 will decline slightly, and the number under age 55 will increase by only 1 percent (U.S. Bureau of the Census, 1989, Table F). As a result, the percentage of the population aged 65 and over is estimated to increase from under 13 percent today to nearly 22 percent by 2030 (U.S. Bureau of the Census, 1989, Table G). A third of the population will be 55 and older. The median age will rise 33 to 42. Given this and global warming, the nation then will look like Florida today.

Demographic projections indicate a growing pool of experienced workers early next century. If labor shortages develop as the influx of young workers declines, then these older workers may provide a potential solution to the problem.

As Levine and Mitchell point out, Social Security work disincentives are already being phased out. How will employer pensions change with future labor market conditions, and, if these work disincentives are eased as well, how will older workers respond?

A recent survey sponsored by the Commonwealth Fund has shed valuable light on the plans and preferences of older Americans. Over 3,500 women aged 50 to 59 and men aged 55 to 64 were interviewed in 1989, and asked detailed questions about their plans and expectations. About 2000 were working and 1500 were not. A major conclusion of the study is that a substantial minority of these older Americans are willing and able to work longer than they have or than they plan to.

William McNaught, Michael Barth and Peter Henderson (1991) have analyzed those who were no longer employed at the time of the survey. Nearly a quarter, representing almost 2 million men and women in these age groups, said that preferred to be working and were capable of doing so if a suitable job were available. The authors then narrowed this sample further, by requiring that they pass a number of specific labor market commitment tests - respondents had to be willing to work in available jobs, need a job for financial reasons, be able to perform at least five of six specific physical tasks, be seeking work, have reasonable wage expectations and be willing to accept difficult job conditions. Even with these additional requirements, respondents representing over 1 million retirees indicated that they were willing and able to work. This is a minority, but a substantial one - nearly 14 percent of those not employed in these age groups.

Quinn and Burkhauser (1991) have analyzed the wage and salary workers who were still employed at the time of the survey. Sizeable minorities (10 percent of the men and 13 percent of the women, representing another million people) said that they expect to stop working earlier than they would really like to.

By comparing the exact age at which people planned to stop working with the age at which they said they would like to stop working, we were able to calculate the number of additional years they would like to work. Over 40 percent claimed that they would like to stay employed for another 3 to 5 years, and another large group (about 40 percent of the men and a third of the women) implied that they would like to work as long as they could. Even if these claims are viewed with some suspicion, there is evidence that many of those who want to work longer would like to do so for a substantial number of years.

It is not obvious what these divergent plans and preferences mean. If people prefer to work longer than they currently plan to, why don't they do so? One interpretation is that they do not want to continue under the terms and conditions of employment that they expect to face, but would like to stay on under different circumstances. This is consistent with the fact that public and private retirement plans often penalize older workers who stay on the job too long.

The Commonwealth study asked several questions about workers' preferences under alternative employment scenarios. People were asked whether they would work longer if their employer pension contributions continued at the same level after age 65, if they were offered a job at somewhat lower pay, but with reduced hours and responsibilities, and whether they would accept a job that required retraining and had different responsibilities and tasks, but the same hours and salary.

Of the 1 million mentioned above, those who would like to work longer than they expect to, over two-thirds answered yes to one or more of these questions. Responses from the entire sample of employed wage and salary workers suggest that about 5 million men and women would be willing to extend their work careers under one or more of the circumstances mentioned above.

There are reasons to be skeptical of questionnaire responses. People may be more likely to say they would worker longer than actually to do so. Economists usually prefer to analyze what people do, not what they say they would do. But when this is done, as Levine and Mitchell point out, the results are the same. Both econometric and survey evidence suggest that retirement choices do depend on the financial options that older workers face.

I can envision two very different scenarios in the future. In the first, Social Security incentives no longer penalize retirement, but many defined benefit pensions still do. Under these circumstances, I suspect that workers would continue to leave their career jobs when pensions dictate, as so many do now, but that increasing numbers would seek post-career employment in new lines of work. Pensions say leave (the career job); Social Security says stay (in the labor market). On the other hand, if employers alter pensions to encourage workers to remain, and increase their flexibility with respect to hours and job characteristics, then the additional labor force participation will be observed on the career job. Either of these scenarios is consistent with Levine and Mitchell's participation predictions, and I find the differences sufficiently interesting to warrant study.

I draw one important policy implication from Levine and Mitchell's paper. One should be wary of making broad policy prescriptions for the future based on demographic and behavioral projections made today. The authors have shown that such forecasts have been notoriously inaccurate in the past.

Labor market shortages may or may not develop early next century. Compositional changes in the population warn us that they might, but whether they do or not depends on the participation decisions that Levine and Mitchell have analyzed, as well as on factors such as immigration policy and macro economic performance. The latter we cannot even explain in the past, much less predict for the future.

And even if aggregate labor market forecasts do come true, they will not apply to all regions and industries. Conditions in the service sector in the southwest may differ from those in manufacturing in the northeast. Current pension incentives may make sense in one area or industry, but not in another. Is it not better to let employers, unions and workers respond to the labor market conditions they face, rather than legislate common characteristics for all?

Levine and Mitchell mention some evidence on changing retirement rules over time. Some defined pension plans increased the financial attractiveness of early retirement during the 1970s and 1980s, the decades during which mandatory retirement was delayed five years and then finally eliminated. When the stick was outlawed, the carrot picked up the slack. These changes were more pronounced in less profitable industries, and for longer seniority workers. These incentives have been used and have worked in the past. There is no reason why they cannot be equally effective in the opposite direction in the future.

4

Can Our Social Insurance Systems Survive the Demographic Shifts of the Twenty-First Century?

Sylvester J. Schieber

EXECUTIVE SUMMARY

This paper assesses the long-term socio-economic and political viability of the Social Security and Medicare programs. The aging and retirement of the baby boom after the turn of the century promises to put new financial pressures on these crucial government programs. It is important that we understand the timing and magnitude of the pressures so that we can do what is necessary to assure that the retirement income security of future generations is on a sound fiscal and equitable social policy basis.

The paper begins by narrowing the focus of the discussion of social insurance to Social Security cash benefits and Medicare. The assessment of the system requires the utilization of generally acceptable measures of financial operations and actuarial projections which are identified. In order to evaluate the long-term viability of the system, it is important to understand how the system is financed, and to assess the magnitude of the financing requirements within the context of overall economic operations and political sensitivity to what can be sustained.

Assessing the Social Security retirement, survivor, and disability benefit programs is done within the context of continuation of existing retirement patterns.

Medicare can only be considered within the context of the U.S. health system generally, and its future needs to be considered in light of the future of the health system.

The conclusions on the long-term viability of the two elements of our social insurance system studied differ from one to the other.

It does not appear that the shift in resources required to meet the general cash benefit promises being held out through Social Security are so large that we cannot make the marginal adjustments needed to maintain the program pretty much along the lines now configured. We should make those marginal adjustments to prevent long-term imbalance in the program as far in advance as possible.

The long-term prospect for Medicare is decidedly pessimistic. It would appear that current projections suggest a future level of benefits that may not be politically sustainable. Putting this conclusion in the larger context of the U.S. health system's inflation and access problems suggests that fundamental issues about the organization and provision of health care services will have to be addressed long before the baby boom reaches retirement age.

INTRODUCTION

This paper attempts to answer the question of whether Social Security can survive the expected demographic changes in our society after the turn of the century as the baby boom generation passes from their working careers into retirement. That this is an issue may be startling to the casual observer of our social insurance system. Just eight years ago, we completed the big overhaul of Social Security that resolved its short-term financial crisis and set it on a course that was hailed as being actuarially sound for the next 75 years. With just one-tenth of that period elapsed and with the system's experience being almost exactly what was predicted, and with the unprecedented accumulations now occurring in the trust funds, it may seem an odd time to be overly concerned about the system's survival.

The prospects for Medicare have not been as bright, at least in recent years, as those for the cash benefits program we call Social Security. But, each time we seem to approach the cusp of crisis in Medicare, the program is amended to push the day of reckoning further into the future. Maybe the continued careful course adjustments can keep Medicare afloat, for who can think of the alternative? And if the financing of Medicare becomes dangerously precarious, we do have the cash benefits trust funds just sitting there.

Yet as we begin to move through the 1990s, the prospects for future problems are beginning to unveil themselves in a fashion that legitimizes questions about the long-term viability of these social insurance programs. After the release of the 1989 Trustees Report, at least one authority declared that the picture on Social Security's financial health was a rosy one for the elderly, but a dim one for the young.[1] Increasingly, there is a feeling in the business community that the federal government's Medicare policies are nothing more than the government promising benefits to the elderly on the one hand, and making employer-sponsored plans pay the bill on the other. There is a growing concern that the shifting of costs from governmentally sponsored health plans to private ones is making the sponsorship of employer plans an untenable proposition. Thus we face the prospect that Medicare is choking its one existing safety valve. Given the general problems of cost inflation, concerns about the quality of care provided, and the limited access that some citizens have to the U.S. health care system, it is important to understand the interrelationship of Medicare to the larger system.

This paper investigates the long-term viability of Social Security and Medicare. These programs are currently solvent and are projected to be so for some time into the future. However, as the baby boom generation ages and begins to pass into retirement after the turn of the century, the larger body of retirees in relation to the number of workers paying into the programs will place new financing pressures on both programs. In the next section of the paper the scope of the discussion is defined. The concepts of social insurance span a large number of programs, but the discussion here will be limited to cover only Social Security cash benefits and Medicare. After the scope of the paper is outlined, the financial measures used in the analysis are discussed. The discussion of measurement methodology is followed respectively by sections on the financial viability of the Social Security cash benefits program and Medicare. In the first of these sections, the viability of Social Security is considered within the context of the general claim on the nation's economic resources that the program poses, and how this is expected to change over the next 75 years. Then, the discussion turns to Medicare where the analysis initially parallels the discussion on the cash benefits program. Given the significant increase in Medicare costs that is expected in coming decades, the analysis is expanded to look at the evolving nature of the U.S. health care system, and the viability of Medicare in this larger context. The last section of the paper turns back to the question that frames the title of the paper, namely, whether our major social insurance programs aimed at the elderly can survive the demographic shifts of the 21st Century.

LIMITING THE DISCUSSION

The terms social insurance and social security are sometimes used interchangeably. Social insurance in this country covers a broad range of programs including unemployment insurance; workers' compensation; temporary disability programs; Old-Age, Survivors, and Disability Insurance (OASDI); and Medicare. Many analysts also include the means-tested income-support programs such as Aid to Families with Dependent Children, Supplemental Security, Income, food stamps, etc., under this broad concept. Some include veterans benefits, public employee retirement, etc., under the social insurance classification as well. For purposes of this paper, a narrowly defined concept of social insurance including only Social Security and Medicare is used.

Undoubtedly the changing demographic landscape of the 21st Century will affect all of the other programs that can be gathered under the social insurance umbrella, but the focus of the series of papers in this conference is on retirement issues which are not germane to a number of programs in the wider definition. Although public employee and military retirement programs are often classified as social insurance programs, they are really employer-sponsored retirement programs providing benefits to retired government employees and their dependents. The implications of our changing demography for employer-sponsored plans is the subject of the paper by John Biggs.

FINANCING SOCIAL SECURITY AND MEDICARE

When the Social Security Act was originally passed in 1935, the program was a retirement program. The original Act called for employees covered by the program and their employers to begin paying equal payroll tax contributions in 1937. The Social Security Act established a separate trust fund into which the payroll tax contributions were to be credited. The accumulation of funds in the trust fund were to be used to pay benefits. The first retirement benefits were to be paid in 1940 to eligible workers who retired at age 65 or above. Under the initial Act, workers who died prior to attaining age 65 were to have their contributions paid to their estates.

Over the years the Social Security Act has been amended many times. On a number of occasions, the Act has been amended to add new benefits. In 1939, before the first retirement benefits were paid, the program was amended to include survivors of deceased workers, and repayment of contributions for those who died prior to age 65 was eliminated. In 1940 the Old-age and Survivors Insurance (OASI) program began to pay benefits to eligible beneficiaries. In 1956 the Social Security Act was amended and the Disability Insurance (DI) program was established. As in the case with the OASI program, equal payroll tax contributions by employers and employees were to pay for the program. Also, a DI trust fund was established to parallel the operations of the OASI trust fund.

In 1965 the Act was again amended and benefits were expanded to include Medicare. The Medicare program was established with two parts, each with its own trust fund that operates like the OASI and DI funds. One part was the Hospital Insurance (HI) program, to cover hospital costs for those eligible. The HI program was funded again by equal employer and employee payroll tax contributions. The Supplementary Medical Insurance (SMI) program covers expenses not covered by HI. The SMI program is funded by a combination of premiums charged to those eligible to participate in the program and federal government contributions from the general fund.

When the initial Social Security cash benefits were being paid, a decision was made not to treat the benefits as regular income for federal income tax purposes. In 1983, when a variety of Social Security Amendments were being considered, the Congress changed the income tax treatment of cash benefits and earmarked the taxes collected to be passed back into the relevant OASI or DI trust funds.

The Social Security Act does not make provision for any of the trust funds affiliated with the Social Security or Medicare programs to operate on a cumulative deficit basis; i.e., the balance in the respective accounts cannot be negative. Since the trust funds can accumulate positive balances, it is not necessary that the programs operate on a cash surplus or break-even basis in any particular fiscal year. The trust funds, however, are restricted in their investment options; they can only buy special issue federal government securities. To the extent that tax collections earmarked for each of the trust funds exceed disbursements, the excess is invested in government IOUs. The extra cash that is collected by the federal government in these situations is diverted to other governmental uses. During periods when the trust fund disbursements exceed the earmarked tax collections, the IOUs are redeemed for cash. The government must raise the cash to fund such redemptions through other taxing or borrowing operations. Currently, the OASDI and HI trust funds are operating on a surplus basis. This situation is not projected to persist indefinitely. As will be discussed later, the SMI trust fund is operated as a term insurance program with the participant premiums and government contributions set on the basis of expected short-term expenditures.

THE LONG-TERM VIEW

Predicting the future is an inexact science, and the further into the future one looks, the more inexact it becomes. For years, actuaries have been estimating the future operations of retirement plans. Social Security has been subjected to continual actuarial review from its earliest conception, up until the present time. Given the crucial role that Social Security's cash benefits and health insurance program have come to fill, and the political nature of the deliberations that often surround them, there is little wonder that the future projections of Social Security's operations come under constant scrutiny, and some periodic criticism.

The primary goal of this paper is to assess the long-term socio-economic and political viability of our Social Security programs. A secondary goal is to avoid getting bogged down in an extended discussion of methodological issues relating to choosing assumptions or making actuarial projections. These combined goals require using commonly available and generally accepted measures of Social Security and Medicare operations.

The Accepted Measures

The structure and ongoing management of the Social Security and Medicare programs provide for regular measurement of the financial status of the system each year. The annual reporting mechanism includes projections of financial operations 75 years into the future. As indicated earlier, the Social Security Act established four trust funds that are central to the financial operations of Social Security and Medicare. These are the Old-Age and Survivors Insurance (OASI) Trust Fund, the Disability Insurance (DI) Trust Fund, the Hospital Insurance Trust Fund (HI), and the Supplementary Medical Insurance (SMI) Trust Fund. The Social Security Act also established a Board of Trustees for these trust funds, including the Secretary of Treasury, the Secretary of Labor, the Secretary of Health and Human Services, and two members of the public. The law requires that the Trustees submit an annual report to Congress on the operations and status of each of the trust funds. The primary public disclosure of the financial measurement and status of the system is found in these Trustees' Reports.

The Trustees' Reports for the OASI, DI, and HI trust funds each include projections of the income, expenditures, and the actuarial balance of the funds over the next 75 years. These projections are developed using four separate sets of economic and demographic assumptions. These assumption sets are designated "Alternative I," the most optimistic set; "Alternative II-A," a somewhat optimistic intermediate set; "Alternative II-B," a less optimistic intermediate set; and "Alternative III," a pessimistic set of assumptions. Over the years there has been considerable analysis of the assumptions used to develop the trust funds projections. Most analysts use the II-B Assumptions and the resulting projections when they discuss the programs. These are considered to be the best estimate of the expected operations of the respective programs.

Over the years, there have been a number of independent reviews of the official projections. The most recent public assessment of the methods and assumptions used in valuing the Social Security trust funds was undertaken by two panels of technical experts convened by the 1991 Advisory Council on Social Security. The first panel, made up of four actuaries and five economists, was asked to review the assumptions and methodology used to project the future financial status of the OASDI programs. The second panel was comprised of four health actuaries and three health economists charged with reviewing the assumptions and methods used to project the status of the Medicare trust funds.

The first panel concluded that the work being done by the staff preparing the annual OASDI projections was "professional and highly competent."[2] Although they suggested the projection methodology being used to value the OASI and DI programs be externally reviewed and validated, they concluded that it appeared reasonable with no discernible patterns of bias. They made no suggestions to change the most important demographic assumptions being used in the "best estimate" (i.e., II-B) projections. They did suggest that the best estimate real wage growth (i.e., wage growth rate in excess of inflation rate) assumption be decreased from 1.3 percent to 1.0 percent; that the ultimate best estimate inflation rate increase from 4.0 percent to 5.0 percent; and that the ultimate best estimate real interest rate (i.e., nominal interest rate in excess of inflation rate) be increased from 2.0 to 2.8 percent. The panel did not suggest changing the mortality assumptions or fertility assumptions being used to value the programs. They estimated that adopting their alternative assumptions would reduce the overall "summarized cost rate" of the OASDI programs from 13.95 to 13.62 percent of covered payroll over the next 75 years of operations, a change of 2.4 percent of total operating cost.[3] This difference is small enough that it would not effect the substance or conclusions of this paper.

The findings and suggestions of the panel of experts looking at HI and SMI were not dissimilar to the other panel. They recommended that the HI projections continue to be done on a 75-year basis and that the same basis be extended to SMI. They concluded the projection work being done by the actuaries at the Health Care Financing Administration was highly competent, and that given the availability of data, no better projection models are evident. They deferred to the Social Security panel on their assessment of demographic assumptions used to value the various programs. They also supported the other panel's recommendations on ultimate real interest rates and inflation rates, but recommended the ultimate best estimate real wage assumption be lowered from 1.3 percent to 0.7 percent.

Both panels recommended the establishment of contingency reserve fund requirements that would have to be considered in the development of long-term cost rates. They also recommended the regular estimation of indicators of the soundness of the trust funds that will prove important for monitoring these programs over time. There is nothing in either panel's report or recommenda-

FIGURE 1
Projected Hospital Insurance Trust Fund Year-end Cash Balances

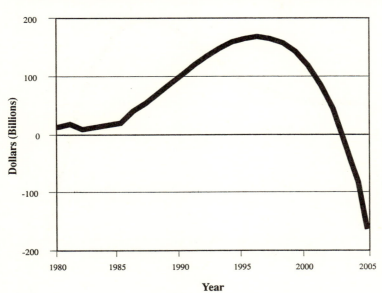

Year

Source: 1990 Annual Report of the Board of Trustees of the Federal Hospital
Insurance Trust Fund:39,54.

---

tions that suggests that using the estimates of program operations by the Social
Security Administration (SSA) or Health Care Financing Administration
(HCFA) actuaries would drastically bias the results of the analysis in this paper.

The Projections

   A simplistic answer to the question of whether our Social Security programs
can survive the coming demographic pressures posed by the baby boom can be
found in a look at the actuarial projections of the systems. Figure 1 shows the
projected year-end trust fund balances for the HI program from the most recent
Trustees Reports'. According to those projections, the HI program is expected to
be inadequately funded to operate beyond 2003. Since these estimates were
developed, Congress has passed the Omnibus Budget Reconciliation Act of 1990
(OBRA 90), which raised the maximum earnings base on which the HI portion of
the payroll tax is paid from $51,300 to $125,000 for 1991. This additional
funding is projected to push the point at which the HI trust fund is depleted about
three years further into the future. The earliest cohort of the baby boom

FIGURE 2
Projected OASDI Trust Fund Year-end Cash Balances

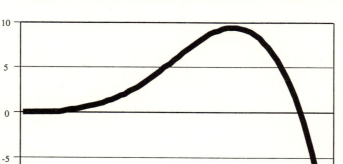

Year

Source: 1990 Annual Report of the Board of Trustees of the Federal Old-Age and Survivors Insurance and Disability Insurance Trust Funds:62,139-140.

___

generation will not be eligible to receive Medicare benefits related to normal retirement until nearly a decade later.

The prospects for the supplementary medical insurance (SMI) program might be considered to be more positive than those facing HI. The SMI program is financed from premium income paid by the enrollees and by general revenue contributions from the federal government. The SMI program is financed on an accrual basis with a contingency margin. The premium rates paid by or for the participants and the actuarial rates setting the government's contributions are set annually. Under this mode of operation the program should always be adequately funded. Since the program is run like an annually renewable term insurance program, no long-term projections of the programs' costs are developed by the HCFA actuaries for presentation by the Trustees in their annual report on the program.

However, between 1980 and 1988 the enrollee premiums for SMI increased at an annual compound rate of 14.3 percent per year and the government contributions by a rate of 17.0 percent per year.[4] During this same period of time the average monthly benefit of a retired worker under Social Security was rising at a rate of 6.0 percent per year (Social Security Administration, 1981 and 1989). This discrepancy raises the question of how long retirees can sustain the rate of growth in the SMI premiums that they have been incurring. Given the federal government's budgetary imbalances the same question applies. Indeed, the Health Technical Panel for the 1991 Advisory Council on Social Security projects that SMI costs as a percentage of GNP will grow from 0.8 percent in 1990 to 2.5 percent in 2020 and 3.2 percent by 2040. Because the SMI costs are projected to be almost equal to HI costs in coming years, any question of the long-term viability of HI has to be equally shared by SMI as well.

In comparison to HI and SMI, the future of the OASDI programs looks rosy. Figure 2 shows the projected year-end balances in the OASDI trust funds for the period 1980 through 2050. During the early portion of this period, the trust fund is projected to grow significantly. In fact it is projected to grow to such an extent that some policy analysts are now arguing that the payroll tax should be reduced, a point that will be analyzed later in this paper. But in the context of Social Security's long-term prospects, as the baby boom passes from their working years into retirement the trust funds will gradually be depleted. They are projected to be completely depleted by approximately 2043.

The Social Security Act does not make provision for the various trust funds to borrow from other sources to make benefits payments. During the fiscal crisis in the cash benefits program during the early 1980s, some interfund borrowing was permitted, but even if it was allowed in the future, the combined funds would still be depleted during the first half of the next century. Thus the projected depletion of the trust funds portends an inability of the programs as now configured to fulfill the promises being held out to future retirees. In theory, if the point was reached that the trust funds were completely depleted, the programs could continue to operate on a cash flow basis. That is, the cash benefits paid out each month would be equal to the cash collections each month minus administrative costs. Those receiving cash benefits would receive partial benefits. Health care providers would receive only a portion of the payments that they would otherwise receive.

If this scenario were to evolve, the national social insurance system could ''survive'' indefinitely, but the prospects for national politicians would be less rosy. The simple answer to the question of whether our social insurance system can survive the demographic shifts of the 21st century is that Social Security and Medicare cannot survive as now configured under current law. But a more complex answer focuses on an implicit extension of the original question. The real question is: Can our social insurance systems be modified in such a way that they provide meaningful retirement income security to the baby boom generation without posing unacceptably onerous burdens on subsequent generations of workers? The answer to that question requires a detailed and separate analysis of the cash and health benefits programs.

THE POLITICAL ECONOMY OF SOCIAL SECURITY

Funding Issues

President Franklin Roosevelt had strong feelings about the financing of Social Security. He wanted the system to be contributory, at least partly because he thought it would provide political insurance for the program. In describing the reasons for using the payroll tax to fund Social Security he said: "They are politics all the way through. We put those payroll contributions there so as to give the contributors a legal, moral, and political right to collect their pensions.... With those taxes there, no damn politician can ever scrap my Social Security program."[6] From 1937 when the first taxes were collected up until the present time, the primary source of revenues for retirement benefits paid under Social Security has been the payroll tax. And indeed, Mr. Roosevelt's political observation has been proven resoundingly over the years.

While the payroll tax has given the public a "virtual equity" in their benefits entitlements, it has also served to act as governor on the level of benefits that can be provided by the system. An extra dollar of benefits provided by the system means that an extra dollar of taxes has to be collected from workers. The heavy reliance on payroll taxes makes the tax rate highly sensitive to the balance of taxpayers to beneficiaries and the benefit levels. Virtually all workers pay the payroll tax on some of their lifetime earnings, and most pay it on all of them.

It is within the context of this governor of a payroll tax system that the long-term viability of Social Security is raised. It seems there is some unspecified limit beyond which our national politicians believe the public will refuse to pay the payroll taxes needed to fund the benefits paid by the system. This point was clearly demonstrated through the 1977 and 1983 Amendments to the Social Security Act. Both Amendments undertook the politically painful process of cutting benefits rather than solving short and long-term funding problems solely on the backs of payroll tax payers, albeit while raising payroll taxes at the same time.

Sharing the Whole Pie

It is possible to argue that using the yardstick of the payroll tax as the measure of our ability to provide adequately for the elderly in our society does not properly reflect our ability as a nation to cope with the pending retirement pressures the baby boomers will present. In 1991, the total expenditures from the OASDI program are expected to be about 4.5 percent of GNP. In 2010, the total expenditure from the OASDI program is expected to be about 4.5 percent of GNP. Between 2010 and 2035, OASDI payments are expected to grow to 6.7 percent of GNP and then stabilize with slight variations between 6.6 and 6.8 percent. The rate of growth in OASDI benefits as a percent of GNP between 2010 and 2035 when the whole baby boom passes into retirement ages is projected to be 1.6 percent per year.

To put the potential growth in OASDI benefits relative to GNP in context, between 1964 and 1989, personal consumption expenditures on recreation in the U.S. grew from 3.8 to 5.1 percent of GNP, a rate of growth of 1.2 percent per year.[7] Between 1960 and 1985, total health expenditures in the U.S. grew from 5.3 to 10.5 percent of GNP, a rate of growth of 2.8 percent per year.[8] As the baby boom retires they will command a bigger share of the GNP than the elderly have traditionally. But the shift in the share of GNP they can claim by virtue of their

OASDI benefits will not necessarily be an overwhelming phenomenon relative to other shifting claims on GNP.

The problem with this analysis is that the funding of the OASDI program is not a generalized claim on the nation's total economic infrastructure. In 1991, earnings subject to the payroll tax are expected to be about 43 percent of the U.S. gross national product (GNP). How the increasing retiree claim on national output is funded for the baby boomers will have important implications on the distribution of income across various segments of society.

From its earliest conception there have been proposals to fund part of Social Security out of revenue sources other than the payroll tax. The Committee on Economic Security that developed the initial proposal for President Roosevelt in 1935 reasoned that as Social Security matured, the federal budgetary costs of old-age assistance would decline. The committee believed that the savings realized in old-age assistance because of an expanding Social Security should be used to subsidize the retirement program. This subsidy was projected to grow to 67 percent of the combined employer and employee contributions by the time the program fully matured in 1980.[9] When President Roosevelt discovered that a large deficit would develop in the proposed program during the 1960s and thereafter, he insisted that the proposal be changed.

Over the years, proponents of other funding sources have repeatedly suggested the use of general revenue funding of some part of the benefits. Suggestions that general revenues be used to fund part of Social Security's benefits were rejected for years because of fears that using them would reduce pressures to restrain benefits or would increase pressures to means-test some part of the benefit. General revenue funding became a partial reality with the 1983 Social Security Amendments which allowed federal income taxation of a portion of Social Security benefits, and earmarked the taxes collected for the trust funds. This year the income taxes collected for the trust fund will be approximately 1.7 percent of the payroll taxes collected. Over time the relative share of the program funded by these earmarked income taxes will increase because an increasing portion of the benefits will be subject to income taxes. But the revenues from income taxes on benefits are projected to grow to only 6.1 percent by 2065.

While the barrier to partial general revenue funding of Social Security may have been broken in 1983, it is unlikely that further general revenue infusions will be made anytime soon given the current relative balances in the OASDI and the general revenue accounts. Indeed, some of the policy makers involved in the development of the 1983 Social Security Amendments are now advising that we reduce payroll tax rates in the short term.

The Dilemma of the Accumulating Trust Funds

The OASDI trust funds are expected to accumulate slightly over $316 billion in tax revenues and interest payments this year. They are expected to have disbursements of $254 billion, and should end the year with $226 billion in assets. The accumulation in the trust funds was anticipated well before the passage of the 1983 Social Security Amendments, although the 1983 Amend-

FIGURE 3
OASDI Payroll Tax Rates Under Two Alternative Scenarios

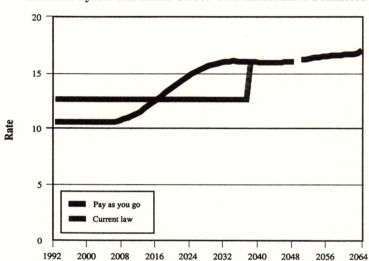

Year

Source: Derived by the author based on information published in the 1990 Annual Report of the Board of Trustees of the Federal Old-Age and Survivors Insurance and Disability Insurance Trust Funds.

---

ments accelerated the process. Under current law, the accumulation in the trust funds should continue through the first quarter of the next century when they would approach $10 trillion, and then begin a gradual decline as shown earlier in Figure 2. The earliest group of the baby boom would reach age 62 in 2008 and the last in 2026.

The primary argument for reducing payroll tax rates now relates to the unfairness of funding general government expenditures through the regressive payroll tax.[10] Some policy analysts, however, argue that the trust fund accumulations are dangerous, because historically the Congress has used excess funds to increase benefits for current beneficiaries.[11] The primary arguments against pursuing rate reductions now relate to the need to increase national savings rates and the desirability of having the baby boomers help provide for their own retirement.[12] The issue of whether or not to decrease the payroll tax now may have some bearing on the long-term question of Social Security's viability and level of operation. This can be illustrated by comparing Social Security under its current funding rules in comparison to an alternative funding schedule.

Comparing Funding Objects

Under current law, the OASDI funds derive income basically from three sources. The primary source of income now is the payroll tax; it will account for slightly more than $300 billion in revenues during 1991. Net interest payments made on the trust fund will be around $23 billion, and income from taxation of Social Security benefits will amount to another $5 billion.[13] The payroll tax rate that feeds the OASDI programs is set by law, currently at 6.2 percent of covered earnings on both workers and their employers. This combined rate of 12.4 percent would apply in perpetuity unless new legislation changes it.

Senator Daniel Patrick Moynihan has recommended that the payroll tax be cut and that Social Security should be funded on a "pay-as-you-go" basis unless the federal government's deficit in its general accounts is brought under control.[14]

You can see the effects of Senator Moynihan's proposal in Figure 3. There is an underlying assumption behind the figure that a contingency trust fund would be maintained at a level equal to one year's benefit payments. If the trust fund is projected to fall below that level, the payroll tax is automatically raised to meet the trust fund target. The flat line in the figure reflects the tax rate in current law. During the latter part of the 2030s the payroll tax under current law would have to be raised if the one-year contingency fund requirement is to be met.

If Senator Moynihan's proposal is enacted, taxpayers would receive an immediate payroll tax cut of between 15 and 20 percent. Shortly after the turn of the century, payroll taxes would have to rise again. Between 2015 and 2020 they would be back up to current rates, and by roughly 2030 they would have to be at least 50 percent higher than at the turn of century. The author of this paper has estimated elsewhere that implementation of a proposal along the lines of the one Senator Moynihan has recommended would reduce his lifetime payroll taxes by approximately $20,000 in 1990 dollars while raising his high school-aged son's lifetime payroll taxes by a like amount.[15] The extent of the lifetime tax reductions or increases for particular cohorts of current or future workers would depend on the age of the individuals in the groups.

But as Charles Schultz has pointed out, "The mere accumulation of financial assets in social insurance trust funds does not, of course, mean that one generation is financing its own retirement and relieving the next of any burden."[16] The net effects of today's Social Security financing decisions depend to a large extent on what we do with the money. John Hambor has postulated the effects of two extreme policies for dealing with the trust fund accumulations.[17] In the first case he provides for a balanced general account of the federal budget in each year in which Social Security tax collections exceed the expenditures from the trust funds. In this instance the OASDI accumulations become net added national savings. The government retires existing federal debt and the freed resources flow through the capital markets into private sector activities. With the proper monetary policy, this would result in lower interest rates and increased investment in capital which would be used to increase national output. During the period of declining balances the process is exactly reversed and the positive effects of the buildup are gradually exhausted. Under this scenario, the baby boom generation would partially fund their own retirement benefits by making the overall capacity of the economy larger, at least temporarily.

In the second scenario, Hambor assumes that the combined OASDI and general accounts of the federal budget are in balance. In this case the general account runs a deficit exactly equal to the OASDI inflow. The trust fund accumulations result in lower nonpayroll taxes for the general citizenry during the period of the trust fund accumulations. The trust fund monies are used to finance current government purchases of goods and services or increased disposable income for income tax payers. Undoubtedly some of the increased after-tax income would leak into the capital markets, but given the relatively low level of private savings in the U.S., not nearly as much as in the first scenario. Without an increase in capital, there is no expanded capacity in the economy and the trust fund is merely a stack of IOUs that future generations will be called on to retire.

In a related study Henry Aaron, Barry Bosworth, and Gary Burtless also studied the effects of actually "saving" the trust fund accumulations. Their simulations were based on a different model than Hambor's, though, in that they assumed the payroll tax would be increased each time the program got out of "actuarial balance" based on a 75-year projection of the systems' operations. The programs are considered to be in actuarial balance if the income rate of the program is within 5 percent of the cost rate over the projection period. The rate would be changed each time the program got out of balance to bring it back into balance for the 75-year projection period. If a policy of this sort were implemented, it would result in much larger accumulations than those now proposed. In fact, under such a regimen, the OASDI trust funds would never be depleted.

In their baseline simulation, Aaron, Bosworth, and Burtless assumed the government always runs a deficit of 1.5 percent of GNP and that the OASDI surpluses or deficits exactly offset balances in the government's general accounts. They then simulated an alternative scenario where all the surpluses bring about added national savings. The deficit in the general accounts in this second simulation was set equal to 1.5 percent of GNP. A partial summary of their results is shown in Table 1. The results of the simulations when the OASDI accumulations are saved are compared to the scenario where they merely offset other government financing imbalances, or where the Social Security program is run on a pay-as-you-go basis.

The results of the simulation analysis suggest that the implications of truly saving the Social Security trust fund buildup would generally be positive. There would be a fairly rapid increase in the level of the capital stock. In results not shown here, they also estimate that the level of wages would rise by nearly 2 percent by the year 2000 and nearly 4 percent over the next 30 years, reflecting the increased worker productivity levels associated with the higher capital stock. The combined increase in economic capacity would drive up net national product and increase general consumption levels.

Table 1.   Economic Effects of Domestically Investing the Social Security Trust Fund Surplus Under a Periodically Adjusted Level Tax Schedule

| Year | General Economy (percent change from baseline) | | | Incremental Social Security Burden (percent of NNP)[a] | |
	Capital Stock	Net National Product	Consumption[b]	Baseline	Higher Savings
1990	0.0	0.0	0.0	-0.1	-0.1
2000	9.4	1.8	-0.8	-0.4	0.3
2010	19.6	3.6	0.8	-0.3	-1.0
2020	23.7	4.2	2.6	1.0	-1.2
2030	21.0	3.9	3.6	1.8	-1.2
2040	16.2	3.2	3.0	1.6	-0.8
2050	13.4	2.6	2.1	1.4	-0.2
2060	12.4	2.5	2.0	1.2	-0.3

Source: Henry Aaron, Barry Bosworth, and Gary Burtless. *Can America Afford to Grow Old? Paying for Social Security.* Washington, D.C.: The Brookings Institution, 1989:78.

[a]The increase in the ratio of OASDI benefits to baseline net national product (NNP) from the 1986-90 average, minus the increase in consumption from the baseline level, expressed as a percent of NNP in the baseline.
[b]Private consumption plus all government expenditures (includes government investment-type outlays).

The most significant result is the estimated decline in the ''Incremental Social Security Burden'' estimated under the higher savings model that was simulated. As discussed earlier, OASDI benefits are expected to grow from 4.5 percent of GNP today to 6.7 percent by 2035. The simulation results reflect changes in the level of resources that will be committed to OASDI as measured against net national product (NNP) instead of GNP. In the baseline case postulated by the authors, the measure is against the level of average commitment in the 1986 period. There is a slight decline in the Social Security burden during the initial period of the simulation because of the size of the baby boom during their working careers relative to the size of the retirement population anticipated over the next decade or two. Beyond that, as the baby boom moves into retirement the relative burden posed by Social Security begins to rise.

Compared to the baseline case, the "higher savings" scenario provides a different pattern. Because of the adjustments to the payroll tax when the system gets out of actuarial balance, there would be a relatively immediate increase in the payroll tax. Since the increased investment effects productivity cumulatively over time, the initial tax increases are reflected as a higher burden on the economy. But once the productivity effects begin to take hold, the net effect of the added savings would be to reduce the overall burden that Social Security would place on the nation's economic capacity. The prospect of a massive governmental trust fund does pose some concerns. If the Social Security trust accumulations were saved while the other governmental accounts were in balance, as John Hambor postulated, it is conceivable that the repurchase of existing federal securities would vitiate an extremely important aspect of our financial markets. If, on the other hand, the government does continue to finance some general operations through borrowing as it has since the end of World War II, the implications would be less significant. Given that the on-budget federal deficit is expected to amount to about 6.7 percent of GNP in fiscal 1991 and averaged 4.6 percent of GNP over the prior 10 years, there is a great deal of room to reduce the deficit without completely eliminating the potential pool of federal securities in which the OASDI trust funds can invest.

Within the current context of massive federal deficits in the general accounts, one concern about the trust fund buildup is that the government is effectively using the regressive payroll tax to fund governmental activities that many policy makers believe should be financed through a more progressive means such as the federal income tax. The interesting aspect of this "problem" is that it has a mirror image that has not been widely discussed. In Figure 4 the contributing sources of income to the trust funds are broken into three major categories. The bottom line reflects the net difference between payroll tax collections each year and the expenditure level in the same year. The middle line reflects the payroll tax collections plus the income taxes collected on benefits and earmarked for the trust funds minus fund expenditures. Finally, the top line reflects total income from the prior two sources plus the interest on the trust fund minus the expenditures.

The extremely powerful effects of compounding interest on the trust fund buildup are clear from the figure. If we leave current law in place, even assuming the trust funds are not "saved," it would result in approximately 20 years of program operations being funded through interest income after the first quarter of the next century. While the tax revenues supporting Social Security exceed the programs' expenditures, the interest going to the trust funds can be paid by merely issuing additional IOUs that the trust funds can hold. But once the tax revenues fall below expenditures, those IOUs have to be converted to real cash in order to meet benefits obligations. Ultimately the IOUs will have to be funded on the basis of general revenue sources, and are likely to be less regressive than the payroll tax. Almost certainly, the revenue sources that would be tapped to fund

FIGURE 4
Contributing Sources of OASDI Trust Fund Balances Over Time

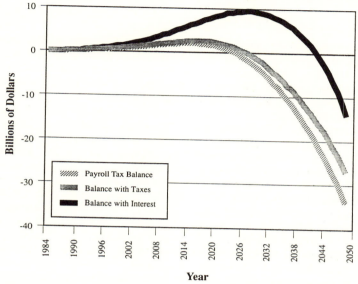

Year

Source: Derived by the author based on information published in the 1990 Annual Report of the Board of Trustees of the Federal Old-Age and Survivors Insurance and Disability Insurance Trust Funds.

these obligations would cover a wider source of income than the payroll tax. If we were to cut the payroll tax right now, it would reduce the regressivity of the funding side of the system now, but it would mean we would have to increase it more than under current law later. In other words, we would be reducing the regressivity of the funding of the baby boomers' benefits during their own working lives while adding to the expected regressive burden of workers who will have to support the system during the baby boomers' retirement.

The generations behind the baby boom are all less than 27 years of age today. When the last of the baby boom turns 65, the children born this year will be not yet be 40 years old. The overwhelming majority of people who will have to support the baby boomers in their retirement have never voted in a public election. Of those that are alive today, few are now prescient enough to care about our national retirement policies and their role in them. At some point, though, the generations behind the baby boom that are called upon to support them in their old age are going to read the economic and political history of the baby boomers' working years. Senator Moynihan may have written the forward to that history when he said: "We are in the process of beggaring the next generation and those that follow."[18] Pursuing Social Security policies today that increase the burden of future generations cannot enhance the long-term viability of the system. They may jeopardize it.

MEDICARE: SOCIO-PHILOSOPHIC AND ECONOMIC CONFLICT

Social Security is a transfer program that gives the elderly, eligible survivors, and qualifying disabled a level of command over goods and services in the national economy. Which goods and services any beneficiary buys with their benefits is determined by their own needs and tastes. The amount of goods and services the beneficiaries can purchase depends on the level of their Social Security benefits, their command of other resources, and the prices of goods and services established by the ordinary workings of the marketplace. Over the years, policy makers have increased the level of Social Security benefits in real terms because they were concerned that the beneficiaries, as a class, did not have sufficient access to goods and services in the marketplace to meet their basic needs. Because of particular concerns that the elderly did not have adequate access to health care services, Medicare was established in 1965 and became effective July 1, 1966. Effective July 1, 1973, coverage was extended to the disabled once they had been entitled to Social Security disability benefits for 24 consecutive months, and to individuals with end-stage renal disease who had been in dialysis for more than two months. Today Medicare covers approximately 34 million people. Roughly 10 percent of them are disabled and the remainder are over age 65.

A Large and Growing Commitment

During calendar year 1970 benefit payments under the HI program were $5.1 billion and those under the SMI program were $2.0 billion. By 1989 benefits provided by the respective programs cost $60.0 billion and $38.3 billion, reflecting compound annual growth rates of 13.8 percent and 16.9 percent. Over the decade from 1979 to 1989, a period in which the disabled were covered throughout, the growth rates were 11.7 percent per year for HI and 16.0 percent for SMI. Over the longer period, total federal government outlays were growing at a rate of 9.7 percent per year and GNP was growing at a 9.0 percent rate. In the shorter period, government outlays were increasing at 8.6 percent per year and GNP at 7.7 percent. Over almost any period selected since its inception, Medicare's growth rate has exceeded that of the federal government in general or the national economy.

One reason for the growth in the cost of Medicare has been the growth in the number of people enrolled in the program. Bringing the disabled into the program in 1973 instantly added about 10 percent more enrollees. Over the last decade the number of enrollees in both the HI and SMI programs has been growing 1.8 percent per year. Some of the growth in the enrolled population may indeed be the result of more people living longer because of the treatment they receive under the Medicare program. Another reason for the growth in costs of Medicare has been the general increase in prices due to inflation. Between 1970 and 1989, the consumer price index reflecting the growth of prices in the general

FIGURE 5
U.S. Health Care Expenditures as A Percentage of Gross National Product

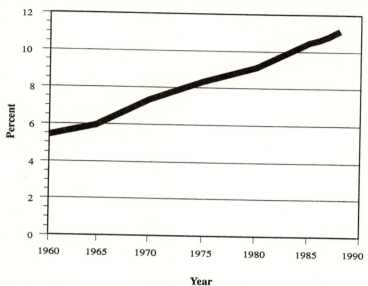

Year

Source: Health Care Financing Administration, Office of the Actuary: Data from the Office of National Cost Estimates, in Health Care Financing Review (Summer 1990), Vol. 11, No. 2:24.

economy was increasing at a rate of 6.3 percent per year. During the period from 1979 to 1989 it grew at a compound rate of 5.5 percent per year. Furthermore, prices in the health industry grew 2.3 percent more per year than the CPI between 1970 and 1989 and 3.7 percent more per year between 1979 and 1989.

One aspect of the growth in Medicare expenditures may be that the program is caught up in an area of economic activity that is progressively claiming more of our national resources. Figure 5 shows U.S. health expenditures as a share of gross national product (GNP) from 1960 through 1988. During this period the share of GNP devoted to health care grew at a rate of 2.7 percent per year. If America experiences the same kind of growth over the next 28 years that it experienced between 1960 and 1988, the nation will devote nearly a quarter of its GNP to health care. If the growth in health costs we have experienced over the past quarter century is projected indefinitely, in about 80 years the entire U.S. GNP will be devoted to the delivery of health care to Americans.

Clearly, the U.S. cannot indefinitely sustain the kind of growth in health care expenditures that the nation has experienced over the past quarter century. But if we look at the aging of the population and its implications for Medicare, the long-term prospects do not look bright. Table 2 shows the projected expenditures of the HI and SMI programs as a percent of GNP for the period 1990 to 2060. The projected share of GNP claimed by Medicare is expected to increase roughly

2.5 times between 1990 and 2020. And by 2020, roughly half of the baby boom will still not have attained the age at which they are eligible for Medicare. Those that are covered by Medicare will still be relatively young, the group of the aged that requires the least health care services on average.

Table 2.   HI and SMI Expenditures as a Percent of GNP, 1990-2060
C
Calendar   Program Expenditures as a Percent of GNP[a]

Year	HI	SMI	HI and SMI
1990	1.15	0.82	1.97
1995	1.39	1.04	2.43
2000	1.62	1.39	3.01
2005	1.80	1.73	3.53
2010	2.04	2.02	4.06
2015	2.36	2.24	4.60
2020	2.64	2.51	5.15
2025	2.96	2.81	5.77
2030	3.22	3.06	6.28
2035	3.37	3.18	6.55
2040	3.42	3.21	6.63
2045	3.43	3.20	6.63
2050	3.44	3.21	6.65
2055	3.45	3.27	6.72
2060	3.46	3.34	6.80

Source: Office of Medicare and Medicaid Cost Estimates, Office of the Actuary, HCFA, December 1990.
[a]Estimates reflect HI and SMI changes enacted in OBRA 90, 1990 II-B Assumptions, and updated HI admission assumptions.

During 1990, an estimated 12.7 percent of the population was age 65 or older. By 2010, the share of the population age 65 or older is expected to grow to 13.8 percent of the population. Over the next 20 years the elderly are expected to increase to more than 21 percent of the total population. We are now in a period where increasing life expectancy is driving up the percentage of the population that is characterized as being old old, or 85 years of age or older. Between now and the time the baby boom begins to retire, the percentage of the population comprised of the young old, between the ages of 65 and 74, and the middle category of aged between the ages of 75 and 84, will remain relatively constant. As the baby boom begins to retire toward the end of the first decade of the next century their compositional effects on the makeup of the elderly population is clear.
    James Poterba and Lawrence Summers have reviewed Medicare expenditure data between 1966 and 1982 to look at the relationship between aging and Medicare costs.[19] They have found that the level of expenditures gradually rises

with age. They found the increases to be relatively consistent from age group to age group across the various years that they studied. In essence, they concluded that the Medicare costs per male recipient over the age of 85 were about twice the cost per male recipient aged 65 or 66. For women, the cost increases were slightly greater, but similar. As the front end of the baby boom moves from being the young old to being an increasing portion of the old old, and as the younger ones move into Medicare coverage, it would seem that the share of GNP needed to sustain the elderly's health care needs would increase at an accelerating rate. The projections suggest the opposite.

Between 1990 and 2010 the share of GNP dedicated to providing Medicare benefits is projected to more than double, according to the HCFA actuaries. The underlying growth rate in the projected share of GNP used for Medicare is 3.7 percent per year. In 2011 the baby boom will begin to reach age 65. Over the next 20 years, assuming current law persists until then, all of the baby boom will come under Medicare protection. During the 20-year period starting in 2010, the share of the population age 65 and over will grow from 13.8 percent to 21.2 percent of the population according to Census Bureau estimates shown in Table 3. Yet the projections of the share of GNP to be devoted to providing Medicare are expected to rise from 4.06 percent to 6.28 percent, representing an underlying growth rate of 2.2 percent per year. As the whole baby boom moves from being the young elderly to being the old elderly we might expect another escalating increase in the resources required to fund the Medicare program. But as we look at the period the baby boom passes across the threshold of being 85 between 2030 and 2050, the share of GNP projected for Medicare grows from 6.28 percent to 6.65 percent, reflecting an annual growth rate of 0.3 percent per year.

Table 3. Number and Distribution of the Population, All Ages and 65 and over in the United States, 1980-2050

Year	Population All Ages (000s)	Total Aged %	65-74 %	75-84 %	85 and Over %
1980	227,704	11.3	6.9	3.4	1.0
1990	249,657	12.7	7.2	4.1	1.3
2000	267,955	13.0	6.6	4.6	1.8
2010	283,238	13.8	7.2	4.4	2.3
2020	296,597	17.3	10.1	4.9	2.3
2030	304,807	21.2	11.3	7.0	2.4
2040	308,559	21.7	9.5	8.1	4.2
2050	309,488	21.8	9.7	6.9	5.2

Source: United States Bureau of the Census. "Projections of the Population of the United States, 1983 to 2080." *Current Population Reports*, Series P-25, no. 952. Washington D.C.: Government Printing Office, 1984.

The reason the growth rate for Medicare as a percent of GNP slows is because the actuaries assume that after the first 25 years, SMI per capita costs grow at the same rate as GNP.[20] The problem with this assumption is that it implicitly eliminates the aging population induced cost increases just at the point we can expect an explosion in the aging population. Given the history of Medicare posing a consistently higher claim on payroll taxes in particular, and other government resources or the GNP in general, these projections have to be taken as a rosy outlook on the prospects of Medicare under current law.

Despite this rosy outlook, the costs of Medicare for taxpayers are projected to increase twice as fast as the costs of paying Social Security's cash benefits between now and the time the baby boom gets to retirement. Over this period Social Security will go from being about 2.3 times the size of Medicare relative to the GNP today to being the equivalent in 2030. As discussed above, the size of Social Security and its projected growth is already a concern. The added problem that Medicare faces in terms of its long-term viability is already is under heavy and growing criticism.

Medicare from the Outside Looking in

Medicare's long-term outlook is further complicated by the overall health care market environment in which it operates. Everyone who pays for health care today is concerned about the general inflation in the system. At least one of those payers, namely the federal government, is big enough and has adequate leverage that it can restrain the inflationary influence other payers face. The problem is that curtailing the inflationary pressures on Medicare, without curtailing the overall inflation rate in the medical care marketplace, merely leads to hyper-inflation in other sections. The federal government, by imposing all its cost-control devices on Medicare, has been shifting costs to the other payers in the health care system. Few, if any, of these other payers have been able to withstand the inflationary forces they face, especially those added by the government's offloading obligations from Medicare.

For years there have been complaints about the effects of the federal shifting of health costs to other payers. Recently estimates have been developed showing how cost controls implemented under the Medicare program affect the cost of providing health care to various consumers under alternative payer arrangements. These are shown in Table 4. It suggests that for each dollar of health care charged against Medicare, the hospital and physician costs involved in providing that care are $1.15. By this estimate, the government is able to shift about 13 percent of the cost of the Medicare program onto other participants in the system. That means the supplier system either has to pass the bill on to other customers, or eat a loss. Dean Coddington, David Keen, and Keith More estimate that the typical indemnity plan, without a network of specified providers vending health services on a negotiated basis, picks up 25 cents of other consumers' costs for each dollar of health care services they purchase. To add insult to injury, according to these estimates, these plans pay another 10 cents of that dollar to make up for past plan losses, and 5 cents because of the plans' administrative complexity. For each dollar expended, the plan is only buying 60 cents worth of health care. The problem will be exacerbated as more and more eligible people become covered under Medicare.

The Congressional Budget Office (CBO) has recently conducted an internal assessment of the impact of legislation on federal spending for Medicare that lends credence to the direction of the article's conclusions.[21] The CBO analysis used two separate methodologies to estimate the annual Medicare savings being realized as a result of legislation enacted from 1981 through 1990. It concluded that Medicare spending is now about 82 percent of what it would have been, had the various legislative measures not been approved. Some of the 18 percent savings may have been realized through more efficient delivery of services to Medicare patients.

Table 4.   Relative Importance of Factors Driving Each Dollar of Medical Cost Borne by Payers

Factor	Medicare	Group and Staff-Model HMOs	IPA-Model HMOs; PPOs	Indemnity: Self pay
Physician/hospital costs	$1.15	$.95	$.70	$.60
Cost Shifting	(.15)	(.07)	.15	.25
Recovery of earlier losses	--	.02	.05	.10
Complexity/overhead	--	.10	.10	.05
Total	$1.00	$1.00	$1.00	$1.00

Source: Dean C. Coddington, David J. Keen, and Keith D. More. "Cost Shifting Overshadows Employers' Cost-containment Efforts." *Business and Health 9*, no. 1 (January, 1991):46.

Given what was happening to the other health care payers, however, it would be far-fetched to believe the medical system was realizing such efficiencies with Medicare patients, while costs were running out of control with the rest of the system's consumers. And this savings is just the effect of legislation enacted during the 1980s.

Medicare's Exposed Flank

Another factor that complicates the issue of Medicare's long-term viability is the currently significant and growing need for added coverage of long-term care for the elderly. As people live to older and older ages, they tend to suffer from increases in functional limitations. In some cases these functional limitations may be minor, and the individual suffering them may still be largely self-reliant. But with increasing age, they often become so disabling that the sufferer requires institutional care. Figure 6 shows the relationship between age and the need for varying levels of help to meet personal needs. The data in the figure were derived by Edward Schneider and Jack M. Guralnik from the 1985 National Nursing Home Survey and *The Supplement on Aging to the 1984 National Health Interview Survey*.[22] Today in-home care is predominantly provided by family members of the individual suffering from the limitations. Based on the projected growth of the elderly population, especially those over the age of 85, Schneider and Guralnik estimate nursing home costs in the U.S. could increase between 2.7 and 4.5 times current costs in real terms between now and 2040. But if you consider the current relative mix between those living at home and getting help and those in nursing homes today, compared to the potential needs for institutional help in the future, the situation could become much worse than these authors project. The elderly today are largely the parents of more children than the baby boomers as parents are having. People with fewer children are going to face smaller likelihood of getting help from family members in dealing with functional limitations than those who have more. The baby boomers almost certainly will face an increasing problem in this regard.

Today, approximately 40 percent of nursing home costs in the U.S. are paid through the Medicaid program. There has been some discussion that employers might respond to the growing need for long-term care insurance by expanding the benefits packages they now offer to their workers and dependents. But most employers already feel so beleaguered with their health benefits programs that it is unlikely that major expansions will occur any time soon in this area. Some policy analysts are now beginning to recommend that a new layer of social insurance be laid on top of Social Security and Medicare to cover this growing need with an estimated near-term cost of 2 to 3 percent of total U.S. wages if the program were fully implemented.[23] Given the potential growth in the need for long-term care in light of the aging population, the cost of such a social insurance program could increase significantly in the future. Schneider and Guralnik's work suggests the costs for the baby boom might be 3 or 4 times those of a program that was fully implemented today.

The Bigger Picture on Medical Care

Medicare is a major player in the health care system, a system that is increasingly under criticism. There is a growing feeling on the part of the public that the U.S. is paying too much for medical care and not getting what it needs in return. There is concrete evidence that can put the feelings about our medical care system into context. This evidence is worth looking at before finally addressing the question on the long-term viability of our social insurance system.

U.S. health care expenditures can be compared to those of its major economic peers to put the American experience in a broader context. Table 5 shows the share of gross domestic product (GDP) dedicated to health care expenditures by the 10 largest Organization for Economic Cooperation and Development (OECD) countries in 1975 and 1989, and the compound annual growth in GDP spent on health care in these countries between the two years.

FIGURE 6
Functional Limitations and Living Arrangements of the Elderly

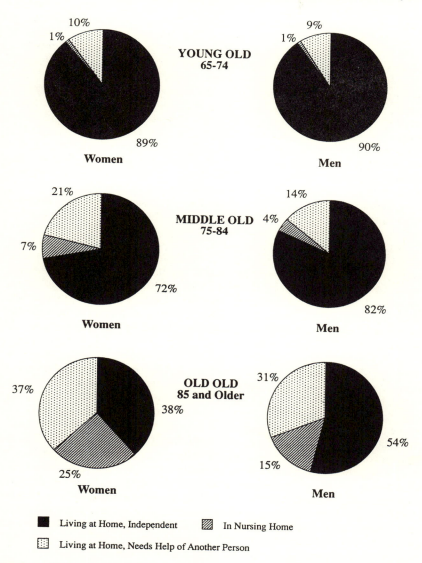

Source: Edward L. Schneider and Jack M. Guralnik, ''The Aging of America, Impact on Health Care Costs,'' *Journal of the American Medical Association*, (May 2, 1990), Vol. 263, No. 17:2337.

Table 5.   Total Health Expenditures as a Percent of Gross Domestic Product for Selected Organization for Economic Cooperation and Development Countries

Country	1975	1989	Annual Growth Rate
Australia	5.7	7.0	1.5
Canada	7.3	8.7	1.3
France	6.8	8.7	1.8
Germany	7.8	8.2	0.4
Italy	5.8	7.6	1.9
Japan	5.5	6.7	1.4
Netherlands	7.7	8.3	0.5
Spain	5.1	6.3	1.5
United Kingdom	5.5	5.8	0.4
United States	8.4	11.8	2.5
Mean All OECD Countries	6.5	7.6	1.1

Source: Data from 1975 and 1989 taken from Organization for Economic Cooperation and Development: *Health OECD, Facts and Trends* (forthcoming), as presented by George J. Schieber and Jean-Pierre Poullier. "International Health Spending: Issues and Trends." In *Health Affairs* (Spring 1991):109. The growth rates shown in the table were calculated by the author of this article.

During 1975, the U.S. spent 8.4 percent of its GDP on health care, more than any of the other largest OECD countries on the list, and 29 percent more than the average level of spending by all the OECD countries. By 1989 the U.S. was spending 11.8 percent of its GDP on health care, 55 percent more than the average OECD expenditure level. Even though the U.S. had started the comparison period from 1975 to 1989 shown in Table 5 with the highest level of health care expenditures, it also realized the highest growth rate over the period. The growth rate in the share of GDP spent on health care in the U.S. over the 12-year period was twice that of the average of all OECD countries.

George Schieber and Jean-Pierre Poullier have also calculated per capita health care spending in OECD countries for 1989. The results for the largest 10 countries are shown graphically in Figure 7. In 1989 U.S. per capita health care expenditures equaled $2,354, compared to an average of $1,102 in the other nine countries shown in the figure, and an average $1,039 in all the other 23 OECD countries. By every measure, the U.S. is spending more on health care than other major industrial countries, and it is doing so at an increasing rate. A possible explanation for the relatively high level of expenditures America makes on health care in comparison to other economically developed countries is that the

FIGURE 7
Per Capita Health Spending in Selected Countries in 1989

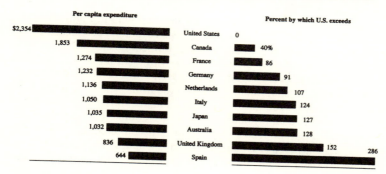

Source: Data from 1975 and 1989 taken from Organization for Economic
Cooperation and Development: *Health OECD, Facts and Trends* (forthcoming),
as presented by George J. Schieber and Jean-Pierre Poullier, "International
Health Spending: Issues and Trends," in *Health Affairs*, Spring 1991:113.

quality of its care is so much better than elsewhere in the world. Certainly, much
of American medical technology is at the leading frontier of medical science.
But, American life expectancy levels at birth and infant mortality rates shown in
Table 6 do not reflect the delivery of superior health care services to the full
spectrum of its population. On the other hand, the results for the United Kingdom
suggest that a socialized health care system at the other end of the organizational
spectrum relative to ours does not guarantee any better outcomes by such
measures.

Infant mortality and life expectancy are, at best, proxy indicators of the quality
of health care being delivered to the various populations encompassed in Table 6.
The problem in cross-national comparisons of the quality of health care is that no
other immediately available measures can be used for comparison purposes.
Some analysts argue that infant mortality and life expectancy rate comparisons
are not indicative of the quality of U.S. health care. They point out that the
American population is more heterogeneous than those of the other countries,
poverty rates among U.S. children are higher than in Japan or Western European
countries, and Americans' drug, drinking, and smoking habits, and other life
style characteristics may contribute to the bad outcomes as measured by U.S.
infant mortality and life expectancy figures.

A key criticism of America's health system is that between 30 and 40 million
people at any point in time lack health insurance protection. Those who have no
health insurance tend to have lower incomes. They include a disproportionate
share of minorities and lower-wage workers and their dependents. These same
individuals often lack sufficient resources of their own to get needed medical
care. Some of them gain access to the health care system through government

programs. Others receive services provided on a charitable basis. Many do not get the care they need.

Another measure of the quality of the health care system in a country is the extent to which the people in the country are satisfied with it. Figure 8 shows the results of a series of nationally representative surveys done across the 10 OECD countries with the highest per capita spending on health care. The United States and Italy exhibit the greatest dissatisfaction with their systems, significantly more than any other nations. Again, these results do not point directly to the structure of America's health care delivery system as being the culprit. While more Americans think their system needs fundamental change, significantly more Italians believe their system needs to be completely rebuilt. The two systems are quite different. The U.S. system is a combination "private/public pluralistic" system, whereas the Italian system is a national health service with a limited private medical sector for people who want a nongovernmental alternative source of services.

Table 6.   Life Expectancy and Infant Mortality in 1990 in Organization for Economic Cooperation and Development Countries

Country	Male Years	Female Years	Infant Mortality Per 1000 Births
Australia	73	80	8.1
Canada	73	80	7.3
France	72	80	8.2
Germany	72	78	8.3
Italy	73	80	8.0
Japan	76	82	5.0
Netherlands	74	81	7.0
Spain	74	80	11.0
United Kingdom	72	78	13.3
United States	72	79	10.0

Source: Mark S. Hoffman, ed. *The World Almanac and Book of Facts.* New York: Pharos Books, 1990:684-770.

The dissatisfaction with the U.S. medical system shown in Figure 8 was based on a survey done in 1988.[24] An article in the July 19, 1990, issue of *The New England Journal of Medicine* reported on two surveys done in 1990, indicating that nearly three out of four Americans favor some form of national health care program.[25] One of the problems with relying on these survey results is the potential biasing of results that can come from the structuring of the questions asked. For example, the question asked in one of the two surveys reported in the July 19, 1990, issue of *The New England Journal of Medicine* was: "In the

FIGURE 8
The Public's View of Their Health Care System in 10 Nations

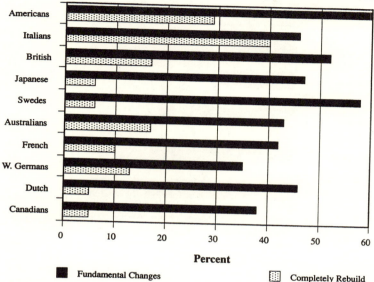

Source: Robert J. Blendon, Robert Leitman, Ian Morrison, and Karen Donelan, "Satisfaction with Health Systems in Ten Nations," *Health Affairs*, (Summer 1990), Vol. 9, No. 2:188.

Canadian system of national health insurance, the government pays most of the cost of health care out of taxes and the government sets all fees charged by doctors and hospitals. Under the Canadian system--which costs less than the American system--people can choose their own doctors and hospitals. On balance, would you prefer the Canadian system or the system we have here in the United States?"[26] While the question clearly stated that the Canadian system "costs less than the American system" and that "people can choose their own doctors and hospitals," it did not list any of the system's characteristics that Americans might perceive as negatives.

The business community is also beginning to show definite signs of becoming restive over the current situation. Nearly 1,800 executives in The Wyatt Company's *Management USA—Leading a Changing Work Force* survey done during the fall of 1990 indicated employee benefits costs are among the most important human resource issues they face in the 1990s, particularly medical benefits cost increases. Figure 9 shows that the executives were five times more likely to list health benefits cost increases as a very important problem than they were to list foreign competition. The executives were three times more likely to list health cost increases as a very important problem than a lack of qualified workers, and

FIGURE 9
Percent of Executives Rating Problems As Very Important

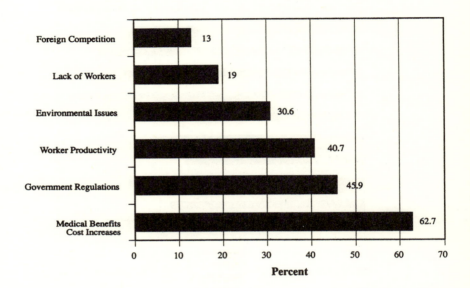

Source: The Wyatt Company, *Management USA_* Leading a Changing Work
Force, 1990.

one-and=a-half to two times more likely to cite health cost increases than
environmental issues, worker productivity, or government regulations.

Some business executives are now beginning to argue that the federal
government should nationalize the health delivery system to relieve business of
this crushing burden. Many executives in firms sponsoring health benefits
programs feel their plans are unfairly bearing the burden of cost shifting by the
government. Others feel that employers that do not provide health benefits to
their workers end up dumping uninsured consumers, who often fail to pay the
full costs of the care provided them, onto the health delivery system. The health
providers then shift these unpaid costs back onto the consumers with employer-
provided coverage. Though some executives have called for nationalized health
insurance, the overwhelming majority are still opposed to it. Among Wyatt's
Management USA respondents, fewer than one in five believe that national
health insurance covering everyone in the United States is the most effective way
to combat rising health costs in this country.

It is possible to dissect and criticize all of the survey questions that relate to
our health care system, but we cannot escape the fact that there is considerable
public dissatisfaction with our current dilemma. Given the projected growth in
Medicare and the potential additional burden of providing the elderly with

FIGURE 10
Percent Indicating There Are Good Things in Our Health
Care System but Fundamental Changes Are Needed

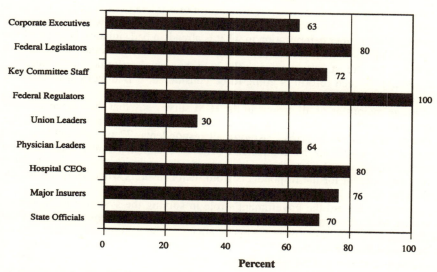

Source: Louis Harris and Associates, Inc., for Metropolitan Life Insurance
Company, *Trade-offs & Choices: Health Policy Questions for the 1990s,* (New
York, 1990:11).

long-term care in the future, the current dissatisfaction with the health care
system has to jeopardize the long-term viability of at least this facet of the social
insurance system.

Health Care for the Elderly

During the fall of 1990, Louis Harris and Associates, Inc., conducted a
national opinion research survey for the Metropolitan Life Insurance Company,
hereafter referred to as the H-M survey.[27] The survey was of employers,
government policy makers, hospital leaders, physicians, union officials, and
health insurers to get their opinions about America's health care problems and
what needs to be done about them. Among other questions, the survey respondents were asked to pick one of three responses most closely representing their
view of the nation's health care system. The essence of the first statement is that
the system is working pretty well and needs only minor changes; the second is
that it has some good elements but needs fundamental change; and the third is
that it is in such bad shape it needs to be completely rebuilt. The percentage of
those from the various groups surveyed picking the middle category can be seen
in Figure 10. Other than union leaders, 70 percent of whom thought the system

needed to be rebuilt, the majority of each group fell in the middle category believing the system needs fundamental change. Given the nature of the problems that have been outlined in this discussion and the consensus that seems to be forming about their seriousness, reform of our health care system is almost certainly going to be a hot legislative issue during the next few years. Given the potential for further deterioration in what is already a bad situation because of the projected growth in costs for providing health care for the elderly, significant reforms are almost certain prior to the baby boomers' retirement and Medicare eligibility. If such reform is going to be considered, it is important to begin to focus on the direction it might take.

Large majorities of all groups in the H-M survey say that they agree strongly or agree somewhat that "everyone should have health insurance, even if this means an increase in taxes." Among all respondents, 72 percent believe most Americans would not be comfortable with a system that limits their range of choice of doctors. Among the various groups, the majority of respondents think this way, except for the respondents from major insurers where only 48 percent thought so.

Attitudes toward the government's role in solving the system's problems are mixed. Most survey participants, 79 percent, disagree that things would get better if the government takes over the management of the health care system. Only a majority of union leaders believe things would improve if the government took over as the manager or administrator of the U.S. health care system. But a majority of respondents in every category believe that an appropriate role for the government is as a rule maker setting the rules for the private sector to manage and administer health care. And 79 percent of all respondents, and 78 percent of corporate executives, believe that government initiatives are needed to solve the problems facing the health care system.

While there is support for the government assuming a role in solving the U.S. health delivery problem, the overwhelming majority of all H-M respondents, 96 percent, believe that the system should continue to involve both the public and private sectors. As reflected in Figure 11, most of the leaders surveyed believe that the system should continue to operate largely through employment-based plans. If the system is still to be employment-based, the issue of employers not providing coverage must be resolved. To accomplish this, 71 percent of all respondents, and from 62 to 91 percent of the various categories of respondents, say that mandated employer-provided basic health coverage would be acceptable. Among corporate executives, 67 percent indicate mandated coverage would be acceptable, with larger firm executives being slightly more willing to accept such mandates than smaller ones. Still among executives of firms with 6 to 25 employees, 60 percent indicate health coverage mandates would be acceptable.

A number of questions in the survey are aimed at the rationing of health care. The first one is a global question: "Do you believe that in order to provide health insurance for everyone and control costs it will be necessary to limit, or ration, the availability of expensive high-tech medical services, or not?" The percentages of those answering yes to this question are shown in Figure 12.

In addition to this global question, a number of specific questions are aimed at

FIGURE 11
Health System Should Continue to Be Employment Based

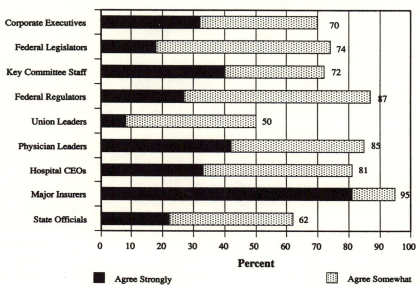

Source: Louis Harris and Associates, Inc., for Metropolitan Life Insurance Company, *Trade-offs & Choices: Health Policy Questions for the 1990s,* (New York, 1990:25).

---

various ways of implementing such rationing. While it may not be a rationing device, 56 percent oppose having to pay more out-of-pocket for their health insurance premiums. The true rationing devices include more cost sharing on the consumer's part, having to join managed care plans, having to get approval of primary care physicians for specialty care, limiting covered care to cost-effective providers, waiting for elective surgery, exclusions of some expensive treatments, and limiting rights to sue for malpractice. In virtually every case the majority of all the H-M respondents support these devices.

While the majority of all respondents favor such rationing or controlled access devices, some groups oppose some of them. A substantial majority, 74 percent, of union leaders oppose limits on covering some expensive treatments. Business executives are split almost evenly on this approach, with 49 percent finding it acceptable and 50 percent unacceptable. A number of groups are opposed to waiting for elective surgery, namely 56 percent of federal legislators, 50 percent of union leaders, 57 percent of the major insurers, and 58 percent of the physicians. Also, 50 percent of the federal legislators and 68 percent of the union leaders oppose increased cost sharing.

Organized labor appears to strongly oppose either implicit rationing devices (e.g., cost sharing) or explicit limits on expensive treatments. Given the political

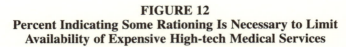

FIGURE 12
Percent Indicating Some Rationing Is Necessary to Limit
Availability of Expensive High-tech Medical Services

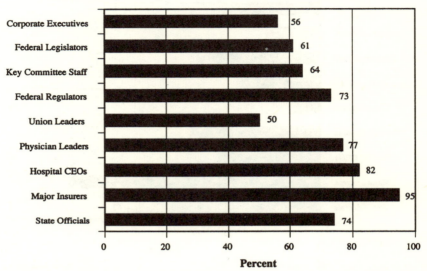

Source: Louis Harris and Associates, Inc., for Metropolitan Life Insurance Company, *Trade-offs & Choices: Health Policy Questions for the 1990s,* (New York, 1990:35).

strength of organized labor, this could be an important hurdle to overcome. If we expand insurance protection to the uncovered and improve the protection of those with inadequate coverage without some governing mechanism on the health care market, we face the prospect of significant new demands on the health care delivery system. This almost certainly would further fuel the inflationary tendencies already inherent in the system, unless we moved to a tightly structured system with extremely rigid price controls.

While various key parties show genuine interest in coming to grips with the health care dilemma and show some flexibility on approaches, no structured model bringing it all together has yet garnered widespread support. Often as we look outward at what other countries are doing in the organization and delivery of health care we focus on Great Britain or Canada. Neither of these countries provides a likely model for the U.S.

In an analysis published later in 1991, Laurene Graig looks at the health care systems of six countries.[28] The U.K. system is government-financed and government-operated, the classic example of socialized medicine, and the bogeyman often characterized as the reason the U.S. does not want to move to a nationalized health delivery system. The U.S. system is characterized by a free-market organization on the delivery side with financing coming from a mix of government programs, employer-provided group insurance, private insurance, and consumer out-of-pocket expenditures. The other four systems fall in between these two, with Canada more toward the U.K. end of the spectrum, and Germany, Japan, and the Netherlands more public/ private mixed systems. Graig's analysis shows that other industrialized countries have been able to organize their health care systems nationally, without having to adopt a monolithic socialized operation. These systems allow consumers freedom of choice in terms of the providers they can turn to when they need care. They have been able to provide universal coverage to their whole citizenry, maintain the popular support of the local populations, while holding both national health care expenditures as a percentage of the gross domestic product and their health cost inflation rates well below U.S. levels.

The common characteristic that the five foreign systems share is that they are willing and able to impose and enforce restraints on their health delivery systems. The U.S., by comparison, gives hospitals and doctors far more freedom to increase the services they provide and the fees they charge for the services they deliver. In most countries, negotiated fee levels set the prices that doctors can charge for services, and they must accept that fee as payment in full. Annual budgets limiting providers' incomes, or graduated tax schedules on fee income above certain levels discourage the system from providing excessive care. In most cases, doctors in the countries studied still are among the highest income professionals in the country.

Pointing out structures that work for other countries is not to say that the United States can or should adopt the national plan that is operating in any of these nations. But the provisions that these countries have implemented in their various national health systems bear considerable resemblance to various provisions that were evaluated in the H-M survey and are seemingly acceptable to broad cross sections of the respondents.

Undoubtedly, America will continue to feel its way for some time on the health care issues. And even if it finds a partial solution to the systemic factors causing health care inflation, cost pressures on these programs will persist. If nothing else, as a society our nation is growing older, and older people require more health care than younger ones. That makes it even more imperative that America begins to bring this problem under control. If it does not, the likelihood that our social insurance system will fail will greatly increase.

WILL OUR SOCIAL INSURANCE SYSTEM SURVIVE?

Retirement in the 21st Century

The phenomenon known as retirement has existed in American society for a long time. The earliest documented records of the prevalence of retirement date back to the late 19th Century. According to the 1870 U.S. Census, an estimated 65 percent of men over age 60 were in the labor force shortly after the end of the Civil War, as shown in Figure 13. Men this age not in the labor force are generally retired. From 1870 through 1930, the prevalence of retirement among

FIGURE 13
Labor Force Participation Rate of Men Aged 60 and Over

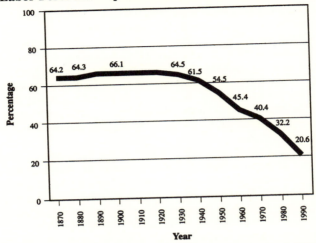

Sources: Roger L. Ransom and Richard Sutch, ''The Decline of Retirement in
the Years Before Social Security: U.S. Retirement Patterns, 1870-1940,'' in Rita
Ricardo-Campbell and Edward P. Lazear, *Issues in Contemporary Retirement*
(Stanford, California: Hoover Institution Press, 1988), Table 1.2:12, and Bureau
of Labor Statistics, Employment and Earnings, (Washington, D.C.: U.S. Government Printing Office, November 1990), Table A-4:9.

men over age 60 held relatively steady, and actually may have declined slightly.
In 1930, about 35 percent of the men over 60 were retired.

The first Social Security retirement benefits were paid in 1940. Today, nearly
all U.S. workers retiring at age 62 or later receive Social Security benefits. In
1940, a sharp increase in federal corporate income tax rates expanded the
incentive for employers to establish pension programs. In the late 1940s,
organized labor won the right to negotiate for pension benefits. The prevalence
of pensions grew rapidly throughout the 1950s and 1960s, especially among
larger firms. At the end of the 1930s, there were fewer than 700 pension plans in
the United States. Today there are nearly 1 million plans in operation. The
overwhelming majority of workers in firms with at least 100 employees are
covered by such plans.

Coincident with the beginning of Social Security and the growth in pensions,
the prevalence of older men in the labor force began to decline, as shown in
Figure 13, and it has continued to do so, until now. The retirement patterns of
women have varied somewhat from those of men because of their different
attachment to the formal work force outside of their homes. The labor force
participation rates of women over 65 have been relatively constant from 1940
until the present time. The labor force participation rates of women younger than

age 65 have been rising, especially recently, because women generally have entered the work force at much greater rates in recent years than they did historically. It appears that women with career tenure patterns similar to normal male tenure patterns are likely to have retirement characteristics similar to their male counterparts.

The long-term decline in the labor force participation rates of older men has been one vestige of our improved standard of living over the last half century. This trend has been so predominant that it will be difficult to reverse. It will be even more difficult if we seek to implement policies that force lower- and middle-income workers to stay in the work force, especially if the upper-income workers can continue to retire at earlier and earlier ages. This will be the case for two reasons. The first is that lower- and middle-wage workers are likely to have less in the way of position-specific skills and they will face greater competition for their jobs from younger workers. Second, if only upper-income workers and the disabled can leave the work force at the ages that society has come to expect, it will establish one more example of the middle class not being able to enjoy what their counterparts in earlier generations have enjoyed, and what they have come to expect.

To a certain extent, the future labor force participation rates of the young old will be dictated by labor market conditions. If there are worker shortages, the resulting higher wages offered to retired workers will bid some of them back into the work force. Under such conditions, it is likely that earning tests on retirement benefits may ultimately be eliminated.

Underlying Social Structure

Discussions about Social Security often turn to the "contractual" nature of the promises that we hold out through the program. One element of the Social Security Act gives lawmakers the capability to change the promises over time in accordance with the general needs and abilities of those who support the program through their tax contributions, and those who receive benefits from the program. Large social institutions like Social Security and Medicare tend to evolve marginally over time rather than in large incremental steps.

Shortly after the turn of the century, the baby boomers are going to start reaching their 60s. As they do so, their aspirations for retirement will be significantly influenced by the retirement experiences of their parents and the intervening cohorts of retirees between them and their parents. If the historical trends in retirement patterns persist as the baby boomers move into their 60s, if the Social Security benefits they receive are those configured in current law, and if the costs of Medicare continue to escalate as projected, the burden on workers to support the baby boom in retirement will reach historic highs. The combined burden of cash and medical benefits may be more than workers will be willing to sustain. This possibility makes it imperative that we keep our eye on the demands our existing promises might impose on future generations. The promises may have to be lowered. If we conclude that reduced promises are necessary, notification of the reductions should be made as early as possible so those affected can have time to adjust their retirement planning accordingly.

Faced with the prospect of changes to retirement plan provisions, many workers will probably prefer lower early retirement benefits rather than pushing back the age at which retirement can commence. While its implementation is still a number of years away and may not be fully understood by those that will be affected, there has been very little outcry about the increase in the Social Security normal retirement age after the turn of the century. This will mean lower initial benefits than they would otherwise receive for the workers affected who want to retire early, but it will not preclude them from getting their Social Security benefits at the same age as their parents could.

The crucial issue in determining whether our social insurance system can survive is what happens to Medicare. The projections reported earlier suggest the elderly would make a significantly larger claim on national resources in the form of medical care as the baby boom reaches retirement age. If this is to occur, other claims on national resources are going to have to be reduced. Since Medicare is run through the public fisc, it is likely that significant increases in Medicare commitments will bring into question public commitments to other programs, raising the potential that our commitment to the elderly could crowd out our commitments to other segments of our society.

It is impossible to predict at this time what our public appetites for national defense, foreign aid, etc., might be 25 or more years from now. We might indeed be willing at that time to reduce other national commitments, especially to the extent they are commitments to individuals or countries outside our own borders. But a large share of our other national commitments is to individuals and programs that benefit other segments of our own society directly.

Reducing public commitments of educational investment in our youth, or decreasing the investment in our national infrastructure, so we can provide ever more expensive health procedures that extend the life of the elderly but that may not improve their overall life satisfaction will pose difficult dilemmas for our policy makers. The projected public cost of providing health care for the elderly and for society in general after the turn of the century suggests that the structure of our health care system will need to change. If it does, it will influence the Medicare commitments.

In the final analysis, it would not appear that the shift in resources required to meet the general needs of the elderly in the future will be so large that we cannot make the marginal adjustments needed to maintain our existing cash benefits retirement program. The Medicare program, on the other hand, would seem to be on a long-term cost path that is not sustainable. This latter problem is only one element in the larger health care dilemma the U.S. now faces.

ENDNOTES

1. A. Haeworth Robertson. ''1989 Trustees Report on Social Security's Financial Health: Good News for the Elderly, Bad News For the Young.'' *Benefits Quarterly* (First Quarter, 1990):1-5.
2. 1991 Social Security Advisory Council on Social Security. ''Social

Security Technical Panel Report to the 1991 Advisory Council on Social Security'':vii.

3. Ibid.:8, 38.

4. Calculated by the author based on data published in the 1990 Annual Report of the Board of Trustees of the Federal Supplementary Medical Insurance Trust Fund. Baltimore, Md: Health Care Financing Administration, 1990:28.

5. Calculated by the author based on data published in the *Social Security Bulletin,* Annual Statistical Supplement 1981:195, and the *Social Security Bulletin,* Annual Statistical Supplement 1989:181. Baltimore Md: Social Security Administration.

6. Arthur M. Schlesinger, Jr. *The Age of Roosevelt,* Vol. 2, *The Coming of the New Deal.* Boston, Mass.: Houghton Mifflin Co., 1959:309-310.

7. Bureau of Economic Analysis. *The National Income and Product Accounts of the U.S., 1929-1982.* Washington, D.C.: U.S. Government Printing Office, 1986:1 and 109, and *The Survey of Current Business* 70, no. 7 (July 1990):40, 53.

8. Office of National Cost Estimates, HCFA. "National Health Expenditures, 1988." *Health Care Financing Review* 11, No. 4 (Summer 1990):24.

9. Committee on Economic Security. *Social Security in America.* Washington, D.C.: U.S. Government Printing Office, 1937:206-207.

10. The Honorable Daniel Patrick Moynihan. "To My Social Security Critics." *New York Times,* February 9, 1990:A-31, and "It's a Matter of Trust, Rosty," *The Washington Post,* March 22, 1990:A-23.

11. See Statement by Robert J. Myers to the Subcommittee on Retirement Income and Employment, Select Committee on Aging, House of Representatives (February 28, 1990):3.

12. Henry J. Aaron, Barry P. Bosworth, and Gary Burtless. *Can America Afford to Grow Old? Paying for Social Security.* Washington, D.C.: The Brookings Institution, 1989.

13. 1990 Annual Report of the Board of Trustees of the Federal Old-Age and Survivors Insurance and Disability Insurance Trust Funds. Baltimore, Md: Social Security Administration, 1990:62.

14. Moynihan, Op. cit.

15. Sylvester J. Schieber. "Accumulating Social Security Trust Funds: Money In Trust or Violation of Trust?" *Tax Notes,* July 2, 1990:88.

16. Charles L. Schultz. "Setting Long-Run Deficit Reduction Targets: The Economics and Politics of Budget Design." In Henry J. Aaron, ed. *Social Security and the Budget: Proceedings of the First Conference of the National Academy of Social Insurance.* New York: University Press of America, 1990:18.

17. John C. Hambor. "Economic Policy, Integenerational Equity and the Social Security Trust Fund Buildup." *Social Security Bulletin.* October 1987:13-18.

18. The Honorable Daniel Patrick Moynihan. "Why We Called for a Surplus." *The Washington Post,* March 7, 1990:A-25.

19. James M. Poterba and Lawerence H. Summers. "Public Policy Implica-

tions of Declining Old-Age Mortality." In Gary Burtless, ed. *Work, Health, and Income Among the Elderly.* Washington D.C.: The Brookings Institution, 1987:42.

20. 1991 Social Security Advisory Council on Social Security. "Report on Medicare Projections by the Health Technical Panel to the 1991 Advisory Council on Social Security":64.

21. Congressional Budget Office Memorandum from Sandra Christensen to Health Staff. "Impact of Legislation (1981-1990) on Federal Spending for Medicare." February 4, 1991:2.

22. Edward L. Schneider and Jack M. Guralnik. "The Aging of America, Impact on Health Care Costs." *Journal of the American Medical Association,* May 2, 1990 263, no. 17:2337.

23. Alice M. Rivlin and Joshua M. Wiener. *Reforming Long-Term Care.* Washington, D.C.: The Brookings Institution, 1987:26-27.

24. Robert J. Blendon, Robert Leitman, Ian Morrison, and Karen Donelan. "Satisfaction with Health Systems in Ten Nations." *Health Affairs* (Summer, 1990) 9, no. 2:185-192.

25. Robert J. Blendon and Karen Donelan. "The Public and Emerging Debate over National Health Insurance." *The New England Journal of Medicine* (July 19, 1990) 323, no. 3:208-212.

26. Blendon, Leitman, Morrison, and Donelan, Op.Cit.:186.

27. Louis Harris and Associates, Inc., for Metropolitan Life Insurance Company. *Trade-offs & Choices: Health Policy Questions for the 1990s.* New York: Louis Harris and Associates, Inc., 1990.

28. Laurene Graig, *Health of Nations.* Washington, D.C.: The Wyatt Company, forthcoming.

Discussions

Dwight K. Bartlett III, F.S.A.

INTRODUCTION

Mr. Schieber's paper is an outstanding one as I have come to expect from this clear thinking, articulate and prolific author. Nevertheless, I do have some comments on the paper as well as additional material and finally a suggested policy recommendation which would require additional research.

On one point of his paper, Mr. Schieber refers to the projections of the Old Age Survivors and Disability Insurance Programs based on alternative II-A as being based on "a somewhat optimistic intermediate set" of assumptions. The economic assumptions included in this set have generally been those currently being used by the Federal Budget people in making their budget projections. At one time it was the practice to make only three projections based on three sets of assumptions, optimistic, intermediate, and pessimistic. A decade ago when I was Chief Actuary of the Social Security Administration, it became apparent that the Federal Budget assumptions were excessively optimistic to be properly characterized as "intermediate." Therefore it was concluded that there should be two intermediate projections using the same demographic assumptions but two different sets of economic assumptions: one being the federal budget assumptions, the other being what the actuaries and economists at SSA believed to be "best guess" assumptions. Therefore the projections on the alternative II-B assumptions have been generally recognized as the "best guess" projections. I note however that the 1991 Trustees' Report returns to the practice of using only three sets of assumptions.

Mr. Schieber also states that general revenue funding of OASDI became a partial reality with the 1983 Social Security Amendments. If he really believes that, I wonder where he believes the money came from that paid for the benefits in the late 1970's and early 1980's when the Trust Fund balances were rapidly declining. General revenues of the government, or as some have quaintly observed, general deficits, were used to redeem the federal securities held in the Trust Funds in order to continue payment of benefits.

Mr. Schieber notes that it is the current consensus that the Trust Funds should be maintained at a level at least equal to the annual benefit payments of the program. This is an increase from what seemed to be the consensus a few years back of 50%. This new figure is based on work done by Richard Foster, Deputy Chief Actuary, SSA. He modeled what would happen to the Trust Fund balances if the current alternative II-B economic assumptions were used in making the projections at the beginning of the period and actual experience emerged equivalent to that the mid-1970's. He further assumed that corrective action in the financing of the program would take Congress five to ten years to implement. His study indicates that a Trust Fund ratio of 100% at the beginning of the period would be adequate, but not excessively adequate, to ride out the adverse experience until Congress acted.

Mr. Schieber opines that the earnings test of OASDI, which has been a favorite whipping boy of conservatives in recent years, will likely be eliminated if labor shortages develop after the turn of the century. He fails to note that the deferred retirement factor, currently at 3%, will be raised to nearly a full actuarial equivalent of 8% after the turn of the century. This may alleviate some of the pressure to eliminate the earnings test at that time.

While he does not quite say so explicitly, I gather from the tone of Mr. Schieber's paper that he favors the currently projected buildup of the OASDI Trust Funds over the next 25 years or so in order to help pay for the benefits of the baby boom generation as they move into retirement. This is a view shared by many economists and is based on the notion that collecting more in social security tax than is required to pay current benefits and expenses results in an increase in net national savings, leading to an increase in capital formation and ultimately to an increase in productivity. While I am not an economist, nevertheless, I find these linkages problematical enough so that I prefer pay-as-you-go financing combined with more nearly pay-as-you-go financing of the balance of the federal budget.

The ultimate burden of the program when the baby boom generation retires will be the benefits that are paid at that time. To make those benefits affordable, we do need to take steps to enhance the productivity of our then economy. It seems to me that the most important contribution we can make to maximizing the economic pie that will exist in the next century is to worry less about how many "widget machines" we are producing today and worry a lot more how well we are educating our young people who will be the workers of the next century.

In deciding whether we can afford our present OASDI program in the next century we need to look at the projected cost of the program not only on "best guess" assumptions but also the effect on those projections of deviations from the assumptions on which they are based.

We are fortunate to have included routinely in the annual Trustees' Report for OASDI sensitivity analyses of the change in the 75 year actuarial balance due to changes in assumptions. The actuarial balance is defined as the present value of future tax revenues less the present value of future benefits and expenses, expressed as a percentage of taxable payroll. The following table illustrates the effect of changing each of the principal assumptions one by one from the intermediate assumption to the pessimistic and to the optimistic assumption. This allows a person reviewing the projections who may feel the intermediate set of assumption are in general appropriate but nevertheless wants to know the impact of a change in one assumption to make that assessment.

The table suggests, on the positive side, that an improvement in the real wage increase will do most for the program, while on the negative side, a more rapid improvement in the death rate presents the greatest risk.

In my opinion the most instructive way to consider the affordability of the ultimate cost of OASDI is to consider its ultimate annual cost as a percentage of Gross National Product. The Trustees' Report contains such projections, and the following table is an extract from the 1991 Annual Report of the Trustees for the OASDI Trust Funds.

Change in 75 Year Actuarial Balance
Due to Changes in Assumptions (in parenthesis)
(As a percentage of taxable payroll)

	Pessimistic	Intermediate	Optimistic
Fertility Rate	-0.45% (1.6)	(1.9 total children born in a woman's lifetime	+0.42% (2.2)
Death Rate Improvement	-0.80 (51%)	(34% decline in age/sex specific death rates over 75 years)	+0.67 (18%)
Immigration	-0.08 (600,000)	(750,000 annual total)	+0.12 (1,000,000)
Real Wage Increase	-0.50 (4.6-4.0)	(5.1% annual increase in wages, 4.0% increase in CPI)	+0.60 (5.7-4.0)
CPI Increase	-0.71 (4.1-3.0)	(5.1-4.0)	+0.20 (6.1-5.0)
Real Interest Rate	-0.48 (1.5%)	(2.3%)	+0.39 (3.0%)

Alternative II Income Rate (13.11%) - Cost Rate (14.19%) = Balance (-1.08%)
Source: 1991 OASDI Trustees' Report

Projected OASDI Benefits and Expenses as Percent of GNP

Alternative	1991	2065
I ("optimistic")	4.82%	5.29%
II ("intermediate")	4.84	6.76
III ("pessimistic")	4.94	9.20

The table shows that even under the optimistic set of assumptions, the program cost will increase modestly, moderately under the intermediate assumptions, and very substantially under the pessimistic assumptions. The increase of about 50% in the program cost as a percentage of Gross National product seems tolerable to me when one considers that the aged dependency ratio, i.e., the ratio of those 65 and over to those 20-64 in our population is projected to increase from 20.9% in 1990 to 41.2% in 2065, nearly a 100% increase.

It is important to note, however, that these costs are just for OASDI and the picture is considerably bleaker when one includes Medicare.

There has been considerable discussion in recent years about the timing for any needed changes in the benefits of OASDI in order to keep the program affordable. Some, particularly those who find the more pessimistic assumptions more creditable, argue that changes should be made now in order to provide future retirees with as much advance notice as possible, so they can do as much advance financial and retirement planning as possible.

My own view is that the financial condition of the OASDI program now is sufficiently strong so that large scale changes are not warranted at present. However, it is quite possible that changes reducing the ultimate cost of the program will be necessary in the future. I would like to propose here a conceptual framework for considering when and how such benefit reductions might be made in the future.

The Employees Retirement Income Security Act of 1974 permits the sponsors of private pension plans to amend those plans so as to reduce benefits, but plan participants at the time of amendment cannot ultimately receive benefits less than they had already accrued up to the date of amendment. I believe the application of such a rule to the Old Age Benefits of Social Security would be appropriate. It seems clear that some changes in the past have not met this rule while others have. For example the making of part of Old Age benefits subject to federal income tax for a higher income individual resulted in an immediate reduction of benefits. I view this as a benefit reduction rather than a tax increase since the tax revenues do not become part of the general funds of government but are added back to the Trust Funds, so it is effectively a form of needs testing for benefits.

On the other hand, the moving of the normal retirement age for old age benefits gradually from 65 to 67 after the turn of the century was long enough delayed so that the actuarial value of accrued benefits of workers affected by the change in 1983 when the change was enacted was not reduced except perhaps for a few very unusual cases. This is true because the additional benefits they would earn for covered employment post 1983 would have value exceeding the loss in value for benefits accrued to 1983 which were affected by the retirement age postponement.

This is a concept which bears further development at another time and place.

Patricia M. Danzon

INTRODUCTION

Syl Scheiber has provided a comprehensive discussion of trends in the costs of the Social Security (OASDI) and Medicare systems. I have been asked to focus my comments on the medical care component. As Scheiber points out, trends in Medicare are closely linked to trends in health care spending, with feed back in both directions. I shall therefore comment on problems and potential solutions for the health care system in general, as well as issues specific to Medicare.

The actuarial forecasts of expenditures relative to planned revenues for Medicare are far more alarming than the projections for OASDI cash benefits. The assumptions underlying the projections appear sound -- indeed, if anything, they are overly optimistic in later years. Under any reasonable set of assumptions, the conclusion is inescapable: medical care for the elderly will absorb an increasing fraction of the income of the working population, unless the structure of Medicare benefits or financing is changed. Expenditures under the Hospital Insurance (HI) and Supplementary Medical Insurance (SMI) programs combined are projected to increase from 1.97% of GNP in 1990, to 6.28% in 2030 and 6.80% in 2060. Moreover, Medicare spending will increase from less than 50% of Social Security cash spending in 1990 to equal the size by 2030. Beyond that point, medical care will absorb over half of the total transfer from workers to retirees.

In fact the HI and SMI projections alone understate the total tax burden on workers to finance health care for the elderly because they exclude Medicaid, which pays for over 40% of long term care costs and covers the SMI premiums and co-payments for the elderly poor. Since Medicaid is financed from state and federal general revenues, long term projections are not routinely made or added to the projected costs of Medicare.

I shall not address here the political feasibility of increasing payroll and general revenue tax rates in order to finance the projected health care costs of Medicare and Medicaid. My comments are concerned with the issues of efficiency and equity that are raised by these projections. Specifically, do current and projected levels of health care spending in general and for the elderly in particular reflect a reasonably efficient allocation of resources, and is the financing reasonably equitable? Does the greater success of other countries in controlling the growth of their health care spending imply that we should adopt their solutions?

SYMTOMS VS. REAL PROBLEMS
IN THE U.S. HEALTH CARE SYSTEM

The U.S. spends a larger fraction of GNP on health care than any other country -- 12 percent, in contrast to under 10 percent for most other OECD countries -- and more per capita in absolute dollars. The U.S. is also alone among developed countries in having roughly 15 percent of the population without health insurance. Widespread dissatisfaction with this situation underlies the growing interest in major system-wide reform. Scheiber appears to favor government-imposed fee schedules and expenditure ceilings for physicians and budget caps for hospitals, similar to those adopted in Canada, Germany and Japan.

While I share the concern over the excesses and inadequacies of the status quo, I am not persuaded by the conclusion, that a system of competing private insurance plans, is fatally flawed and that government controls on total expenditures are a good idea.

Spending more on health care is not necessarily bad: the optimal level is clearly not zero. But concern over health care costs is well-founded -- in general and for the elderly in particular -- if the marginal benefit would be higher if resources were reallocated from health care to other uses such as education, capital investment or consumption. The criteria I adopt in evaluating the status quo and proposed alternatives are efficiency and equity, not control over total spending.

How Meaningful are the Statistics?

Underlying the criticisms of health care spending in the U.S. relative to other countries is the implicit assumption that Americans spend more but get the same level of health care. This conclusion is often based on international comparisons of mortality and morbidity that fail to control for a host of other factors that affect health, including education, nutrition, stress and genetic factors. But the more fundamental objection is that the available mortality and morbidity data cannot measure the multidimensional value to consumers of many of the health services that are routinely more available in the U.S. These benefits include the information that comes from more frequent use of MRI scans and other diagnostic techniques; greater access to elective procedures such as hip replacements that reduce pain and improve well-being, particularly for the elderly; greater freedom of choice of physician, location and timing of treatment. There certainly is waste in the U.S. health care system, and many services cost more than they are worth, because of distortions in insurance markets that are discussed below. But the extreme view, that Americans just pay more for the same level of health benefits, ignoring real but unquantifiable benefit differences, is clearly mistaken.

Second, accounting costs of budget-constrained systems such as Canada's understate the real costs. There are significant hidden costs in the form of nonoptimal patient time costs, foregone benefits due to rationing by queuing, and the excess burden of tax-based financing. If these hidden costs are accounted for, the overhead costs of the Canadian system, over and above spending on medical services, is probably higher in Canada than in the U.S. (Danzon, 1992).

Third, some of the benefits of U.S. spending on R&D for pharmaceuticals, other medical technologies and information systems, accrue to other countries. Countries with budget-constrained health care systems pay less than their "fair" share of the joint costs of R&D that benefit consumers worldwide. Not all R&D spending on drugs or other medical technologies is worthwhile. But on balance, other countries surely benefit from U.S. spending in these areas and these benefits are omitted from simple international comparisons of health care spending.

THE REAL PROBLEM: DISTORTIONS IN THE STATUS QUO

To the extent that there is waste and gross inequity in the U.S. system, this is driven largely by misguided public policy rather than fundamental flaws in competitive private insurance markets. Neither the U.S. nor any other country has tried a well-designed, undistorted system of private health care financing. The U.S. system is heavily influenced by government tax policy and other cost-increasing regulations, and by lack of appropriate interventions to assure that coverage is universal and affordable.

Tax subsidy to employer health insurance

Chief among the distorting government policies is the tax rule that employer contributions to health insurance are tax-exempt income to employees. This exemption applies to federal and state income and payroll taxes. The implied tax subsidy increases with the employee's marginal tax rate, from zero for workers who pay no tax up to 50 percent or more for higher income employees, with an overall average around 33 percent. For example, for an employee in a 33 percent marginal tax bracket, $100 of employer-provided health insurance effectively costs only $67 in terms of after-tax income. This subsidy is sufficient to more than offset the administrative load on health insurance. Consequently most workers are better off having insurance even for routine medical expenses, not just for large, unpredictable expenses which are the usual object of insurance.

This tax subsidy plays a critical role in the inflation and the inequities of the U.S. health care system. It leads employees to choose very comprehensive plans with relatively low levels of co-payment and, until recently, few other mechanisms for controlling costs. Even co-payments are tax-subsidized under flexible spending accounts which are common in most large firms. High tax-induced levels of health insurance in turn have made consumers insensitive to prices, fuelled demand for quantity and ''quality'' of services and for cost-enhancing technologies, and undermined demand for cost-reducing technologies.

The structure of the tax-subsidy is also fundamental to the inequities and coverage gaps of the U.S. system. Because the value of the subsidy rises with the employee's marginal tax rate, it is highly regressive and is of little or no value to lower income families. Moreover because the subsidy applies only to employer contributions, those who do not obtain insurance through employment face are excluded. This exacerbates the cost- differential due to higher administrative costs and regulatory costs in the non-group market. Further, the employment-focus of the subsidy has probably stunted the formation of other insurance-purchasing groups, such as banks, which could offer some of the scale economies of group purchasing but have little incentive to develop such plans when most of the population is better off getting insurance through the workplace.

Insurance regulation

State regulation of insurance has also increased the cost of insurance. Most costly are mandated minimum benefit laws, which require that commercial insurance plans cover specified services such as alcoholism treatment, chiropractors, psychologists, in vitro fertilization, acupuncture, etc. There are over 800 state mandates in 1991, very few of which have been subject to a cost-benefit test. In addition, several states require commercial insurers to absorb deficits in high risk pools. These costs must ultimately be passed on to policyholders in the price of insurance.

The burden on cost-increasing regulations falls most heavily on individuals and small firms, because self-insured employer plans are exempt under ERISA. State regulation has certainly contributed to the dramatic trend towards self-insurance in recent years and to the number of small firms that do not offer plans.

Regulation has also been used to limit competition in ways that increase provider incomes and raise costs for consumers. Laws against the corporate practice of medicine stunted the growth of HMOs for many years. Freedom-of-choice laws in some states limit selective contracting to form preferred provider organizations (PPOs), that have demonstrated ability to reduce costs. Limits on consumer co-payments for using out-of-plan providers obstruct the formation of point-of-service plans. Managed care has been undermined by restrictions on utilization review procedures.

In unconstrained insurance markets, plans compete by offering consumers a menu of choices that trade-off lower premiums, on the one hand, against co-payments, restrictions on choice of provider, and provider-targeted financial incentives to restrain excess use, on the other hand. There is no free lunch in health insurance: consumers cannot have unrestricted choice, total financial protection and low cost in public or private systems. Private insurers compete by devising plans that offer consumers their preferred trade-off between cost and coverage. But competition cannot work if insurers are barred by regulation from using the strategies essential to control costs.

The partial public safety net

Although some 15 percent of the U.S. population does not formally have either private or public insurance, in fact they have quasi-insurance through an informal and haphazard, publicly-subsidized safety net. This safety net includes public hospitals, public clinics, uncompensated care (partly tax-financed through the tax-favored status of not-for-profit hospitals), and the Medicaid "spend down" for the near poor who become eligible for Medicaid if they incur large medical expense.

Given this safety net, the decision not to buy insurance may be a rational decision for many without employment-based coverage. Although this quasi-insurance may entail lower quality of care and the embarrassment of relying on charity, it may be the best option for those without employment-based coverage, if the alternative is to pay a high price for an individual policy, with no tax subsidy, mandated benefits that may be of relatively low value and a high administrative load.

MEDICARE SPECIFIC SOLUTIONS

Miracle cures and Improved cost-effectiveness

The only hope for a substantial reduction in expenditures without reduction in real benefits is to find either prevention or cure for the major disease categories where our current therapies are costly and tend merely to prolong survival without cure. Miracle preventive or curative therapies for cancer, cardiovascular problems and Alzheimer's top the wish list. Certainly we cannot count on medical breakthroughs to solve the fiscal problems. But as pressures mount worldwide to regulate prices of pharmaceuticals, the long term effects on incentives for R&D and hence on health care costs should be borne in mind.

A related, only slightly less utopian search for a solution that cuts costs without cutting benefits is the outcomes research in which HCFA is currently investing heavily. The hope is to find definitive evidence that some high cost treatments are no more effective than lower cost alternatives. I am skeptical partly because preferences for the risks and possible outcomes of alternative treatments differ -- some people are willing to take high risks or incur pain or time costs for a chance of cure, others are not. In that case the optimal treatment for a given condition depends on the patient's preferences. This type of research, while useful, is unlikely to provide a clear mandate for eliminating a large fraction of high cost care.

Universal reduction in covered benefits

More realistically, achieving significant savings will require eliminating some services that have real value to recipients. In that case, Medicare could follow the example of the Oregon Medicaid program and attempt to ration on the basis of some measure of benefit relative to cost. The goal in Oregon is to rank health interventions by a benefit/cost ratio and then allocate the fixed budget to yield maximum benefit per dollar spent, denying coverage for services that are low on the priority list. While this approach is consistent with the principles of efficient allocation of fixed budgets, it begs some obvious and difficult questions: how to devise a common benefit measure that permits comparison across procedures that address different medical conditions and have very different health state outcomes; how to make interpersonal comparisons, when specific services target specific subgroups of the population; and how to determine the total budget to be allocated to health care for the subsidized population.

While one may disagree with the details of the implementation of this process in Oregon, the willingness to state clearly the inevitable allocative and distributive issues that arise in allocating health budgets sets a commendable example to other social insurance programs, particularly Medicare.

Selective Increase in Contributions

One factor contributing to the increase in Medicare expenditures relative to OASI cash transfers is that cash benefits become increasingly means-tested over time, whereas Medicare remains a universal entitlement program, regardless of the recipient's income or tax contributions to the system. Over time the cash transfers to the high income elderly diminish because one half of benefits are subject to income tax for individuals with income above $26,000 ($32,000 for couples). Since this limit is not indexed, its bite increases with inflation, making the cash component of Social Security increasingly means-tested in all but name. This reinforces the sharply declining marginal benefit schedule for cash payments. Indeed, of the reforms adopted in 1983, taxation of benefits was the second largest source of savings, after raising the retirement age (Thompson, 1983).

In contrast to Social Security cash payments, Medicare benefits are unrelated to income or payroll tax contributions (except to the extent that states cover co-payments and SMI premiums for the very poor under Medicaid). Indeed, higher income beneficiaries probably obtain greater per capita benefits from Medicare (controlling for health status) because they are more likely to buy supplemental insurance. Supplemental coverage that covers Medicare co-payments undermines the incentive effect of co-payments and increases use of medical care. Most of the cost of this additional care falls on the Medicare program, since the supplemental policy covers only the co- payments. This tendency for Medigap coverage to increase costs for Medicare is well known. The obvious solution is to tax Medigap policies, to reflect the expected costs that they impose on the basic program. So far such proposals have not succeeded, but they deserve consideration.

A second feature of Medicare that is very costly and raises serious questions of distributional equity is the provision of full benefits to dependents without additional contributions. This implies a windfall to nonworking spouses, relative to single individuals and two worker couples. The OASI program entails a similar redistributive effect, but dependent benefits are only 50 percent of the benefits of the primary beneficiary and the marginal benefit schedule is sharply declining. The cash windfall to nonworking spouses is therefore proportionately less at higher income levels, although not absolutely less. However everyone who is eligible for OASI receives full Medicare benefits, regardless of contributions. Thus spouses who never worked get identical benefits to spouses who worked and paid payroll taxes all their working lives. As the tax burden on working generations increases, this structure -- that is probably regressive in its impact and discourages labor force participation -- becomes increasingly indefensible.

If we continue to have a publicly run insurance program for the elderly, financed by payroll taxes, then a universal program makes sense, which implies extending coverage to non-contributing dependents. However that does not justify the current system. One solution is to maintain universal benefits but require workers to contribute in proportion to their expected number of dependents covered. A simpler alternative is to require modest premium contributions from retirees, to both HI and SMI, that are inversely related to the duration of payroll contributions over the individual's working life. Low income retirees would be protected through the Medicaid buy-in and by relating income support under the SSI program to income net of Medicare premium contributions. This or any other change in benefits or increase in retiree contributions should be phased in gradually. But such changes are certainly worth considering as an alternative to further increases in payroll tax rates.

Are fee schedules the solution?

If the objective is to control total budget costs of Medicare, the most effective alternative is full capitation. Full capitation of providers is the only solution to the unbundling problem. It also creates fewer distorting incentives for shifting care between inpatient and outpatient settings than the current alternative, of DRG reimbursement of hospitals and fee schedule payment of physicians, with overall expenditure targets. So far, enrollment of Medicare beneficiaries in HMOs has been at the option of the beneficiary. The result has been minimal cost savings and possibly some increase in costs, because of biased selection and the practice of tying payments to HMOs to the level of per capita costs in the fee-for-service sector. Thus as long as participation in capitated plans remains optional, it holds no great hope of controlling costs. Mandating that beneficiaries enroll in capitated plans amounts to turning the Medicare entitlement into a voucher. This approach has practical difficulties but is worth considering.

Instead of moving in the direction of increasing the freedom of Medicare beneficiaries to "voucher out" of Medicare, in 1992 HCFA moves to paying physicians based on a resource-based relative value fee schedule. This is similar in principle to the fee schedule approach used in other countries that appear to have been successful in controlling health care costs, including Canada, Germany and Japan. The experience of these countries that have used tightly controlled fee schedules has been a rapid growth in volume and reduction in length of visit. The "solution" has been total expenditure caps or rules that relate the price increase in year t inversely to expenditures in year t-1.

Although total budget costs have risen less rapidly in countries using fee schedules than in the U.S., it does not follow that tight, government- imposed fee schedules are a more efficient approach to cost control than the mix of co-payments, managed care, capitation and other strategies that are used by private insurers. Budget-constrained health care systems have significant hidden costs that do not appear in measured accounting costs. Physicians respond to low fees by cutting the duration or quality of visit. But each visit entails travel and waiting time for the patient. Unmeasured patient time costs due to the proliferation of short visits are a significant hidden cost of tight fee controls. For example, the average patient in Japanese makes twelve physician visits a year, each of only five minutes duration, whereas the average American makes only four visits but average duration is 15-20 minutes. Assuming that each visit entails at least one hour of travel and waiting time, the patient time costs of physicians' services are three times higher in Japan than in the U.S. Health care systems such as Canada's that rely on budget caps to control hospital expenditures incur a significant hidden cost in the form of foregone benefits due to rationing by waiting. Moreover, although tax-financed public monopoly systems are often said to incur much lower insurance overhead expense, in fact the excess burden from raising taxes greatly exceeds the premium collection expense incurred by competitive private insurers in the U.S.

In general, rationing by prices and by information-driven systems, which are the norm in competitive private insurance markets, is more efficient than rationing by patient time costs or by queuing, which are the methods adopted in several of the countries that appear to have been more successful in controlling health care costs. There is a distributional objection to rationing by prices, but this can be addressed more efficiently by subsidizing the purchase of health insurance for the poor.

Concluding Comments

In conclusion, I agree with Syl Scheiber that it makes sense to address Medicare reform as part of a more general reform of our health care system. I am concerned about the relentless rise in expenditures, but only because it is symptomatic of underlying inefficiency. I am also very concerned about the inequity of the status quo. But I do not favor turning to the budget constraining mechanisms that have been adopted in countries such as Canada, because they address the symptom rather than the underlying cause of the problem; they also generate large inefficiencies that entail real although hidden costs. Rather, I recommend eliminating the major causes of inefficiency and inequity in the present system. This requires mandating that all individuals obtain coverage; implementing a universal system of fixed and progressive tax credits in place of the current open-ended and regressive tax subsidies confined to employment-based coverage; and eliminating regulations that impede competition (Pauly, et al., 1991). Given this basic structure, there is no reason to expect major "failure" in private insurance markets that would warrant turning to more regulatory alternatives.

NOTE

1. Individual insurance premiums are tax-deductible only if total health expenditures exceed 7.5 percent of adjusted gross income, which is rare.

5

The Impact of the Demographic Transition on Capital Formation

Alan J. Auerbach
and
Laurence J. Kotlikoff

INTRODUCTION

The population of the United States is aging. As of 1990, about one fifth of the total U.S. population was over 55 years old.[1] In fifty years that figure will be close to one third. This aging will be particularly acute among the older old. Currently, those over age 75 represent only 5 percent of Americans. By 2040 this figure is projected to grow to about 12 percent.

At the same time that the elderly fraction of the population is increasing, the relative population of young people will be declining. While well over half the population was under age 35 in 1990, this figure is projected drop to just over 40 percent by the year 2040.

This aging of the population, which is attributable to declining rates of fertility and mortality, has a range of implications for the level and composition of national saving and capital formation in the United States over the next several decades. In this paper, we review a variety of these implications and discuss the policy issues that they raise.

In considering these issues, we will focus primarily on the United States. However, one should keep in mind that many other countries are simultaneously undergoing demographic transitions as strong or stronger than the United States. In Japan, for example, the demographic transition is occurring at a more rapid pace. Almost a quarter of the Japanese population is currently 55 or older; by 2010 almost a third of the Japanese population will be 55 or older compared with only a quarter of the U.S. population. The existence of such a demographic transition in many of the industrialized countries means not only that the lessons learned for the United States may apply much more broadly, but also that the pattern of international capital flows that one might associate with a single country's demographic transition may not arise when several countries undergo such a transition simultaneously. We discuss this point further below.

WHAT ARE THE ISSUES?

The demographic transition affects capital formation because of differences in household behavior over the life cycle. In the simple life-cycle model of household saving, individuals engage in a pattern of "hump" saving, drawing down resources in childhood and again in old age, with both of these periods of net dissaving being financed by saving during pre-retirement adulthood.

Perhaps the simplest measure of how saving should be affected by the demographic transition is the dependency ratio of children and the elderly to the remainder of the population. According to midrange forecasts of the Social Security Administration (presented in Aaron et al, 1989, Table 1-1), the dependency ratio (those over 64 and under 20 to those between 20 and 64) of the United States will rise from .695 in 1990 to .806 in 2040, with the growth in the share of elderly swamping the reduction in the share of children in the overall population.

From this very simple trend, one might predict a decline in the saving rate, as a smaller fraction of the population will be savers and a greater fraction of the population will be dissavers. However, this conclusion is sensitive to the exact specification of saving behavior and the pattern of the demographic transition. Therefore, the first issue we address is what different models of saving would predict for household saving over the next several decades. We begin with a review of the ability of such models to explain recent trends in saving behavior and discuss other evidence concerning the applicability of different models. We then consider their predictions of saving rates during the coming decades.

The demographic transition may also affect national saving through changes in government behavior. An increasing share of government spending is in age-related categories, and one would expect spending of old-age pensions and health care to rise with the increase in the elderly population. As we shall discuss, the implications these spending increases will have for national saving depend not only on how the spending is financed but also how the private sector reacts to the government's fiscal policy. This relates not only to the horizons of households (the extent to which they are "Ricardian" consumers) but also the extent to which government social insurance programs may reduce household precautionary saving.

The interaction of government and household saving has another, political dimension, relating to the increasing political power of the elderly. A growing elderly population will not only increase the need for certain types of social insurance spending, but may also be able to shift the burden of such spending onto other generations, including those not yet alive. This, in turn, may have a further, depressing effect on the rate of national saving.

The pay-as-you-go method by which we calculate the budget of the social security system may contribute to such as shift in the burden, as short-run "surpluses" may increase the pressure to reduce current social security taxes or increase benefits. This is but one example of the problems of measuring "government saving." We shall discuss these problems and how they are influenced by the demographic transition.

As individuals age, they may alter not only their level of wealth but also its composition. Only under restrictive circumstances would one expect the saving and portfolio choice decisions to be independent. As the horizon of a household becomes shorter and its size and composition changes, we would expect changes in the riskiness of the assets it holds as well as changes in the size and type of housing, which represents about half of the U.S. private capital stock. The changes in government fiscal policy may also have implications for asset composition.

Finally, there is the issue of international capital flows. As the United States saving rate changes during its demographic transition, this should give rise to changes in the capital account and, therefore, offsetting changes in the current account. The magnitude of such changes, and the implications for domestic capital formation and the composition of domestic production, are the subject of our last section.

RECENT SAVING BEHAVIOR AND THE ROLE OF DEMOGRAPHICS

Table 1 is a useful point from which to embark on a discussion of saving and demographics. The table presents U.S. net national saving rates for the past six decades. The net national saving rate is the most comprehensive measure of our nation's saving rate. It arises from subtracting U.S. private plus government consumption from U.S. net national product and then dividing by U.S. net national product. This saving rate tells us the fraction of the economy's net output that is put away each year to provide for the future.

The figures in the table are based on both the National Income Accounts measures of net national product, private consumption, and government consumption and corrected versions of these numbers. In constructing the net national saving rate it is important to measure private and government consumption correctly. Nevertheless, the U.S. Commerce Department's National Income and Product Accounts treat the purchase of durable goods by consumers as well as investment by the government as current consumption. Fortunately, however, the Commerce Department also provides data that can be used to calculate correct measures of private and government consumption and investment.

Both the corrected and uncorrected measures of the net national saving rate show a marked drop in U.S. saving in the 1980's. According to the corrected measure, the U.S. saving rate averaged only 7.2 percent during the period 1980 through 1985. This average is about three fifths the corrected average saving rate of the 1970's and just over half the corrected average rate of the 1950's and 1960's. The corrected saving rate for the first half of the 1980's is indeed so low that it is even less than the average saving rate in the 1940's, during which the U.S. engaged in massive wartime military spending. While we have not calculated corrected saving rates since 1985, the uncorrected data suggest that the corrected rates for the full decade would be even lower than those in the first half.

Can demographics explain the recent drop in U.S. saving? Our past research based on a variety of models suggests that the answer is no. Our simplest model

(Auerbach and Kotlikoff 1990a) starts with the assumption that the relative consumption and income profiles of individuals remain constant over time and, starting from some benchmark year to fix the levels of consumption and income, measures the changes in consumption and income due exclusively to changes in the age structure of the population.

Unfortunately, this methodology predicts that the national saving rate should have increased during the 1980's. For example, if one uses 1970 as a benchmark year (using the uncorrected saving rates for the benchmarking procedure), predicted rates of national saving for the remainder of 1970's stay very close to the actual rates of national saving, but those predicted for the 1980's rise to an average of 12.8, far from the actual average value of 4.3%.

One potential culprit that comes to mind is government consumption spending. Table 1 shows that the government sector (federal, state, and local) did consume a somewhat larger fraction of national output in the 1980s than in the previous three decades, but this increase is too small to account for more than a very modest decline in the rate of U.S. saving.

Rather than the result of increased government consumption, the decline in national saving is due to increased rates of private consumption. The second and fifth columns of Table 1 show this clearly. These columns give corrected and uncorrected measures of the private sector saving rate, defined here to equal the share of net national product less government consumption not consumed by the private sector. Net national product less government consumption seems the appropriate disposable income concept for the private sector since it represents the annual output left over after the government has consumed. It is this disposable income that the private sector can either consume or save. Regardless of whether one corrects the basic data for consumer durables and government investment, it is clear that the private sector saving rate has fallen dramatically in the 1980's. According to the corrected data, the private sector saving rate averaged 16.2 percent over the period 1950 through 1979. In contrast, from 1980 through 1985 the private sector saving rate averaged only 9.3 percent.

What has changed to lead the private sector, namely households, to switch from consuming 84 cents of every dollar of national output not consumed by the government to consuming 91 cents of every dollar of national output not consumed by the government? The answer many economists will offer← you is the government's intergenerational policy in the 1980's. The conventional argument is that by cutting taxes and running large budget deficits the government allowed current generations to consume more at the expense of future generations. However, there are considerable problems with this explanation. First, even if one assumed that households increased consumption by nearly all of the increase in the measured government deficits in the 1980's, this would explain only about half of the drop in national saving between the 70's and 80's, and a far smaller fraction of the gap between the actual saving rate and the much higher one predicted for the 80's. Second, models of household saving such as the life-cycle model would predict that households should have saved a considerable fraction of the extra disposable income generated by the deficits. Finally, the deficits themselves may have overstated the net fiscal transfers to current generations. For example, although their impact did not appear immediately in measured deficits, the 1983 Social Security amendments considerably reduced the future benefits of current young and middle age generations.

Another alternative explanation of our failure to predict the recent decline in saving is our model's assumption of fixed consumption and earnings profiles. However, even in models that allow the age profile of saving behavior to respond to demographic changes, we have obtained similar predictions of a rise in saving in the 1980s.

One alternative approach begins with the same initial consumption and earnings profiles, but in forecasting saving behavior over time incorporates the alternative implications of three different savings models[2] (Auerbach, Cai and Kotlikoff 1990). Each model predicts an increase in saving during the near future. An entirely different approach, based on a general equilibrium simulation model of the United States in which households obey a life-cycle model of consumption augmented by a bequest motive, also finds that saving should have been higher during the 1980s than in earlier decades (Auerbach and Kotlikoff 1990b).

Thus, rather than reflecting demographics or government policy in any apparent way, the drop in national saving in the 1980s seems to reflect a change in basic consumer behavior that is not captured well by any of a variety of models of aggregate saving. This may reflect an unobserved shift in consumption behavior, perhaps due to changing attitudes about the future or a reduced perception of need for precautionary saving.

WHAT IS THE "RIGHT" MODEL OF SAVING?

None of the models of saving we have used do very well in explaining the drop in U.S. saving rates during the 1980's. Is this due to a temporary shift in behavior in the 1980's, or does it reflect more fundamental failings in the way we model behavior? In anwering this question, it is useful to consider other evidence regarding the behavior of different models.

Most empirical analyses of saving are based on some variant of the Life-Cycle/Permanent Income Hypothesis, which specifies that households save to smooth consumption in the presence of income that fluctuates due to life-cycle labor supply patterns as well as other factors, such as macroeconomic fluctuations. Among the questions that are most relevant when one is considering a demographic transition are:

1. the extent to which households follow the pure life cycle model in old age by decumulating wealth;
2. the role of children in the household's consumption planning; in particular, the determination of bequests; and
3. whether household saving responds to changes in government and private ension programs.

These questions quite closely related, of course. Households that are saving for bequests may not reduce their wealth in old age, and may save more to offset increases in pay-as-you-go social security benefits. However, there are also independent factors at work. For example, households without any bequest motive may still maintain assets in old age for precautionary purposes.

There are many studies in the literature on each of these questions, and the results to date are not conclusive. While not all studies have found that households decumulate assets during retirement, several studies have (including King and Dicks-Mireaux 1982 and Diamond and Hausman 1984). This decumulation of household wealth is in addition to the automatic decumulation of the value of annuitized social security and pension benefits. However, the reduction seems too small to rule out considerable saving for precautionary expenditures and bequests.

The indication that bequest saving may be present is corroborated by the finding of Kotlikoff and Summers (1981) that the pattern of life-cycle saving generating by consumption and labor earnings over individual life cycles can explain only a fraction of observed household wealth. While many empirical studies have attempted to test the Ricardian equivalence proposition often associated with a strong bequest motive, the determinants and strength of bequest behavior are still not well understood.

Dating to the work by Feldstein (1974), there have been several papers measuring the impact of social security wealth and pension wealth and saving. While most studies have found that households do reduce personal saving in response to increases in pension or social security wealth, there is considerable uncertainty over the magnitude of these offsets. The findings to date suggest that the pure life-cycle model without bequests cannot fully account for observed savings behavior. However, the exact nature of the bequest motive, and the extent to which households respond to accumulations of public and private pension wealth, remains somewhat uncertain.

CAPITAL DEEPENING AND THE DEMOGRAPHIC TRANSITION

Whatever the cause, the sobering lesson of the 1980's is that economists still have a very limited understanding of U.S. saving behavior. This does not necessarily imply that the models we have are useless for considering the changes one might expect from future demographic change. We are, after all, conducting a ceteris paribus experiment. While we may not be able to explain all or even most of the variance in saving rates over time, our analysis of the contribution of demographic change to the determination of the saving rate may still be valid. However, if our economic models fail to capture fully current behavior because of the modelling of demographic effects, they may also be misleading concerning future behavior.

Nevertheless, given our current state of knowledge, economic models of demographics, saving, and capital deepening (increases in capital per worker) are informative if only for demonstrating the potential effects that demographic change could have on the accretion of American wealth. With this objective in mind, we consider the results from a variety of models.

General Equilibrium Analysis

We begin with results from our previous paper comparing demographic transitions in the United States and Canada (Auerbach and Kotlikoff 1990b). The simulation results are from the Auerbach-Kotlikoff Demographic Simulation Model, henceforth, the AK Model. The AK model is a numerical simulation model for studying the general equilibrium effects of the demographic transition.

The model's agents live for 75 years, the first 20 of which are spent as children. At age 21 each individual in the model becomes an adult and a parent. Adults in the model have to decide how much to work, how much to spend on their own and their children's consumption, how much to bequeath to their children at the end of their lives, and when to retire. These households view the present value of net social security benefits as wealth, although they do adjust bequests in response to this wealth. The decisions of these adults, when aggregated over the different generations of adults alive at a point in time, determine the total supplies of labor and savings to the economy.

Solution of the model requires that the time path of wage rates and interest rates be such as to make the supplies of labor and savings in each year equal to the demands for these productive factors by the model's firms. The model is solved over a 250 year period and also has an elaborate specification of the government sector. Most parameter values of the model are based on empirical studies of household behavior, while remaining free parameters are adjusted to make the model fit the observed post war data for the U.S. as closely as possible. In addition the model's annual birth rates are chosen to reproduce the past and projected demographic structure of the U.S. population.

For every simulation, projections begin in 1960, with the assumption that a steady state (including a steady state population) existed in that year. We then run the model forward through an historical period (ending in 1985), benchmarked to actual data, in order to allow simulations from the present onward to incorporate the current non-steady-state population structure. Table 2 presents the results of three simulations. We will discuss the alternative simulations below, and concentrate on the "base case" results provided in the table's first column.

The base case assumption includes a continuation of current fiscal policy, by which we mean that each component of government spending will remain fixed per member of the group covered by the spending program. Changes in required tax revenue are assumed to come from variations in the rate of consumption taxes. For purposes of these simulations, we have also assumed that the social security system will run on a pay-as-you-go basis without any significant trust fund accumulation.

The model is benchmarked to the actual national saving rate in 1960. As we have already noted above, it predicts a rise in the saving rate during the 1980s that is similar to the one predicted by our calculations based on fixed earnings and consumption profiles. Thereafter, the model predicts a steady decline in the national saving rate, falling from 12.2% in 1985 to 5.8% in 2050, before increasing slightly to a steady state value of 6.3%.

This predicted gradual decline in the saving rate is what one would expect given the gradual increase in the dependency ratio. A declining saving rate means slower growth in the accumulation of U.S. wealth, and, ignoring the import of foreign capital, it also means slower growth in the accumulation of capital (plant, equipment, inventories, and improved land). The reduced rate of growth of U.S. capital over the next 50 years would be more troublesome were it not also the case that the supply of labor will also grow at a reduced rate. This slower growth of labor supply should not be surprising since the aging of the population means that an increasing fraction of the population will be retired. On balance, it turns out that the growth rate of labor supply will fall by more than the growth rate of capital, and the ratio of capital to labor is predicted to rise. Hence, the drop in saving rates notwithstanding, economic models in general, and the AK model in particular, predict capital deepening associated with the demographic transition. Perhaps a more intuitive understanding of this point arises from considering that in 2040 there will be more older people relative to young and middle age workers and it is the older members of society who own the most wealth (capital).

The fact that capital will become increasingly abundant relative to labor means that the return to capital (real interest rates) will decline over time, while the return to labor (real wage rates) will increase over time. Beyond the model's normal growth in wages due to total factor productivity, the simulation predicts an increase of about 7% in the after-tax real wage between 1990 and 2050. This implication of the demographic transition is good news for future workers, but bad news for the current baby boom generation. It means that when the baby boomers retire they will earn a smaller return on their accumulated savings, while their children and grandchildren are earning higher real wages (the return to labor).

The increase in pre-tax wages will also improve the government's fiscal position by expanding tax revenues. As a consequence, the government will be able to cut non-social security tax rates. As Table 2 indicates in the AK model the demographic transition will permit a drop by four percentage points in consumption tax rates. Alternatively, had we kept consumption tax rates constant the AK model would have permitted almost a three percentage point drop in the income tax rate.

The "good" news for our children and grandchildren with respect to real wages and non-social security tax rates is offset by the "bad" news on social security tax rates. As the table shows, the social security tax rate in the Base Case, which does not take into account the 1983 Social Security Amendments, rises from 8.0 percent in 1990 to 12.8 percent between 2030 and 2050.[3] While the accumulation of a social security trust fund will obviate the need for such a future rise in social security tax rates, the trust fund is being accumulated through higher tax rates today. In either case, the demographic transition has necessitated a rise in payroll tax rates to maintain the viability of the social security system, although the incidence of the burden on different generations is quite different.

How robust is the central prediction of this model, that the saving rate will decline steadily for several decades from the 1980s? An alternative general equilibrium modelling approach, in Cutler et al (1990), provides quite similar predictions. Their simulations are based not on the aggregation of life-cycle households but rather on the assumption of a single, infinite-horizon family choosing its optimal consumption path. For simulations that begin in 1970 (i.e. that start the household's consumption response to the demographic transition in 1970, compared to the AK model's start in 1960), they find a saving rate that peaks in 1980, falls by about 5 percentage points to a low just before 2030, and then recovers slightly. Given the differences between the models, these predicted patterns are quite similar.

Partial Equilibrium Models

The previous models study the effects of demographics on saving using general equilibrium simulation analysis. Other estimates from our own work, using a partial equilibrium approach (fixed interest and wage rates) predict that the saving rate will first rise for several years before beginning the decline that is common to all models. In our study based on fixed earnings and consumption profiles (Auerbach and Kotlikoff 1990a), we found that the savings rate should begin to fall around the year 2010. Our alternative simulations also based on the actual consumption and earnings profiles but imposing additional constraints implied either by the infinite horizon or life-cycle consumption model (Auerbach, Cai and Kotlikoff 1990) predicted that saving rates would peak sometime between 2000 and 2010.

There are many potential sources for the differences between the general equilibrium models' predictions of an immediate decline in the saving rate and the partial equilibrium models' prediction of saving rates first increasing for several years. One explanation is the absence of general equilibrium changes in factor prices from the partial equilibrium models. In a previous study in which we imposed the partial equilibrium constant-factor-price assumption on some of the simulations with our general equilibrium model (Auerbach et al 1989), we found a smaller predicted drop in the saving rate between the years 1985 and 2010 (1.5 percentage points versus 2.8 percentage points). This may be due to the fact that with rising real future wages, households in the general equilibrium models save less at the onset of the demographic transition. However, this effect explains only part of the difference in predicted saving rates between the general and partial equilibrium analyses.

A second explanation may have to do with the consumption profiles used. While the general equilibrium simulations are based on consumption and earnings profiles generated by the assumption of household utility maximization, the partial equilibrium studies use actual consumption and earnings data by age to generate the consumption and earnings profiles. It is not immediately clear why this difference should be responsible for the difference in predicted savings behavior, but it deserves further investigation.

SAVING AND CHANGES IN GOVERNMENT POLICY

Thus far, we have focused on changes in household saving that are likely to come about as a result of the demographic transition that the United States is currently undergoing, and have ignored changes in government policy that may alter national saving directly or the saving behavior of households.

Many government spending programs, in addition to old-age pensions, are targeted toward the elderly; Medicare is the most prominent example. On the other hand, a significant share of local government spending is on schools, targeted toward the young. Hence we would expect offsetting pressures on different components of the overall government budget as the population ages.

In the ''base case'' simulations in the first column of Table 2, which we have already discussed, we assumed that all government spending remained fixed (except for normal productivity growth) relative to the targeted population; for example, Medicare spending per qualifying individual is kept constant. Hence, increases in the elderly as a fraction of the population increases Medicare expenditures per capita, overall.

To see how much pressure this maintenance of services puts on the budget, we considered an alternative simulation, presented in the second column of the table, in which overall spending was kept fixed per capita. As a comparison of the columns indicates, the extra expenditures necessitated by a maintenance of services is not great, forcing a rise in the consumption tax of about .7 percentage points in the year 2050. The reason the increase is this small is that, while the elderly receive a considerable level of government spending per capita, so do the young, who become a smaller fraction of the total population as the transition proceeds. In addition, our simulations assume unchanging relative prices. To the extent that health care costs continue to rise relative to other expenditures, the shift toward an elderly population could be considerably more expensive to finance.[4]

Even more significant, however, are the expenses of maintaining the Social Security system's old-age survivors and disability insurance (OASDI) pension program. Our base case simulations indicate that, under pay-as-you-go financing, maintenance of benefit levels would require an increase of 60 percent in the payroll tax rate associated with OASDI. The third column of the table presents a simulation of the impact of increasing the retirement age gradually from 65 to 67, as called for by the 1983 changes in the social security system. As a comparison of the first and third columns of the table shows, this reduction in the present value of benefits is projected to increase national saving noticeably, while at the same time reducing the necessary increase in payroll tax rates. By the year 2010, for example, the saving rate is projected to be .6 percentage points higher as a result of the increased retirement age.

Even with the planned increase in the retirement age, the payroll tax will need to rise to finance benefits. In the simulations presented, this rise is timed to satisfy pay-as-you-go balance in the system. In reality, payroll taxes have already risen, and the economy has been accumulating a considerable trust fund to help pay for future benefits, with annual increments in the neighborhood of $100 million per year recently.

What effect will this accumulation have on saving? The answer depends on whether the trust fund accumulations have additional effects on fiscal policy. In isolation, they represent a powerful government saving program, as households currently alive are being forced to help pay the cost of future benefits. Although we have not performed simulations of this exact pattern of trust fund accumulation, trust fund simulations in Auerbach and Kotlikoff (1987) do suggest that accumulations of this magnitude would have a considerably larger impact on the national saving rate than would the gradual rise in the retirement age just discussed.[5]

The key issue, however, is whether the presence of such a large accumulating trust fund will lead to reduced levels of government saving in other areas. Given the practice of using the budget deficit as a measure of fiscal policy, the presence of such a large ''surplus'' may lead to a belief that fiscal policy is relatively ''tight'' and that taxes may be cut or spending raised, either in the social security system itself or elsewhere in the budget. This is an issue both of politics and measurement, the issues to which we turn next.

MISREADING FISCAL POLICY
DURING THE DEMOGRAPHIC TRANSITION

While our nation's aging may not change our government's objectives, the aging process may wreak havoc on traditional measures of fiscal policy and, if more appropriate measures are not developed, lead to a misreading and misdirection of fiscal policy. The U.S. deficit is a case in point. In the next two decades the U.S. is projected to run significant surpluses arising, in the main, from an influx of social security receipts. Had the U.S. historically chosen different labels (words) for its social security receipts and payments, the projected surpluses in the next two decades would not necessarily arise.

To see this, suppose that we accounted for the social security system in a different way than we do. At present, the government accounts for social security each year by measuring the cash-flow surplus or deficit of each year's contributions over benefits.

Suppose, instead, that we viewed the social security system as a combination of fair annuities plus net (positive or negative) additional transfer payments to benefit recipients, calculated as the difference between what fair annuities based on contributions would has been and what benefits actually are. This system is economically equivalent to the present social security system, but its budgetary implications would be quite different. Contributions themselves would not be included in budget calculations, for they would be offset by the liability to pay future annuities that the government incurs simultaneously. Only the excess benefits being received by current beneficiaries would appear. Since current benefit recipients are, in the aggregate, receiving substantial lifetime transfers (net of the present value of payroll taxes), this would result in a major increase in the deficit that excludes social security, instead of the massive surpluses currently being reported.

It is important to stress that these two policies are not simply identical from each generation's perspective in some present value sense, but are also identical in terms of the timing of the flow of net receipts and payments from the private sector to government.

The arbitrary nature of accounting conventions affects the deficit in many ways. As the preceding example indicates, however, the demographic transition influences the signal that any particular accounting convention provides. The use of a cash-flow approach to accounting for social security leads to the incorrect message that current generations, including those about to retire, are generating large surpluses for the current young and future generations.

These ''surpluses'' (of the social security system) of the 1990s may lead politicians to view fiscal policy in the 1990s as tighter than in the 1980s and provide them with an excuse to loosen fiscal policy. ''Loosening'' fiscal policy here means either increased government consumption spending or increased intergenerational transfers from future generations toward current generations, as would normally be provided by a tax cut.

Indeed, since social security revenues were included in the deficit measure in evaluating compliance with the Gramm-Rudman deficit targets, these revenues have already provided politicians with an excuse for running looser fiscal policy than if social security receipts and expenditures were left out of the Gramm-Rudman calculus. The implications for capital formation of the spending of such ''surpluses'' is discussed further in Aaron et al (1989).

Loosening of U.S. fiscal policy over the next two decades will likely be detrimental to U.S. capital formation and leave fewer resources available to ease the burden of rising dependency ratios in subsequent decades.

What is needed as an alternative to the arbitrary deficits is a generational description of fiscal policy that indicates in present value the amount of net lifetime taxes the government plans to extract from different generations. Such generational accounts would be invariant to pure labelling changes in policy. Unlike the deficit, which entirely ignores the future, generational accounting requires one to make a variety of assumptions about future economic and fiscal variables. We have made an initial calculations of such accounts (Auerbach, Gokhale and Kotlikoff 1991).

IMPLICATIONS OF A SHIFT IN POLITICAL POWER
TOWARD THE ELDERLY

Even with a correct assessment of fiscal policy, the fiscal policy that is actually chosen could be greatly influenced by the growing political power of the elderly. Today 28 percent of the voting age population is over 55; in 2010 the figure will be 36 percent; and in the 2040 it will be 42 percent. The recent passage and almost immediate repeal of a program to tax the elderly to pay for new catastrophic insurance coverage that would benefit them demonstrates that the elderly have an effective political voice. So too does the record of the elderly over the past two decades in raising their relative income positions.

Between 1970 and 1984 the median real income of the elderly households rose by 35 percent. In contrast, the average real income of households age 25 to 64 rose by less than one percent. Boskin, Knetter, and Kotlikoff (1985) point out that much of this improvement in the relative income position of the elderly reflects an increase in social security benefits.

Increasing transfers to the elderly by increasing the burden on future generations will, under all but the purest view of Ricardian equivalence, reduce national saving. Even if these transfers are from younger generations currently alive, the effect will likely be a decline in national saving: the life cycle hypothesis suggests that the elderly have higher marginal propensities to consume than the young, and some recent evidence confirms this (Abel, Bernheim and Kotlikoff, 1991).

In addition to garnering larger government transfers, the elderly may affect the accumulation of U.S. capital by altering the composition and level of government consumption. There are numerous government consumption programs geared toward the elderly that could be initiated or expanded. The government could, for example, initiate a retraining program for the elderly to get them back into the labor force. Or it could provide the elderly with free transportation for shopping, etc. The list of reasonable sounding ways to redirect the government's consumption toward the elderly is, indeed, quite long.

To consider the potential impact of such political shifts on saving, we conducted two simulation experiments in our paper assessing the affects of demographics on saving using earnings and consumption profiles (Auerbach and Kotlikoff 1990a). In one experiment, we considered the effect of an increase in consumption of those over 65 by 5 percent and a decrease in consumption by those under 45 by 5 percent. Roughly speaking, one may view this as simulating the effect of cutting taxes on the elderly by 5 percent of income and raising taxes on the young by 5 percent of income. Aside from the effect of generally lowering saving rates, this policy would, according to our simulations, also sharpen the decline in the national saving rate as the elderly fraction of the population increases, by about .6 percentage points in the year 2010.

A second, admittedly extreme, simulation exercise considered the impact of focusing all age-specific spending on the elderly. In particular, we asked what would happen to national saving if all age-specific spending were on programs for individuals over age 65 and that the level of such spending per elderly individual were constant through time. In this case, the large growth of the elderly fraction of the population leads to a huge increase in projected government expenditures, with a decline in the national saving rate of several percentage points. While considering an extreme case, this simulation does illustrate the potential importance of politically-driven shifts in the composition of government spending.

The extent and type of government investment might also be altered in a government largely controlled by elderly voters. For example, given their shorter time horizons the elderly may be less interested in longer term government investments for such items as environmental preservation.

AGING AND THE COMPOSITION OF NATIONAL WEALTH

One may identify several effects that the changing age structure of the population may have on the composition and ownership of national wealth. One, associated with the international capital flows that changes in national saving may induce, is the share of national wealth owned by foreigners. We return to this below. The remaining channels through which aging may affect wealth composition involve the changing portfolio choice of households over the life cycle and the financial policy of government as it reacts to the changing demographic structure. We consider the household effects first.

Household Portfolios

One would expect household portfolios to change over the life cycle. As age increases and time horizons shorten, one might see an increase in liquid assets and annuities in household portfolios, with households seeking to finance current and near-term consumption. Moreover, with the decline in family size associated with children reaching adulthood and, frequently, a spouse's death, households might also reduce their demand for housing.

There is some evidence, that households shift from less liquid assets, such as private businesses and real estate, to more liquid assets, such as checking accounts and marketable securities, as age increases. Such results were obtained for the United Kingdom by Shorrocks (1982), using Inland Revenue data from the mid-1970s. Ioannides (1989), studying the Federal Reserve Board's 1983 Survey of Consumer Finances, estimated quadratic relationships between wealth shares and age, finding that holding of "other real estate" declined with age while holding of "business assets" had an inverted U-shape holding pattern with respect to age. Holdings of money market funds strictly increased with age, while holdings of checking accounts and stocks and bonds all followed a U-shape pattern.

Individually purchased annuities do not represent a major share of household portfolios. This does not include the annuities provided by social security and private pensions, which represent a significant fraction of household wealth that increases as households approach retirement. However, an important question is how households would react to reductions in these provided annuities. For example, if social security benefits were cut substantially, how much of this reduction in annuities would households replace through their own purchases? As mentioned above, the evidence on the responsiveness of private wealth to changes in public and private pensions ranges from full to only partial offsetting. Given that a significant fraction of households have very low wealth aside from their social security benefits (e.g. King and Dicks-Mireaux 1982, Diamond and Hausman 1984), the responsiveness by the private sector would, presumably, depend on how benefits were cut; a move to means-testing might elicit a greater private response than an across-the-board cut in benefits. The response would also depend on the degree to which these public annuities are pereceived as substitutes for available private sector assets.

One particular area in which annuity markets have not developed as fast as might have been predicted is in "reverse annuity" mortgages, where the household uses its housing equity to support an annuity, with the seller of the annuity receiving the house in payment upon the death of the purchaser. As the household ages, one may distinguish two reasons for it to reduce its ownership of housing. First, it requires less housing consumption. Second, it may wish to hold its wealth in more liquid and/or annuitized form.

Though there are life-cycle effects of home ownership, the transactions costs associated with moving may limit the ability of aging households to reduce housing consumption. In light of this, one might still expect households to convert their illiquid housing wealth into more liquid form, as through remortgaging the house. For the elderly, the reverse annuity mortgage appears to be the ideal vehicle for this conversion, but little such conversion occurs. Recent research (e.g. Venti and Wise 1990) argues that this is because elderly households do not really wish to reduce their housing equity: even when they move, their equity does not typically go down. While there may a decline in housing equity in the few years before death (e.g. Sheiner and Weil 1990), households appear to retain a significant amount of housing equity until death.

Even if the elderly do not reduce housing demand significantly, the aging of the population may still affect total housing demand through a decline in the formation of new families by young adults. Based on cross-section estimates of housing demand, Mankiw and Weil (1989) argue that the rapid increase in real housing prices in the 1970's can be attributed to the postwar baby boom's transition to adulthood. They infer that housing demand and prices should fall in the coming decades.

In summary, the aging of the U.S. population may lead to an increase in the fraction of wealth held in liquid assets, though this should depend on the level of annuities provided by public and private pensions in the future. In addition, when all effects are considered, the share of housing in household portfolios is likely to fall as well.

Government Assets

The mirror image of the growth of publicly-provided annuities is the growth of government's liability to pay these annuities. Many have argued that the growing social security trust fund may have important implications for asset markets, as this massive accumulation must be invested until it is eventually run down in the middle of the next century. However, one may easily overstate the importance of this trust fund for the composition (as opposed to the level) of national saving.

First of all, one must recognize the ability of the private sector to shift its portfolio in response to government portfolio choice. As government shifts it purchase of assets, the incipient changes in relative rates of return will bring forth offsetting private sector responses. This factor alone has led others to conclude that how the surplus is invested is not a particularly important issue (e.g. Aaron et al 1989). However, as in the case of private pensions, one must also look beyond the assets that the trust fund holds to the liabilities that the trust fund is intended to offset.

If one assumes that future benefit payments do not depend on the contemporaneous balance of the trust fund (a problematic assumption itself, but a useful starting point), then a change in the composition of the trust fund's assets also changes the nature of the implicit liability of future taxpayers. If taxpayers take this into account, they may wish to offset the government's portfolio shift with one of their own. For example, if the trust fund shifts to a riskier portfolio of assets, one might initially expect this to lead to a greater social assumption of risk. However, this government shift implicitly saddles the private sector with the added risk of the residual needed to pay benefits in excess of trust fund accumulations. Forward looking households might then wish to purchase the safer assets the government disposed of, without any increase in yield, in order to restore the character of their expanded portfolio, inclusive of the future implicit tax liabilities.

This argument is nothing more than an application of the Modigliani-Miller theorem to government finance. It is vitiated by several factors. A change in the trust fund balance may have real effects on benefits actually paid. Perhaps more important, the horizon of taxpayers may be considerably shorter than would be needed for a significant offset to occur. However, to ignore this effect completely also seems unjustified.

International Capital Flows

A variety of studies (discussed above) have projected that the demographic transition will have a significant impact on U.S. national saving rates. In an open economy, this can spill over into the current and capital accounts. Since the current account surplus (and the capital account deficit) equals the excess of national saving over national investment, we would expect increases in national saving to lead to improvements of the current account balance and reductions in capital inflows: more national saving should reduce the rate at which foreigners have increased their net holdings of U.S. assets.

It is difficult to know exactly how large these effects will be. In one of our studies (Auerbach and Kotlikoff 1990a), we estimated the current accounts for the next several decades that would be consistent with the saving rates our simulations predicted and the assumption of a constant world interest rate (and hence a constant domestic capital-labor ratio). We found quite significant increases in the projected current account, by between 3 and 4 percentage points between the current decade and the one commencing in 2010, which translate into annual numbers that are even larger than recent U.S. current account deficits.

These estimates of a strong swing toward surplus remain even when we assume that world interest rates would gradually fall by 3 percentage points between 1990 and 2050, as might be expected from the simultaneous aging and increased capital intensity of the economies of many developed countries. However, in assuming perfect substitutability of the assets of different countries, these estimates may greatly overstate the flows that will actually result. In addition, they are based on simulations that project saving rates to rise into the next century before falling while, as we have discussed above, other studies project a more immediate onset of the decline in rates of national saving.

CONCLUSIONS

The demographic transition underway in the United States may have a significant effect on our national saving rate and on the international capital flows that such saving may generate. Analysis of these effects is difficult because it requires projections far into the next century based on models of behavior for which historical validation is limited. However, research has shown that demographics may have powerful effects on national saving.

Although there is considerable uncertainty about the "right" economic models to use for analysis of household behavior, one of the greatest unknowns is how the political process will change as an increasing fraction of the voting population is elderly.

Table 1.   Net National Saving Rates and Household Saving Rates Corrected and Uncorrected

Period	Corrected Measures			Uncorrected Measures		
	$\dfrac{(Y'-G'-C')}{Y'}$	$\dfrac{(Y'-G'-C')}{Y'-G'}$	$\dfrac{G'}{Y'}$	$\dfrac{(Y-G-C)}{Y}$	$\dfrac{(Y-G-C)}{Y-G}$	$\dfrac{G}{Y}$
1940-1949	.086	.101	.271	.055	.059	.274
1950-1959	.133	.167	.203	.092	.116	.211
1960-1969	.130	.166	.215	.089	.116	.226
1970-1979	.118	.152	.223	.085	.109	.222
1980-1985	.072	.093	.230	.050	.064	.223
1980-1989	na	na	na	.043	.054	.225

NOTES TO TABLE 1

Definitions

Uncorrected Measures:
  Y - NIPA measure of net national product.
  G - NIPA measure of government consumption.
  C - NIPA measure of personal consumption.

Corrected Measures:
  Y' - Y plus imputed rent on consumer durables and government tangible assets (excluding military equipment) less depreciation on the stock of consumer durables and government tangible assets (excluding military equipment).
  G' - G less government expenditures on tangible assets (excluding military equipment), plus imputed rent on the government's stock of tangible assets (excluding military equipment).
  C' - C less consumer expenditures on durables plus imputed rent on the stock of consumer durables.

Imputed rent on an asset is calculated as annual depreciation plus 3 percent times the stock of the asset. Annual depreciation of consumer durables and government tangible assets as well as the stocks of consumer durables and government tangible assets are reported in the U.S. Dept. of Commerce's Fixed Reproducible Tangible Wealth in the United States, 1925-85.

Table 2.   Demographic Simulations from the AK (1990b) Model

Nat. Saving Rate	Base Case	No Age-Specific	2 Yr Inc in Soc Sec
1960	9.8	9.8	9.8
1985	12.2	12.2	12.2
1990	11.7	11.7	12.0
2010	9.5	9.4	10.1
2030	6.5	6.6	7.2
2050	5.8	5.9	6.3
Long Run	6.3	6.3	6.6
Consumption Tax Rate			
1960	9.8	9.8	9.8
1985	8.3	8.3	8.2
1990	8.6	8.6	8.4
2010	5.7	5.5	5.2
2030	5.8	5.2	4.9
2050	5.5	4.8	4.5
Long Run	5.3	4.6	4.1
Social Security Tax Rate			
1960	7.1	7.1	7.1
1985	7.6	7.6	7.5
1990	8.0	7.9	7.9
2010	10.2	10.2	8.0
2030	12.8	12.8	10.2
2050	12.8	12.8	10.1
Long Run	12.3	12.3	9.9

ENDNOTES

1. This and other projections for the U.S. and other countries come from Auerbach et al (1989), and were compiled from Social Security Administration projections for the United States and comparable statistics for other countries.
2. The three models were of an infinite horizon households, several life-cycle households, and a reduced form time series model incorporating demographic variables.
3. These social security tax rates should be viewed as the sum of employer plus employee social security taxes. The reason that the model's social security tax rates are lower than the actual social security tax rates is that the model assesses social security taxes on all earnings: i.e., there is no earnings ceiling in

the model.

4. Aaron et al (1989; p. 50) report that, from 1974 to 1985, overall HI (Medicare) spending would have risen by 177% had the cost of hospitalization payments risen at the same rate as the general price level. In fact, HI spending rose by more than 400% over this period!

5. For alternative simulations of the impact of the trust fund accumulation on national saving and welfare, see Aaron et al (1989).

Discussion

Alicia H. Munnell

Alan Auerbach and Laurence Kotlikoff have done their assignment; they have predicted the impact of the upcoming demographic shift on saving and capital formation. They conclude that the significant projected increase in the elderly and the young relative to the working-age population will substantially depress the national saving rate beginning around the year 2010. Their conclusion rests on the standard life-cycle model where households accumulate wealth in their working years and then draw down their wealth to support themselves in retirement. According to this theory, the demographic shift should produce a dramatic increase in the number of dissavers relative to savers and this development should substantially reduce national saving. Who can argue with that logic?

While the logic may be flawless, the importance of demographics as opposed to other factors in determining national saving deserves some consideration. In fact, three things should make us somewhat cautious about incorporating a lower saving rate into our national strategic planning.

The first, which the authors acknowledge themselves, is the evidence from the 1980s. Their model, as well as several others, suggests that, based on demographics, the saving rate should have increased during the 1980s. The projected rise in private saving should have occurred because the large decline in the proportion of the population that was young swamped the increase in the proportion that was old. But instead of a projected rate of 12.8 percent, saving averaged 4.3 percent for the decade. This means either that demographic factors are not very important or that other influences overwhelmed the demographics. The difficulty is that economists have been at a loss to explain the behavior of national saving during the 1980s. Studies have explored the impact of capital gains from equities and housing, the effects of higher real interest rates, a reduction in the need for precautionary saving, the effect of slower income growth, and a host of other factors as possible reasons for the precipitous decline in saving. Unfortunately, to date the puzzle remains unsolved. However, the fact that models based on demographics were off by nearly 200 percent in projecting the 1980s saving rate suggests that forecasts for the future should be taken with a grain of salt.

The second argument for caution in interpreting the results is the fragility of the evidence documenting the importance of demographics. The strongest piece of evidence comes from a series of cross-sectional studies comparing international differences in saving rates (Modigliani 1970, Feldstein 1980, Modigliani and Sterling 1983, and Horioka 1989). These studies, which were originally undertaken to determine the impact of social security on saving, generally found a statistically significant negative relationship in the late 1960s and early 1970s between the proportion of a country's population that was either young or old and the country's saving rate. The regressions also implied that the negative effect of the proportion of aged was twice that of children - a perfectly plausible result. As an offset, the studies showed that a tendency to retire early raised saving among the currently working population. The difficulty with these international results is that they do not stand up well with the revision in data that has occurred since the original studies were completed. Moreover, Bosworth (1990) found that the results were very sensitive to which countries were included in the analysis. They also fail the predictive test in that they all suggested a strong increase in saving for the industrialized countries in the late 1970s and early 1980s that never materialized.

A third reason to interpret Auerbach and Kotlikoff's results with a grain of salt is that the case for a demographic impact on the saving rate rests on the assumption that the rate of saving for each age group remains relatively constant over time. A recent paper by Bosworth, Burtless, and Sabelhaus (1991) suggests that this assumption may not be valid. Using data from two sets of cross-sectional surveys (the 1972-73 and 1982-85 U.S. Bureau of Labor Statistics' Consumer Expenditure Survey (CES) and the 1962-63 and 1983-86 Federal Reserve Board's Survey of Consumer Finances (SCF)), they find that the variation in saving rates for different age groups across time may well exceed the variation among age groups at one point in time. Their findings are reproduced in Table 1. Simple regressions reported by the authors indicated that between 84 percent and 95 percent of the drop in national saving was due to the decline in the saving rate within age groups. Clearly, changes in the age distribution of households and in the relative incomes of households in the various age categories had only a slight effect.

Whereas the Bosworth, Burtless, Sabelhaus results are very interesting and bear on the material in the Auerbach-Kotlikoff paper, they too must be interpreted cautiously. The reason is that Bosworth, Burtless, and Sabelhaus base their results on only a subsample of the original SCF survey; they chose this route to deal with the problem created by changes in household status when estimating saving as the difference in wealth between two points in time. In order to avoid the gains in wealth that result from a former single person marrying or the loss of wealth from an intact couple divorcing, they limited their subsample only to those units with no change in marital status. They also eliminated people whose own business represented a significant share of their assets. In both the SCF and the CES they eliminated households where the head was younger than 25 and people for whom saving was greater than income. With all these exclusions, the samples are no longer representative of the population.

Their solution reflects not only potential measurement problems with the surveys, but also how little we know about saving; theirs was a desperate response to the fact that the saving rate by age varied widely depending on which households were included or excluded from the sample. Even within age groups, saving rates differ considerably. Our inability to explain this variability was documented in a recent study by two economists intimately involved with the Survey of Consumer Finances (Avery and Kennickell 1990).

Using a variety of models, they were able to explain only 7 percent of the total variation in the level of saving among the members of the Survey of Consumer Finances. Saving at the individual level appears to be very idiosyncratic and varies enormously among households. However, ignoring or discarding households with peculiar situations or extreme saving rates cannot be the solution, since Avery and Kennickell found that households where saving exceeds two standard deviations from the mean accounted for 43 percent of total saving in the survey.

The important point is that the economics profession does not really understand saving or saving behavior. This means that we cannot explain variation among households at one point in time. It is not surprising, therefore, that we cannot explain the variation over time. Since we cannot identify the major factors affecting the fluctuations in the nation's saving rate, we cannot possibly isolate the impact of demographic shifts from other phenomena. This means that any exercise that focuses on demographics as the main determinant of future saving rates should be viewed very cautiously.

Let me comment briefly on one other part of the Auerbach-Kotlikoff paper that seems to be drawing a great deal of attention, that is, the issue of generational accounts. On a theoretical basis, additional information that displays how government taxing and spending policy affects different generations would be useful. This does not mean, however, that the current accounts, arbitrary as they may be, do not provide adequate information on how the government allocates its resources and how it affects today's economy. Even though the classification of any particular spending or revenue item may be somewhat arbitrary, the fact that the classification is consistent over time does allow our cash-based accounting system to provide meaningful information on trends.

My reservations concerning the generational accounts are twofold. The first is philosophical and a little sentimental. In recent years, some people have spent a lot of time pitting the old against the young and fostering a sense of intergenerational warfare. In my view, this tactic is destructive. Our society consists of families with members from a variety of generations; health care for the elderly benefits middle-aged children who no longer have to carry the primary burden for their parents. But generational accounts focus on who receives the benefit directly and ignore the indirect benefits to others.

The second problem is more serious and more fundamental to the whole approach. Any system of accounts that projects revenues and expenditures into the future must discount these streams back to the present in order to make them comparable. Discounting requires assuming an appropriate rate; rates can and do vary from 1 percent to 8 percent. The particular rate adopted determines the entire pattern of burden and reward. The alternative is to present calculations for a series of rates, but then the results will vary so much that they will reveal very little. In short, generational accounts are interesting, but should be interpreted cautiously.

Table 1.   United States Household Saving Rates by Age of Head, 1962-85.

Survey Age Groups

Year	25-34 (1)	35-44 (2)	45-54 (3)	55-64 (4)	65+ (5)	Total (6)
Survey of Consumer Finances						
Saving Rate:						
1963	14.7	11.3	17.2	14.2	11.2	14.0
1983-85	13.6	10.1	10.3	10.6	2.5	9.5
Change	-1.1	-1.2	-6.9	-3.6	-8.7	-4.5
Age Distribution:						
1963	21.5	20.7	20.8	17.0	19.9	100.0
1983-85	20.5	18.4	18.3	15.4	27.4	100.0
Relative Income:						
1963	104.0	125.5	124.5	91.8	50.6	100.0
1983-85	90.5	130.8	129.5	100.4	66.6	100.0
Consumer Expenditure Survey						
Saving Rate:						
1972-73	9.5	12.1	16.8	22.9	14.9	15.1
1982-85	9.6	8.6	10.5	15.8	11.5	10.8
Change	0.1	-3.5	-6.3	-7.1	-3.4	-4.3
Age Distribution:						
1972-73	22.6	18.7	20.2	17.5	21.0	100.0
1982-85	25.8	21.1	15.5	16.0	21.6	100.0
Relative Income:						
1972-73	95.0	119.9	126.5	104.9	58.0	100.0
1982-85	94.1	120.3	124.5	102.7	67.5	100.0

Source: Barry Bosworth, Gary Burtless and John Sablehaus, ''The Decline in Saving: Evidence from Household Surveys,'' 1991, The Brookings Institution, mimeo.

Caution, then, is the main message of my comments today. The caution, however, does not so much reflect a failing on the part of Auerbach and Kotlikoff, but rather of the entire economics profession. It is amazing that we know so little about something as important as the forces that determine saving and capital accumulation. Gary Burtless has remarked that the state of the art here differs markedly from that in labor, where economists have learned a great deal over the past 20 years about how people respond to changes in wage rates and other phenomena. In the saving area, we now have a lot of cross-section as well as time-series data, from which we should be able to begin to sort out the forces that determine individual and national saving; documenting our ignorance may be the first step toward progress.

6

Implications of Demographic Change for Design of Retirement Programs

John H. Biggs

This paper speculates on the influences of demographic changes on private pension plan design in the early part of the 21st century. For concreteness of exposition, I will take the point of view of the Board of Directors of a newly formed company that has grown rapidly to a relatively large size (at least 1,000 employees), and has decided in the year 2020 to establish a pension plan. This point of view abstracts from the variety of historical forces that influence an existing pension plan of an organization with a significant history -- accordingly, the paper does not attempt to cope with the rich detail and considerations that changes in such a plan would entail. As this Board, with assistance from its advisors, considers the basic design of its plan, the question is: how will its decisions be influenced by the demographic changes that will have occurred since 1990?

The demographic changes that are likely to occur over the next thirty years are described in other papers presented in this Symposium. This paper selects from these changes the following trends which seem to the author as likely to be the most significant to pension plan designers in 2020:

(1) The general aging of the population - the "Florida effect" - in which the whole country takes on the present (1990s) age profile of the State of Florida - will be a major feature. Specific important aspects will be: younger employees will be in relatively short supply, and employees between ages 60 and 70 will be much more numerous than in 1990. (See Figure 2, Age Distribution of the U.S. Population: 1987, 2000, 2010, and 2030 in Preston, ch. 2, p 24.)

(2) The "squaring of the mortality curve," due to lower mortality rates among those 65 to 80 years old, will produce a rapidly growing super-old group - over 85. (See Preston, op. cit., who questions attempts to infer

biological limits to the life span, thereby raising the possibility of still more rapid growth of the over-85 population.) Medical costs and long-term health care for this older population will be a continuing concern for the younger workers and their employers.

(3) Improved health for all ages, but especially for senior workers between ages 60 and 75, may have a major impact on labor force participation rates at the higher ages. (See Levine and Mitchell, ''Expected Changes in the Workforce and Implications for Labor Markets,'' ch. 3, which forecasts a higher labor force participation among older workers for a variety of reasons, primarily economic with substantial doubt expressed as to the role of poor health in causing early retirement.)

(4) Although it is not always seen as a demographic change, some improvement in labor productivity can be reasonably expected by 2020, with implications for the design of our national Social Security and private pension systems. (Auerbach and Kotlikoff, in ch. 5 of this volume, analyze the various models that might forecast changes in capital formation due to demographic changes.)

BROAD OBJECTIVES OF THE PENSION PLAN

What are the likely changes in the broad purposes of a private pension plan in the next three decades? First, one may ask: Will private pension plans continue to play an important role in income maintenance in retirement? Will federal tax policy continue to encourage the voluntary establishment of pension plans and, more narrowly, of employer-sponsored pension plans in the private sector? Or, at the other extreme, will establishing and maintaining pension plans be required for employers? Will tax policy shift toward encouraging individual taxpayers to make provision on their own for retirement (via the IRA model), perhaps with diminished use of the employer as the main vehicle?

A related issue is whether paternalism - to the extent it exists today - will still be a guiding motivation for employers. The history of private pension plans in this country has been one of identification by employers of the joint employer-employee interest in having a plan, and of their establishing that plan for the benefit of employees. Will this equation still be the right one for the year 2020? Will employers still operate plans that may give employees financial incentives to retire, as now, or will they instead give them incentives not to retire? Will new institutions have been developed to replace mandatory retirement? How will greater lifetime wealth (assuming economic progress over a generation) be consumed over a life cycle? Will the quality of work of older employees be improved by longevity and health care improvements?

Similarly, how will employers relate to the U.S. health care system in the future? Will increasing longevity and innovations in medical care technology have raised the present value of future postretirement medical care costs to the point where employers believe they must leave this burden with the retiree or the government, or will new solutions to medical care access and delivery have been sought and implemented by the year 2020?[1]

The above questions are among those which demographic change will force the designers of pension plans to consider in 2020. The character of these queries suggests that the appropriate description of this paper is more "speculation" than scientific prediction. Nevertheless, the effort is useful, if only to shape discussion today of what our current national retirement policy should be concerned with tomorrow.

First, consider the question whether pension plans will exist in 2020 and extrapolate what will be the effect by then of current trends in federal regulation and tax policy. Although these issues might seem fairly remote from demographic forces, they are so important to pension plan design that their effects would swamp any demographic forces. Further, their own course in history will also surely be driven by population demographics.

Thirty years - or a generation - is a relatively long period in terms of U.S. pension development, and rates of change in the pension plan environment do not appear to be slowing. If one contrasts 1990 with 1960, one finds enormous change in pension coverage, in the economic role of pensions in providing retirement income, and certainly in the analysis of pension issues.

For example, in terms of public policy interest, hardly an issue of the Wall Street Journal appears without some pension coverage. In terms of economic research, a number of important organizations have emerged. For example, the Pension Research Council, a pioneer in pension policy analysis, is now joined by other major research organizations, including the National Bureau of Economic Research and the Brookings Institution. In addition, the Employee Benefit Research Institute, a fairly new organization, now provides the pension community with extensive public policy research and information.

An area of significant development in the last thirty years has been the federal treatment of pension plans. This public policy attention - whether in terms of taxes or of substantive regulatory (ERISA) or institutional (PBGC) controls - has developed from a very small base to a major national concern. One must question whether the regulatory and tax structure that was originally designed to encourage retirement plans has become so complex - in order to extend coverage and to prevent abuses of tax-deferred privileges - that the establishment of new pension plans may be becoming uneconomical for even the medium-sized employer (Clark and McDermed 1990). Accordingly, I have selected for illustration a 1,000-employee firm, to represent an employer that is sufficiently large to support the costs of designing and operating a pension plan in the environment of the 2020s.

If one is to project forward from 1990 to 2020 the extraordinary growth rate of the complexity of pension regulation, one must conclude that an employer in 2020 would simply not even consider adopting a pension plan. Even a modest projection of growth in the numbers of pages of tax rules (comparable to demographic projections of population growth) must lead to the conclusion that long before 2020 a pension regulation "population bomb" will have exploded, obliterating any possibility of truly effective or economical compliance with those regulations. What can be done to slow this inhibiting growth in complexity?

The key objective of federal retirement policy has not been so much a regulatory one per se, or a concern to extend pension coverage, as it has been a concern to prevent employer-based plans from abusing the benefits of tax deferral in favor of owners, managers, or highly compensated employees.

Elsewhere, I have suggested that the key to resolving this problem is to base the tax benefit on the individual taxpayer rather than the employer (Biggs 1985). This idea is a simple one and solves many equity issues regarding tax policy. Any employer contribution to a pension plan is "attributed" to the employee and becomes taxable income (as is done now for costs of group life insurance above a fixed-dollar floor amount). No elaborate nondiscrimination rules need apply to such an employer plan, since the pension contribution is no different from any other salary payment, applying equally to all employees in proportion to wages or salary. The employee would then be allowed to apply the contribution to a plan for pension savings, and to exempt such attributed income in his or her own tax return, up to an appropriate fixed limit.

Looking at this problem in a different way, do we need a different base from that of the employer for enhancement of retirement plan coverage? According to recent 1988 data published by the Employee Benefit Research Institute (EBRI), only about half of all private wage and salary workers are now employed by firms with pensions, and actual worker participation of workers in such plans is less than half (EBRI 1989). Further, firm size makes a substantial difference in whether pension coverage is available. Again, using the above EBRI data, the proportion of wage and salary workers at firms with 100 or more employees who were covered for pension plans was 79% in 1988, compared with the coverage rate in smaller firms (under 25 employees), which was 17% (EBRI 1989). To give the absolute contrast, the underlying numbers are significant: of 59 million workers in large firms (employing 100 or more), 46 million were covered; of the 22 million workers in small firms (employing under 25), only 4 million were covered. It would seem odd, then, to expect that a system of tax benefits for pension plans under which the employees of large companies gain most of the tax benefits would continue for long.

Sometime between now and 2020, therefore, one might predict a pension tax revolution under which critics of modest coverage rates and of an even more highly regulated system would be heeded by Congress. If the subsequent change is (1) to a broad-coverage employee-based tax benefit or (2) to no tax benefit of any kind for retirement savings, then the Board of Directors of our hypothetical 2020 company will have a much-attenuated motivation for adopting a pension plan on today's model. It is interesting, however, to speculate about employers' behavior under such unfamiliar conditions, since private employers may still be motivated to make it practicable for employees to retire at a reasonable age with reasonable benefits. Therefore, it seems reasonable to suggest that one possibility to implement such objectives would be to develop a new type of plan for a required allocation of a portion of employees' salary to a separate funding mechanism <u>restricted</u> for specific use in providing retirement income. (More about this later.)

Along with the question of retirement income, there also goes the question of health care coverage in retirement. Already employers are deeply concerned about the escalating costs of retiree health care. This concern has been heightened by the immediacy of the changes in accounting for retiree health care liabilities that have been adopted by the Financial Accounting Standards Board (FASB). Even without these changes in required accounting, employers by 2020 would have long-since realized that an open-ended health care commitment to retirees constituted an unacceptable financial obligation. Extrapolation to 2020 of the last thirty years of medical care experience and costs would produce bizarre results. Should even a portion of this extrapolation occur, however, employers will surely have been forced to curtail employer-based retired-life medical care plans.

But perhaps, by 2020, other health care options - national in scope - would have been explored and adopted. The U.S. health care system is now the most expensive in the world, costing 40% more per capita than that of Canada, the country in second place, and as much as double the cost in other advanced nations (Hilts 1991). It seems likely that within just a few years new approaches will be considered, and that our newcomer to pension plan design in 2020 will have the benefit of this experience and will, undoubtedly, address in a combined way the issues of retirement income, acute medical care after retirement, and, perhaps especially, long-term institutional care needs of retired employees.

The classical purpose of a pension plan is to give senior employees an incentive to retire - and the means - at an age that is acceptable and desirable to the employee and that is appropriate for the employer. Finding equilibrium in that decision has had an interesting history in pension plan practice. Mandatory retirement was intended to bring about the needed balance. To some individual employees, however, the requirement was harsh and failed to take individual differences into account. However one may feel about the propriety of government intervention in prohibiting mandatory retirement, it is hard to believe in 1990 that there will ever be a return to that practice.

Clearly, the Florida effect and the squaring of the mortality curve will lead employers to be less interested in reducing the labor force by encouraging employees to take retirement at age 65 or even earlier. Although some might disagree, I believe that presently it is the general view of corporate senior management that the quality of the work force is improved if the compensation arrangements and the culture of the company can encourage many employees to retire voluntarily in their late 50s and early 60s, so that very few, if any, remain at.work past age 65. The demographic changes by 2020 - the baby-boom followed by the baby-bust - would seem almost certain to cause that view to shift to a higher cluster of ages. And, under 1983 amendments, the age for full retirement benefits under Social Security will gradually increase from age 65 beginning in 2003 until reaching age 67 in the year 2027 and beyond (Commercial Clearing House 1990).

Employee tastes, on the other hand, will not necessarily be driven to prefer higher retirement ages. Indeed, improved health and higher lifetime wealth accumulations may well produce stronger preferences for post- retirement leisure. Much research is now being done on what influences the retirement decision (Quinn, Burkhauser, and Myers 1990; Kotlikoff and Wise 1989).

At present, partly because many of those who may have had a full lifetime of pension plan participation are just beginning to retire, private pensions play a lesser role in retirement security than they might be expected to in the future. According to 1986 data from the Employee Benefit Research Institute and the Social Security Administration, while 27% of the U.S. population age 65 and over now receive money from private pensions, only 7% of those people rely on company pensions for at least half of their retirement income. At the same time, 91% of the population age 65 and over currently receive benefits from Social Security, and 62% report that Social Security benefits constitute at least half of their income (Uchitelle 1990).

As for Social Security benefit amounts, the average monthly benefit amount for a person newly awarded benefits in 1988 as a retired worker was $507 and for spouses, $251. For persons already receiving benefits in 1988, the average monthly benefit amount for retired workers was $537, and for spouses, $277 (U.S. Dept. Health and Human Services 1989).

By the year 2020, we might expect private pension benefits to have further matured and therefore to play a stronger role than now in retirement income support. Other developments may also influence pension design in the future, since our society will have had several decades of experience with the behavior of a relatively better-off elderly population. Also, our experience with "uncapped" retirement ages will no doubt have sharpened our understanding of the effect of retirement-age attitudes on labor force participation. Obviously, these developments will play a significant role in the future design of retirement incentives and programs under private plans.

One final note to tie together several of the above points: One may fairly assume some continuing, or perhaps residual, employer paternalism by the year 2020, as employers will want to be sure that long-service employees at the higher ages will have the wherewithal actually to retire. No employer will be willing to force terminating employees into poverty in old age (nor do I believe that our community institutions will permit it by then - although I may be unduly influenced in making this assertion by my experience in higher education, where virtually all employers have sound pension plans).

Accordingly, even if tax benefits have been eliminated or shifted from employer-based plans to individual taxpayers, the remaining, albeit attenuated, interest for our hypothetical employer may well be to provide for some form of carrot or stick to make sure his employees have retirement assets. Clearly one source of income will be based on the continuing commitment of the federal government under the wage-related Social Security benefits based on wage taxes under FICA statutes. Another major (and dependable) source could well be a system that would direct a significant portion of employees' lifetime compensation to an annuity fund that could be used only upon retirement from the labor force.

DEFINED BENEFIT OR DEFINED CONTRIBUTION PLAN

The most fundamental design question for a company's pension plan is whether to shape it in the form of a defined benefit plan, a defined contribution plan, or some combination of the two. This will still be true in 2020 unless some regulatory change not now foreseen should occur.

There is substantial recent evidence for the growing use of the defined contribution form of plan as opposed to the defined benefit form: first, serving as the basic pension plan of an employer and, second, as a companion or "secondary" plan to a defined benefit plan. (See Table 3, page 6, of April 1989 EBRI brief; over just the five-year period, 1980 to 1985, under primary plans defined benefit participants have <u>declined</u> from 29.7 million to 28.9 million while defined contribution participants have doubled from 5.8 million to 11.6 million; and under secondary plans, defined benefit participants drop from 400,000 to 100,000 while defined contribution participants rise from 12.7 million to 21.7 million.) There have been some attempts to analyze the reasons for this trend. Clearly the differential burden of regulation is an obvious suspect (see Clark and McDermed (1990). Another view is that of Gustman and Steinmeier (1989), who see a major cause as the result of employment shifts toward jobs more likely to be covered by a defined contribution plan. Significantly, they do not challenge the drama of the word "stampede" in their paper's title. Whether the defined benefit plan will be seen in 2020 as a "dinosaur" (or to continue the stampede metaphor, perhaps a "buffalo") will depend upon a number of political and social developments beyond the scope of a paper on demographics. It is the contention, however, of this paper that demographic trends over the next thirty years are likely to weigh in the balance in favor of the defined contribution expression.

In 2020, the relative supply of skilled new entrants to the labor force will be markedly lower than today (see Preston); job mobility among young skilled workers will be no less than today, competition for trained employees under age 40 will be intense. The large cohort of baby boomers will be moving into their retirement years; by about 2011, the first of the baby boomers will have reached age 65. Given these demographics, one can see employers designing compensation and pension systems that (1) will attract the younger employee, and (2) will shift from providing early retirement incentives to providing incentives to older employees to work on for a few years longer while at the same time building up additional resources for a later and longer retirement period.

Both of these objectives, I believe, will be better served by the defined contribution form. I will not repeat here the analysis of the pattern of benefit accruals that occur under a defined benefit plan. But the defined benefit approach, which results in a "back-loading" of accruals that favor long-service employees, imposes a very substantial loss of benefits on the employee who makes several job changes in a lifetime career.

Furthermore, defined benefit plans often incorporate provisions for incentives to retire early (Kotlikoff and Wise 1989). The expression of this early retirement incentive is more flexible under the defined benefit plan form than the defined contribution: additional years of service can be offered, the actuarial reduction can be curtailed, or eligibility dates can be altered and all such changes fit easily into the plan's basic structure. Financing such incentives under a defined benefit plan - especially if overfunded - can be done in a number of ways, many involving no "cash flow" losses even if accounting cost increases. The defined contribution plan on the other hand is less flexible: additional money must be added and it has no period over which to accumulate. Corporate treasurers see cash depleted and accounting costs are hard to spread.

In contrast to these current advantages of the defined benefit form, the changed objectives in 2020 may lead to preference for the defined contribution form. The defined contribution form, which has no back-loading, thus providing additional visible extra compensation to younger employees, is a more flexible arrangement for providing deferred retirement incentives. Investment income, additional employer contributions, and a reduced life expectancy all automatically lead to an increased annual income for each year deferred. Typically, the retirement income will double between age 65 and 70. No significant additional cost is borne by the employer. Some employers today, who prefer a younger work force, regard this incentive effect of the defined contribution arrangement as perverse. But the changed labor force demographics of the year 2020 may change "perverse" to "preferred."

Two additional trends should be specifically emphasized, even if they are not strictly classifiable as demographic.

First is the growing awareness of the loss in pension wealth to employees who make several job changes, referred to above. As noted, the defined benefit plan derives logically from a labor relationship typified by long career service with one employer, strong incentives to reduce labor force mobility, especially at ages 40-55, penalties for early withdrawal (vesting rules), and little concern for former or shorter-service employees (no portability).

Continued high job mobility among young skilled employees and growing comprehension by labor force participants of the economic values of pension plans, and influences on those values, will lead to a preference for defined contribution types of plans, since they are capable - if made widely available - of producing similar benefits for similar careers regardless of employment history. They are more easily structured to provide for portability. And their vesting schedules tend to be shorter than defined benefit plans (a five-year vesting rule for young, mobile employees in a defined benefit plan produces some inefficiently small equities that must then be maintained for several decades).

The second trend with important implications is the growing social preference for more personal control over pension assets, perhaps even more broadly, over all personal finances. Although anecdotal, the professional experience of our longer-service benefit counselors at TIAA-CREF is illuminating. They recall the days in, say, the 1960s and 1970s, when plan participants showed only moderate interest in their TIAA-CREF accumulations; when once-a-year benefit illustrations were deemed quite sufficient information on the progress of their pensions; when little interest was shown in asset allocation (choose 50% of allocations to the fixed annuity and 50% to the variable annuity - and then forget it); when settlement of the annuity at retirement was a simple one-time event (not involving today's multiple settlements with additional possibilities of choosing among different Assumed Interest Rates (AIRs), estate planning deferrals, and so on); and when just passing interest seemed to be shown in investment performance.

Today, in contrast, we have quarterly reports, 24- hour-a-day services to provide valuation quotes, PC programs to help plan retirement settlements and asset allocations, the possibility of varying AIRs and a very large staff of telephone counselors. Evidence of the trend is available in other forms: the growing sophistication of our courts in evaluating pension wealth in divorce settlements; 401(k) plans that permit many investment options and frequent transfer opportunities.

This trend would suggest, however, that employees prefer a plan in which they can reflect their own investment preferences, and their retirement income settlement arrangements, and in which they can design their retirement asset portfolios consistently with their other assets.

An interesting official statement of the above view was given by David George Ball, assistant secretary for pension and welfare benefits of the U.S. Department of Labor, in a speech on February 19, 1991, before the College and University Personnel Association. Introducing a regulation interpreting Section 404(C) of ERISA - perhaps the first federal effort to regulate defined <u>contribution</u> plans exclusively since ERISA was passed in 1974 - Secretary Ball described the administration's broad philosophy on pension plans (Ball 1991):

> This is a theme which underlies our approach to retirement issues. That theme is economic empowerment which is, in many ways, a trend away from institutional control and toward self-reliance. Economic empowerment recognizes that there must be more personal savings and more personal control over one's own life.

By 2020, our imaginary employer will be faced with a Social Security system that will doubtless still be a defined benefit plan, and certainly one that will provide, as it does now, relatively more generous income replacement ratios than did Social Security at the time the defined benefit plans were born - i.e., in the decades just after the Second World War when Social Security was still relatively immature. (See Scheiber, in this volume, who raises doubts about whether the current generosity of benefit levels can be maintained.)

Thirty years from now, "paternalism" in pensions may belong exclusively to the government by means of the mandated and universal Social Security system. There may be little willingness by employers to protect employees from their bad investment decisions, even from misuse of cash options at retirement, with the view taken that the employer has shared in the cost of the Social Security pension, which cannot be "squandered." In fact, some employers now are shifting to combination plans with very much this view: first provide a minimum level of defined benefit and, secondly, involve the employee by installing a defined contribution plan or matched savings plan - (either 401(k) or 403(b)) -

with great employee latitude (even a cash option at retirement) in making allocation and investment decisions under the plan.

One should not conclude this subject without noting (as mentioned earlier) the severe regulatory bias that is developing against employer-sponsored pension plans, especially against defined benefit plans. Even a modest extrapolation of trends of the last decades must present a very gloomy prognosis for the defined benefit plan. The underlying forces (primarily social concerns on discrimination) leading to overregulation will also curtail defined contribution plans, but the form of control is less destructive. Additionally, one wonders about the viability in the next decade of the PBGC mechanism and the ability of our state and local governments to meet their defined benefit commitments. Substantial failure of these institutions would destroy confidence in the defined benefit promise, thereby accelerating the trend toward independently funded defined contribution plans.

TARGET AGE AT RETIREMENT

We like to say at TIAA-CREF that - in recent years - our participants are retiring earlier and later. The age when fewer are retiring is age 65. Although a preference for early retirement continues to be evident, the effect of changing attitudes of older workers has led to a few more retirements of people in their late 60s and a few in their early 70s. (See the excellent analysis by Levine and Mitchell in this conference volume, in which they review the historical decline in labor force participation rates for older workers, and analyze economic factors that may lead to an increase in such rates by 2020.) Forecasting the equilibrium in 2020 is difficult; one can confidently predict only that our hypothetical Board of Directors in 2020 will no doubt spend more time discussing this question than heretofore. The purpose of this paper, however, is to make an informed judgement of how such demographic changes may affect pension plan design.

As stated above, one would not predict for the future a return to the use of mandatory retirement ages, just as one would not predict a return to sex-distinct annuity rates in pension plans. It is not only our national dislike of age discrimination, as expressed in the 1970s' and 1980s' legislation, that leads to this view. One can also argue that the growing preference for employee control of retirement funds and retirement arrangements also works against assigning to either an employer or a group (e.g., a union) the decision-making power to require one uniform model for automatic retirement.

Obviously, the demographics of relative population cohort size, the improved health of the "young" old (see Crimmins in this volume, who argues that no such improvement has yet occurred), and the economic incentives built into Social Security and private pension plans will lead to greater potential for labor force participation after the traditional retirement ages. But pressures to lower the ages at which workers retire will come from employees who may prefer to allocate more of their increased lifetime wealth to retirement consumption - again taking the optimistic view that future generations will have more real lifetime wealth to distribute than the current generation (again, see Levine and Mitchell, who present a brief argument that the aging of the baby boom will not depress their wages substantially). Employers may find it harder to recruit young, skilled, and trained employees, and may at times find that senior employees, as a group, are not substitutes for younger workers - especially in demanding professional and high- technology types of jobs. Accordingly, older workers with appropriate skills may be offered incentives to continue work.

The resulting design of retirement arrangements - based on new patterns of retirement behavior and new needs of employers for workers - will doubtless be more complex, allowing for much more variation in retirement age. The employer will still have in mind a central age tendency - perhaps still mid-60s, or perhaps centering on Social Security's age for full benefits - but will explicitly design flexible early and later retirement ages. An objective important to many employees would be that sufficient assets should be available so that an employer could put in provisions for ''ad hoc'' early retirement incentives. The plan will probably not punish financially those who elect to retire after the ''central age tendency.'' However, managers may worry about the employee who is age 80 and who refuses to retire; ''firing'' older employees whose managerial product has declined entails ''costs'' not in the usual economic model.

Perhaps the most interesting demographic effect on the design of the retirement age for private pensions will be an indirect one, derived from governmental policy related to Social Security retirement (as discussed elsewhere in this Symposium). Unless Social Security benefits are dramatically curtailed, or the age for full benefits raised further than already scheduled, or FICA taxes significantly increased, then in 2020 the cost of paying for the baby boom retirees will be very much on the public's mind. Within a few years benefits will exceed outgo as the system begins to receive benefit applications from the baby boom retirees. The consolidated federal budget will be subject to <u>losses</u> from the Social Security outgo beginning about 2030, instead of <u>gains</u> as is occurring in the 1990s. (See Figure 2 in Scheiber's paper in this volume.)

Consequently, many proposals will no doubt be advanced for increasing taxes and reducing benefits. But surely another approach, and perhaps the most practicable, will be to find ways to encourage the baby boomers to work to later ages and thereby defer the start of Social Security benefits. This will take the form, as is already enacted currently, of providing for benefit increments for working past age 65, and, as scheduled for 2022 and beyond, of raising to age 67 the age for full benefits. But it may also take the form of various incentives or requirements by the government that <u>private</u> retirement plans encourage later retirement: rigorous enforcement of age discrimination laws; tax incentives for individuals to delay retirement; or even specific plan design components. The designers of a new plan in 2020 will have to respond to those needs.

Another evolving point of view may lead the Board of Directors to see the retirement age as less a target variable - as specified in a typical defined benefit plan - and more a dependent variable determined by the adequacy of assets accumulated for retirement. If one assumes that the culture of a company puts pressure on low-productivity employees to retire, they will tend to do so voluntarily, but only if retirement income financial assets are sufficient to replace the human capital earnings given up. This basic humane employment principle may in the future be the key motivation behind a generous employer-required or funded pension arrangement.

ELIGIBILITY AND CONTRIBUTION REQUIREMENTS

The eligibility and contribution features of pension plan design will not change significantly unless federal tax policy changes. The need to have a competitive package for young employees will lead to more relaxed service requirements - a most-aggressive provision, for example, would provide immediate participation upon employment in a fully vested defined contribution plan, with an interesting menu of investment choices. Some present-day employers are already using such liberal incentives to attract highly desired senior executives - many of whom are ''depression babies'' - who are in relatively short supply. One can argue that such provisions in the future may well be extended to other classes of employees who are also in short supply.

If federal tax policy continues to favor the employer as the source of the pension plan contribution, then it is unlikely that demographic effects will much change the present level of required and voluntary employee contributions to pension plans.

VESTING AND PORTABILITY

Competition for younger employees will be an inducement to employers to liberalize these two related provisions: moving to still earlier vesting and providing for preservation of pension benefits in convenient ways through transfers of pension accumulations and rights to later employers or to pension custodial accounts. The combined effect of both pension preservation and portability, of course, may seem somewhat perverse for employers since the threat of benefit forfeitures to reduce employee turnover would obviously be diminished. This loss of ''golden handcuffs'' is, of course, reinforced by the trend toward the defined contribution and away from the back-loaded defined benefit plan.

Perhaps by 2020 our society's retirement policy (expressed in tax and labor law) will be rationalized sufficiently to prevent or discourage severely the usual spending by terminated employees of vested pension benefits received as lump sums. Our government's current schizophrenia on this issue was highlighted last year when the Treasury opposed a proposal to make it more difficult to cash out vested accumulations on the ground that the government needed the immediate tax revenue from such cash- outs. In the meantime, the Labor Department was voicing the importance of pension preservation and portability. These are contemporary conflicts. In the future, pension vesting and portability design features will become significant only to the extent that public policy can assure maintenance of permanent retirement funds.

INFLATION PROTECTION

How designers of pension plans provide - or more often today, fail to provide - for inflation is one of the most interesting aspects of evolving pension plan design. I would predict much more explicit and complete protection in 2020 than today, but this change will be driven more by experience with pension plans than by demographics per se. Demographics will have two effects: (1) those about to retire will face longer lives and, hence, greater need for postretirement protection of income from inflation; and (2) they will also face medical care costs for a long retirement period, including long-term care needs. Both of these will substantially add to concern about postretirement inflation.

While pension plans were young and growing - during the postwar decades - the primary focus on the effects of inflation was on active employees. Accordingly, final-salary defined benefit plans, instead of career-average plans, became the pattern. Pensions were protected against loss of purchasing power through adjustments during employment years. The costs of this approach do not seem to have been excessive, since the small depression-era demographic cohort was working its way through these years. For postretirement inflation protection, several forms, although limited in scope, were used: (1) ad hoc adjustments when employers felt sufficient incentive and profitability to make them; (2) a very few explicit formula-driven commitments; and (3) for medical coverage, an open-ended commitment by some employers to provide retirees with inflation-adjusted medical coverage similar to that provided for active employees.

The shift in design in 2020 will be to much more explicit and, in the case of medical benefits, limited funding of postretirement benefits. The baby boomers will be retiring and will have (1) longer life expectancies; (2) higher costs for acute medical care; and (3) greater risks of an eventual need for long-term custodial care. If defined contribution plans then dominate the pension scene, at least in the private sector, the design concern will be to fund payout arrangements that can use underlying assets in a way that helps incomes adjust to future inflation.

I suspect that designers of pension plans in 2020 will be as reluctant as they are now to commit their corporate financial life to a guarantee of future inflation protection. But assets that can provide some inflation protection will be more widely used: real estate, common stocks, government bonds indexed to inflation (if they exist), and corporate securities that are linked to inflation by the issuer of the security. Those assets that are not inflation linked - fixed income securities and real estate related loans - will be used to support annuity forms that do not immediately pay out their full income - i.e., that pay out the real income and reinvest the inflation premiums. An example of this approach is the graded payment method of annuity income, under which the earnings on a portfolio of fixed income assets in excess of a 4% payout rate are added back to principal so as to increase subsequent payouts accordingly.

With respect to long-term care, perhaps the most fundamental way to cope with those needs is to provide adequate levels of real income to retirees. The present fixed nominal incomes that actually represent declining real incomes can hardly prepare one for the significant extra financial burdens that may have to be borne in advanced age when special needs for extra care are manifest. Provision of constant real income is obviously important for retirees' basic support; level real incomes may be sufficient by themselves to cover long-term care costs.

However, some employers will add explicit insurance arrangements for long-term care, either directly in the pension plan or, as is done now by a growing number of employers, by sponsoring a voluntarily purchased plan.

There will no doubt be much change by 2020 in the federal government's role in providing long-term care. The elderly will be more numerous and even more potent as a voting force than today. But quality differentials between government-financed and privately financed care will doubtless exist and, presumably, many Americans will still provide for the care of elderly members of their families without government support.

A final note on inflation: the demographics of 2020, the "Florida-ization" of America, may lead to a firmer political opposition to inflationary governmental policies, fiscal and monetary. As the large and more vocal senior voting segment of the population comes to depend on financial capital (eroded by inflation) and not human capital (augmented by inflation), severe punishment may be in store for those elected officials who propose economic policies leading to inflation. Accordingly, the demographics of 2020 may lead to an environment that is less inflationary and easier for plan designers to cope with.

DEATH AND DISABILITY BENEFITS

As the postwar baby boomers move through their 50s and 60s, the continuing need for survivor benefits (occasioned by early death) and for disability income benefits (occasioned by illness or injury) will remain an important social issue. It is hard to imagine the plan designers in 2020 bringing to our Board of Directors a pension plan design that does not fully and explicitly cover the important design features of disability and survivor benefits.

If individual and group life insurance arrangements lose their tax-benefited features, there will be much more interest in providing such benefits through the pension mechanism. The strong presence of Social Security survivor and disability benefits, with $50,000 of tax-free group life, and tax-free inside buildup of individual life insurance, have all inhibited the growth of disability and survivor benefits in pension plans. By 2020 this situation may well be altered. One could be optimistic in suggesting that improved population health (albeit difficult to improve for younger ages) will lead to lower-cost insurance plans for disability and premature death, thereby making generous provision for such needs more affordable for employee benefit plans.

BENEFIT FORMULAS

The historic trend toward salary-related pension plans and away from flat-rate plans will undoubtedly continue. It's hard to see the demographics in 2020 leading to a return to plans that state benefits as dollars per year of service as an appropriate design.

One possibility that can be foreseen is a renewed growth in interest in Social Security integration, but with a different motivation. I would contend that the primary interest historically has been the employer's interest in adjusting the private pension benefit to reflect the presence of the Social Security benefit.

An opposing point of view has been argued by Zvi Bodie (1989), who sees

Social Security integration in private pension plans as insurance against the possibility that Social Security benefits may not be paid. As of today, I doubt whether this view identifies an explicit or even implicit interest on the part of very many employers, since few plans would provide the larger benefit if Social Security benefits were to disappear.

But by the year 2020 a possible weakening in confidence in the future of the Social Security system could become a factor in employer plan design. The gap between FICA tax income and Old Age, Survivors, and Disability Insurance outgo will be visible and growing, and many will fear a diminished capacity of a smaller active work force to carry the Social Security burden. Accordingly, employees who are covered under private pension plans may look to their employers for private insurance, in Bodie's sense; that is, employees will expect private employers to step in with increased outlays if social insurance benefits are curtailed. This could be an acceptable cost to employers as a group, since the absence of such a substitute benefit might lead to a significant increase in payroll taxes to fund the social insurance alternative.

CONCLUSIONS

This paper is an attempt to foresee some of the possible pension plan design responses to the demographic forces of the early 21st century. Symposium discussants and others will doubtless see other responses of private pension plans to the elemental forces of population changes. Hopefully, this paper and these discussions will help inform us as to how to prepare for that future.

ENDNOTE

1. A recent survey of chief executives of the nation's largest companies by the Gallup Organization for the Robert Wood Johnson Foundation that 91% of chief executive believe that a fundamental change or complete rebuilding of the health care system is needed. The survey also found that 73% of the executives believe that the problems could not be solved by companies working on their own, with the two main issues being control of the cost of health care and access to the system for more people (Hilts 1991).

Discussions

Emily S. Andrews

INTRODUCTION AND REVIEW

Forecasts of the future are always fraught with danger, particularly for those of use who are likely to live to see the day. John Biggs takes a thoughtful first step towards assessing the future of retirement programs in the early 21st century. He outlines many of the key issues involved, including the aging of the work force, longer life expectancy, and improved health. He also discusses the impact of changes in employer motivation (more paternalism or less) and changes in employee motivation (a desire for greater financial control). Perhaps the two key elements of his analysis are his focus on large 1,000-plus employee firms and his concern with the aging of the work force.

While Biggs is relatively circumscribed in his speculation, he suggests that employers will be less interested in encouraging early retirement and will be more interested in defined contribution plans. These conclusions are hard to refute as general propositions.

I would disagree with at least one of Bigg's assertions, however. Despite rhetoric to the contrary, U. S. Census Bureau data on job tenure over the past two decades do not indicate any movement towards greater work-force mobility. Nonetheless, this assertion is not key to his arguments.

Biggs also discusses the problems inherent in influencing retirement ages without the stick of mandatory retirement. While Biggs doubts that mandatory retirement will be permitted, the fact that he raises the issue at all is interesting since it has only been an active concern in recent years to those whose constituencies are in higher education.

Biggs expands his analysis to discuss retiree health care, inflation protection, long-term care, death and disability benefits, and benefit formulas. In general, he does not foresee any dramatic changes although he envisages change in government policy towards long-term care.

All in all, Biggs prognosis is conservative; my own prognosis is probably no less so. I believe, however, that several factors not mentioned by Biggs will be crucial determinants of the impact of demographic change on retirement programs. Furthermore, recent trends in benefit design can be used to motivate our insights into future trends in benefits.

My discussion will focus on several demographic and economic trends not emphasized by Biggs and on recent changes in plan design. A forecast of the future will be presented based on this appraisal. My analysis is intended to expand upon the material provided by Biggs, and not necessarily to create an independent alternative vision of the future

The area in which I can provide no guidance is that of legislation. We have all read about potential legislative proposals to tax pension-fund income, index benefits, improve portability, and prohibit lump-sum distributions. We have also read recent reports on how to expand access to health insurance coverage and how to fund retiree health-insurance benefits. Proposals continue to be offered on the financing of Social Security. Most recently, concerns have been raised about the future of the PBGC and the security of annuities provided by insurance companies. I believe that it takes more than an economist's poor tools to predict outcomes in any of these areas. Hence, my further discussion assumes that in terms of legislative change, all other things will remain equal.

ADDITIONAL DEMOGRAPHIC AND ECONOMIC ISSUES

Future benefit design will be influenced by more than the aging of the labor force. While Biggs' paper is suggestive of some of these issues, he focuses on the benefits provided by very large employers. This obscures several important economic and demographic economic trends that are as likely to influence plan design. Furthermore, the interaction of demographic changes with the structure of the economy should be more explicitly considered.

Labor Market Issues

The future structure of the labor market will influence plan design from the perspective of the firm's personnel-policy objectives and from the perspective of employees' preferences. Several aspects of the labor market bear scrutiny insofar as they will influence benefits in the future.

Women and Minorities

One of the most important labor market trends has been the shift towards nontraditional workers and away from prime-age white men. Nontraditional workers include women and minorities. These groups entered the labor force in increasing numbers in recent decades. In, 1970, 38 percent of the labor force was female. That fraction rose to 43 percent in 1980, and 45 percent in 1990. Similarly, the proportion of nonwhite workers in the labor force rose from 11 percent in 1970 to 12 percent in 1980, and 14 percent in 1990. These trends are expected to continue.

From the perspective of the employer, nontraditional workers are likely to have different employment and earnings patterns compared to prime-age white men. The earnings of both women and minorities are currently below those of white men. Insofar as relative earnings reflect the productivity of different groups of workers, employers may have different expectations about their patterns of labor-force mobility and retirement. Consequently, employers would want to establish different types of employee benefits as their work forces became more diverse.

Moreover, nontraditional workers may not desire the same types of benefits as prime-age white men. For instance, the tax advantages from deferred compensation accruing to nontraditional workers will be less than the those accruing to prime-age white men, if, on average, nontraditional workers face lower marginal tax rates. In addition, different population groups are likely to have different patterns of consumption and saving. These differences may affect their benefit choices as well.

For example, sex, marital status, and the presence of children will all have an impact on the mix of benefits that workers prefer. For instance, married women in two-earner families may be able to balance their benefits against their husbands', perhaps desiring less health insurance or a different kind of pension. Similarly, families with children may be more interested in child care and health insurance relative to deferred compensation, in contrast to the benefit mix preferred by single women and men.

The Growing Service Sector

Another key labor market trend over the past several decades has been the increase in service-sector employment relative to manufacturing. Employment in services increased from 20 percent of private-sector employment in 1970 to 24 percent in 1980 and 31 percent in 1990. Over the same period, employment in manufacturing fell from 35 percent of private-sector employment in 1970 to 24 percent in 1980 and 21 percent in 1990. This dramatic two-decade decline in manufacturing meant that the number of workers in manufacturing was virtually constant over the period despite large gains in employment.

Firms providing services are less likely to have pension plans than those in manufacturing. In addition, the types of plans provided in different industries are not the same. Data from the Department of Labor based on Form 5500 for 1985 show that 51 percent of all pension plan participants in manufacturing have coverage under a primary and secondary plan compared to only 20 percent of plan participants in services.

Department of Labor data from Form 5500 also show that there were 194 participants, on average, in primary manufacturing pension plans compared to an average of 21 participants per primary plan in services. Data for 1985 showed that 69 percent of participants in plans with fewer than 100 participants had defined contribution plans as their primary plan. By contrast, only 21 percent of participants in plans with 100 or more participants had defined contribution plans as their primary plan.

In other words, a continuing shift in employment to the service sector may lead to the establishment of smaller plans and to the establishment of more defined contribution plans. This shift is only part of the story, of course. Other evidence suggests that plans in the service-providing sector have been getting larger. And, although the evidence does not support the contention that employment in firms with fewer than 100 participants has been growing, the possibility of shifts away from firms towards smaller entities bears scrutiny.

While smaller firms are clearly less likely to provide pensions, in 1987 6.7 million employees were covered by primary plans with fewer than 100 participants. Since smaller firms make up a substantial share of employment, under favorable economic conditions, their role in pension provision might grow.[1]

The Cost of Doing Business

The costs of employee benefits can also be expected to influence plan establishment, plan continuation, and plan provisions. The costs of regulation have been highlighted in a study prepared for the PBGC by Hay/Huggins (1991). The study created indices for total administrative expenses and for ongoing operating costs (excluding special one-time expenses associated with the need to conform the plan to regulatory change. Estimated annual cost increases ranged from 8 to 11 percent depending on the size of plan considered. The study also indicates that the relative cost of administering a defined benefit plan has increased relative to the cost of running a defined contribution plan. The primary cause of the relative-cost increase is identified as the Tax Reform Act of 1986. It is difficult to imagine that sizable cost increases and shifts in relative costs would not influence plan provision and plan design.

Another factor that must be taken into account in today's environment is the pressure of cost increases in other components of compensation. In earlier years, benefits made up a relatively small percentage of the compensation package. Pension contributions were the largest component. Recent increases in the costs of health care have changed that equation. Whereas health insurance accounted for 31 percent of employer outlays for voluntary benefits in 1970, its share has risen to 53 percent by 1989.

Furthermore, Warshawsky (1991) cites estimates from several sources on the dollar value of the accrued liabilities for retiree health insurance for all private corporations in the U.S. These estimates range from $100 billion to over $300 billion. These near and long-term pressures on total compensation costs will surely lead to a reevaluation of the types of retirement benefits provided.

CURRENT TRENDS IN PLAN DESIGN

The combination of labor market and cost factors can be evaluated within the context of current trends in plan design that are obvious from tabulations based on federal data. First, there appears to be a slow shift away from any pension plan coverage. Certainly, the most radical change in plan design would be no plan. According to Census Bureau data, the percentage of workers aged 15 and older participating in a pension plan declined from 44.9 percent in 1979 to 40.8 percent in 1987.

Similarly, data prepared for the Health Insurance Financing Administration (HCFA) indicate that employer-sponsored health insurance coverage declined from 57.3 percent of workers in 1980 to 53.7 percent in 1990 (based on adults who worked the previous year)(Fu Associates, 1991). While the statistical significance of each of these declines may be questioned, few could argue that participation has been steadily rising.

During the same time period, we have witnessed a shift towards primary defined combination plans. Ippolito (1991) indicates in a recent study that this shift was concentrated among plans with fewer than 1,000 participants. He finds that the movement towards defined contribution plans among large single employers was primarily attributable to employment shifts. By contrast, the movement towards smaller defined contribution plans appears to have been additionally influenced by changes in administrative costs, personnel policy, and/or employee preferences.

Another change in the nature of pension plan provision has been the increasing trend among employers towards secondary (and tertiary) plan coverage. In 1975, 21 percent of primary plan participants had secondary plan coverage as well. By 1987, that percentage had increased to 39 percent. Tertiary plan coverage increased over the same period from 4 percent of primary plan participants to 13 percent.

Coupled with the movement towards secondary plan coverage was the strong growth in 401(k) plans. Cash or deferred arrangements (CODAs) are popular with both employers and employees for the same reason -- they permit pretax employee contributions. The number of 401(k) plans grew from 1,703 in 1983 to 45,054 in 1987. CODAs covered 28 million participants in 1983 and 35 million participants in 1987. By 1987, 38 percent of all defined contribution plan participants were in 401(k) plans. The growth of 401(k) plans has been slower in recent years but has far from abated.

Changes also might have been expected to have taken place over the past two decades in the key provisions of defined benefit plans. These provisions include normal retirement ages, early retirement ages, benefit formulas, and Social Security integration. Department of Labor tabulations of BLS data on plans sponsored by medium and large employers generally paint a picture in which change have been minimal. Between 1982 and 1986 some shift towards earlier early retirement ages may have taken place. The most striking change, however, is the increase in the percentage of full-time participants covered by plans with integrated formulas. This percentage rose from 45 percent in 1982 to 62 percent in 1986. The easy explanation for this change is that employers have become more cost consciousness in recent years.

IMPLICATIONS FOR PLAN DESIGN

Demographic and economic trends can be coupled with trends in plan design to form a economically motivated scenario of the future. The future labor force will not only consist of older workers but will consist of nontraditional workers -- women and minorities. We can hypothesize that some of the changes in plan design may already have been a result of these demographic shifts. For instance, both the movement towards defined contribution plans and the provision of secondary plans would appeal to younger workers and two-income families. While flexible benefit plans have not gained as wide popularity yet, they may expand slowly to meet the needs of a more diverse work force.

As the shift towards services continues, the distribution of pension plans will resemble those offered in the service sector. The full service sector is actually more heterogenous than suggested earlier. This heterogeneity is particularly apparent in the types of jobs offered. Taking hospitals as an example, some jobs are very highly remunerated, while others pay salaries close to the minimum wage. Nonetheless, both services (narrowly defined) and the service sector (broadly defined and including finance, insurance, real estate, and communications) seems to be typified by the greater use of defined contribution plans. Further analysis of service-sector plan provision by plan size would provide an extremely useful guide for the future.

Thus, based on labor-force movements alone, I would predict that the use of defined contribution plans in either a primary or secondary capacity will continue to grow. With their expansion, the issue of retirement will become more pressing for employers. Defined contribution plans do not have as strong retirement incentives as defined benefit plans. Benefit accruals in defined contribution plans are not backloaded and plan assets can be cashed out upon job change. Employers will be less able to use their pensions to target retirement. If this personnel-policy function diminishes, there may be even greater incentives for employers to provide 401(k) plans that encourage employee contributions thereby cutting compensation costs, providing a desirable benefit, and encouraging personal financial responsibility on the part of their employees.

The costs of benefit provision will also continue to influence plan design in the future. If the increases in health care costs continue, coupled with relatively slow gains in economic growth, their economic influences on plan provision can be expected to prevail. These cost factors will lead to several outcomes. First growing businesses will be less likely to establish pension plans even when they expand to over 100 employees. Second, when plans are established, they will be more likely to be defined contribution plans in view of their relative administration-cost advantages.

Third, defined contribution plans will be even more likely to be 401(k) plans. Employers can share costs with employees using cash or deferred arrangements enabling workers to accumulate greater assets for the future.

The increasing costs of employee benefits will also affect the provisions of existing defined benefit plans. Companies with 10,000 or more employees are extremely unlikely to abandon defined benefit plans. Employers could be expected to integrate plans that are not currently integrated with Social Security to reduce plan costs.

Another change in the structure of defined benefit plans that employers might made would be to reduce the generosity of the benefit formula. This could be done in conjunction with other changes in benefits similar to those made for federal employees. In that case, defined benefit plan annuities were reduced and additional benefits were made available through a pretax savings plans similar to a private-sector cash or deferred arrangement. Large employers that have not already instituted secondary defined contribution plans and/or have not provided a 401(k) plan could change their benefit packages and reduce direct employer costs by this strategy. A mix of benefits from both defined benefit and defined contribution plans could also be used by employers to better meet the needs of a more diverse work force.

Another change that defined benefit plans could adopt would be to increase the ages specified under the plan for both early and normal retirement. A change in the age of normal retirement would, in effect, reduce the benefits provided retirees at specific ages and, hence, reduce the financial incentives to retire. This is exactly what was done through the 1983 Social Security amendments - - a benefit reduction in the guise of a change in the normal retirement age. Although firms still appear to be encouraging early retirement, the shifting demographics of the labor force may mean that early-outs are no longer desirable by the year 2021. Furthermore, phased-in changes in the age of retirement are probably unlikely to affect the labor market behavior of younger cohorts.

Changes in employer-provided retiree health insurance benefits are likely to have an even greater impact on the age of retirement than changes in defined benefit plan provisions. After FASB 89, many employers may prospectively eliminate retiree health insurance or change the benefit promise from a package of health plan services to a fixed dollar amount to be used to purchase health insurance. Workers contemplating retirement before age 65 who do not have retiree health insurance coverage may be less likely to relinquish their jobs if they find they can no longer purchase effective health insurance on their own or obtain insurance through alternative non-career employment (part-time or part-year).

These speculations are premised on the assumption that economic growth will remain relatively sluggish but positive, following trends established in the 1970s and 1980s. Should our current recession be a precursor to an even less favorable economic environment, many more plans are likely to terminate and few employers are likely to establish new plans. If terminations were more likely among smaller employers, an interesting shift would take place as the proportion of participants with primary defined benefit pension plans would increase reversing the trend of the past decade.

Barring this type of economic disaster, the trends in benefits are probably clear. First, the participation rate is likely to remain stable or decline. Second, the trend towards defined contribution plans is likely to continue through the growth of secondary plans and the increased use of defined contribution plans for primary coverage. The popularity of 401(k) plans will be maintained with these plans commanding an increasing share of the market. Finally, as employers seek to reduce costs across-the-board, implicit reductions in benefits through changes in plan provisions and explicit changes in retiree health benefits are likely to lead to later retirement ages. All in all, retirement programs will be leaner and meaner than they are today.

ENDNOTE

1. In 1983, 36 percent of employment was in firms with more than 1,000 employees, 17 percent was in firms with 99 to 1,000 workers, and 47 percent was in firms with fewer than 100 employees.

Anna M. Rappaport, F.S.A.

INTRODUCTION

This conference includes papers and discussions that express a number of differing viewpoints. The academic members of the conference generally have presented findings backed by research. My comments and observations are based on a study of issues related to demographics and their implications for financial security systems over the last twenty years combined with many years of practice as an employee benefit consultant. They should be interpreted as a practitioner's view. My comments about employers are heavily influenced by experiences in working with employers and in helping them develop employee benefit strategies.

Mr. Biggs presents a number of ideas that provide a basis for an interesting discussion. I disagree with him on a number of points, particularly with the extent to which he views defined contribution plans as more desirable than defined benefit plans. I will discuss our areas of disagreement as well as try to provide additional insights.

Mr. Bigg's paper discusses the issue of demographic change and looks at the hypothetical position of a newly formed employer in the year 2020. He assumes that the employer will adopt a pension plan to cover about 1,000 employees. In this discussion, I will comment on the following issues raised in Mr. Bigg's analysis:

- Demographic trends and other factors which must be discussed with these trends.

- The retirement age issue.

- The concerns of employers already sponsoring pension plans, emphasizing issues that affect employers of different sizes.

- The total retirement package.

- The choice of defined benefit vs. defined contribution plans.

We should note that Mr. Bigg's choice of a relatively large new employer is useful in that it permits a focus on where future employers might be if they did not have to deal with reality. However, this will be a relatively rare situation. Most organizations will be existing organization with a past, a culture and a set of benefits, so that they have to deal with that past. These conditions make the issues far more difficult to deal with.

Newer organizations tend either to be smaller or to be spinoffs from existing companies, often created by leveraged buyouts. Small new companies have start-up issues and are different from the 1,000-life company described in Mr. Bigg's example. Spinoffs from existing companies have to consider both the tradition of the company they came from, and additionally, they often have very large debt burdens (if they are created using the financial vehicles currently in vogue). It is important for the Pension Research Council and this conference to deal with the broader issues and not to limit our consideration of plan design to new employers under unusual conditions.

DEMOGRAPHIC TRENDS, THEIR DISCUSSION AND OTHER FACTORS MUST BE CONSIDERED

I agree with Mr. Biggs that the aging of the population and squaring of the mortality curve are extremely important issues to consider. It is unclear to me that improved health for all ages is ahead, and I am most interested to hear what other discussants at this conference have to say about longer life, extended working life, postretirement long-term care and their impact on postretirement financial resources.

Family structure and divorce is another important area of demographics when looking at the pension system and how well it works overall for the population. Traditional pension plans work best when either (1) each individual earns a personal benefit independent of family status and is in the paid labor force, or (2) there are stable families and the same family exists during the times when benefits are earned and paid. In our society, many people meet neither of these conditions.

There is an issue of how well pensions work for individuals who are partial or total homemakers and later become separated from the primary breadwinner in the household. There is also the issue of benefits after death. Karen C. Holden, in a paper titled "The Lifetime After Retirement: Wives and Lengthening Widowhood,"presented at the Society of Actuaries Symposium on the Future of Retirement, stated that women in their thirties and forties today will on average spend fifteen years as widows. This takes into account the difference in male and female life expectancies and typical age differences between husbands and wives. Dr. Holden also documents the fact that income typically drops during widowhood. It is important to take into account the needs of women with mixed career patterns and of widows when we look at retirement plans and how they may operate in thirty years.

Mr. Biggs asserts that the supply of skilled new entrants to the labor force will be markedly lower in 2020 than today. This seems to me to be an unwarranted assumption because:

(a) The cohort in question has not yet been born, and many of the Baby Boomers (particularly some of those who have two-career families) seem to have delayed the point at which they had children, rather than not having them at all. We do not really know how many children will be born in the next decade.

(b) Skills are partially a function of the educational resources in place. Americans have recognized substantial difficulties and challenges with the educational system, but these may be overcome by 2020 so that skill levels rise substantially. In addition, retraining of the existing work force is likely to increase markedly.

(c) We do not know what the skill requirements will look like in thirty years. Technological development increases the skill requirements of some jobs while other jobs require less skill or may be shifted to robots.

(d) Additionally, it is totally unclear what will happen to immigration policy over a thirty year period.

This commentator believes there is no basis to project a deficit of skilled new entrants to the labor force in thirty years. A comment has been made that competition for trained employees under age forty will also be intense. Some of the same reservations also apply to that comment. In addition, it is not clear what the total need for workers will be in the U.S. in thirty years.

Mr. Biggs brings in the non-demographic factor of productivity improvement for consideration. Other related non-demographic issues include:

- The globalization of business and the need for companies to achieve competitive production costs when considered on a worldwide basis.

- The impact of the federal deficit on public policy.

- The impact of restructuring American business in the late 1980s and the early 1990s, which is likely to improve productivity as mentioned by Mr. Biggs, but may have other effects also.

THE ROLE OF REGULATIONS

While regulation is certainly not a demographic issue in the real world, it interacts with demographic issues as employers make plan design changes. Mr. Biggs points to the tendency of changes in pension regulation to make it increasingly difficult for employers to sponsor pension plans, with the problems being more severe for defined benefit plans.

He points out that if the trends continue, it may be virtually impossible to sponsor a traditional defined benefit plan. This trend is an extremely important issue. It should not be viewed as inevitable, but rather we must find a way to protect the pension system. We should note that as the population ages, public pressure for favorable pension regulation and defined benefit plans may build.

A related issue is taxation. However, because the population is aging, there may be public pressure to counter this effect. It is very possible that pension and benefit taxation will become less favored over time.

THE RETIREMENT AGE ISSUE

A critical issue for the retirement plans of the future will be the nation's retirement age policy and employers' human resources policy regarding retirement ages. Mr. Biggs discusses this topic under the heading ''Target Age at Retirement.''The policy of the nation in the last few decades has been to facilitate retirement in the early 60s, but to support the right of employees to work longer. These policies have been supported by the following actions:

- Social Security benefits are available for retirement beginning at age 62. Full benefits are available today at age 65, and that age will gradually increase to 67 for people born in 1960 or later.

- Medicare is available at age 65. This can be interpreted as implicitly reflecting a policy position that employer coverage ought to be provided until age 65, and that medical benefits become a societal responsibility at age 65.

- Support for employer-sponsored pension plans and regulation to protect plan participants through a variety of legislation, including the Internal Revenue Code, ERISA, REA and other legislation. At the same time, national retirement policy often seems to be inconsistent and fragmented and driven by deficits and tax policy.

- Abolition of mandatory retirement and stringent requirement with regard to age discrimination in employment.

- Increases in the Social Security late retirement credit.

- Increasingly stringent requirements for pension accruals and participation at older ages.

The effect of public policy is to create and reinforce the rights of individuals to work longer, while at the same time, facilitating retirement in the early 60s. As Mr. Biggs points out, the age structure of the population is changing. People are able to work to ages beyond typical retirement ages. Mr. Biggs states that the squaring of the mortality curve will lead to a diminution of employers' interest in encouraging employees to take retirement at age 65 or earlier. He indicates that employers are almost certain by 2020 they will want employees to retire at a later age. A key issue is when this will happen, and what form employer policy will take. A related question is whether Social Security retirement ages will increase more, and how benefits will change.

The crunch on federal resources is likely to lead to long-term reductions in benefit levels and/or increases in retirement ages (a form of benefit reduction). One viewpoint would suggest that retirement should be possible at a wide range of ages, so that individuals would have a choice based on preferences and resources. Another view would be that the current age should simply increase. Another view would be that employers will be less involved in the retirement decision; people will retire when they are so inclined and have resources. Or, as an alternative to retirement, they might simply scale down their level of work, but continue working, possibly in a new job or career. Many individuals do this type of thing today. This is a major issue with regard to the future of retirement, and on that is not being addressed very much in an institutional setting today.

Mr. Biggs discusses the experience of TIAA-CREF with regard to retirement age, and points out that people are retiring earlier and later today. He indicates that fewer people are selecting age 65 and that there is increasing support for more individual control over both when they retire and how they invest funds. I believe that the population covered by TIAA-CREF may be different from the population at large. This should be considered before this experience is used to represent a broader population, and possibly extrapolated. University faculty may prefer to retire at older ages than people in many other jobs because they have greater freedom and flexibility. They have the potential for more leisure time that many older people who are not ready for full retirement desire. It should also be pointed out that the job performance of university faculty is less subject to measurement than the performance in many other jobs, and that tenured faculty cannot be terminated from their jobs except in very unusual circumstances.

Mr. Biggs states that pressure to lower the age of retirement will come from employees who may prefer to allocate more of their increased lifetime wealth to retirement consumption. It is unclear to this commentator that lifetime wealth will increase, or that if it does, it will increase consumption during the retirement period. Many people prefer other alternatives for leisure. It appears very possible that today's elderly will be better off than future generations of elderly, and that many individuals will be forced to work longer in order to have the resources to retire. If responsibility for providing retirement income shifts from the employer to the employee, this will vary greatly by individual, but overall, Americans are very low savers. Individuals in their twenties today are spending a higher proportion of their income for housing than in the past, and the real earnings of younger people are not increasing as rapidly as in the past. It is unclear to this commentator where increased wealth comes from.

A number of factors may make retirement more difficult in thirty years than it has been in the last decade (and than it is likely to be in the next decade). These include:

- A generation that has had to spend more of its assets for housing, but has experienced less appreciation in housing values when compared to the retirees of the 1980s and 1990s.

- A generation who, in many cases, had their children later (even though there are fewer of them) so that they were stilling paying college expenses at a high cost as they near retirement ages.

- A generation with increased responsibility for aging parents who are living longer and who are still alive as their children enter their 60s, and sometimes even their 70s.

- A generation whose employers are less generous in the benefits they offer.

- A generation who has seen Social Security benefits flatten out and not keep pace with inflation.

Mr. Biggs points out that employers will find it harder to recruit young, skilled and trained employees, and will find that very senior employees, as a group, are not substitutes for younger employees--especially in demanding professional and high technology jobs. But senior employees may indeed be substitutes, and that would work best from the employee point-of- view if the jobs are designed with more flexibility. One of the great unanswered questions of the 1990s is how effective employers and society will be in helping displaced workers rebuild skills and reenter the system.

OUTLOOK FOR SOCIAL SECURITY BENEFITS

Mr. Biggs asserts that Social Security benefits in 2020 will continue to be relatively more generous than in the early days of Social Security. He does not say whether it will be more generous than today. I seriously doubt that this will be more generous, and if anything, I think they will be considerably less generous when the combination of Social Security and Medicare are considered together. This is likely to be a result of increasing pressures on the federal budget and a lower ratio of contributors to beneficiaries in the Social Security system.

THE CONCERNS OF EXISTING EMPLOYERS WITH EMPHASIS ON ISSUES AFFECTING DIFFERENT SIZED EMPLOYERS

Mr. Biggs does not examine the issues facing existing employers with existing plans, but these issues will be vital in sorting out the future of retirement plans. Retirement plans generally reflect the culture and tradition of organizations, but they often are the product of long-term human resources policy. For many employers, expected pension benefits are a substantial part of their assets, and they have built up expectations about retirement over many years. Larger employers commonly issue annual benefits statements that have increased pension awareness and expectations. Decisions to make fundamental changes in retirement benefits are difficult and should not be taken lightly.

Benefits philosophy is often defined as a spectrum. At one end of the spectrum is entitlement and at the other, a compensation orientation. Few employers are at the extremes of the spectrum; most common are someplace in the middle. The entitlement-oriented employer in 1990 is likely to offer a retirement package with a fairly generous final average pay plan, and retiree health benefits with substantial employer support, often supplemented by a matched savings program.

The compensation oriented employer in 1990 is likely to offer a defined contribution plan without retiree health, or with minimal company support for retiree health. Part or all of the defined contribution plan may be tied to profits and/or paid as a match on the employee's savings. Retirement is often viewed as a responsibility shared by the employer, employee and government. The matched savings component of the package supports the employee share of the responsibility. The level of employer support varies greatly by company. Newer organizations are more likely to have compensation oriented and rely on defined contribution plans.

For larger, well-established employers, particularly in traditional industries, the most common pattern of retirement benefits is a defined benefit plan based on final average pay, plus retiree health and matched savings. There is a heavy orientation to entitlement and support for career employment underlying this type of benefit program.

Unions are also an important factor, both in influencing new benefit plan designs, and in making it more difficult to change existing designs. Companies commonly cover unionized (and sometimes other hourly) groups with defined benefit plans with flat dollar formulas while salaried groups are covered by final average pay plans. Negotiated plans are more often flat- dollar plans, with periodically negotiated increases in the benefit per year of service. Defined benefit plans covering unionized groups may be either single-employer plans or industry-wide multiemployer plans. Unions prefer flat dollar plans so that they can negotiate increases.

Company attempts to change pensions and/or reduce or eliminate retiree health benefits may also become a factor in new unionization.

As of the early 1990s, many of the traditional entitlement-oriented employers are trying to shift more to a compensation orientation. However, most large employers still try to encourage and support career employment. These are some of the changes larger employers appear likely to make during the next decade:

- Continued use of defined benefit plans as the base level of retirement benefit.

- Increased emphasis on the matched savings component of the retirement program.

- Increased choice in employee savings vehicles and defined contribution plans.

- Reduced support for retiree health benefits as some companies discontinue their plans, while those who keep their plans increase retiree cost sharing and introduce features like age and/or service linked contributions.

- Reductions in early retirement subsidies, and more program designs that encourage later retirement.

- Limitations on withdrawal of funds for non-retirement purposes in response to expanded federal regulations.

For smaller employers, the situation in the early 1990s is very different. Small businesses start often--some grow and many others go out of business. Those that grow are likely eventually to offer some type of pension benefits. Smaller employers with one or a small number of owners were likely to offer defined benefit plans in the past. These plans helped the owners shelter assets for retirement from taxation. However, changes in federal tax and employee benefit laws have significantly reduced the opportunity of owners to shelter assets for retirement and have imposed many new restrictions on pension plans.

The changes in pension law over the last decade have driven small employers away from defined benefit pension plans to a significant extent. The costs of operating such plans are exorbitant for very small employers, and many of these plans have terminated. Small businesses more commonly provide defined contribution plans, but many will offer no pension benefits at all in the future. Medium-sized businesses with up to about 500 employees are also shifting away from defined benefit to defined contribution plans. As a practical matter, they may also have great difficulty in offering retiree health benefits.

Retiree health benefits are seldom offered by small businesses. Smaller employers must be able to insure active employees' health benefits, and many have trouble securing satisfactory coverage. Insurers who are reluctant to cover small employers' active employees are unlikely to want their retirees. Career employment is not really an issue for employees of small businesses.

Developments for small employers are likely to include:

- Movement away from retirement benefits.

- Use of defined contribution plans, where benefits are offered, including IRAs and SEPs.

- Reliance on packaged products offered by insurance companies, mutual funds or banks.

- Cancellation of retiree health benefits where they are currently provided.

- Lack of a defined retirement policy.

The Total Retirement Package

A key question is whether in the future, pension plan design, acute medical care and long-term care will be addressed in an integrated fashion. An increasing number of employers are recognizing the importance of doing this today. At the same time, several barriers impede full integration of these benefits. These barriers include:

- Major differences in tax treatment, nondiscrimination rules and other regulations applying to this range of benefit programs.

- Major differences in tradition and customs among employers.

- Major differences in funding approaches for different benefits.

- Employers' perception that if they offer long-term care, they must cover those benefits through insurance to avoid long-term obligations.

- Community priorities and practices that provide pensions on a very common basis, retiree health less frequently, and long-term care even less often.

It remains to be seen whether these benefits are integrated and how.

THE DEFINED BENEFIT VS.
DEFINED CONTRIBUTION PLAN CHOICE

My colleagues and I have been involved in many studies to examine the possibility of converting defined benefit plans to defined contribution plans. Generally, at the end of the study, the company decides not to change. Why? Where are all of the promised benefits of the defined contribution plan?

Our experience can be summarized as follows: When financial considerations and risk are the key drivers of a company's decision about plan structure, and when benefit level is unimportant, the company is likely to move to a defined contribution plan. However, that is a rare situation. Most companies' benefit decisions are driven by human resources policy. They generally decide to continue their defined benefit plans because these plans provide the most effective means to provide adequate benefits to career employees without excessive spending for those who leave early. These issues are discussed further below.

Mr. Biggs indicates that there is little doubt that in 1990 the defined benefit plan is in decline, with few new plans being formulated and many existing ones being abandoned. He does not cite the difference in experience between small and large employers in this regard. A December 1990 study by Richard A. Ippolito published by the Pension Benefit Guaranty Corporation, titled, "Pension Plan Choice, 1979-1987: Clarifications and Extensions,"indicates that the number of workers covered by a primary defined benefit plan fell substantially. The study states that:

"The aggregate results, however, commingle two contrary trends relating to plan size. Among plans with more than 100, but fewer than 1,000 participants, there was a clear shift in preferences away from defined benefit plans. The data support two potential explanations for these preference changes: increases in administrative costs; and the introduction of a new type of pension plan introduced in 1979 legislation. The study did not include plans with fewer than 100 participants. Among plans with more than 1,000 participants, there was no evidence of a shift in preferences away from defined benefit plans. In fact, there was a small shift in favor of these types of plans.''

The 1979 legislation referred to was the authorization for 401(k) plans, which permit employees of for-profit employers to save pre-tax dollars for retirement and pay tax on those dollars and the investment earnings on them when they are paid out as benefits. This development called into question the future of defined benefit plans.

We can look at the future and the likely role of defined benefit plans for larger employers if we look at the rationale for retirement plans and the decisions employers make in choosing plan type.

For small employers, there is not much to decide in looking at defined benefit plans. The complexity of regulations has driven the administrative cost up so that the minimum cost of operating such plans is out of reach for most very small employers.

For other employers, the next question concerns attitude about the financial risk related to retirement plan sponsorship. Some employers are unwilling to bear financial risk, and in such cases, the defined contribution plan is the logical choice. However, this choice is generally made at considerable cost. Defined contribution plans generally pay out more dollars than defined benefit plans to those who leave early. For an employer targeting a specific benefit level at retirement age, defined contribution plans tend to be more expensive for each dollar of retirement benefit delivered than defined benefit plans. Defined contribution plans are generally more expensive for another reason. The investments commonly utilized for the two types of plans differ, and defined benefit plans typically are invested in riskier investments with greater long-term returns on assets.

Where risk is not the key driver of the plan structure decision, human resources philosophy comes into play. There are two key philosophical issues: Is the employer more oriented to entitlement (paternalism) or to compensation? Also, how important are encouraging and supporting career employment, and paying out retirement dollars to long-service employees who leave at retirement age? Defined benefit plans as structured in 1991 are the most cost-effective way to pay adequate retirement benefits to career employees and to minimize payments to those who leave at earlier ages. They also offer employers the flexibility to offer early retirement windows and to make retroactive adjustments in benefit levels as circumstances change. They provide defined levels of income, which facilitate orderly retirement. The employer can control the level of early retirement benefits through the plan design. For these reasons, larger employers are likely to continue offering such benefits.

Mr. Biggs argues that from a human resources management point of view: "One would see employers designing compensation systems that (1) will attract the younger employee, and (2) provide an incentive to older employees to work on for a few years longer. Both of these motivations are better served by the defined contribution plan.''

With respect to attracting younger employees, there are probably more efficient methods of accomplishing this than defined contribution pension plans. It is the commentator's opinion that pension plans are not a significant factor in attracting younger employees, regardless of form, but it is clear that younger employees benefit more from most defined contribution plans and that they generally prefer them. With respect to the second issue, defined benefit plans offer more flexibility in permitting an employer either to include or exclude incentives to retire at various ages. They also permit control of the benefit level relative to pay. One of the attributes of defined contribution plans is that the employee bears the investment risk as well as all inflation risk, so that benefits relative to pay can be much higher or lower than expected at the time plans were designed many years earlier. If benefits are much higher, the plans probably serve as an incentive to retire early, whereas if benefits are lower, they serve as an incentive to retire later.

In considering the issue of later retirement, the relative incentive between defined benefit and defined contribution plans depends on the benefit adjustment method used by the defined benefit plan. The defined contribution plan will continue crediting investment income to the participant, and generally will also call for continued contributions. Once the fund is large, investment income is considerable, and so long as the funds remain in the qualified retirement plan, the investment income is tax deferred. This can be an incentive to delay retirement. In contrast, defined benefit plans are required to continue crediting service, but are not required to offer actuarial increases after normal retirement age. Most plans do not offer actuarial increases; doing so is opposite to most employers' human resource policies today. This is somewhat of a disincentive to delayed retirement. If employers wish to encourage delayed retirement, they have the option to include actuarial increases to benefits.

Mr. Biggs points out that labor force mobility continues to increase, and that such mobility leads to employee, employer and societal preference for defined contribution plans. I do not agree with this statement. It seems to me that whether the employer will prefer such plans depends on priorities and objectives, and that an employer who wishes to reduce turnover will prefer defined benefit plans. In contrast, increased mobility may force us to focus on pension issues related to mobility. This may lead to restrictions on use of lump-sum distributions for non-retirement purposes and more focus on pension portability. Depending on the nature of future changes in requirements, new rules could push employers toward defined benefit plans or toward defined contribution plans.

Mr. Biggs perceives a growing preference among the population for personal control over pension assets and cites TIAA-CREF experience as proof that such control is desirable. Certainly, choice and control are popular with employees, but experience would not support the assertion that they are always used well. When lump sums are paid out before retirement, the funds often are spent rather than rolled over into other retirement plans. This happens so often that restrictions on distribution options are a likely area for future legislation.

In addition, it is the experience of many defined contribution plans that when employees have choices of investment options, 75 percent or more of the funds are invested in fixed income choices with guaranteed principal, even though long-term returns on equities are substantially greater. (TIAA-CREF may have different experience, but it does not have a typical participant population.) Participants who follow this investment pattern are seeking the same kind of security offered by defined benefit plans.

We should note one other fact about control. Control probably means more individual responsibility and may mean lower retirement benefits in the end. In an environment of increased employee control, employers faced with limited resources are less likely to invest dollars in retirement benefits. Retirement savings responsibility would be shifted disproportionately to individual employees, which is not in their best interest.

Mr. Biggs gives a gloomy prognosis for defined benefit plans from a regulatory outlook. I agree with that point, provided that past trends continue. I am hopeful, however, that this will not be the case, and as indicated above, I would hope that this trend can be reversed. As the Baby Boom matures, they will have a strong incentive to see this trend reversed.

Mr. Biggs strongly supports the use of defined contribution plans and sees them as growing in prominence in the future. Based on the past and present records of retirement benefits and employee behavior (and needs), I believe that defined benefit plans will continue to play an important role in human resources planning and that a much more balanced viewpoint is appropriate.

7

Trends in Health Among the American Population

Eileen M. Crimmins
and
Dominique G. Ingegneri

INTRODUCTION

This paper will address the issue of recent and future trends in health among the American population middle aged and older. At the outset it is useful to acknowledge that not all researchers agree as to the direction of changes in health in the recent past and this disagreement leads to shaky ground on which to predict the future. Acknowledging this, however, we will attempt to join the theory and the data concerning health change in the past into a plausible picture which indicates that in recent years there has been no substantial improvement in self-reported health among the American population. In fact, the 1970's appear to have been years of some deterioration in health; and the first part of the l980's appear to be years of relative stability in health with some hint of improvement in the most recent years. We have yet to experience any sustained period of improvement in reported health among the middle aged and older population.

In the first section of the paper we will describe the changing relationship between morbidity and mortality in recent years and how this has led to disagreement among researchers as to the expected direction of change in health over the past 25 years. Next we will turn to the issue of measuring change in health. In the third section of the paper we will present data on observed changes in health over a twenty year period. Finally, we will discuss the implications of the recent changes in health for the future.

Why is there a question as to whether health is improving or deteriorating?

Some may wonder how it is possible to question the direction of trends in health when it is obvious that remarkable strides have been made in extending life in recent years. Life expectancy at birth was 74.9 years in 1988, up from 70.2 in 1968; remarkable improvement in only twenty years. Not only has life

expectancy at birth lengthened but improvement has also occurred at unprecedented rates at the oldest ages with life expectancy at age 65 increasing by about
two years over the same period. It is the very factors which have produced the
remarkable declines in mortality since the mid-1960's which call into question
whether people in 1990 are healthier than those in the 1960's as well as longer
lived.

Throughout much of this century mortality has declined rapidly in the United
States. Since the late 1960's, however, the causes of death responsible for the
mortality decline have differed from earlier mortality declines. From 1900
through the 1950's mortality decline was largely due to reduction in death rates
from infectious diseases. Since the mid 1960's, mortality decline has been due
primarily to the reduction of chronic diseases especially heart disease (Crimmins,
1981). This switch in causes of mortality decline from infectious to chronic
conditions may have resulted in a new relationship between trends in mortality
and trends in health of the surviving population.

The decline in mortality that preceded the late 1960's came about either
because people no longer got diseases like polio, measles and smallpox or
because people were treated and cured of diseases like tuberculosis and scarlet
fever. People no longer got diseases because of public health measures that
improved sanitary conditions, because they were inoculated or vaccinated
against a number of conditions, or because with economic development the
conditions of everyday life and the resistance of the population to disease
improved. They were cured of diseases contracted because of the improvement in
treatment of infectious diseases.

Over the long run, deaths were reduced from these diseases because both the
incidence of the diseases and the case fatality rates were decreased. If mortality
decline occurs either because people do not develop diseases or because people
are cured of diseases they otherwise would have died from, the health of the
surviving population should be improved. Health of the population probably
improved when mortality from infectious diseases accounted for most of the
mortality decline.

When mortality decline is due to reduced death rates from chronic diseases, it
is not clear that the improvement in mortality should be accompanied by
improvement in health of the surviving population. If mortality declined because
people did not get chronic diseases, or got them at an older age, or because
people were cured of chronic diseases, we would expect improved health with
declining mortality. However, while we may be able to increasingly avoid or
delay death from a number of chronic diseases; we are unable to ''cure'' or
prevent most chronic diseases. Once one has a disease like heart disease, one has
it for life. The question then becomes are people less likely to get diseases or less
likely to get them by a specific age or are people just as likely to get diseases
today but more likely to survive once they have disease. In the first case,
morbidity or ill health in the surviving population could be lower with declining
mortality; in the second case, it would undoubtedly be higher.

Three views on likely change in health in recent years

It is disagreement as to whether mortality has declined because people are not getting diseases or are getting them later or whether people are merely surviving longer with diseases which leads to different views as to the likely change in health in recent years. Fries (1980) is perhaps most responsible for the idea that improved mortality will be accompanied by lower morbidity and certainly for terming this occurrence the "compression of morbidity." He expects that the "rectangularization of the survival curve will be accompanied by rectangulariza-tion of the curve showing the age of onset of chronic disease." This means that as mortality declines the age at onset of morbidity will both be delayed to later ages and compressed into a shorter period of time at the end of life. Using the terminology of the preceding section, Fries believes that the incidence of chronic disease has and will be reduced as mortality from chronic disease declines.

The opposite view is expressed by Kramer (1980) and Gruenberg (1977) who argue that when mortality decline is due to reduced death rates from chronic conditions, chronic disease prevalence will increase as mortality rates are lowered. While death from chronic disease is being prevented, they feel that the lowered mortality rates are not the result of either a reduced incidence of chronic disease or a reduction in the rate of disease progression but of reductions in death from what they call the "lethal sequelae" of these conditions. Thus, they believe that the case fatality rate has decreased but that this has occurred at an advanced stage of disease progression so that it has resulted in an unhealthier population - an argument termed "the failure of success."

Manton (1982) has proposed a position somewhere between the two outlined above. He describes the relationship between mortality and morbidity when life expectancy is increasing as "dynamic equilibrium." This means that the "severity and rate of progression of chronic disease are directly related to mortality changes so that, correlated with mortality reduction, there is a corre-sponding reduction in the rate of progression of the 'aging' of the vital organ systems of the body." Manton seems to accept the idea of Fries that mortality decline may be accompanied by decline in incidence of some diseases but he feels, like Kramer and Gruenberg, that the bulk of the recent mortality decline was due to decreases in the case fatality rate. Manton, however, feels that the reduced mortality has been due to saved lives at earlier stages of disease progression than Kramer and Gruenberg. This leads Manton to expect that mortality decline will be accompanied by increasing prevalence but decreased severity of chronic disease within age groups.

To sum up these three views we turn to the basic epidemiological equation which views morbidity prevalence or how much sickness exists at a point in time as a function of incidence and duration of illness. The implications of the three theoretical approaches for the relationships between mortality decline on meas-ures of incidence, prevalence, and duration of morbidity are shown in Table 1. Manton's idea that duration be separated into two ways of increasing duration - eliminating the lethal consequences and decreasing the rate of progression of disease - is included for clarity.

Table 1.   Three Theoretical Views as to the Direction of Morbidity Change with recent Mortality Change in the U.S.

	Prevalence	Incidence	Duration[*]	
			Sequelae	Rate of Progression
Fries	↓	↓	=	↓
Gruenberg, Kramer	↑	=	↓	=
Manton	↑	=↓	↓	↓

[*] ↓ in sequelae or rate of progression is ↑ in duration
Source: Crimmins, E.M. (1990).

Two of the views described above lead to expectations of increased prevalence of morbidity or sickness in the population when mortality declines from chronic conditions. One leads to an expectation of less morbidity in a longer-lived population. Lower prevalence would occur when mortality decline occurs because disease incidence is reduced, or fewer people of a given age have developed a disease. Higher prevalence exists where incidence is not changed but mortality declines because diseases are managed and treated so that they do not progress as rapidly to death. When this happens individuals live longer with diseases increasing the proportion of persons with disease in the population.

Other Factors Affecting the Relationship Between Trends in Mortality and Trends in Health

While these researchers have carefully described how they see mortality change and morbidity change relating for diseases that cause death, there are two reasons why none of the above scenarios is likely to adequately describe the observed relationship between mortality and health change. Each of these reasons lends support to the notion that health would not necessarily improve with mortality. One is that the discussion is really limited to the relationship between change in mortality and ill health from diseases which are killer diseases like heart disease, cancer, and cerebrovascular conditions. Morbidity from lethal diseases is only a part of the ill health suffered by older Americans. Investigations of health among middle aged and older Americans have shown that many of their health problems come from diseases which are not major causes of mortality. In fact, people rarely, if ever, die from a number of diseases which are among the major causes of health and disability including arthritis, musculoskeletal impairments, vision or hearing loss, and Alzheimer's disease (Verbrugge, 1984; Crimmins, 1990). Because such a significant proportion of poor health is caused by non-lethal causes, there is no reason to expect that changes in mortality and morbidity will be as closely related as the three scenarios outlined in Table 1 suggest.

The theoretical arguments presented above ignore the interactive process between diseases and conditions and their effects on the distribution of frailty or capacity to resist disease or the progression of disease of the surviving population. Individual frailty can arise either from genetic endowments or past insults to one's ability to resist diseases. As mortality declines, those saved from death do not tend to be persons of average constitution but a weaker and frailer group who would have perished under a more severe mortality regime (Alter and Riley, 1989; Poterba and Summers, 1987). Thus, with more mortality decline the population becomes more heavily weighted with a frailer group more susceptible to a whole host of diseases and conditions than the average survivor in the population. This effect should increase morbidity or ill health among survivors in a period of declining mortality.

Empirical Studies Examining the Trend in Health

To this point, we have discussed largely theoretical rather than empirical approaches to the issue of changing health. A large number of empirical studies based on national data have reported deterioration in the health of middle-aged and older Americans (Colvez and Blanchet, 1981; Verbrugge, 1984, 1989; Crimmins, Saito, and Ingegneri, 1989; Crimmins, 1987, 1990; Riley, 1990). Most of these report on health change during the 1970's but Riley has found continued deterioration in health between 1982 and 1986. Ycas (1987) on the other hand found that the deterioration in health reported in the 1970's had stopped in the 1980's.

There are also a number of studies that argue for no substantial change in health among the older population in recent years. Poterba and Summers (1987) argue for little change in average level of health on the basis of the frailty argument; they do however expect an increase in the variance in the health of the population. Other researchers who have concentrated on the older population have found little change using some measures and samples of the population (Schneider and Guralnik, 1987). It is difficult to find researchers presenting evidence of improving health. The one study that argues for improving health of the older population examines change in measures relative to other ages rather than absolute health (Palmore, 1986).

This phenomenon of deterioration in reported health is also found in a variety of other countries: Canada (Wilkins and Adams, 1983), Great Britain (Riley, 1990; Bebbington, 1988), Japan (Riley, 1990), and Australia (Mathers, 1990). In addition evidence from the Alameda county study which follows multiple cohorts indicates that more recent cohorts who have experienced lower mortality have higher rates of disability and a higher prevalence of diseases at specific ages (Kaplan, 1991).

Empirical Evidence on Health Change in Recent Years in the U.S.

Now we turn to empirical evidence in trends in health. While we present evidence similar to that discussed above, ours is fairly unique in that annual data are presented for a twenty year period. In order to test the theoretical approaches discussed above it will be useful to examine indicators of prevalence, incidence, age at onset and duration of ill health along with measures of frailty of the population. The only data source that allows study of detailed measures of health over any period of time is the National Health Interview Survey. This is a national survey ongoing since 1957 from which data representative of the noninstitutionalized population of the United States are produced annually. Every year over 100,000 individuals who live in 40,000 households are interviewed. Data tapes are available annually since 1969. Because of major changes in survey procedures and questionnaire format introduced in the 1982 survey the results are comparable within the periods 1969 to 1981 and 1982 to the present (Kovar and Poe, 1985; U.S. Department of Health, Education, and Welfare, 1975). For many indicators some incomparability is introduced across the 1981 to 1982 years and caution must be exercised in examining trends across these dates. We have adjusted the figures used in this paper to take into account the procedural changes but still recommend caution in interpreting change from 1981 to 1982.[1]

Limitation of Activity.

The major indicator of the prevalence of ill-health available in the NHIS is the "Limitation of Activity." This measure is an indicator of long-term disability in the population which reflects the general functional ability of a population. It is the percent of the population that is "unable" or "limited" in ability to carry out its normal activity because of a chronic health condition.[2] The percent limited in activity for each of four age groups in each year from 1969 through 1988 is shown in Figure 1. The two age groups in the top panel could be considered the working ages; the two in the bottom panel would be the retired ages. The general pattern is an increase in activity limitation or a decline in health from 1969 through the mid 1970's, followed by a six to eight year period of stability, and then a hint of the beginning of a downturn or some improvement in health in the most recent years. This is true for those 45 to 74. The one age group that does not follow this pattern is those 75 years of age and over. This age group experiences neither a clear increase nor decrease in morbidity over the period.

We can also examine change in the incidence of activity limitation and the duration of limiting activity in order to see the reason for the change in prevalence. Unfortunately, these indicators are only available for the survey from 1969 through 1981. The incidence of activity limitation is constructed here as the number of people becoming limited in the last year among those who were not limited at the beginning of the year. The incidence of limitation increased in the age groups for those 45 through 74 from 1969 through the mid-1970's (Figure 2). About the time the prevalence of activity limitation became stable, in the mid

FIGURE 1
Percent of the Population (by Age) Limited in Activity
due to a Chronic Health Problem: 1969 - 1088

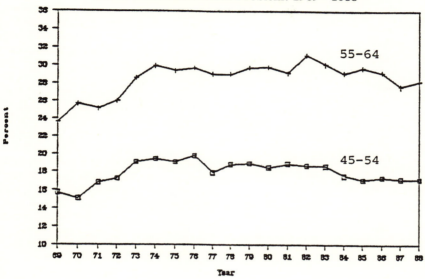

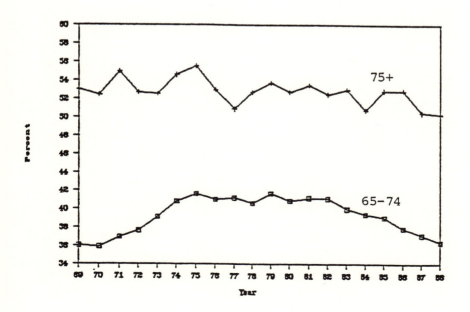

FIGURE 2
Annual Incidence of Activity Limitation due to a Chronic Health Problem
(by Age): 1969 - 1988

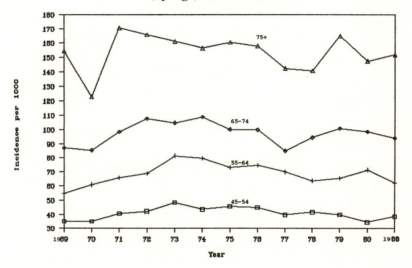

1970's, the incidence stopped increasing. This means that the increase in the prevalence of limitation was due in part to the fact that an increasing number of people were falling sick in each age group each year during the early 1970's. There appears to be some slight trend toward decrease in the incidence after 1973.

The duration of limitation or average length of time that people have been limited has increased steadily over the years from 1969 through 1981 for those above age 54 (Figure 3). For most of the age groups the average duration of limitation was between 6 and 6 1/2 years in 1969. In 1981 the average was closer to 7 1/2 years. This would coincide with increased survival over the period for people with limitation. For those in the 45-54 age range, there is no consistent trend in the duration of limitation but it does appear to be slightly downward between 1970 and 1978. Age at onset of limitation remained almost unchanged for all age groups between 1970 and 1981 (Figure 4).

The pattern of increasing prevalence of activity limitation up through the mid 1970's would seem to arise from both an increase in the incidence of limiting activity and an increase in the survival of limited people. After the early 1970's the increase in incidence was slightly reversed but the increase in duration - undoubtedly resulting from a continuing increase in the survival of those with limitation - continued. It is this increase in duration which probably results in the stability of the prevalence measure up through the beginning of the 1980's. At the end of the 1970's there appears to be some slight trend toward decreasing incidence and some leveling off of the increase in duration but virtually no change in the age at onset of limiting conditions over the entire period.

FIGURE 3
Duration of Activity Limitation (in Months) by Age:
1970 - 1981

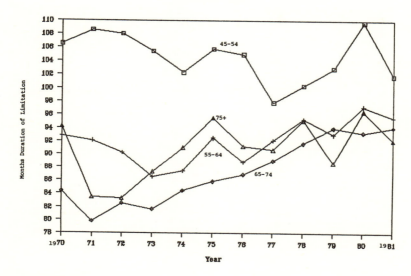

Restricted Activity Days.

Another indicator of the prevalence of ill-health is the number of days in a year that a group must restrict its activity because of any form of ill-health either a short-term or a long-term illness. This indicator is annualized even though the basic questions refer to a two week reference period before the interview. A restricted activity day is a day on which your activities are adjusted because of a health problem. Trends in this indicator for each of the four age groups are shown in Figure 5 (Panel A).

The number of restricted activity days generally increases for each age group up through the mid 1980's after that there is, again, a hint of a decline. Using this indicator of health, the trend to deteriorating health lasted longer than it did using the activity limitation indicator.

In order to get a better idea of the reason behind the trend for the mean number of activity days and to examine the issue of change in the variance as well as the mean in a measure of health, we examine the change at either end of the continuum of restricted activity days: those who experience no restricted activity days and those for whom every day is a day of restricted activity. If the increase is due solely to change at the upper end of the continuum, it would be an indicator of increasing frailty or severity of illness among the population. If there is increase only in the percentage of people having some disability but not having all days disabled, one would tend to think that health was worsening among the healthier members of the population. It appears that the overall increase in the

FIGURE 4
Mean Age at Onset of Activity Limitation by Current Age: 1970 - 1981

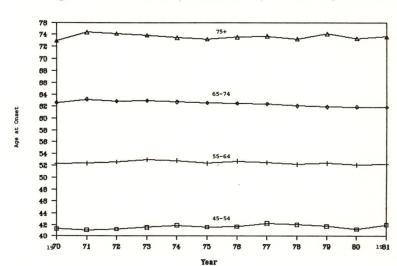

mean throughout most of the period comes from both a decrease in the percent of each age group that experiences no restriction in activity (Figure 5, Panel B) and an increase in the percentage of the population with fourteen days of restricted activity in the past two weeks (Figure 5, Panel C). This indicates that the increase in the mean comes from a combination of factors: more people experiencing some illness and more people being ill for the entire reference period, both movements toward worse health. Interestingly, the recent change in direction in the trend in restricted activity days seems to result from change in the direction of the trend in each of these indicators. In the last few years, there are more people with no restricted activity days and fewer people with all restricted activity days.

It is possible to examine change over time in the number of severe restricted activity days: days when one spends at least half the day in bed because of a health problem (Figure 6). There appears to be a very small and insignificant increase in the number of bed days for most age groups through the 1970's. Indicating little trend in ill health severe enough to keep one in bed.

We can examine change in either end of the continuum of bed days: no bed days and 14 bed days during the reference period. Again, we want to see if while the mean is stable there is change in the ends of the continuum. There is some slight decrease in the percentage of most of the age groups with no days up through the 1980's but the percentage changes are quite small. The trend in the proportion with 14 bed days is barely discernible but slightly upward, at least into the 1980's.

There are some consistencies and some inconsistencies in the story told by the data so far. The consistencies lie in the general incidence and prevalence trends

FIGURE 5
Mean Annual Restricted Activity Days, Percent with 0 Days, and Percent with 14 Days (by Age): 1969 - 1988

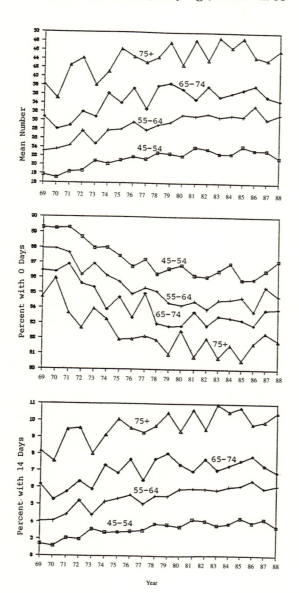

FIGURE 6
Mean Annual Bed Disability Days, Percent with 0 Days, and Percent with 14 Days (by Age): 1969 - 1988

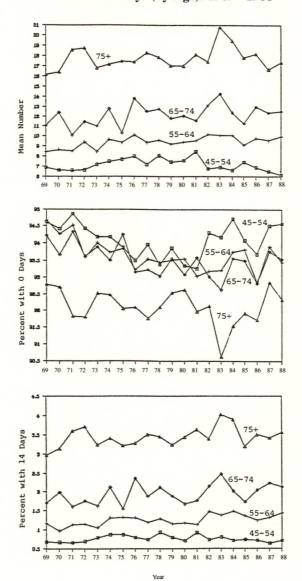

Year

over time while the inconsistencies derive from the actual timing of shifts in the trends depending on the indicator of health. Limitation of activity peaked earlier than restricted activity days and seems to be more clearly improving in recent years.

Table 2.   Percent of the U.S. Population 65+ Having Difficulty Performing Specific Functions: 1962, 1975, 1986

	YEAR		
FUNCTION	1962	1975	1986
Dressing	8.7	9.7	6.0
Bathing	10.2	9.7	10.0
Going out of House	10.1	13.5	11.6
Preparing meals	11.8	9.3	7.4

Source: Authors' tabulation from 1962 and 1975 National Surveys of the Older Population collected by Ethel Shanas; 1986 National Health Interview Survey.

Frailty.

Now we turn to other indicators of frailty and severity of ill-health. We would like to see if we can find an indication of systematic change in the amount of frailty in the older population over time. No similar indicators are available at multiple points in time for the younger population. The indicators of activity limitation and restricted activity days are measures of health problems that do not necessarily indicate long-term frailty. Most surveys of the health of the older population, however, now include fairly standardized measures of the abilities to perform personal care activities (known as activities of daily living or ADL functions) and activities which allow for independent living (known as Instrumental Activities of Daily Living or IADL functions). People who are unable to provide their own personal and home care are the frailest in society. There is a growing consensus that this is the best way to measure health when one is interested in the issues of independence and institutionalization at least among the older population.

In order to examine trends in frailty we will examine change over three dates in the proportion of the noninstitutionalized population 65 years of age and older that is unable to perform each of four specific activities.[3] The first three are usually included in ADL activities and include: dressing, bathing, and going out of the house. The last function, preparing meals, is usually included with IADL activities. The three dates at which comparable data are available are 1962, 1975, and 1986. For the first two dates the data are from the Surveys of the Older

Population collected under the direction of Ethel Shanas. Data for 1986 are from a special supplement to the National Health Interview Survey.

If one looks at the change between 1962 and 1986, there is significant decrease in inability to dress and prepare meals and no significant change in ability to go out or bathe. This pattern suggests slightly improving functioning or less frailty but there really is little consistency in the pattern of change over the whole 24 year period. These data lend little support to those who have emphasized the role of increasing frailty or dependency when frailty is thought of as the weakest members in the population.

Are the Data Reflecting Trends in "Real" Health or Only "Reported" Health?"

It is possible that the data do not reflect changes in "real" health but rather changes in "reported" health. All data are self- reported and all definitions of health are somewhat subjective. Are there other explanations of the observed trends that would result only from changes in assessment or reporting of health?

Two possibilities have been suggested; the importance of which, we believe, can be discounted. In the first of these, Barsky (1988) has suggested that deteriorating health among Americans can be explained by changing assessment of health. He believes that increasing fixation on health has caused us to become "worried sick." We worry so much about health now that we are more likely to see ourselves as sick than in the past. This explanation, however, does not fit with the observed time trend as there is no evidence that Americans were fixated on their health in the 1970's but lost the fixation in the 1980's; nor does it fit with the fact that the same phenomenon has been observed in a variety of countries; nor does it fit the pattern of increasing prevalence of most types of diseases not just more subjectively defined diseases. The second hypothesis has been suggested by researchers at the National Center for Health Statistics, the organization responsible for both monitoring trends in the nation's health and collecting the data utilized here (Wilson and Drury, 1984). Because researchers at NCHS could not believe that health could be deteriorating, they suggested that their improved survey procedures and design were resulting in an increased reporting of ill health. We do not feel that this is likely to be the explanation because the pattern of increased disability during the 1970's and improvement in the 1980's is also found in the CPS disability surveys in the U.S. as well as in data from other countries. In addition, Bound and Waidman (1990) have estimated that the likely effect of such changes, if they exist, would be quite small.

Another explanation of the increase in reported ill health during the 1970's that was favored by economists who examined trends in reported health for only the working age population was that the trend represents the availability and generosity of disability payments (Parsons, 1980). Certainly the time trend in work disability does match the timing of changes in generosity and ease of obtaining benefits. Disability benefits were easier to obtain and more generous in the 1970's than they had been earlier; policy changes made them more difficult to obtain again in the 1980's. More recently, economists studying work disability have reduced the weight given to changing disability benefits in explaining the time trend while still seeing it as a part of the explanation (Wolfe and Havemann, 1990; Bound and Waidman, 1990).

This explanation does not account for reported deterioration in health among non-workers as well as workers nor in the similarity of trends for other countries. In addition, this explanation assumes that additions to the disabled roles in the 1970's were malingerers who were then removed from the roles in the 1980's; however, attempts to investigate the assumption that the additions to the disabled came from the able-bodied (Bound, 1989; Crimmins and Pramaggiore, 1988) have tended to show that the increases in the disabled population in the 1970's came from a population with the same health levels as the already disabled rather than a healthier population. Bound (1989) has also shown that those removed from the disability pool in the 1980' s were not able to return to work. At this point, I think people still believe that disability policies have had some effect on the working-age trend in reported health but that the effect was overestimated in early studies. It is certainly possible that it accounts in part for increases and then improvement in ill-health and incidence seen in the data.

There are those who emphasize the idea that accommodation to health problems may have changed among the American population. People now may be more willing to change their lives at an earlier phase of the disease in order to prevent progression of the disease (Verbrugge, 1984, 1989; Bound and Waidman, 1990; Wolfe and Haveman, 1990; Crimmins and Pramaggiore, 1988). We have found some evidence to support this as an explanation of the rise in disability among the older working age population in the 1970's. Between 1969 and 1980, the percentage of men who suffered from any limiting condition who also reported that they currently worked decreased remarkably (Figure 7). Between 1969 and 1980, this percentage fell from 73 to 61 for those 45 to 54 years of age, from 61 percent to 47 percent for those 55 to 61 years of age, and from 47 to 29 percent for those 62 to 64 years old. There is little change in this percentage after 1980. We assume this increasing accommodation to disease could probably be explained by a gradual phasing in of the disability program. A period during which both doctors and patients learned of the existence of the program and the possibility of non-work with benefits. While this growing willingness to accommodate to diseases would be related to increases in disability, it is not clear that it would cause reported increases in the amount of limited activity. It does, however, indicate the possibility of a period of growing accommodation to health problems that could be related to increasing reports of ill-health.

One final explanation of the observed trend in health that would explain changes in ''reported'' health that could occur while ''real'' health remained unchanged is that peoples' self assessments of their health have changed not because of internal change as suggested by Barsky but because of external clues from their contact with the medical establishment that led them to believe that their health worsened in the 1970's and then improved in the 1980's. The time trends in hospital discharge rates for the population 45 years of age and over

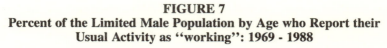

FIGURE 7
**Percent of the Limited Male Population by Age who Report their
Usual Activity as "working": 1969 - 1988**

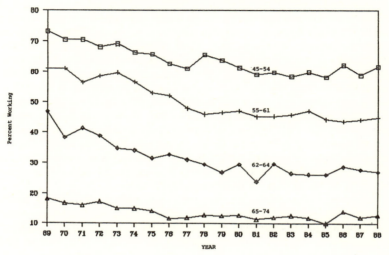

change in a fashion that resembles the time pattern of changes in self-assessments of health (Figure 8).

We realize that there is real danger in assuming this direction of causality between reported health and health-care utilization but there is remarkable similarity in the observed trends for the two series. Hospitalization indicators are one measure of the severity of treatment people have received and doctors' assessments of peoples' health because people do not generally choose to admit themselves to hospitals. While we have some idea of what caused the reversal in the direction of the trend in hospital usage, no one has suggested that it is related to improving health but rather to issues of payment and technology. Changes in doctors' views of their patients' health are not important to this argument but a change in the likelihood of being hospitalized may be interpreted as a change in health by laymen who would be likely to think a condition less serious if it is treated outside of a hospital.

Future Trends in Health

The uncertainty about the reasons for any past change in health leaves us little basis for projection of the future. What we have learned from the recent past is that improvement in mortality does not have to be matched by improvement in morbidity. The relationship between morbidity change and mortality change depends on the stage of the disease process at which intervention occurs. This stage has changed over recent decades and is likely to continue to change in future decades.

FIGURE 8
Percent of the Population by Age Hospitalized in the Past Year: 1969 - 1988

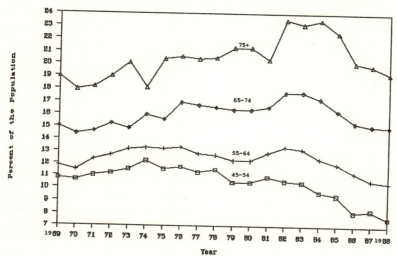

When researchers and clinicians turned their full attention to chronic conditions in the early 1960's, they began by examining ways to treat people in order to lessen the likelihood that people would die or become increasingly debilitated by disease. This involved treatment and research on existing diseases. As time has passed, our understanding of the disease process and our research focus has moved back toward the inception of the disease for many conditions. Certainly, a very high proportion of research effort is now concentrated on identifying risk factors and attempting to delay or prevent the development of diseases. When we can increasingly prevent or delay the disease process, the disease incidence will decrease and the age at onset of diseases will increase. At this point the population should experience improving health.

It is possible that this process has begun in the 1980's. The life style risk factor changes which were adopted by large numbers of the population in the 1970's - increased exercise, decreased smoking, decreased consumption of fat - may be beginning to show results.

In addition, medical technologies are beginning to show promise of more fruitful early intervention for a number of major killer diseases. Clearly, research into ways to prevent the development and progression of non-fatal diseases must be increased in order to be able to make severe inroads into current levels of disability. Currently, however, there appears to be little we can do to prevent the progression of some of the more important non-fatal diseases like arthritis and musculoskeletal conditions.

The basic epidemiological approach that we've used here - that of looking at prevalence, incidence, and duration of illness - is useful for examining change over time in a population but it ignores the return to good health from poor health which is an important aspect of any individual's pattern of change in health. Recent studies of health change in the older ages have employed a dynamic perspective to examine health change in both directions - getting sick and getting well (Crimmins and Saito, 1990; Rogers, et al., 1990). These studies have demonstrated the importance of rehabilitation to wellness in affecting the overall level of health in a population. Emphasis on rehabilitation or the return of lost functioning which can accompany chronic disease is also important in determining the societal level of good health.

ENDNOTES

1. The changes instituted in 1982 had striking effects on the level of ill-health reported for some age groups on both limitation of activity days. In addition, even a cursory glance at the time trend data for limitation of activity indicates that 1977 was an unusual year. A special supplement on disability was added to the main survey during this year to be administered to those with some limitation of activity. It appears that the interviewers found fewer people limited in activity in order to reduce the number of supplements they would have to administer.

The method applied to determine the adjustment for the series of limitation of activity was to regress the annual proportion reporting limitation of activity for each age group on year, year squared, a dummy variable for 1977, and a dummy variable for the time period from 1982 through 1988. The adjustment was made using the coefficients for the 1977 dummy and the 1982 through 1988 dummy.

For each series the equation resulted in an R^2 greater than .90. Adjustments were made when the probability level of the coefficient was .1 or smaller.

The procedure for adjusting restricted activity days was similar except that no indicator for 1977 was included in the regression.

2. 'Normal activity' consists of both what are called major activities and secondary activities. Major activities consist of working, keeping house, and in later years (for those over 69) of performing personal care functions. The percent limited in these major activities can vary by age and sex because of the strength and stamina required for the activity. Thus levels are not always comparable across age-sex groups. 'Secondary activities' consist of other activities such as involvement with community, church, or friends.

3. While each survey contained numerous additional questions about functioning ability, more items were not included in the analysis either because of incompatibility in question or response category format or because questions asked in one year were not asked in another.

Discussions

Eric R. Kingson

COMMENTS

Professor Eileen Crimmins' and Dominique Ingegneri's paper does an excellent job of summarizing perspectives and literature about whether current and projected declines in age-specific mortality rates are and will be accompanied by improvements or decrements in the health of middle-aged and older persons. It also presents informative findings from their research on this topic.

As a discussant for this paper I will first summarize some of what we learn from their interesting paper. Then I will identify several questions and issues that I believe need to be addressed.

WHAT WE LEARN FROM THE PAPER

First, from their analysis and review of the literature we learn that in spite of large increases in life expectancy at birth and at older ages from 1968 through 1988, the health of middle-aged and older Americans, on average, does not appear to have improved. We also learn that this trend is consistent with trends in Canada, Great Britain, Japan, and Australia. The discussion and analysis suggests that recent declines in mortality rates which have been driven primarily by reductions in death rates from chronic illnesses have "resulted in people with health limitation living longer" through these people may not "be very severely impaired" (Crimmins and Ingegnen, 1991). Ironically, They point out, it is "the very factors which have produced the remarkable declines in mortality since the mid-1960's which call into question whether people in 1990 are healthier...as well as longer lived" (Crimmins and Ingegneri, 1991).

Second, we learn of the complexity surrounding the relationship between morbidity and mortality trends. The authors note that to the extent that age-specific mortality rates decline as a result of decreases in infectious disease (as was the case in the first half of the century), then the health of the population should also improve. However, potential health outcomes for the surviving population are more ambiguous when improvements in life expectancy result from reductions in death rates from chronic diseases (as has been the case since the mid-1960's). This is because mortality reductions could be associated with, for example, reductions in the prevalence of chronic diseases or with lengthened periods of survivorship after the onset of such diseases. Morever, the relationship between morbidity and mortality is more difficult to disentangle for two other reasons. As mortality declines, the surviving population tends "to be a frailer group" who is more susceptible to a whole host of diseases." Also, much of the health and disability problems of older persons are a function on non-lethal chronic diseases such as arthritis as opposed to "killer" chronic diseases such as cancer. Thus, reductions in case fatalities from prevention or treatment of killer diseases may actually increase the risk on "non-killer" chronic illnesses (Crimmins and Ingegneri, 1991).

Third, the paper helps clarify the basis for disagreement among those interpreting and forecasting trends in the health of middle-aged and older persons. Such disagreements, we are told, revolve around differing views as to whether it is the postponement of chronic illness or the ability of people to live longer in spite of such ailments which is largely responsible for declining death rates. These differences also revolve around views as to the relative severity of chronic disease prevailing during different periods. At one pole of the debate, there are those who believe that the older population is likely to be both longer lived and healthier because mortality declines are being driven by the prevention, the delay of onset or conceivably the curing of chronic diseases (Crimmins and Ingegneri, 1991). James Fries theory that morbidity is and can be further compressed to shorter periods at the end of life is based on the view that preventive interventions can prevent and delay the onset of chronic illness as well as on the assumption that the human life span is fixed (Fries, 1989). At the other pole, the "failure of success model" suggests that the incidence and rate of chronic disease progression has been stable while case fatalities declined. The result has been to extend the period of survival with chronic illness, thus resulting in a longer lived population with a greater prevalence of chronic disease. Other positions fall between these two poles. For instance, Manton's "dynamic equilibrium" theory causes him "to expect that mortality decline will be accompanied by" more, but less severe, "chronic diseases within age groups" (Crimmins and Ingegneri, 1991).

Fourth, we learn from their careful empirical work that there is no clear trend in the health of the middle-aged and older population from 1969 through 1988. Their analysis of National Health Interview Survey data also suggest that the health of these groups declined during the 1970s and stabilized in the 1980s. These findings are based primarily on analysis of trends for several indicators of health status-including limitations in activity due to chronic health problem, inability to perform one's major activity, incidences of new activity limitations, duration of activity limitations, mean annual restricted activity days, and mean number of bed disability days. These findings based on reports of health status leads to the conclusion that mortality reductions have resulted in people with chronic ailments living longer.

QUESTIONS AND ISSUES NEEDING FURTHUR EXAMINATION

Thankfully, the authors leave their discussants opportunity to raise and begin to address a few questions.

My first question concerns what we should conclude from their and others research about the likely ability of retirees of the future to work longer, given that the substantial literature which addresses these issues is far from conclusive (see Butler, 1982; Feldman, 1983; Feldman, 1991; Fries, 1991; Guralnik, 1991; Manton, 1983; Verbrugge, 1991).

Fries (1991) outlines three possibilities that can affect the ability to work: 1) that life expectancy increases but disabling conditions occur at roughly the same ages with the consequence that we simply add "infirm years to life"; 2) that the average age of disability and life expectancy increase by the same amount, thus increasing the potential number of working years; and 3) that life expectancy increases with the average age of disability increasing by even more, thereby substantially increasing the number of years older people of the future are able to work. Other possibilities exist. Feldman (1991) suggests that life expectancy may increase, especially for persons of higher socioeconomic status, and that the age of onset of disability may, in general, increase for persons of higher socioeconomic groups but not for those of lower status. In other words, there may be bifurcation by social class of the ability to work longer.

Experts such as Fries have suggested that the effective worklives of future older persons will be further lengthened because medical knowledge will reduce the onset of chronic illness, because shifts from manufacturing to service industry employment will reduce occupational trauma and prevention of risk factors are likely to result in a healthier and more functionally independent older population.

On the other hand, there is considerable evidence that we simply do not know whether late-middle-aged and older persons are and will be able to work longer. The authors' findings and review of the literature suggest that we do not know. So do others. Feldman's analysis shows that "disability rates for the population aged fifty-five to seventy show no evidence of a decline in work incapacity" during the recent period of declining mortality (Feldman, 1991). In fact, as several other authors observe, "Empirical evidence for reduced disability in the face of increasing life expectancy is difficult to find" (Kane, Radosevich and Vaupel, 1990). Yet these same authors also point out that "experienced clinicians have noted that the health status of elderly persons seem to have improved greatly in the last two decades." They speculate that we may be experiencing simultaneous increases in the proportions of very healthy elders as well as impaired elders.

The future invites speculation. Biologist Edward Masoro has found that restricting the caloric intake of rats "markedly increases life span, retards a broad spectrum of age-associated physiological changes, and delays or prevents most age-associated diseases" (Masoro, Katz and McMahan, 1989). If these findings have human application, then they would lend support to the view that older people of the future may be able to work longer. (They also suggest we may be hungrier.) Another view suggests that today's elderly and those of the next twenty years may be transition generations--experiencing both greater longevity and greater morbidity. But, as later cohorts of the elderly benefit more from biomedical breakthroughs and more healthful behavior it is possible that most older people may experience a longer life with substantially less disabling disease (Harootyan, 1990; Takeuchi, forthcoming). Others suggest that today's social structures have not caught up to the already changing capacities of older persons and are thus "generally failing to make room for those many workers who as they age, continue to be capable and are not ready for full retirement" (Riley, 1990). Matilda Riley notes that while "the twentieth century has been the era of increasing longevity, the twenty-first century will be the era of social opportunities for older people to age in new and better ways.''

Given all these views, what are we to conclude about the ability of older persons to work longer in the future?

My second question--which is really more of a suggestion --concerns whether there is more need to examine variations in health status and trends between advantaged and disadvantaged populations. Is it possible that we are concentrating too much on aggregate morbidity and mortality trends and missing an important part of the story about the ability of today's and tomorrow's older people to work? I am curious about what differences might arise in Professor Crimmins' analysis of morbidity trends if they were further disaggregated--not only by age groups--but also by race and income class. Related to this, it may be that their analysis would be further strengthened if it were disaggregated according to gender.

There is need to examine changes in mortality and work capacity in ways that take into account the great heterogeneity of middle-aged and older persons. Feldman's analysis (1991) provides an example of the importance of doing so. He finds that the decline in the death rate for men with at least one year of education was substantially greater than for those with less than eight years of education from 1960 to 1980. More significantly, wide difference exist in reported work disability rates between such groups:

> Data from the latter half of the 1970s show, at every age, wide differences in disability rates. For instance, for men in the sixty-five to sixty-seven age interval, 31 percent of those with less than twelve years of education, 18 percent of those with twelve years of education, and 12 percent of those completing one or more years of college were reported as being unable to work because of health. Survey data suggest that these differences have not diminished over time, which is certainly consonant with data on the relationship between socioeconomic status and incidence and prevalence of various chronic diseases. (Feldman, 1991)

Failure to examine differences across various groups may lead to one-dimensional policy instruments which are not sensitive to the multiplicity of circumstances surrounding the abilities and needs of older persons. For example, Rose Gibson (1986) suggests that a very needy large group of late midlife black workers who are gradually exiting the labor force primarily because of work-limiting health conditions are largely ignored by major retirement research and therefore deprived of the program and policy planning and policy that emerges from such research.

The third question concerns whether self reports of health status such as the type Professor Crimmins is using provide a reliable source of information. The short answer is provided by Martynas Ycas (1987) in his review of findings on health trends near the age of retirement. After reviewing some of the limitations of such data, he concludes that the National Health Interview Survey--which

Crimmins uses--'' is easily the best source of health and limitation trend data.''

The longer answer requires some elaboration of the possible limits and strengths of data on reported health and disability status. Health indicators based on self-reports are sometimes criticized on the grounds that they are not separate from what they are measuring--labor force behavior (Chirikos and Nestel, 1981). ''Poor health'' can be viewed as an acceptable reason for leaving or reducing work effort, and so incentive exists to use it as a rationalization to mask other reasons for retirement. Also, it has been noted that declarations of ''poor health'' or ''work-limiting health conditions'' do not always have the same meaning for all members of a sampled population (Chirikos and Nestel, 1981). Moreover, questions in longitudinal surveys are not always comparable across years and subjective notions of ''health'' and ''disability'' may vary over time.

Measures based on specific functional limitations have generally been preferred to those based on more subjective health reports. Even so, studies find self-reports of health and physician ratings of health significantly correlated (La Rue, Bank and Hetland, 1978). Sheppard (1977) concludes that self reported health status should be taken at face value and Andrisani (1977) finds that men age 45 to 59 who reported work limiting health conditions in 1966 were two to three times as likely to have died by 1972 than those who did not report limitations. More recently Howard Iams and John McCoy (1991) find that self-reports of health status in 1982 (e.g., number of disorders, degree of functional limitation, incidence of selected disorders and health as a reason for retiring) are significantly associated with dying prior to 1989 for a sample of newly retired-worker beneficiaries drawn from the 1982 New Beneficiary Survey. They conclude that their findings ''contradict the argument advanced that self-assessed health may be unreliable because it is more socially acceptable to stop working for presumed health reasons ... than for other reasons.''

My final question concerns the lessons which should be drawn from their and others' research to guide retirement and pension policy.

I have few candidates. They may have others. First, their conclusion that recent health trends do not point to a clear direction for future health trends for older persons provide reason for caution about policy interventions which are based on the assumption that middle-aged and older persons are and will be healthier.

Second, I think their findings lend support to the view that raising the age of eligibility for full Social Security benefits and reducing the value of benefits to those retiring at earlier ages cannot be justified on the grounds that older persons of the future will be able to work longer. Moreover, the costs imposed by this change will fall more heavily on those future workers in poor health than on those in good health (See Sammartino, 1987). Increasing the age of eligibility for full benefits may be justified on financing grounds or on grounds that life expectancies at age 65 are increasing. However, it should be recognized that doing so involves compromising the program's social adequacy goal. To the extent that providing widespread protection against loss of income--especially to lower and moderate income workers--is a valued goal, then corrective interventions should accompany increases in the age of eligibility for full benefits and reductions for receipt of early retirement benefits under Social Security. For example, the age of eligibility for Supplemental Security Income retirement benefits might be <u>lowered</u> as Social Security retirement age changes are phased-in.

Third, to the extent that encouraging healthy persons to work longer is a valued policy goal, I believe their findings point to a greater need for more surgical interventions via employer decisions and public policy. Certainly, firms have at their disposal mechanisms (e.g., wage incentives, flexible work and retirement options) which can be employed as needed to encourage longer work. Moreover, consideration could be given to reducing private and public-employee pension incentives for the voluntary early retirement of healthy persons. Finally, I believe their discussion implies that consideration should be given to directing more resources at research and the promotion of behavior which may potentially help prevent or delay the onset of chronic illness.

To conclude, I appreciate having this opportunity to comment on Eileen Crimmins' and Dominique Ingegneri's informative and excellent paper.

Marc M. Twinney, Jr., F.S.A.

INTRODUCTION

I would like to complement Dr. Crimmins and her colleague on their paper. It seems to me to be quite different from many of the Symposium papers we have discussed. Her analysis seems to be more complete, perhaps because the data and evidence are more adequate.

One of her conclusions has considerable impact for business and others who bear the burden of paying for health care. This is that "... mortality decline (especially at older ages) has resulted in people with health limitations living longer." In other words, this means that because there will be more "old" people in the population, there will be a greater need to provide health care of all kinds. Dr. Crimmins also expressed this school of thought as follows: "As mortality declines, those saved from death do not tend to be persons of average constitution but a weaker and frailer group who would have perished under a more severe mortality regime ... a group more susceptible to a whole host of diseases and conditions than the average survivor in the population."

What does this mean to business and to others who pay the health care bills? For employers who provide health care during employment and after retirement, as my company does, the consequences in increased costs are extremely serious.

As my discussion focuses on costs and its future trends, I would also point out that the company, like much of American business, is striving to provide people with adequate health care, especially for catastrophic illness. We think abandonment of health care benefits is not the answer to the cost problem. On the other hand, we cannot ignore costs in a worldwide automotive industry. Our global competition has a sizeable advantage in this cost element. The question is -- How long into the future can the company and the country afford the costs of present benefit plans and health care system?

To give you an idea of the competitive cost situation in one industry, here is the health care story in terms of costs per unit manufactured. In the U.S., our costs are now approaching $700 per vehicle manufactured. This is about double the costs for health care in the next group of competitors -- those new U.S. plants established by foreign companies. Foreign plants outside the U.S. have even lower costs. That means the U.S. manufactured product must absorb these costs as losses or try to pass them on to customers. Though U.S. consumers may wish to buy American products, not very many would be willing to pay $300 more when they purchase a car or truck. This difference is growing and the growth shows little sign of slowing by the 21st century.

My remarks will start with cost aspects in total and for the older population, enlarging on observations made earlier in the Symposium. I will then discuss the costs not paid by Medicare, the portion paid by the employer. Then I will turn to the new accounting treatment of costs and how this magnifies the problem.

TOTAL U.S. HEALTH CARE COST AND INFLATION

Comparing the growth in national health care costs with the increases from medical and general inflation is instructive. For the period 1970 to 1990, national health care expenditures grew 880%, over 40% more than medical inflation and 85% more than general prices as measured by the CPI. But this is not the largest growth sector related to health care. If we add the business-paid health care expenditures to the picture, we would find they have risen over 1200% during this period, another 40% faster than the total U.S. health care growth. (Table 1)

HEALTH CARE SPENDING AND WEALTH PER CAPITA BY COUNTRY

Mr. Schieber's paper told us about the relationship between health care spending and gross domestic product in each country. He also suggested that per capita spending and per capita gross domestic product should be compared to adjust for higher U.S. per capita income. Such a comparison shows that United States' spending is clearly out-of-line with other countries -- even when it is adjusted for national income. The United States spent about $600 more per capita than it should based on the average relationship among 22 OECD countries in 1989. This is a large difference -- about one-third higher than the $1800 indicated as equivalent to the OECD average for the U.S. and its national incomes advantage. (Table 2)

COMPANY HEALTH CARE COSTS BY GROUP

Next we turn to the company's health care costs in 1990 by insured groups. These are large costs even for a company as large as Ford. Health care costs are regularly one of our two largest costs of doing business. Blue Cross/Blue Shield is our second largest supplier.

The active employees make up 64% of the Company-paid costs and the retired employees, 36%. The cost for the retirees eligible for Medicare included in these percentages is only the part paid by the Company. If an estimate of the Medicare paid benefits is included, the total costs for retiree benefits would increase from $430 million to $810 million. This is more than the $760 million spent on the active employees who outnumber retirees roughly by 4 to 3. Let's focus further on these retiree costs. (Table 3)

NEW ACCOUNTING FOR RETIREE HEALTH CARE COSTS

For those who are not familiar with FASB, it is the acronym for the Financial Accounting Standards Board. FASB is the independent organization that sets accounting standards for generally accepted accounting practice in the United States. If a company wants to issue securities, it must publish financial statements prepared and audited in conformance with these standards.

FASB has ruled that, beginning in 1993, corporations must show on their books the accrued costs for retiree health care -- similar to the way pension costs are recorded -- rather than account for them as pay-as-you-go costs as most companies do now.

According to the actuaries and accounting firms, this change will increase a company's cost by 3 to 7 times the present pay-as-you-go costs, depending upon the maturity of the company. This change will compound the high cost base previously discussed.

The most important factor in measuring future health care costs is the health care trend rate. These rates are examined next.

HEALTH CARE TREND RATES

The health care trend rate is the long-term annual rate of increase in the benefit costs. These rates are developed from national experience and company-specific experience, and by type of coverage or service. The long-term trend rate must be developed separately from the cost related to increasing age for measuring accounting costs because the aging increase can be isolated accurately in actuarial projections. The trend rate is also developed separately from the projected population so that population variation can be projected for a specific group. This means that these trend rates are different from -- somewhat lower than -- the gross rates used in other contexts.

The trend rates reflect all of the other elements contributing to the health care cost increase. These include medical (price) inflation, utilization, intensity (mix), technology and quality of care changes, and regulatory requirements. They exclude possible changes to Medicare or the plan of benefits.

- Nationally, the trend rates have tended to be relative high -- about double the annual rate of increase in other prices as reported in the CPI. The automotive industry rates resemble the national trends.

- Let us look at what actuaries have been saying about measuring these trends. The trend rates are highly volatile from year-to-year, especially the changes from mix, technology, quality and regulation. They have very low creditability -- worse then the stock market trends according to some actuaries. This results from so much of the growth (up to 50%) resulting from random changes in mix, technology and quality of care. Only the long term gives the rates any reliability approaching that of other actuarial rates. But it is in the long term that there is the least agreement.

- Many actuaries believe that the current high rate of increase cannot continue indefinitely. This is based on the growing portion of gross national product that would be consumed by health care expenditures if growth rates since 1967 when Medicare and Medicaid came into being continue unchecked. We have already seen that the United States spends one- third more for health care than the average per capita relationship outside the U.S. These actuaries assume there is a natural limit at some point and that health care expenditures cannot exceed some percentage of gross national product.

- Other actuaries are not so sure. Actuaries at the Health Care Financing Administration charged with making the long term projection for

Social Security and other government programs detect no slacking in the forces driving the rates, among which are the proportions of the population suffering from chronic conditions that are treated but not cured.

- Given the lack of creditability, let alone certainty, in the trend rates, the actuaries may defer to the standard of conservatism in accounting when the measurements are too uncertain. This standard calls for the assumption of lowest forecast so that the most likely costs would be recognized.

HEALTH CARE COSTS BY ATTAINED AGE

The health care cost increase by age appears to be more uniform by year of age from group-to-group then the general trend rate. A typical assumption being made is an increase in the gross benefit payments by year of age of 2.5%, until age 65, 3% from age 65 to age 85 and zero after age 85. During the 25 years from the company's average retirement age of about 60 to age 85, this means that annual costs will double from this source alone.

The zero rate assumed after age 85 raises a question that I cannot answer. I would speculate that data for higher ages is still too sparse to verify the rate of increase. This suggests that the force of mortality becomes the dominant factor at these ages. By the way, the increase in the mortality rate in annuity tables during the same 25 years from age 60 to 85 is about eight times.

NATIONAL HEALTH EXPENDITURES AS A PERCENTAGE OF GNP

The Health Care Financing Administration has estimated that total U.S. health care costs will reach $1.5 trillion or 15% of the GNP, by the year 2000. Other health economists have projected the costs will reach $2 trillion, or 20% of the GNP, by the year 2000.

If the health care trend continues unchecked, the prospect is presented of health care crowding out other national priorities and of American business becoming less competitive in the global market. These are outcomes to be resisted, thus raising the question of changing the health care trend rate in some acceptable way. (Table 4)

TAMING THE HEALTH CARE TREND RATE

Returning to the retiree cost accounting aspects, the efforts at altering the effects of the trend rate would appear to fall into three categories.

- Assumptions and Limits. This category has already been referred to. It includes the plans of business and actuaries to assume a reduced rate of increase in the trend over time -- ultimately declining to the level of inflation rates in other prices or in medical services only. Elaborate arguments are made for limitations as a percentage of the gross national product. While much of this reasoning seems cogent, it still seems to fall more into the category of hope than action and defers the real solutions to the problem.

- Voluntary Caps and Retiree Cost Sharing. These approaches include changing a company's cost by sharing the cost increases with service users as a group. The AT&T and Communication Workers recently entered into this kind of arrangement and many firms consider three party support to pay the costs as superior to two party. This has been the arrangement from inception in general, in the oil industry and for selected companies in other industries such as defense contracting. This solution has the potential of diminishing the trend to some degree but there is no agreement among experts about its possible effectiveness.

- System Reform - Improved Financing, Equity and Efficiency. The system of delivering and paying for health care is under increasing scrutiny. To be effective in taming the health care trend, three principles are usually mentioned for reform:

  - Improved financing -- a mechanism that spreads costs equally over the total economy.
  - Equity -- coverage of all the people with consistent quality of care.
  - Improved efficiency -- elimination of ineffective and inappropriate care, reduction of unnecessary expenses, including malpractice extremes, and imposition of national budgets to contain costs.

Whether this is enough to achieve reform is also challenged. For example, in writing about the limits on medical progress, Daniel Callahan expressed the following: "For perhaps the health care problem is not quite what appears on the surface, just a matter of improved financing, equity, and efficiency. Perhaps it is a crisis about the meaning and nature of health, and about the place that the pursuit of health should have in our lives."

Whether true reform will be made in a timely fashion is one of America's biggest challenges for the 21st century.

Population Aging and Retirement Policy: An International Perspective

Robert L. Clark

INTRODUCTION

All developed countries have experienced significant aging of their populations since 1950. The primary determinants of the increase in the proportion of national populations in the older ages is the result of declines in fertility rates and reductions in mortality rates at older ages.

Population aging has important implications for the cost of social security systems. The role of social security programs and their costs are also influenced by the existence of employer pension plans and national retirement policies. Government tax policy affecting individual savings also affects the reliance on and need for social security retirement benefits. This paper begins with a review of past population aging in several developed countries and considers projections of the pattern of continued aging through the first quarter of the twenty-first century.

The direct discussion of population trends and retirement programs is restricted to six countries. Countries included in the analysis are Japan, the United States, France, Germany, the Netherlands, and the United Kingdom. These countries are of interest in their own right as specific examples of the development of national retirement programs in the context of population aging. In addition, they provide clear examples of population trends and development of retirement programs that have occurred in the other developed countries. The German example is based on pre- unification population projections for West Germany and the West German social security and pension systems.

The review of social security systems concentrates on worker retirement benefits and does not attempt to examine disability insurance, unemployment programs, or medical insurance. While these programs, especially medical insurance, are also affected by the changing age structure of the population, space constraints of this paper do not permit an assessment of all aspects of public programs influenced by population aging. However, some of the cost data reported throughout this analysis include disability expenditures combined with those for retirement benefits. In addition, the relationship among disability, unemployment, and retirement insurance programs is briefly examined.

Expenditures on retirement and survivors components of the national social security systems represent a growing share of Gross National Product (GNP) in most developed countries. Simanis (1990) reported information on the proportion of GNP spent on old-age, survivors, and disability insurance (OASDI) in the countries in our sample in 1980 and 1983 (See Table 1). The highest GNP share for OASDI programs was in the Netherlands which allocated 14.5 percent of its GNP to these programs in 1983. This was followed closely by Germany with 12.5 percent. In contrast, France (8.2 percent), the United Kingdom (7.4 percent), and the United States with (7.0 percent) devoted substantially less to OASDI programs. Japan had by far the lowest GNP share for these programs allocating only 3.2 percent of its GNP to OASDI. Table 1 also indicates that the cost of OASDI programs rose substantially between 1980 and 1983. The projected aging of these populations that is described below will continue to drive up the real and relative costs of retirement programs in these countries.

Table 1.   Expenditures on Old Age, Survivors, and Disability Insurance as Share of Gross National Product

Country	Share of GNP Spent on OASDI	
	(Percent)	
	1980	1983
France	7.5	8.2
Germany	11.4	12.5
Japan	2.5	3.2
Netherlands	13.8	14.5
United Kingdom	5.9	7.4
United States	6.2	7.0

Source: Joseph Simanis, "National Expenditures on Social Security and Health in Selected Countries," Social Security Bulletin January 1990, pp. 12-16.

This report examines the existing social security systems and problems they face in response to the shifting age structures of national populations. First, the structure of social security retirement programs in each of these countries is briefly described along with a review of major changes in them during the past two decades. For example, the United States and Japan enacted major amendments to their programs in an attempt to reduce future costs. In contrast, programs in western Europe reduced ages for early retirement during the past 20 years in an effort to reduce national unemployment rates. Recent legislation in several of the European countries has eliminated some of these early retirement provisions and begun to address the problem of rising costs of their social security programs. Past and pending changes in social security programs are then examined in relationship to the projected demographic changes. The importance of labor force participation rates and national retirement policies on the cost of social security programs is examined.

The significance of employer pensions in providing retirement income is governed, in part, by the generosity of the national social security system. Private pensions exist in each of these countries; however, their structure differs substantially across the nations in our sample. The employer pension system in each of the six countries is briefly described. The interaction between employer pensions and social security is assessed along with a review of potential changes in the pension systems in the twentieth first century.

Primary conclusions for this analysis are:

1. Population aging is continuing to occur in all of the countries examined in this study. The pace of population aging will accelerate in all countries during the first quarter of the twentieth first century. In Japan, the Netherlands, and Germany, a rapid increase in the elderly population will occur between 2000 and 2010. Similar increases will occur in France, the United Kingdom, and the United States beginning in the second decade of the twenty-first century.

2. Population aging will substantially increase the cost of social security systems in all developed countries. This follows directly from the rise in the number of retirees relative to the number of workers.

3. The expected cost increase can be moderated by raising the age of eligibility for retirement benefits and providing incentives for older persons to remain in the labor force. Projected costs can also be lowered by reducing the generosity of annual benefits. Over the past 15 years, Japan and the United States made modifications in their social security systems aimed at reducing projected future social security expenditures. The western European countries are only now beginning to address the problem of rapidly rising future costs of social security.

4. Employer pensions are linked to social security programs and are also affected by the aging of the population. Employer pensions will continue to evolve and be influenced by national retirement policies, demographic changes, and policies affecting private savings.

5. Public/private differences in retirement age policy are beginning to emerge. Governments, concerned about the rapidly rising costs of social security, favor raising the age of retirement. Firms, concerned about worker productivity and labor costs, are still interested in maintaining relatively young retirement ages.

6. Early retirement provisions in Europe which were instituted to remove

older workers from the labor force in an attempt to lower unemployment rates are being eliminated. These programs are inconsistent with sound retirement policy in an aging society.

POPULATION AGING IN DEVELOPED COUNTRIES

After the conclusion of World War II, fertility rates increased sharply around the world. The length of national baby booms varied considerably ranging from only three years in Japan to over 15 years in the United States. Since the ending of the baby booms, fertility rates have dropped markedly in all developed countries.[1] This pattern of fertility has dramatically altered the age structure of national populations and produced the population aging in the developed countries. Declines in mortality rates at older ages have raised life expectancy during retirement. The increase in life expectancy at older ages exacerbates the trend toward aging of the populations and increases the costs of social security retirement programs. In flows of young immigrant workers have moderated the pace of population aging in some areas.

The aging of the populations of the six countries in our study are shown in Table 2 which indicates the percent of the population in each nation age 65 and over. The population projections are based on the medium variant projections produced by the United Nations. In 1950, France and the United Kingdom had the oldest population with 11.4 and 10.7 percent of their population 65 and over. Japan was the youngest population with only 4.9 percent of its population 65 and over. At this time, Japan's population resembled that of a developing country with fewer older persons and more youths (45.8 percent of the population was between 0 and 19 years of age). Other relatively young populations were those of the Netherlands with 7.7 percent age 65 and over, the United States with 8.1 percent, and Germany with 9.4 percent.

Over the next 40 years, the older populations in each of these nations steadily increased. The most rapidly aging populations were those of Germany, Japan, and the Netherlands. The slowest rate of aging was experienced by France. These demographic changes resulted in Germany and the United Kingdom having the highest proportion of persons 65 and older in 1990. The age structure of the Japanese population was transformed during this period from one resembling a developing country to being similar to the other developed countries being examined.

Between 1990 and 2010, Japan is expected to experience the most rapid population aging among the developed countries. Japan had only a short post-war baby boom. Fertility rates have fallen drastically since 1950 reaching 1.53 in 1990. At the same time, there has been a sharp increase in life expectancy at age 65. These two trends have produced a rapid aging of the Japanese population. The proportion of the population 65 and older in Japan is projected to increase from 11.7 percent to 19.6. Germany faces a somewhat smaller but still substantial increase in its elderly population; the percent of the population 65 and over will increase from 15.4 in 1990 to 20.4 percent in 2010.

The other four countries are expected to have only modest increases in their elderly populations during these twenty years. However, the pace of population aging in these other four countries accelerates after 2010. Between 2010 and 2025, the proportion of the population age 65 and over rises by 6.2 percentage points in the United States from 13.6 to 19.8 percent. Increases in the proportion of the population age 65 and older of 6.1 percentage points in the Netherlands, 5.1 percentage points in France, and 3.7 percentage points in the United Kingdom are forecasted.

Table 2.   Actual and Projected Percentage of Population 65 and over: 1950-2025[a]

Year	France	West Germany	Japan (Percent)	Nether- lands	United Kingdom	United States
1950	11.4	9.4	4.9	7.7	10.7	8.1
1960	11.6	10.8	5.7	9.0	11.7	9.2
1970	12.9	13.2	7.1	10.2	12.9	9.8
1980	14.0	15.5	9.0	11.5	15.1	11.3
1990	13.8	15.4	11.7	12.7	15.4	12.6
2000	15.4	17.0	15.9	13.6	15.2	12.8
2010	15.7	20.4	19.6	15.2	15.7	13.6
2020	19.3	22.2	23.7	19.4	18.2	17.5
2025	20.8	24.1	23.9	21.3	19.4	19.8

[a]Population projections are based on medium variant projections of the United Nations.
Source: United Nations, Global Population Estimates and Projections, 1990, diskette version.

The populations of Germany and Japan will continue to age during this period. The proportion of the Japanese population over age 65 is projected to increase from 19.6 percent in 2010 to 23.9 percent in 2025 while in Germany the proportion rises from 20.4 to 24.1 percent. These projections may underestimate the extent of population aging in the developed countries. Several country specific projections indicate more rapid population aging than that shown in Table 2. The unification of Germany may slow the rate of aging compared to these projections as the East German population had a higher fertility rate than that prevailing in the West.

The continued increase in the proportion of older persons in the populations of these countries increases the financial pressure on their social insurance programs. This point is highlighted by calculating the ratio of persons 65 and over and hence of retirement age to persons 20 to 64 and deemed to be of working age. Such ratios are often referred to as old age dependency ratios. While these ratios can be modified to take into account a variety of other factors, the simple population dependency ratio illustrates the point of the demographic effect on the future cost of social security retirement programs.

Table 3 illustrates the increases in the old age dependency ratios for each of the countries in our sample between 1950 and 2025. The pattern of increases is similar to that shown in Table 2; however, the magnitudes of the increases are much greater. Once again, Japan and Germany are shown to be the most rapidly aging countries. Between 1950 and 1990, the ratio of persons 65 and over to those 20 to 64 almost doubled in Japan increasing from 10.0 percent to 19.0 percent. Between 1990 and 2025, the ratio will more than double again rising to 42.9. Slightly smaller increases are forecasted for Germany.

If all persons aged 20 to 64 were in the labor force and all persons aged 65 and over were retired, these increases in the ratios shown in Table 3 would translate directly into tax rate changes necessary to finance national retirement programs.

Although this is clearly not the case, these sharp increases in the ratio of retirees to workers along with the maturing of social security systems have been the primary causes of the cost increases for national retirement programs during the last half of the twentieth century. During the first quarter of the twenty-first century, demographic changes will be the driving force behind the projected spiraling costs of these systems.

The demographic effect on the cost of social security will be moderated by the increasing proportion of women who are expected to be in the labor forces of the developed countries. Another factor that will offset the rising cost of providing benefits to retirees is the reduction in the proportion of the populations that are less than 18 that accompanies the aging of the populations. Thus, to some degree, higher costs of providing income to a growing elderly population can be financed by reductions in the proportion of national income needed to provide benefits to children.

The impact of population aging on national retirement programs results in increases in real and relative expenditures for these programs. Table 4 shows that the real government expenditures on social security[2] in each of these countries is expected to increase sharply in the next 35 years. These estimates of future pension expenditures are based on a study for the International Monetary Fund (IMF) completed in the mid 1980s (Heller, et al, 1986).

The projections are based on a series of demographic and economic assumptions. The base line demographic assumptions are determined by official national population projections available in the early 1980's. Economic assumptions in long range projections are subject to considerable uncertainty. The future growth rates in gross domestic product used in these projections ranged from 2.8 percent per year in Japan to just over one percent in Germany. Projections of pension expenditures are based on program provisions prevailing at the time of the study and all future changes that were already incorporated into existing law in the early 1980s.

Table 3.   Actual and Projected Percentage of Population 65 and Over to Population 20 to 64[a]

Year	France	West Germany	Japan	Nether- lands	United Kingdom	United States
			(Percent)			
1950	19.5	15.7	10.0	14.1	17.8	14.1
1960	20.8	17.9	10.6	17.0	20.1	17.7
1970	23.8	23.1	11.7	18.8	23.2	18.8
1980	25.0	26.8	15.0	20.1	27.0	19.8
1990	23.5	24.1	19.0	20.6	26.2	21.3
2000	26.3	27.2	25.9	21.9	25.7	21.4
2010	26.3	34.1	34.0	24.5	26.3	22.1
2020	33.6	37.5	43.1	32.5	30.9	29.9
2025	37.0	42.2	42.9	36.7	33.7	35.1

[a]Population projections are based on medium variant projections of the United Nations.
Source: United Nations, Global Population Estimates and Projections, 1990, diskette version.

As would be expected from the information in Table 3, the projected increase for Japan is much larger than the other developed countries. Table 4 shows that real social security expenditures in Japan are expected to increase from an index of 100 in 1980 to 1,314 in 2025. In contrast, increases in the United Kingdom, the United States, France, and Germany are only expected to reach 290 to 325. As a percentage of gross domestic product, social security expenditures are expected to more than triple in Japan[3] while rising by less than 55 percent in these other developed countries.

During the last ten years, fertility and mortality trends have caused demographers to revise their population projections. More rapid population aging is now forecasted than was assumed in the IMF report. The IMF analysis was based on a forecast of the proportion of the population age 65 and older for France in 2025 of 15.8 percent while the current United Nations projection is 20.8 percent. Increases in the proportion of persons 65 and older are noted for every other country in our sample except the United Kingdom (Germany: IMF 19.4 percent, UN 24.1 percent; Japan: IMF 21.2 percent, UN 23.9 percent; United Kingdom: IMF 19.4 percent, UN 19.4 percent; United States: IMF 19.5 percent, UN 19.8 percent). The increase in expected population aging implies that the expenditure projections shown in Table 4 are underestimates of the increases that are now expected with the most recent demographic trends.

Table 4.   Projection of Governmental Expenditures on Social Security and Government Employee Pensions

Country	1980	2000	2010	2025
	Index of Real Social Security Expenditures			
France	100	175	230	325
Germany	100	180	218	300
Japan	100	430	787	1,314
United Kingdom	100	159	199	290
United States	100	145	178	306
	Index of Ratio of Social Security Expenditures to GDP			
France	100	110	115	130
Germany	100	129	140	154
Japan	100	229	307	319
United Kingdom	100	115	124	144
United States	100	92	90	110

Source: Peter Heller, Richard Hemming and Peter Kohnert, Aging and Social Expenditures in the Major Industrial Countries, 1980-2025 (Washington, D.C.: International Monetary Fund, 1986), p. 31.

SOCIAL SECURITY SYSTEMS

The social security retirement programs in the six countries are briefly described in this section. The emphasis is on benefit levels and the age of eligibility for early and normal retirement benefits. Population aging increases the cost of any specific social security system. Reductions in average annual benefit levels and raising the retirement age are two methods of reducing future cost increases. Each of these methods have been or will be employed by developed countries to reduce the required increases in social security contributions.

Each of the six countries in our sample has responded to the projected cost increases by amending their retirement programs.[4] Legislation in the United States (1977), in Japan (1985), and in the United Kingdom (1986) significantly reduced projected future costs by lowering future benefits through the modification of benefit formulas. The United States (1983) and Germany (1989) have scheduled increases in the age for full benefits and higher reductions in benefits at early retirement. France and the Netherlands have increased contribution rates and proposals in France would increase years of service for full benefits along with increasing the years included in determining the earnings base.

FRANCE

The French social security system was established in 1910. The basic social security system covers all wage earners and salaried employees except those in agriculture, mining, railroads, public utilities, the public sector and the self-employed. Workers in these sectors are covered by special systems. The basic system covers approximately 70 percent of all employees. Retirees receive an earning-related benefit that depends on years of service and age that retirement benefits begin.

The retirement benefit is based on the higher of average annual covered earnings indexed by wage growth during the highest ten years since 1948 and preceding either age 60 or retirement. The normal retirement age for both men and women is 65; however, persons can retire at age 60 with unreduced benefits provided that they have at least 37.5 years of coverage.

Retirees who are 60 and have 150 quarters (37.5 years) of coverage can receive a full or unreduced benefit equaling 50 percent of their earnings base. The maximum benefit attainable for a single retired worker in 1990 was $11,375 while the minimum benefit for fully qualified persons was approximately $5800.[5] Retirement benefits are increased on January 1 and July 1 of each year by a percentage based on the increase in wages.

The benefit formula is

$B = AEARN * N/150 * K$

where $AEARN$ = the 10 year average of indexed earnings,

N = the number of quarters of coverage up to 150,

and K = the generosity parameter. K is equal to 0.5 if age is 60 or more and N is 150 or more. Thus, a retiree aged 60 with 150 quarters of coverage receives a benefit of 50 percent of $AEARN$.

Persons between 60 and 65 without 150 quarters of coverage can receive a reduced benefit. The benefit is reduced by 1.25 percentage points per quarter of the lesser of the number of quarters of covered earnings below 150 or the number of quarters remaining to age 65. Thus, for retirees beginning benefits at age 60, the minimum retirement benefit is 25 percent of the earnings base (50 - [20*1.25]).

Certain persons with less than the required 37.5 years of coverage can receive a pension at age 60 that is not subject to the reduction factor. These include women who are caring for a family and women who have raised children.

No retirement pension is paid prior to age 60; however, a special "pre-pension" may be paid to persons age 55 or older who retire in order to be replaced on their job by an unemployed person. The paying of "pre-pensions" was introduced to increase employment opportunities for younger persons by reducing the supply of older persons seeking employment.

The age for full benefits with 150 quarters of coverage was reduced to 60 in 1983. Consideration is now being given to increasing the age for unreduced benefits to 65. Proposals considered in 1990 would gradually raise the age for full benefits back to age 65.

The pension is not increased for continued employment after age 60 unless the person does not have the full 150 quarters of coverage. For these workers, the pension is increased with continued work but only up to the point that the retiree has accrued 37.5 years of coverage. There is an earnings tests that reduces benefits if beneficiaries continue to work.

The systems are pay-as-you-go financed by employer and employee contributions. At the beginning of 1990, the employer contribution rate was 8.2 percent of earnings up to $22,600 while the employee contribution rate was 7.6 percent of earnings up to the limit.

GERMANY

The German social security system was instituted in 1889. All wage earners and salaried employees are now covered by the national social security system.[6] There are separate systems for salaried and wage earners; however, both have the same provisions. Prior to 1968, salaried employees earning in excess of the social security earnings ceiling were not required to be covered by social security; however, most such employees voluntarily enrolled in social security.

The social security system is financed by employer and employee contributions. In 1989, employer and employee contributions were 9.35 percent of earnings up to DM 73,200 each. Beginning in 1957, the system was changed from a funded system to a pay-as-you-go system.[7]

The normal retirement age for social security benefits is 65 with 5 years of covered employment; however, persons reaching age 63 with 35 years of coverage are eligible to receive an unreduced retirement benefit. Benefits can be received between 63 and 65 only if earnings are below DM 1,000 per month. This earnings test is eliminated at age 65. Deferred retirement past age 65 up to age 67 increases benefits by 0.6 percent per month.

Retirement benefits are determined using the following formula

.015 * N * Wage Ratio * Base Wage

where N = years of social security coverage. In addition to working in covered employment, years of covered service can be achieved by certain activities that are considered socially important such as raising children and education.

Wage Ratio = Employee's Covered Wage/National Average Covered Wage. This ratio is calculated for each year of earnings. The ratios are averaged over the entire working career. The ratio cannot exceed 2.

Covered Wages = Wages up to that year's social security ceiling.

Base Wage = An amount determined each year by the government. In 1989, this amount was DM 29,814 or approximately $18,000. At one time, the base wage was the average of the national average wage for the three years prior to the year of computation; however, the current figure is set somewhat lower than this average.

The current average social security benefit represents about 50 percent of average gross earnings of workers in the same year. This represents about two-thirds of the average net earnings of all employees. The maximum attainable benefit for a single retired worker in 1990 was $25,142. Since 1957, benefits have been increased annually based on the increase in average earnings so that current pensioners share in the gains in real earnings.

Prior to 1972, the age of retirement was fixed at age 65 for men and 60 for women.[8] The Pension Reform Law of 1972 enabled a variety of individuals to select early retirement with no actuarial reduction in benefits. These include retirees who are 63 with 35 years of coverage, unemployed women age 60 with 10 years of coverage in the last 20 years, persons age 60 who are disabled with 35 years of service, and persons who are age 60 with 15 years of coverage and have been unemployed for at least 12 of the last 18 months. In response to these changes in requirements to receive social security benefits and high levels of unemployment, the labor force participation of men aged 63 dropped from 67 percent in 1970 to 27 percent in 1980.

From 1984 to 1988, preretirement pensions were available for certain persons. In 1989, a partial pension was introduced to replace the preretirement pension. Partial pensions are available to workers age 58 who have worked full-time for the last five years but now reduce their hours by half but not below 18 hours per week. The employer continues to pay the worker half salary and pays a partial pension of a minimum of 20 percent of earnings. The partial pension is reimbursed by the government if the employer hires an unemployed person to fill the partial vacancy.

In December 1989, legislation was enacted to reduce the benefits for early retirees. Between 2001 and 2006, the retirement age for unreduced pensions is scheduled to rise to age 65 for men and women. Early retirement at age 62 will be permitted but will result in a reduction in benefits of 3.6 percent per year of retirement prior to age 65. The present provision allowing unreduced benefits at age 63 with 35 years of service is removed and women will no longer be able to retire at age 60 with 10 years of contributions in the last 20.

Unification of East and West Germany required many changes in the social and economic policy of the two countries. For the most part, East Germany was merged into the West German systems of labor laws and social security. The impact of unification on the social security system will primarily depend on its effect on the rate of economic growth, however, the impact of the introduction of younger East Germans will moderate the projected demographically induced rise in social security costs arising from the decline in the ratio of contributors to beneficiaries.

JAPAN

The Japanese social security system consists of the National Pension which pays a flat benefit to most persons and five additional earnings related programs.[9] Most private employees are covered by the Employees Pension Insurance program. Other earnings related systems cover agricultural workers, private school teachers, national public workers, and local public workers. Benefits from all the social security systems are adjusted annually to reflect increases in consumer prices.

The National Pension was established in 1961 as a pension for self employed persons. In 1985, this program was expanded to cover all workers and to provide a basic or flat social security benefit to all retirees. The program is financed by individual contributions of 8,400 yen per month ($57) in 1990 for self employed persons and people not currently employed. Employees and their spouses are covered by the National Pension through their contributions into the earnings-related pension plans.

The Employees Pension Insurance program was established in 1941. It is financed by equal employer and employee contributions that total 14.3 percent of covered earnings in 1990 for men and a slightly lower rate for women. The contribution rates for women are scheduled to be raised to those of males during the next several years. Contribution rates have more than doubled since 1970 when the combined tax rate was 6.2 percent. Qualified companies that establish a company pension may contract out of the Employees Pension Insurance program.

Prior to the 1985 social security amendments, the monthly benefit from the National Pension was equal to 1,680 yen times the number of years of coverage. A phased-in reduction of benefits was enacted in 1985. The new formula ultimately will be 1,250 yen or $8.50 (in 1984 prices) times the number of years of coverage. The transition will be completed in 2005. The benefit is indexed for price increases. The maximum benefit attainable in 1990 was $4,683

Full benefits from the National Pension are received at age 65. Early retirement benefits may be accepted at age 60; however, benefits are reduced for each year prior to age 65. Benefits accepted at 60 are only 58 percent of the age 65 benefits. Delayed retirement increases benefits. Delaying the start of benefits to 70 results in a benefit that is 188 percent of the age 65 benefit. This schedule of age specific benefits imposes a greater than actuarial reduction for retirement prior to 65 and a greater than actuarial increase for delayed retirement after 65. Despite these adjustments for postponing the acceptance of retirement benefits, most persons begin their pension prior to age 65.

Prior to 1985, the Employees Pension Insurance program provided both a flat benefit and an earnings related benefit. The pre-1985 flat benefit was 2,400 yen per month times years of covered employment. The 1985 amendments brought employees into the National Pension system and will ultimately reduce the flat benefit to 1,250 yen per month times years of coverage.

Prior to 1985, the earnings-related benefit from the Employees Pension Insurance program was 1.0 percent of average insured earnings per year of coverage. This formula is being reduced to 0.75 percent per year of coverage. The reduction is phased in over a 20 year period. The maximum attainable benefit for a single retired worker in 1990 was $15,297. Full benefits are awarded at age 60; however, benefits are reduced by an earnings test if the persons continues to work. The earnings test is eliminated at age 65. The government has proposed raising the age for benefits to 65, however, this has been rejected by the Diet on several occasions.

The 1985 social security amendments were a major effort to reduce the projected costs of social security in Japan. The changes substantially reduced the benefits future retirees will receive. Despite these changes, the contribution rates are projected to more than double in the next 35 years. The government continues to press for an increase in the age for retirement benefits under the Employees Pensions Insurance program to further moderate cost increases.

THE NETHERLANDS

The Dutch social security system was established in 1913. Since 1957, all residents have been compulsorily covered by social security for retirement and survivor benefits. Since the beginning of 1990, the system has been solely financed by employee contributions. Employees pay 14.3 percent of earnings up to a maximum of around $22,000 per year.

Social security pays a flat pension benefit to men and women at age 65. There are no provisions for early retirement and no gains from delaying the acceptance of social security past the age of 65. The pension is paid whether or not the person actually stops working; there is no retirement test for benefits.

The benefit is equal to about 60 percent of national average earnings. The maximum attainable benefit for a single retired worker in 1990 was $8,654. In addition, retirees receive a holiday bonus equal to 8 percent of their benefit in May of each year. The social security benefit is targeted to maintain a married couple's income at the level of the minimum legal wage net after taxes. Benefits are normally increased in January and July of each year to maintain this relationship.

In the case of older couples, each person has an independent right to their benefit. Combined benefits for the couple are about one third higher than the benefit for a single retiree.

To receive an unreduced retirement benefit, a person must have been covered by social security for 50 years between the ages of 15 and 65. Benefits are reduced by 2 percent for each year coverage falls short of 50 years.

UNITED KINGDOM

Social legislation was enacted in the United Kingdom in 1908.[10] Historically, the English social security program provided only a flat benefit to all retirees. These benefits are paid through the National Insurance Scheme. In 1978, the State Earnings-Related Pension Scheme, an earnings-related benefit program, was introduced. This pension system replaced the previous earnings-related pension program which was in effect from 1960 to 1975.

The social security system is financed by employer and employee contributions. Contribution rates are a function of the level of annual earnings - higher tax rates are paid for persons with higher earnings. In 1990, maximum employer contribution rates were 10.45 percent on earnings up to a maximum of about $30,000. This rate was paid for employees with annual earnings of $15,000 or more. Maximum employee contributions for workers with lower earnings were 9.0 percent of earnings up to the earnings ceiling. No tax was paid for workers with annual earnings of less than $4,000.

Companies with an approved private pension may contract out of the earnings-related social security program. Contracting out of the earnings-related benefit implies that the firm offers an employer pension at least as good as the social security system benefit. If the firm or worker contracts out of the earnings-related portion of social security, contributions are reduced for both the employer and the employee.

The flat benefit is paid to men at age 65 and women at age 60. To receive a full pension benefit, men must have had 44 years of coverage and women 39 years. In 1990, the maximum attainable benefit for a single retired worker was $4,065.

The earnings related benefit formula is:
1.25 percent of the average of the highest 20 revalued annual earnings subject to this plan time years of coverage after April 1978. Thus, the maximum is 25 percent of the highest 20 years of earnings. Since only years of covered employment in this system are counted, it will be 1998 before the system fully matures and retirees can begin to accrue the maximum benefit. After 1998, the number of years used to determine average earnings will be increased. The highest attainable benefit for a single retired worker in 1990 was $3,952. The benefit for 1990 retirees is based on only 12 years of service (1990-1978, the first year of the program). Benefits are increased annually to reflect increases in consumer prices.

Currently no early retirement benefits are paid. Until 1988, an early retirement plan was in effect. This plan allowed the payment of retirement benefits to men prior to age 65 and women prior to age 60 provided that the retiree was replaced by an unemployed person. Delayed retirement results in increases in the retirement benefit. Both the flat and earnings related benefits are increased by 1/7 of one percent for each week benefits are postponed beyond age 65.

The Social Security Act of 1986 introduced a series of modifications into the system designed to reduce future costs. These included a reduction in the earnings-related benefit for persons retiring after 1999. The reduction is phased in over a 10 year period and lowers the benefit formula from 1.25 percent of earnings to 1.0 percent. At that time, the full earnings benefit will be 20 percent of average revalued earnings. Companies are encouraged to contract out of the earnings-related system. Membership in a firm pension plan cannot be compulsory. Instead employees must have the choice of opting out of the company plan and establishing a personal pension with an insurance company or remaining in the earnings related component of social security.

The United Kingdom is attempting to control social security costs by eliminating early retirement benefits and reducing earnings-related benefits. In addition, the government is encouraging the privatization of earnings-related benefits. Both companies and individual workers are allowed to withdraw from the earnings component of social security and establish a private retirement benefit.

UNITED STATES

Social security legislation was enacted in the United States in 1935. Although initially covering only employees in industry and commerce, one system now covers virtually all wage earners and salaried employees, self-employed, and most government employees. In general, the social security system has maintained relatively small trusts covering year-to-year fluctuation in revenues and expenditures. The 1983 amendments increased tax revenues and reduced benefits sufficiently so that annual income is projected to exceed annual expenditures producing large increases in the value of the trust funds for the next 30 years. With no further changes in the tax and benefit structure, these surpluses would be depleted in the following 20 years.

The retirement benefit is determined by multiplying a progressive benefit formula times average indexed monthly earnings. For persons who attain age 62 in 1991, this formula is 90 percent of average indexed monthly earnings up to $370, 32 percent of covered earnings between $370 and $2,230, and 15 percent of average earnings above $2,230. Average earnings are calculated from the highest 35 years of indexed earnings between age 22 and 62; only earnings after 1951 are counted.

Although the formula does not directly penalize workers with fewer years of coverage as in many countries, workers who do not have earnings in at least 35 years will have a lower average earnings and hence a lower benefit, although not proportionately so. For the middle income worker, social security will provide a retirement benefit at age 65 that is approximately 42 percent of earnings. The maximum attainable benefit in 1990 was $11,700.

The program provides an earnings-related benefit to retirees who have accumulated 40 quarters of coverage. An unreduced pension is paid at age 65 with early retirement benefits available beginning at age 62. Early retirement benefits were first available in 1956 for women and 1961 for men. Benefits are reduced by 5/9 of one percent per month when first claimed prior to age 65. Despite this reduction, about two-thirds of retirees begin their benefits prior to age 65. Delaying the acceptance of benefits between 65 and 70 increases the social security benefit by 3 percent per year.

Historically, benefits are subject to an earnings test that reduces benefits if retirees continue to work. Under present law, the earnings test does not apply to persons 70 and over. Until 1990, benefits were reduced one dollar for every two dollars of earnings. In 1990, the earnings test was modified for persons aged 65 to 69 so that benefits are reduced one dollar for every three dollars earned above a specified level. This reduction in the penalty for continued work was intended as an incentive to older persons to delay retirement. Benefits are increased annually to reflect the increase in consumer prices.

The retirement and survivor benefits of the social security system are financed by equal employer and employee contributions of 5.6 percent on earnings up to a specified maximum. The earnings maximum was $53,400 in 1991. The tax rate has increased from 1.0 percent on the first $3,000 between 1937 and 1949 to 3.65 percent on the first $7,800 in 1970 to its present level.

Legislation in 1977 substantially reduced the projections of future costs by correcting a problem in the indexation of benefits that was increasing the replacement rate over time. In 1983, legislation was enacted to further reduce the projected future costs of retirement benefits. The social security amendments moved scheduled tax rate increases forward, for the first time made half of social security benefits subject to the income tax for retirees with relatively high income, raised tax rates for self-employed, and raised the earliest age for full benefits for future retirees. The age of eligibility for unreduced benefits will be increased from 65 to 67 between 2003 and 2027. Early retirement benefits can still be accepted at age 62; however, the benefit will ultimately be only 70 percent of the unreduced benefit instead of the current 80 percent.

The 1977 and 1983 social security amendments dramatically improved the financial status of the program. Despite the reduction in benefits and the higher minimum age for full benefits, expenditures for OASI are projected to rise sharply. Between 1990 and 2010, immediate projections indicate that expenditures will be just under 10 percent of payroll. These same projections have costs rising between 2010 and 2025 from 10 percent to 13.5 percent of payroll. Projected cost continued to rise to almost 16 percent by 2065. Without additional changes in the benefit structure, contributions rates must eventually be raised as the trust funds are depleted.

DEMOGRAPHY, RETIREMENT AGE, AND THE COST OF SOCIAL SECURITY

The above review of social security programs is summarized in Table 5 which presents the key characteristics of these national retirement programs. These data revealed that all of these countries have some form of early retirement options and that over time people have opted to accept benefits at ages prior to the normal retirement age. In some of the countries the normal retirement age has been set below age 65 and this has further encouraged the acceptance of benefits at relatively young ages.

Faced with continuing high unemployment rates from the mid 1960s to the 1980s, many European countries employed social security as a tool for reducing unemployment rates. Some programs were simply trying to reduce the supply of workers competing for jobs while others tied the availability of early retirement benefits to the retiree being replaced by an unemployed person.

The use of social security retirement programs to combat unemployment problems increased the cost pressures on pension programs throughout Europe. Presumably, governments in these countries felt that reduced costs in other programs such as unemployment insurance and the gains in political stability associated with lower unemployment rates justified these policies.

[a]Benefits are either a flat benefit based solely on years of coverage or are earnings-related benefits that depend on average covered earnings and years of service.

[b]The National Pension provides a flat benefit to retirees while the Employees Pension Insurance program pays an earnings-related benefit. Items in parentheses refer to the earnings-related benefits.

[c]The United Kingdom has both a flat benefit and an earnings-related benefit program. The values in parentheses refer to the earning-related benefits.

[d]Some countries continue to have differences in the age or service requirements for women. In most cases, these differences are gradually being eliminated in accordance with the EEC directive on equal treatment for men and women.

[e]The normal retirement age without 37.5 years or coverage is 65. Reduced benefits can be started as early as age 60 if the retiree does not have 37.5 years of service.

[f]The normal retirement age with between 5 and 35 years of service is 65. Early retirement is available for certain groups of unemployed, disabled, and those with long service.

[g]Maximum benefit in U.S. dollars payable to fully insured single worker retiring at the normal retirement age. The benefit in national currency was converted to U.S. dollars using exchange rates of January 15, 1990. EBRI (1990), p5.

[h]In most countries, earnings test is eliminated for older retirees; 65 in Germany and Japan and 70 in the United States.

[i]All countries have some mechanism to increase retiree benefits. These adjustments are based either on price increases or wage increases.

Disability pensions have also been employed to reduce the number of older persons who remain in the labor force. By interpreting the concept of disability more broadly, more older persons become eligible for a disability pension before they could receive a retirement benefit. Mirkin (1987) provides a detailed listing

Table 5.   Social Security Characteristics

Characteristic	France	Germany	Japan[b]	Netherlands	United Kingdom[c]	United States
Type of Benefit[a]	Earnings	Earnings	Flat (Earnings)	Flat	Flat (Earnings)	Earnings
Requirements for Normal Benefits [c]: Men[d] Age	60[e]	63[f]	65 (60)	65	65	65
Yrs of Coverage	37.5	35	25	50	44 (60)	10
Max. Benefit[g] (U.S. Dollars)	$11,375	$25,142	$4,682 ($15,297)	$8,654	$4,065 ($3,952)	$11,700
Early Retiremt Age	60[e]	60[f]	60 (none)	No	No	62
Earnings Test[h]	Yes	Yes	No (Yes)	No	No	Yes
Delayed Credit	No	Yes	Yes (No)	No	Yes	Yes
Benefit Adjustment[i]	Wages	Wages	Prices	Wages	Prices	Prices
Contract-Out	No	No	No (Yes)	No	No (Yes)	No

of changes in European pensions to encourage early retirement. He reviewed changes in retirement programs linked to unemployment and disability. These changes can be compared to those in the United States where disability standards were tightened and legislation in 1983 raised the minimum age of eligibility for full benefits beginning in 2003.

These changes along with other economic and social conditions have contributed to the rapid decline in labor force participation rates of older persons. Table 6 illustrates the decline in participation rates for men 65 and older in the six countries between 1950 and 1985. The largest declines have occurred in France, Germany and the Netherlands. Only about one in every twenty men 65 and over in these countries remains in the labor force. Rates are somewhat higher in the United Kingdom (10.6 percent) and in the United States (18.2 percent); however, the participation rates for Japanese men are much higher than for any other developed country in the world.[11]

Table 6.   Labor Force Participation Rate of Men Aged 65 and Older

Country	1950	1960	1970 (Percent)	1980	1985
France	37.2	26.1	15.0	6.0	5.6
Germany	27.5	21.4	16.7	4.9	4.7
Japan	54.5	54.5	54.5	45.8	42.7
Netherlands	31.5	20.4	11.4	4.5	4.2
United Kingdom	34.4	26.6	18.8	11.0	10.6
United States	45.0	33.9	25.5	19.1	18.2

Source: United Nations, World Demographic Estimates and Projections, 1950-2025, New York: United Nations, 1988.

In effect, these data indicate that the retirement age in most developed countries is closer to age 60 than age 65. For example, in the United States more than half of the men age 62 are not in the labor force. To reflect this observation, the ratio of beneficiaries to workers is revised. Table 7 presents the trend in the ratio of persons 60 and over to those 20 to 59. These ratios can be compared to those in Table 3 which presents the ratio of persons 65 and older to those 20 to 64.

Table 7.   Actual and Projected Percentage of Population 60 and Over to Population 20 to 59[a]

Year	France	West Germany	Japan (Percent)	Nether-lands	United Kingdom	United States
1950	30.3	25.3	16.5	22.4	27.9	22.5
1960	33.1	29.8	17.4	26.9	31.8	27.3
1970	37.0	37.8	18.8	29.2	37.2	29.2
1980	32.8	35.7	22.8	29.6	39.7	30.0
1990	35.4	35.9	30.6	30.1	38.1	30.8
2000	37.0	43.7	39.4	31.6	37.0	30.0
2010	41.4	49.0	54.2	39.6	41.3	34.7
2020	50.1	58.0	59.4	49.6	46.6	47.3
2025	54.6	68.5	60.0	56.4	53.3	53.4

[a]Population projections are based on medium variant projections of the United Nations.
Source: United Nations, Global Population Estimates and Projections, 1990, diskette version.

This ratio reflects the number of beneficiaries per 100 workers if age 60 is the retirement age instead of 65. In 1990 this revised ratio is 35.9 percent in Germany and 30.6 percent Japan. By 2025, the ratios are projected to rise to 68.5 percent in Germany and 60.0 percent in Japan. The doubling of these ratios is one of the reasons the contribution rates in Germany are projected to increase from 18.7 percent in 1990 to 40 percent of earnings in 2030 (Schmaehl, 1989) and in Japan, projections are that contribution rates will increase from 14.3 percent in 1990 to 31.5 percent of earnings in 2020 (Clark, 1990).

Raising the age of eligibility would reduce the future costs of these social security programs. Government estimates indicate that if the age of eligibility for benefits in Japan were raised to 65 for both men and women a contribution rate of 26.1 percent in 2020 instead of 31.5 percent would be sufficient to finance benefit payments. Thus, raising the age for full retirement benefits would lower the expected contribution rates by 5.4 percentage points.

These data indicate the importance of the age of eligibility for retirement benefits in determining the cost of social security programs. This cost factor increases in significance with population aging. In a speech to the 1991 Annual Meetings of the National Academy of Social Insurance, Dalmer Hoskins, Secretary- General of the International Social Security Administration identified the demographic pressure on the cost of European social security systems and its relationship to early retirement incentives in these systems as one of the most important problems they will confront in the coming years.[12] Key points of the analysis of social security and the implications of population aging are:

1. The pace of population aging will quicken over the next 20 years; first in countries like Germany and Japan and then in the other developed countries.

2. For any given level of retirement benefits and age of retirement, population aging increases the cost of social security. Contributions in many of the developed countries may double in the next 35 years.

3. Most social security systems offer early retirement options. Across the developed countries, a majority of persons accept early retirement benefits.

4. The European countries have exacerbated the potential cost increases of their social security programs by offering special early retirement incentives in an effort to reduce unemployment.

5. In reviewing worldwide trends in social security between 1985-87, Haanes-Olsen (1989) concluded that "In Western Europe, .. there is concern that present social programs cannot be maintained at their current levels but must be restructured." Reasons for this conclusion were the aging of the populations, continuing high unemployment rates, and early retirement. The current analysis indicates that increases in the age for full and reduced benefits must occur if the future costs of social security systems are to remain within acceptable limits.

6. Several countries have already enacted legislation raising the age for full benefits for future retirees. In other countries proposals are now being considered. The success of these efforts to actually increase the minimum age for full benefits is still to be determined.

PRIVATE PENSION PLANS

Private pension plans are prevalent in most developed countries.[13] Each of the six countries in the present study has an extensive network of employer or occupational pensions. These supplemental pensions are regulated by the national governments in all of the countries. Substantial differences in benefit provisions, plan management and financing, and government regulation are found in the employer pensions of these countries.

Employer pensions are mandatory for all employees in France. In Japan and the United Kingdom, operation of an approved pension plan allows firms to contract out of the national earnings-based social security program. In most countries, pensions are optional to the employer; however, if a pension is offered it must meet government guidelines.

In most countries, pension coverage is more likely for workers with high incomes and those who are employed in large firms. Patterns of pension coverage depend on the generosity of social security benefits and whether the social security benefit is a flat benefit for all retirees or is earnings related. The link between employer pensions and national pensions also depends on firm-based retirement policies and how these are linked to national retirement policies.

During the twentieth century employer pensions developed along side of maturing social security systems. Adequate retirement income for most workers required both pension and social security benefits. In the coming decades, population aging will cause national governments to reduce social security benefits and increase tax rates to support these benefits. In addition, there will be upward pressure on the age of eligibility for benefits. The key question for employer pensions is how will they be adjusted in response to these changes.

This section briefly describes the employer pension system in each of the six countries. Specific attention is paid to the relationship of employer pensions to social security benefits, costs, and age for eligibility. The impact of population aging on employer pensions is also discussed.

FRANCE

French workers are covered by mandatory private pension plans that supplement social security benefits. Initially, many of these plans were established through collective bargaining agreements; however, they have been extended to cover all workers by legislation. For coverage purposes, workers are divided into four categories; cadre employees (managers, supervisors, and technical employees), assimilated cadre employees (technicians, foremen, and senior salaried employees), article 35 employees (lower paid assimilated cadre employees), and non-cadre employees (all other employees). All jobs are ranked by a system of pension points which determine membership in the various categories. Plans covering each type of workers are coordinated by different pension associations.

Cadre employees have been mandatorily covered by supplementary pensions since 1947; all other employees have been covered since 1962. Together with social security benefits, the mandatory supplementary plans generally provide an adequate level of benefits for employees with earnings below the social security contribution ceilings. For workers with high earnings, additional pension income or private savings is needed.

The pension benefit is based on a points system. The benefit is calculated as the total number of employee's pension points times the pension point value for that year. Pension points are accrued by contributions by the employee and his or her employer along with any credit for periods of disability, unemployment, or sickness. In some cases, the number of children raised can also add to a person's total of pension points. The number of points earned each year are based on the employee's earnings-related contributions divided by the reference salary. The reference salary is an index of the average covered earnings for all members in each year.

The normal retirement age for these supplementary pensions is 65 for men and women; however, beginning in 1983, an unreduced pension could be started at age 60 if the worker has 37.5 years of coverage with participating firms. The eligibility requirements match those for social security benefits. Early retirement benefits with an actuarial reduction are available at age 55. These pension plans increase benefits on January 1 and July 1 of each year in accordance with increases in the pension point value. These increases allow benefits to rise in conjunction with price and real wage increases. Employees have an immediate vested right to all pension credits accumulated under these supplementary pension plans. Credits are portable across employers within the pension system.

Both the employer and employee contributions are required to finance the supplementary pensions. Contribution rates are a function of the level of earnings. In 1990, the contribution rate was 2.88 percent for employers and 1.92 percent for employees on earnings up to the social security limit of $22,600 in 1990. For earnings between $22,600 and $90,000 the contribution rates are 7.02 percent for employers and 2.34 percent for employees.

The national plans are financed on a pay-as-you-go basis with no accumulation of pension funds. The aging of the population reduces the number of workers relative to retirees in these plans. As a result, future pension benefits will have to be reduced or contributions must be increased substantially. This can be seen by referring to Tables 3 and 7. The use of pay-as-you-go financing makes the French pension system especially sensitive to population aging.

GERMANY

Although the German social security system provides relatively high levels of benefits, most employers provide supplementary pension coverage. Large employers are more likely to offer such coverage than small firms. Generally, comparable benefit programs are offered to salaried and hourly workers.

The average social security benefit after a full working career is between 40 and 45 percent of final earnings of workers with earnings below the earnings ceiling. Most supplementary pension plans provide benefits to raise this to between 50 and 60 percent of average final earnings. Pension benefits and other plan provisions vary widely across the country. For the most part, firms have adopted defined benefit plans. Pension benefits are typically final earnings plans although flat benefits are common where the benefit is a function of years of service and the job. Most plans do not require employee contributions.

National pension regulations govern vesting requirements, taxation of employees on employer's contributions, early retirement provisions, benefit insurance, and post-retirement increases in benefits. Pensions being paid to retirees are to be reviewed at least three years for possible adjustment that should be equal to the change in prices since the last adjustment. Vested deferred benefits typically are not increased until they become payable. Vesting requires 3 years of participation and 12 years of service or 10 years of participation and age 35.

Four types of funding are common in Germany. These are book reserves covering about two thirds of employees with an employer pension, support funds covering one quarter of participants, pension funds covering one fifth of participants, and direct insurance covering about 10 percent of participants. It is not uncommon for firms to employ several of these funding options.

In direct insurance plans the firm sets up a contractual relationship with an insurance company and names the employees as beneficiaries of the policies. In this case, employer contributions are considered taxable income to the employee. The employer may assume the employee's tax liability.

Pension funds can be run by the employer or more commonly, an association of employers. These funds must cover at least 200 persons. If the firm uses book reserves, employees are given a specific promise that benefits will be paid. No funds or reserves outside the company are accumulated.

In 1974, a comprehensive set of pension regulations were adopted in Germany. These regulations cover many of the same issues as ERISA in the United States. For example, 100 percent vesting is mandatory after 10 years and age 35. Pensions in the course of payment must be reviewed every three years and increased by the full increase in the cost of living.

JAPAN

The Japanese system of private retirement plans consists of lump sum severance pay plans and employer pensions.[14] One or both of these types of retirement programs are offered by 90 percent of firms. As in most countries, large firms are more likely to provide at least one of these retirement benefit options than small firms.

The lump sum severance plans are the traditional retirement benefit in Japan. Typically, one benefit formula covers all workers in a firm. The benefits depend on years of service and the reason for leaving the firm. Persons who quit receive a lower payment than persons who leave due to employer actions or policies. The difference between these two payments declines with additional years of service. The average lump-sum payment to a male college graduate leaving the firm at age 60 in 1988 was 3.5 years of annual salary. Book reserve funding of these plans is the norm.

Annuity pensions are relatively new in Japan. The development of Japanese pensions was stimulated by legislation in the 1960s. There are two types of pensions: tax qualified pension plans or employees pension funds. Plans in both systems are defined benefit pensions providing fixed term or life annuities.

Tax qualified plans were introduced in 1962 with the passage of legislation giving favorable tax treatment to pension contributions. Tax qualified plans must be funded through life insurance companies or trust companies. Plans are regulated by the Ministry of Finance. To establish a tax qualified pension an employer must have 15 or more employees.

Benefits are based on years of service and use either a flat benefit or earnings related formula. Virtually all of these pension often have lump sum options and a very high percentage of retirees select lump sum distributions. Workers who leave the plan prior to retirement receive a lump sum settlement as there is no practice of deferred vested benefits. Tax qualified plans are primarily adopted by smaller firms. In 1989 there were 79,000 plans covering 8.5 million employees.

Beginning in 1966, employers could establish employees pension funds. To institute such a pension, a firm must have 500 or more employees in a single firm or be part of a multi-employer group with at least 3,000 employees. In 1989, there were 1,259 funds covering 8.3 million workers. These pension plans are regulated by the Ministry of Health and Welfare.

Benefits from employees' pension funds are composed of two components. A substitutional component is directly linked to the earnings-related social security benefit provided by the Employees Pension Insurance program. In exchange for lower social security contributions, the firm assumes responsibility for the earnings- related benefit. In 1990, social security contributions were reduced by 3.2 percent for men and 3.0 percent for women if the company established an employees pension fund.

In addition to this contracted-out benefit, the pension must provide a supplementary component that is at least 30 percent of the substitute benefit. The company typically pays an unindexed pension benefit. The social security system pays the cost of indexing the contracted-out benefit to increases in prices. These plans are covered by a pension benefit insurance system that guarantees the payment of benefits to retirees.

Virtually all Japanese firms have mandatory retirement requirements. Previously, 55 was the typical age for mandatory retirement. The government has strongly encouraged firms to raise the age of compulsory retirement. During the past decade, the modal retirement age has risen to 60. With seniority-based earnings and final pay retirement plans, the increase in retirement ages has tended to increase labor costs. Firms are responding by reducing the rate of growth in earnings after age 55 and by limiting the proportion of earnings that apply in the determination of retirement benefits. The expected increase in the age of eligibility from 60 to 65 for social security benefits also will have important implications for the Japanese pension system.

THE NETHERLANDS

The Dutch social security system provides a flat benefit to retirees that equals approximately 60 percent of national earnings for workers with 50 years of credited service. Due to the nature of the flat benefit, most firms offer supplemental pensions. Plans may be for individual firms or industry-wide. Zweekhorst (1990) reports that there are 78 industry-wide pension funds covering over 1.5 million workers. Most large companies operate separate firm plans. There are approximately 1,000 single employer pension funds covering 700,000 employees. Additionally, companies can purchase insurance contracts for their workers. There are about 100,000 employees covered by these plans. Approximately one million public servants are covered by the pension fund for public employees.

All supplementary pension plans are regulated by provisions of various pension legislation. Regulations limit the amount of equity in the pension fund and the ownership of stock of the plan sponsor.

The normal retirement age is 65 for men and women although some plans allow women to retire at age 60 without penalty. Early retirement options are not commonly part of the pension plans. This is partly due to the fact that social security benefits can not be started prior to age 65. However, about half of all firms offer early retirement options outside the pension plan. These plans typically provide up to 80 percent of earnings to retirees between 60 and 65.

Benefit formulas typically range from 1.25 to 2.0 percent of average salary per year of service with most plans using 1.75 percent. A maximum of 40 years of credited service is used to determine benefits in most plans. Benefits are usually integrated with social security to prevent extremely high replacement rates.

Retirees who have had a full career of 40 or more years will receive a combined benefit equal to about 70 percent of earnings. Most plans use earnings-related formulas based on final average earnings over the past 3 to 5 years; however, many plans still use career average salary. Zweekhorst (1990) estimates that 73 percent of plans use final pay formulas and 18 percent adopt career average formulas.

Benefits are vested after a minimum of one year of service. In most plans, deferred vested pensions are indexed. This indexation raises vested future retirement benefits to reflect wage and price increases. Once pensions are received, they are regularly increased in response to rising prices. Virtually all beneficiaries received an increase between 1984 and 1988.

Despite the high level of employee contributions to social security, pension participants generally are required to contribute to their supplementary plan. Contribution rates are typically 3 to 5 percent of covered earnings.

UNITED KINGDOM

Historically social security has provided a relatively low replacement rate to all but low income workers. This follows from the use of a flat benefit set near the subsistence level. The need for additional retirement income has produced wide spread coverage by employer and personal pensions.

Pension plans may contract out of the earnings-related component of social security but not the flat benefit. The contracted-out benefit cannot be less than the social security earnings-related benefit. When the earnings-related benefit is contracted out, social security contribution rates are reduced. The normal retirement age is set to be 65 for men and 60 for women.

Pension plans can be either defined benefit or defined contribution plans (money purchase). Defined benefit plans are the most common type of pensions. The most common benefit formulas use final average earnings. Defined contribution plans have been allowed to contract out the earnings-related social security benefit only since 1988.

The maximum pension allowed is two thirds of final earnings. Since 1988, participation in a supplemental pension cannot be mandatory. Employees have the right to remain in social security or start an individual retirement plan. These new personal pension plans are portable from one job to another. They are defined contribution plans. Since 1988, 3.5 million employees have started personal pension plans.

Pensions in payment are regularly increased to reflect price increases. One survey found that in 1989 62 percent of plans had guaranteed increases, 36 percent awarded ad hoc increases, and only 2 percent gave no increases.

About 80 percent of British pension plans require employee contributions with the average contribution rate being 4 percent. Employees can make additional, voluntary contributions to increase retirement benefits. Benefits are vested after two years of participation. Vested benefits are revalued over time. The rate of increase in benefits is the increase in the cost of living up to a maximum annual increase of 5 percent.

UNITED STATES

The pension system in the United States has developed during the twentieth century along side of a maturing social security system. Historically, most large, unionized firms have adopted defined benefit plans while smaller nonunion companies are more likely to provide defined contribution plans. Between 1940 and 1980, coverage rates increased from 14 percent of all workers to around 50 percent. Since 1980, the proportion of the labor force covered by a pension plan has declined somewhat.

Because of the progressive benefit formula for social security benefits and their tax advantages, higher income workers have a higher demand for pension coverage. Coverage rates also are higher for union members and workers in large firms. Substantial variation exists in the coverage rates by industry and occupation.

Most defined benefit plans use earnings-based benefit formulas and most of the plans using these formulas are based on final average earnings to calculate benefits. Plans governed by collective bargaining agreements typically determine benefits as a flat amount or as dollars per year of service.

Pensions are highly regulated. Beginning with the Employee Retirement Income Security Act of 1974, the federal government set minimum vesting and funding standards, required considerable reporting of pension finances, and mandated the purchase of insurance to guarantee benefits in the event of plan termination. During the 1980s, regulations have been regularly revised to extend the scope of government oversight.

Since the mid-1970s, there has been a pronounced trend toward greater use of defined contribution plans. This movement has been the result of continued regulation that has raised the price of offering defined benefit plans relative to defined contribution plans. The trend toward greater use of defined contribution plans has also been caused by structural changes in the economy.

In general, normal retirement ages vary between 60 and 65, although some plans offer full retirement benefits that are a function only of years of service. Virtually all pension plans have early retirement options. In most cases, early retirement reductions are substantially less than the actuarial equivalent benefit.

Less than 5 percent of private pension plans offer an automatic indexation of benefits. However, many plans provide regular ad hoc increases. These increases tend to be significantly less than the increase in prices. Vested deferred benefits are frozen at the time a worker leaves the firm. There is typically no indexation of these benefits for either wage or price increases.

PENSIONS, SOCIAL SECURITY, AND POPULATION AGING

Employer pensions developed along side of maturing social security systems throughout the twentieth century. During the same period, national economies developed, real incomes increased, and employment shifted away from self-employment, and agriculture toward manufacturing. The role of employer pensions is closely linked to that of social security, firm personnel policies, and national socioeconomic conditions. The primary objective of both programs is to provide adequate retirement income and to facilitate orderly, planned retirement. However, both types of plans are often structured to achieve other objectives such as increases in the probability that older workers will retire.

Population aging will necessitate major changes in social security systems in all developed countries. The key question for this study is how will employer pensions respond to the aging of the labor force and the changes in the social security system. This section assesses several of the most important of these possible changes.

1. How will pensions respond to changes in social security? The importance of employer pensions depends on the average generosity of social security benefits and whether these benefits are earnings-related or flat-rate. Obviously, the higher the replacement rate from social security, the less important role there is for pensions. Flat-rate social security benefits create a need for additional benefits for workers with higher career earnings. In some countries, pension benefits are integrated with social security benefits. In these cases, reductions in social security benefits would lead to higher pension benefits unless the pension plan is revised.

The likely reduction of replacement rates from social security will increase the need for additional retirement income. This will create an opportunity for employer pensions to expand. Working against increased pension benefits is the rising payroll tax rates necessary to support social security. Will firms and workers be willing to devote even more of potential income to retirement programs so that pensions can fill the gap being created by social security? In countries such as France where employer pensions are also pay-as-you-go, the financing problem is even greater.

2. How will pensions respond to higher retirement ages? In most countries, normal and early retirement ages for pensions are closely linked to those of social security. Population aging necessitates that governments consider raising the normal retirement age for social security benefits. How will firms respond to this increase?

Over the past three decades, many developed countries have lowered normal retirement ages or introduced early options for social security. For the most part, employers accommodated these changes by lowering the retirement ages in their pension programs. The decline in retirement ages was consistent with firm personnel policies that attempted to reduce the number of older workers.

The increase in social security retirement ages and the desire by governments to increase the proportion of older persons who remain in the labor force now seems to go against the continuing desire by firms to promote early retirement. This dichotomy of interests will be an important aspect of pension policy in the twenty-first century.

3.   How will pensions respond to further governmental regulation? In an effort to safe guard pension benefits, most governments have enacted pension legislation that regulates many important aspects of pension plans. Such regulations obviously alter the structure of pension plans but may also affect the likelihood that firms will offer a pension.

Evidence suggests that the decline in pension coverage and the shift from defined benefit to defined contribution plans in the United States is influenced by regulatory policies. Thus, the ability of governments to achieve certain objectives through regulations is limited by the possibility of firms opting out of the pension system. Of course, governments could make employer pensions a mandatory form of compensation.

4.   How will pensions respond to the aging of the labor force? The aging of the labor force may have direct implications for employer pensions. In the past, firms have adopted pension provisions to encourage older workers to retire. This personnel policy was based on the higher labor costs associated with older workers, with many years of job tenure. In addition, the general belief that productivity begins to decline after a certain age also stimulated firms to encourage early retirement.

Most of these polices were adopted at a time when there were large cohorts of young persons entering the labor force and the relative price of young workers was low compared to older workers. The aging of the population is accompanied by sharp declines in the size of cohorts of young workers. Thus, firms will have a more difficult time hiring young workers and their relative wage will tend to rise. At the same time, the cohort of older persons will be larger and this should tend to depress their relative wage.

These projected demographic events and the accompanying changes in relative wages should increase the demand for older workers. Whether employer attitudes toward employing older workers change is a significant factor in determining future changes in pensions. Only if employers are seeking to retain older workers will they voluntarily adjust their pension plans. Only if older persons remain active workers can the retirement age for social security be raised without causing substantial declines in income at older ages.

5.   How will the public and private retirement programs of Europe develop during the 1990s with the continuation of economic unification? The preceeding discussion has illustrated the substantial diversity in retirement programs among European countries. The increased coordination among the European nations may produce a more homogeneous set of social security programs and employer pensions. Given the major differences in these programs today, it is likely that these retirement plans will retain their diversity into the twenty-first century.

ENDNOTES

1. In the United States, the total fertility rate fell from a high of over 3.5 during the late 1950's to 1.74 in 1976. Since the mid 1970's the fertility rate has increased slightly reaching 2.05 in 1990.

2. These data include all government expenditures on social security and for government employee pensions paid by national and local governments.

3. The proportion of gross domestic product devoted to pensions in Japan is projected to increase from 4.2 percent in 1980 to 13.4 percent in 2025 (Heller), et al, 1990).

4. This discussion draws on information in Gordon (1988), The Wyatt Co. (1990), Foster (1990), EBRI (1990), and U.S. Social Security Administration (1991) among other general discussions of social security systems in these countries.

5. The maximum attainable benefits reported for each of the six countries are reported in EBRI (1990). They represent the maximum benefit payable to a fully insured single worker retiring at the normal retirement age. National currency is converted into U.S. dollars using exchange rates as of January 15, 1990. All other values reported in the chapter are converted using the average exchange rate that prevailed during the first quarter of 1990.

6. The discussion covers only the West German social security system prior to unification. Efforts to merge the systems of East and West Germany are now underway (see Furer and Lang, 1990).

7. Accumulation of assets in the social security funds was, in part, a function of post-war inflations that increased the nominal asset prices. In fact, the social security systems had only a limited degree of funding (Schmaehl, 1989).

8. For a discussion of the movement toward equalization of treatment of men and women in the German social security system, see Puidak (1987).

9. For a detailed discussion of the Japanese social security programs, see Clark (1990).

10. Hill (1990) provides an interesting historical review of the develpment of social security in the United Kingdom.

11. The high participation rates of older Japanese men occurs despite the availability of social security benefits at age 60, about half of the labor force being covered by a private pension, and relatively high average per capita income.

12. OECD (1988) examines the challenges to social security posed by populatin aging in the developed countries.

13. This discussion is based on information in The Wyatt Co. (1990), Foster (1990), and Turner and Dailey (1990) along with several other general reviews of international pensions. For Horlick (1980).

14. Clark (1990) provides a detailed discussion of Japanese pensions.

Discussions

G. Lawrence Atkins

INTRODUCTION

Developed nations share a population aging phenomenon in the next few decades that is forcing a re-evaluation of social security programs, the cost of public support for early retirement, and the role of older workers in the economy. Robert Clark's paper <u>Population Aging and Retirement Policy: An International Perspective</u> provides an extensive description of population aging in six developed countries and their varied responses to retirement age and benefit levels in their social security programs.

A review of Dr. Clark's paper produces a number of interesting conclusions. First, the developed countries share a phenomenon of population aging that is surprisingly consistent in the burden that it will pose for these economies in the future. There are certainly differences among the countries in the rate and timing of aging in the 75-year period from 1950-2025. The rates of increase in the concentration of the 65 and older population vary from a mere doubling in France and the United Kingdom to a fourfold increase in Japan. And while Japan is experiencing its greatest surges during the 1980s and '90s, Europe and the United States are expected to experience their most rapid increases after 2010. Nonetheless, all of the countries are undergoing substantial population aging, and all will reach the year 2025 with one-fifth to one-fourth of their populations age 65 and older.

Second, despite general similarities in population aging, different countries have reached very different results in setting social security retirement ages and funding private pensions. These variations are due, in part, to the varying mixes of public and private programs in each country. Some countries rely heavily on social security and manage retirement age policy through these benefits. Germany and France, for example, have relatively high social security replacement rates and small occupational pensions. Neither country has funded private pension plans -- France has ''pay-as-you-go'' financing and Germany funds with employers' book reserves. Both countries adjust social security retirement ages for some groups in an attempt to meet varying retirement needs through a single public program. Other countries, such as the United States and the Netherlands, with lower social security replacement rates and more significant funded private pensions, adopt uniform social security retirement ages and use the flexibility of the private sector benefits to meet the needs of various groups.

Third, these countries have ended up with different labor force participation rates for older men, that, at least in some countries, present problems for the cost of social security programs in the future. These differences appear related to a mixture of cultural values and the structure of public sector and private sector benefits. Continental Europe has a strong tradition of reducing unemployment among older workers through disability and early retirement programs. France's ''pre-pension'', Germany's ''partial pensions'' and the Netherlands' liberal disability benefits have helped to produce the lowest labor force participation rates (4 to 6 percent) for men aged 65 and older. The United States, with an ethic of continuing work and less sympathy for older workers, limits public early retirement and disability benefits and relies on private-sector benefits to meet cyclical needs to reduce older worker unemployment. The U.S. has a comparatively high rate of participation (18 percent). Japan has the highest rate of participation (43 percent) despite having the earliest public retirement age and strong private- sector early retirement policies. Japan's high labor force participation seems instead largely due to unique cultural values and a pattern of second careers for older workers.

Finally, all of the countries have begun to respond in some fashion to the problems population aging will pose for their retirement programs. While differences exist in the timing and sequencing of social security retirement age and benefit changes, most of the countries have begun reducing early retirement subsidies or raising retirement ages to manage rising costs in the systems. For example, Germany, which added early retirement benefits for a variety of groups in 1972, began reducing early retirement benefits in 1989. France lowered its age for full benefits as recently as 1983 and is now considering raising it again. Japan has proposed a retirement age increase, and the United Kingdom is considering eliminating early retirement benefits. Only the United States has actually enacted an increase in the age for full benefits, from 65 to age 67, phased-in after the year 2000.

As we near the 21st century, however, it is surprising how few countries have made any significant policy changes in anticipation of the demographic phenomenon they share in the next 25 years. Even the United States, with its social security retirement age increase, has barely begun to face the challenge of supporting a larger aged population by the year 2025. The options for all of these countries are limited and become more limited as time passes. In general, there are three options: greater economic growth, delayed retirement and increased labor force participation of the elderly, or reduced retiree well- being.

GROWTH

Economic growth as a solution relies on a rise in worker productivity to sustain a larger future retired population at today's level of relative economic burden. A fifty percent increase in individual worker productivity will enable the same worker who today supports one-third of a retiree's benefits to support one-half of a retiree's benefits in thirty years with no increase in relative burden. Thus, the ability of these countries today to raise personal savings and domestic investment capital and spur economic growth will have a direct affect on their ability to sustain a larger retired population in the future.

Savings may be created, in part, by pre-funding retirement income programs. Surprisingly, however, developed countries seem to have done relatively little to accumulate retirement assets to offset future retirement income liabilities. Pre-funding of the social security system itself is one option, but most developed countries do not now pre-fund their social security programs. A few, the United States included, prefund a portion of the social security system, although the U.S. in the aggregate is expanding its debt rather than creating savings. Pre-funding occupational pensions is another option. The United States is particularly accomplished at encouraging personal savings through occupational pensions, with nearly $3 trillion of assets currently accumulated in pension plans. Most developed countries, however, appear to have done little to pre-fund occupational pensions either. France, for example, has mandated private pensions that are not pre-funded. Germany's pensions are largely funded with corporate book reserves, meaning that employers expect to pay pension benefits out of future earnings.

While growth may be the most desirable solution, it may also be the most difficult to affect. First, as noted above, growth is a function of overall fiscal and economic policy and not just social security or retirement income policy. Government policies in other areas may easily offset the effects of social security or private pension "savings". Massive United States federal budget deficits currently consume all of its social security "savings" and more, leaving social security with little more than a ledger entry, and forcing the U.S. to borrow over $90 billion a year (as of 1990) from foreign investors. In fact, some analysts argue that the availability of excess social security tax revenues are making it easier for the U.S. Congress to overspend in other programs.

Second, creating real government savings through publically financed programs is almost a hopeless task for democratic institutions. The discipline to reduce spending and raise taxes to balance public budgets is itself difficult and unpopular. Raising taxes above the cost of current government operations in order to increase the government's ownership of domestic capital is even more difficult to justify, and too much to expect of a popularly- elected legislature.

Most importantly, economic growth is a function of a complex interplay of factors, only some of which are amenable to public policy. With tremendous advances in global transportation and communication, increasing shares of the world's investment capital and its economic growth can be expected to shift to emerging nations with large low-paid labor forces and relatively low production costs, reducing the rate of growth in the mature industrial economies of developed nations. In addition, many of these developed nations have responded to slowed growth and higher unemployment by expanding eligibility for social security and private pension benefits, creating an added competitive burden for their domestic industries.

While developed nations may want to rely upon economic growth as their preferred solution to sustaining the burden of an aging population, realistically they will be forced to adopt other policies as well. There are two other general options: either keep older workers in the labor force for longer periods, or reduce future retirement benefit levels.

WORK

Countries choosing to avoid the unpleasantness of social security benefit cuts will pursue a policy of eliminating early retirement incentives and encouraging delayed retirement, in an effort to reduce the proportion of older persons receiving public benefits. The United States, for example, moved in this direction in 1983 by enacting a future increase in the age for social security benefits from 65 to 67 and a reduction in benefit payments at early ages, coupled with reductions in the earnings limit and increases in the delayed retirement benefit. The intent was to increase the economic incentives for work and reduce the incentives for retirement at any particular age up to age 70. (The 1983 changes can also be viewed as a benefit cut at any particular age relative to prior law, although supporters have argued that in conjunction with rising life expectancies, the retirement age change adjusts lifetime benefits to match those provided earlier cohorts).

The problem with work as a solution is that governments may have a limited ability to influence the demand and supply of older workers. Demand is a particular problem. The availability of jobs for older workers is a primarily a function of the health of the economy. In slack economies, older workers are the last to find employment and are bid out of the labor force either at public expense or at a cost to the economy through private benefits.

While public benefits have been used in Europe to offset the effects of plant shutdowns and remove displaced workers from the labor force, private-sector responses have prevailed in the United States, although the private-sector costs have in some cases been transferred to the government. Labor force reductions in the United States during the recession of the early 1980s produced special retirement incentives which, in some industries, burdened firms with substantial unfunded pension costs. These added costs later helped force some of these companies into bankruptcy and transfered unfunded pension obligations to the federal pension insurance program (the PBGC) and through it to other companies that pay pension insurance premiums.

Even if jobs are readily available or can be created, there is an important question of the extent to which retirement age changes and economic incentives in retirement plans can influence the labor supply decisions of older workers. Individual preferences for work or leisure, the difficulty of late- career job changes and overall mobility of the workforce, the health status and educational attainment of older workers, and career expectations may have more to do with age of retirement than the structure of retirement incentives.

Uniform national retirement policy implemented through heavily- weighted public benefits becomes a crude and inefficient mechanism to influence labor supply. If the benefits influence behavior at all, they are likely to have too much influence, encouraging the productive and unproductive to retire together. Explicit early retirement incentives in the German and French social security systems, for example, appear to have left practically no males in their labor forces older than age 65. Broad eligibility rules for disability insurance programs have a similar effect. Countries that pay benefits for "partial disability" draw older workers from the labor force who could still work under more restrictive disability standards. The Netherlands, with its broad disability definition, has as few men over age 65 still working as Germany or France.

The alternative to a uniform national rule is a relatively "age- neutral" public policy. Age-neutral policy defers retirement age issues to the private-sector. It either allows private firms to structure benefit incentives that will stimulate labor supply to meet their own cyclical needs for older workers, or it frees individuals from economic incentives altogether and permits labor supply decisions to be made on other grounds.

The concept of an age-neutral public policy is that by providing equivalent public benefits at different ages, financial incentives for retirement at particular ages (within a reasonable age band) are eliminated. The United States has moved in the direction of age-neutral public policy through a variety of changes. The 1983 Social Security Amendments raised social security's delayed retirement credit to produce an actuarially- equivalent benefit that yields the same lifetime benefits at any retirement age from 62 through 70. Recent private pension law changes eliminated benefit funding rules that provided federal tax benefits for early retirement subsidies. Additional federal age discrimination laws have sought to limit private pension subsidies offered only to early retirees and not available to older workers.

In general, U.S. policy has favored the use of employer-structured incentives to manage the labor supply to meet fluctuations in demand. While public policy in the United States has prohibited mandatory retirement by firms, it has generally left firms free, within limits imposed through age discrimination and pension rules, to structure window plans or provide special supplemental early retirement benefits that may accomplish similar objectives through financial incentives. In the U.S. model, private pension incentives have a much more significant effect on decisions to retire than social security retirement ages. Roughly two-fifths of American men who receive social security early retirement benefits at age 62 are already retired by that age. While early retirement in the U.S. is influenced by health status and job availability, among other things, the availability of employer- provided benefits at early ages is certainly a major factor.

Gradually, however, U.S. policy is shifting toward enhancing individual flexibility in making retirement decisions. Age discrimination laws have increasingly aimed at prohibiting targeted retirement incentives. Increasing defined benefit plan regulation and complexity, combined with a growing concern about pension portability has shifted the growth in employer pensions toward defined contribution plans. These plans reduce the employer's ability to influence retirement decisions by accumulating individual retirement assets, the value of which is generally unaffected by an individual's retirement age. In addition, there has been growing interest in encouraging individual asset accumulation for retirement unrelated to employment (such as individual retirement accounts (IRAs). All of these approaches meet two objectives. They mitigate the employer's influence over retirement age choices and labor supply, and they provide benefits that are unaffected by an individual's choice of retirement age.

Countries that have encouraged early retirement with generous social security benefits and other public policy initiatives now find they may have gone too far in reducing the labor force participation of older men. Substantial public policy changes in the reverse, however, may have an equally clumsy effect on the incomes and labor force participation of older workers. Increasingly, countries are choosing to reduce the influence of public policy to permit private-sector pensions to be more responsive to firm-level or individual needs, and permit older worker labor supply to be more responsive to cyclical patterns in the economy. In a flexible system, the structure of retirement benefits is reduced and the demand for labor is increased as a factor influencing retirement decisions and the ability of workers to remain employed for longer periods in old age.

Flexible retirement policy also reduces the ability of the government to influence a long-term pattern of increased labor supply among older men as a response to the demographic transformations in the society. In addition, financial incentives provided through public and private retirement benefits are only one factor affecting retirement decisions of older workers in developed countries in the future. Weight also has to be given in public policy to efforts that would influence health status, attitudes about work and leisure, the demand for labor, and other cultural and economic factors that contribute to retirement decisions.

BENEFIT REDUCTIONS

A country that cannot grow its way out of its demographic burden and is unable to create the additional jobs needed to retain older workers in the labor force, will be faced with a Hobson's choice. They can either reduce the relative incomes of younger workers through taxes in order to sustain the incomes of retirees or reduce the incomes of retirees through retirement benefit cuts, relative to younger workers.

Economies that are in this predicament because they have failed to outgrow their demographic burden will have little choice. An increase in taxes will only further their economic problems. A reduction in retiree benefit levels will be the favored solution. But the reduction in income for retirees will also have its consequences for the economy -- contributing to declining real income levels, lower levels of consumption and savings, and a general decline in the standard of living.

We need only look to Eastern Europe to see this predicament clearly today. Poland's social insurance system now provides one-fourth of the personal income in the country, financed by a 43 percent tax on firm payrolls. The average benefit, however, provides barely a subsistence level income. Poland's responses to low levels of productivity have been to provide public early retirement and disability benefits to large portions of the workforce. Future growth in the economy will be hampered by high social insurance taxes on firms (or later on wages), yet there is little room in an impoverished country to reduce benefits or reduce the number of early retirement or disability beneficiaries. At the same time, Poland faces its own population aging in the future (growing from 2.2 to 1.76 workers per beneficiary between 1990 and 2020). This situation will be greatly aided by economic growth. In the meantime, Poland will be forced to modify benefits, change the conditions for early retirement and disability, and build programs to help pensioners return to the workforce. Implementation of the changes will have to be especially cautious to avoid damaging their fragile democracy.

Dr. Clark suggests, in his paper, that a future reduction in social security benefits might encourage an offsetting expansion of private pension benefits. This seems an implausible scenario. Where pensions are not pre-funded (as in France and Germany) a benefit increase would be financed as a current business cost, not unlike the burden that forced cuts in social security benefits in the first place.

Where pensions are pre-funded, a projected increase in pension benefits would require a comparable increase in pension funding and thus in national savings in the decades before the demographic burden materializes. The higher level of savings and investment in the economy generated by higher pension contributions could well help bring about the productivity improvements needed to avert future social security benefit reductions. The need for reductions is a sign of the inability of the economy to generate the necessary savings, including the pre-funding of additional pensions, that would foster growth.

Even if additional funding for pensions were consistent with an economic condition that necessitated reductions in social security benefits, private pensions would prove to be a poor substitute for public benefits. While social insurance in the United States covers virtually all workers and thus nearly all of the population, private pensions at their best have only covered half of today's workforce. Lack of coverage, lack of portability of occupational pensions across jobs, and restrictions that interfere with the accumulation and vesting of pension benefits all serve to reduce to unacceptable proportions the number of workers who would be entitled to receive supplemental benefits from pension plans.

CONCLUSIONS

Dr. Clark's paper is a fascinating and well-structured presentation of the dimensions of population aging in a few select developed countries and of the implications of population aging for retirement age policy and the structure of public and private retirement income programs. While he gives great weight to modifications these countries have made or will need to make in public retirement ages and benefit structures, he gives only passing mention to the underlying economic challenge.

In a developed world that has encouraged early retirement, reduced labor force participation, retained high unemployment rates, and now faces a growing proportion of older persons in the population, the ability to sustain this demographic shift will depend upon raising current levels of savings and investment in order to induce future economic growth. Ironically, some of these countries have required or permitted the development of unfunded private pension plans that do not contribute to current investment but have created additional obligations to be fulfilled through future economic output. This is even true, to an extent, in the United States where all of social security's reserve accumulation and even a portion of private pension savings is offset (or consumed) by huge and growing government deficits.

The ideal solution for the future would be to find the current discipline to increase contemporary savings and investment in order to build the labor productivity that can sustain an older and more dependent population. This argues for a retirement policy that provides greater flexibility for employers and individuals to modify their retirement incentives and decisions to respond to economic conditions in the future. It also argues for a reduced role for government in providing generic early retirement and disability benefits that induce far-reaching changes in the labor supply of older workers.

Robert J. Myers

Dr. Clark has presented a very interesting and important paper on population trends in six countries over the next 35 years as they affect retirement policy under social security systems and private pension plans. It is somewhat unfortunate that the data do not relate to the next 40-50 years, because the upward trends shown will not possibly have reached their fruition in as short a period as 25 years.

Age 65 is used as the borderline between the two categories, working population and aged population. Then, two measures of the extent of aging of the population are used, namely, the population aged 65 and over as a percentage of the total population and also as a percentage of the population aged 20-64. On the whole, the latter seems a somewhat better measure as to the financial burden of the retired population on the working population. Perhaps, however, it might have been better to have a variable, and increasing, age borderline over the years.

The extent of aging of the population shows somewhat the same general picture in all countries except Japan. Thus, in the five other countries involved, the aging situation shows a plateau in 1980-2000 and even until 2010 in France and the United States, and thereafter accelerates sharply in the remaining years up to 2025. This is a clear reason why consideration of demographic problems should not be myopic and be confined to only a few near- future years. Future prognostication of most elements in our social and economic lives is fraught with uncertainty, but this is certainly not the case as to the age structures of populations.

Although Dr. Clark did not point out the special situation in Japan, I believe that such is clearly present. Specifically, no plateau in the aging trend occurs in the 1980's and 1990's, but rather a significant steady upward trend is present. The likely reason for this is that Japan was a very high- mortality country before World War II and after then had a quite sudden improvement in mortality (in part as a result of public health measures sponsored by the military occupation). As a result, the effect of rapidly declining mortality at all ages resulted in steady increases in the aging of the population.

Dr. Clark well points out that the aging of populations is due both to decreases in fertility and to reduction in mortality at the older ages. I might point out, however, that reductions in mortality at the younger and middle ages also add to this effect, because a greater number of people then live to old age. Also, it is interesting to note that in the past decade a small, but significant, increase in fertility has occurred in the United States and in some other countries; this can have some counteracting effect on the aging of the population in the future.

Quite obviously, the aging of the population in all of the countries considered will put serious financial strains on their social security programs and their private pension plans. A somewhat partial offsetting effect is that, with fewer children, there will be lower child-support costs. In my opinion, the solution to the unfavorable cost effect of the aging trend is clearly to raise the Normal Retirement Age (the age at which full- rate benefits are first payable). Japan and the United States have already done this, and further action in the former country in this direction seems to be under way. It is noteworthy that the four European countries are at last recognizing the long-term problem involved and are reversing the previous short-sighted views that lowering the retirement age was desirable to combat unemployment.

In my view, the United States may well have to raise the NRA beyond age 67, at least to age 68, and possibly over the long run to age 70. Japan, which had an NRA of 60 for men and 55 for women in its earnings-related program until 1986, but then is gradually increasing the age for women to 60 over a 15-year period, is attempting to have a uniform age of 65, which would both move in the direction of higher retirement ages and also provide equal treatment by sex.

Digressing a moment, it is interesting to note that, in a country as scientifically advanced as Japan, the reduction figures for early retirement and the increase factors for delayed retirement in its National Pension Scheme (flat universal benefits with an NRA of 65) are inequitable. The reduction facor is 58 percent at age 60, and the increase factor at age 70 is 188 percent, whereas the true actuarial factors would be approximately 70 percent and 140-150 percent, respectively. Further, the factors do not increase on a monthly basis by age at initial claim, but rather only annually. Rather surprisingly, the vast majority of the beneficiaries take the poor actuarial bargain of claiming benefits at age 60 rather than the wise actuarial choice of waiting until age 70 (assuming that they could afford to do so). But they do have the foresight almost universally to claim benefits at about the time of their birthday, rather than waiting a number of months and having the same reduction (or increase) factor.

The United Kingdom is in a rather peculiar situation as to retirement ages at the present time. Until recently, the NRA was 65 for men and 60 for women both in the Social Security program and in private pensions. However, the principles of the European Economic Community require equal treatment by sex in this respect, and the courts can enforce this for private pensions, but it is not so effective for governmental social security systems. As a result, private pension plans have gone to a uniform basis for the NRA by sex -- generally (and, in my opinion, wisely) to age 65 for everybody.

Although the U.K. government is well aware of the need to raise retirement ages, it is on the horns of a dilemma in equalizing the NRA by sex; to lower to age 60 for men would be too costly and to raise to age 65 for women would produce great complaints from them. The solution, of course, as always in such cases, is to raise the NRA for women gradually over a period of time, and perhaps on a deferred basis. In the meantime, an anomalous situation has occurred for private pension plans which attempt to have equal treatment by sex when they permit early retirement before age 65, by giving bridging payments to men aged 60 to 64 to equalize for the situation of larger social security benefits for women at those ages. The EEC courts have rejected this "equalizing in the aggregate" procedure as being unfair discrimination when only the private pension plan is considered.

I am contrained to point out certain myths and misstatements present in Dr. Clark's paper as it deals with the U.S. Old-Age, Survivors, and Disability Insurance program, as follows:

1) OASDI is stated to be financed on a pay-as-you-go basis both in the past and in the future. Although this was so on a de facto basis in the 1960s and by legislation in the 1970s, it was not the case before the 1960's, nor is it estimated to be so during the next 50 years, when a mammoth fund will be built up and then depleted (after which, if the benefit structure is left unchanged, and tax rates are increased appropriately, OASDI again will be on a pay-as- you-go basis). As an aside, I might mention my strong view that the financing of OASDI should be changed so that it will be, at all times, on a pay-as-you-go basis.

2) Actuarial early-retirement reduction factors are stated to be penalties. Such is not the case, because they have been determined on an equitable basis -- just as persons who buy whole-life insurance policies at older ages pay more than those who do so at younger ages, and this is not considered a penalty.

3) The paper states that the 1977 Amendments significantly reduced costs by lowering future benefits. In a sense this was true, because changes were made to rectify a faulty run-away benefit- computation procedure, but the intent was to maintain benefit levels at what was previously intended.

4) It is stated that the 1983 Amendments moved the program toward universal coverage. While it is true that some small extension of coverage occurred then, the vast majority of the movement toward universal coverage occurred much earlier -- essentially in the 1950 and 1954 Amendments.

5) It is not brought out that the benefit formula for 1991 that is described is for persons who attain age 62 then, or who become disabled or die before age 62 in 1991.

6) The Average Indexed Monthly Earnings for those attaining age 62 in 1991 and after is stated to be computed from earnings at ages 22 - 61, whereas actually it is computed over the best 35 years of indexed earnings after 1950.

7) The NRA is stated as rising above age 65 beginning in 2000. Actually, this first occurs in 2003, because the NRA for persons attaining age 65 in 2000-02 continues to be 65. This misstatement appears widely, even by the Social Security Administration itself! A correct usage of the year 2000 is that the NRA increases beyond age 65 for persons who attain age 62 in that year.

In summary, Dr. Clark clearly demonstrates the need for all developed countries to begin raising the NRA for both social security systems and private pension plans. Likewise, labor and management should find ways to provide attractive employment opportunities for persons age 60 and over, even if it means that these will be with shortened work weeks and reduced responsibility -- as has been done in Japan.

Bibliography

Aaron, Henry J. (1982). *Economic Effects of Social Security.* Washington, D.C.: Brookings.

Aaron, Henry J., Barry P. Bosworth and Gary Burtless (1989). *Can America Afford to Grow Old? Paying for Social Security.* Washington, D.C.: The Brookings Institution.

Abel, Andrew, Douglas Bernheim, and Laurence, J. Kotlikoff (1991). *"Do the Average and Marginal Propensities to Consume Rise with Age?"*

Ahlburg, D.A. and J. Vaupel. (1990) "Alternative Projections of the U.S. Population." *Demography.* Vol 24(4):639-52

Alho, J. (Forthcoming). "Stochastic Methods in Population Forecasting." *International Journal of Forecasting.*

Alter, G., and J.C. Riley (1989). "Frailty, Sickness and death: Models of Morbidity and Mortality in Historical Populations," *Population Studies* 43:25-46.

Andrews, Emily and O.S. Mitchell (1986). "The Current and Future Role of Pensions in Old-Age Economic Security." *Benefits Quarterly* 2:25-36.

Andrews, Emily S. (1989). *Pension Policy and Small Employers: At What Price Coverage?* Washington, DC: Employee Benefit Research Institute.

Andrews, Emily S. (1992). "The Growth and Distribution of 401(k) Plans." *Trends in Pensions.* John A. Turner and Daniel Beller, eds. Washington, D.C.: U.S. Government Printing Office.

Andrisani, P. J. (1977). Effects of Health Problems on the Work Experience of Middle-Aged Men. *Industrial Gerontology.* 4:97-112.

Antos, J., W. Mellow, and J. E. Triplett (1979). "What is a Current Equivalent to Unemployment Rates of the Past?" *Monthly Labor Review.* March:36-46.

Auerbach, Alan J. and Laurence J. Kotlikoff (1990a). "Demographics, Fiscal Policy, and U.S. Saving in the 1980s and Beyond," in L. Summers, ed., *Tax Policy and the Economy,* v. 4. Chicago: University of Chicago Press.

Auerbach, Alan J. and Laurence J. Kotlikoff (July 1990b). "Tax Aspects of Policy Towards Aging Populations: Canada and the United States," *NBER Working Paper # 3405.*

Auerbach, Alan J. and Laurence J. Kotlikoff (1987). *Dynamic Fiscal Policy.* Cambridge, England: Cambridge University Press.

Auerbach, Alan J., Jagadeesh Gokhale and Laurence J. Kotlikoff (1991). "Generational Accounts - A Meaningful Alternative to Deficit Accounting," in D. Bradford, ed., *Tax Policy and the Economy*, v. 5. Chicago: University of Chicago Press.

Auerbach, Alan J., Jinyong Cai and Laurence J. Kotlikoff (1991). "U.S. Demographics and Saving: Predictions of Three Saving Models," in *Carnegie-Rochester Series on Public Policy*.

Auerbach, Alan J., Laurence J. Kotlikoff, Robert P. Hagemann, and Giuseppe Nicoletti (1989). "The Economic Dynamics of an Aging Population: The Case of Four OECD Countries," *OECD Economic Studies*.

Avery, Robert B. and Arthur B. Kennickell (1990). "Measurement of Household Saving Obtained from First Differencing Wealth Estimates." Presented at the Twenty-First General Conference of the International Association for Research in Income and Wealth, August 20-26, 1989 (Revised February 1990).

Bailey, M.N. (1987). "Aging and the Ability to Work". In *Work, Health, and Income Among the Elderly*. Ed. G. Burtless. Washington, D.C.: Brookings.

Ball, David George (1991). Statement before the College and University Personnel Association, 19 February 1991. Unpublished.

Barsky, A.J. (1988). *Worried Sick*, Boston: Little, Brown, and Co.

Bean, Frank D., Jeffrey S. Passel, and Barry Edmonston (1990). "Undocumented Migration Since IRCA: An Overall Assessment," :251-265 in Frank D. Bean, Barry Edmonston, and Jeffrey S. Passel, *Undocumented Migration to the United States: IRCA and the Experience of the 1980s*. Washington, D.C.: The Urban Institute Press.

Bebbington, A.C. (1988). "The Expectation of Life Without Disability in England and Wales," *Social Science and Medicine* 27:321-326.

Bennett, N. and David E. Bloom (1990). "Plotting Our Destiny: Interpreting Our Demographic Trajectory." *American Planning Association Journal* Spring :135-39.

Biggs, John H. (1985). *A New Look at the Regulation and Taxation of Private Pension Plans*. St. Louis, Mo.: The Center for the Study of American Business, Washington University. Working Paper no. 91.

Blau, F.D. and M.A. Ferber (1986). *The Economics of Women, Men, and Work*. Prentice-Hall. Englewood Cliffs, N.J.

Blendon, Robert J. and Karen Donelan (1990). "The Public and Emerging Debate over National Health Insurance." *The New England Journal of Medicine* (July 19) 323, no. 3:208-212.

Blendon, Robert J.; Robert Leitman, Ian Morrison, and Karen Donelan (1990). "Satisfaction with Health Systems in Ten Nations." *Health Affairs* (Summer) 9, no. 2:185-192.

Bodie, Zvi (1989). *Pensions as Retirement Income Insurance*. Cambridge, Mass.: National Bureau of Economic Research. Working Paper no. 2917.

Boskin, Michael, Michael Knetter, and Laurence J. Kotlikoff (1985). "Changes in the Age Distribution of Income in the United States, 1968-1984," mimeo (October).

Bosworth, Barry, Gary Burtless and John Sabelhaus (1991). "The Decline in Saving: Evidence from Household Surveys." The Brookings Institution, mimeo.

Bosworth, Barry (1990). "The Global Decline in Saving: Some International Comparisons." Brookings Discussion Papers in International Economics No. 83, The Brookings Institution.

Bound, J. (1989). "The Health and Earnings of Rejected Disability Insurance Applicants," *American Economic Review* 79:482-503.

Bound, J. and T. Waidman (1990). "Disability Transfers and the Labor Force Attachment of Older Men: Evidence from the Historical Record," NBER Working Paper, No. 3437.

Bourgeois-Pichat, J. (1986). "The Unprecedented Shortage of Births in Europe." *Population and Development Review.* Vol 12, Supplement:3-25.

Buck Consultants. Actuarial Report, Projected Postretirement Valuation and Assumptions (1990)

Bumpass, L. (1990). "What's Happening to the Family? Interactions between Demographic and Institutional Change." *Demography.* Vol 27(4):483-98.

Bureau of Economic Analysis (1986). *The National Income and Product Accounts of the U.S., 1929-1982.* Washington, D.C.: U.S. Government Printing Office:1 and 109, and *The Survey of Current Business (1990).* 70, no. 7 (July):40, 53.

Burkhauser, Richard V. and Joseph F. Quinn (1983). "Is Mandatory Retirement Overrated?" *Journal of Human Resources* 18:337-358.

Burkhauser, Richard V. and Joseph F. Quinn. (1989) "American Patterns of Work and Retirement". In *Redefining the Process of Retirement: An International Perspective.* Ed. W. Schmahl. New York: Springer Verlag:91-113.

Burkhauser, Richard V. and Jennifer L. Warlick (1981). "Disentangling the Annuity from the Redistributive Aspects of Social Security in the United States." *The Review of Income and Wealth.* (December) 1981:401-421.

Burtless, G. and A.H. Munnell (1991). "Does a Trend Toward Early Retirement Create Problems for the Economy?" In *Retirement and Public Policy.* Ed. A. H. Munnell. Washington, DC: National Academy of Social Insurance.

Burtless, G. and R. Moffitt (1984). "The Effect of Social Security Benefits on the Labor Supply of the Aged." In *Retirement and Economic Behavior.* Eds. H. Aaron and G. Burtless. Washington, D.C.:The Brookings Institution:135-171.

Butler, R. (1982). Testimony before the National Commission of Social Security Reform, Washington, D.C. (June 21).

Cain, G. C. (1979) "The Unemployment Rate as an Economic Indicator." *Monthly Labor Review.* March:24-35.

Callahan, Daniel(1990). What Kind of Life: The Limits of Medical Progress. Simon and Schuster.

Chapman, S. H., M.P. LaPlante, and G. Wilensky (1986). "Life Expectancy and Health Status of the Aged." *Social Security Bulletin* (October):24-48.

Chirkos, T.M. and G. Nestel (1981). "Impairment and Labor Market Outcomes: A cross-sectional and Longitudinal Analysis." In *Work and Retirement.* Cambridge, Massachusetts, MIT Press.

Christensen, Sandra (1991). Congressional Budget Office Memorandum from Sandra Christensen to Health Staff. "Impact of Legislation (1981-1990) on Federal Spending for Medicare." (February 4):2.

Clark, Robert L. and A. McDermed (1990). *The Choice of Pension Plan in a Changing Regulatory Environment.* Washington, D.C.: American Enterprise Institute Press.

Clark, Robert (1990). *Retirement Systems in Japan,* Homewood, Ill.: Irwin for the Pension Research Council.

Coale, A.J. and M. Zelnik (1963). *New Estimates of Fertility and Population in the United States.* Princeton, N.J: Princeton University Press.

Coale, A.J. and S. Watkins (1986). *The Decline of Fertility in Europe.* Princeton University Press. Princeton, N.J.

Colvez, A., and M. Blanchet (1981). "Disability Trends in the United States Population 1966-76: Analysis of Reported Causes," *American Journal of Public Health* 71:464-471.

Commercial Clearing House (1990). *1990 Social Security Explained.* Chicago, IL: CCH.

Committee on Economic Security (1937). *Social Security in America.* Washington, D.C.: U.S. Government Printing Office:206-207.

Condran, G., C. Himes and S. Preston (1991) "Old-age Mortality Patterns in Low-Mortality Countries: An Evaluation of Population and Death Data at Advanced Ages, 1950 to the Present." *Population Bulletin of the United Nations.* No 30:23-60. United Nations. New York.

Congressional Budget Office (1987). *The Changing Distribution of Federal Taxes: 1975-1990.* Washington, D.C.: G.P.O.

Coopers and Lybrand (1989). Retiree Health Benefits: Field Test of the FASB Proposal. FERF Research.

Crimmins, E.M. (1987). "Evidence on the Compression of Morbidity. *Gerontologica Perspecta,"*1:45-49.

Crimmins, E.M. and M. Prammaggiore (1988). "Changing Health of the Older Population and Retirement Patterns Over Time," In *Issues in Contemporary Retirement,* R. Ricardo-Campbell and E. Lazear, Eds., Stanford, CA: Hoover Institution Press.

Crimmins, E.M. (1981) "The Changing Pattern of American Mortality Decline, 1940 - 1977, and its Implications for the Future," *Population and Development Review*7:229-54.

Crimmins, E.M. (1984). "Life Expectancy and the Older Population: Demographic Implications of Recent and Prospective Trends in Old Age Mortality." *Research on Aging.* Vol 6(4):490-514.

Crimmins, E.M. (1990). "Are Americans Healthier as Well as Longer- lived?" *Journal of Insurance Medicine* 22: 89-92.

Crimmins, E.M. and Y. Saito (1990). "Getting Better and Getting Worse: Transitions in Functional States Among Older Americans," Paper presented at the 1990 Annual Meetings of the Population Association of America.

Crimmins, E.M., and D.G. Ingegneri (1991). "Trends in Health Among the American Population." Paper prepared for the Pension Reseearch Council Symposium entitled "Demography and Retirement: The 21st Century," (May 9 - 10).

Crimmins, E.M., Y. Saito, and D.G. Ingegneri (1989). "Changes in Life Expectancy and Disability-free Life Expectancy in the United States," *Population and Development Review*. 15: 235-267.

Cutler, David M., James M. Poterba, Louise M. Sheiner, and Lawrence H. Summers (1991). "An Aging Society: Opportunity or Challenge?" *Brookings Papers on Economic Activity* 21:1, 1-73.

Daniels, C.E. and J. D. Daniels (1991). "Factors Affecting the Decision to Accept or Reject a Golden Handshake." *Benefits Quarterly*. Vol. VII, No. 2: 33-46.

Danzon, Patricia M. (1991). "The Hidden Costs of Budget-Constrained Health Care Systems." Mimeo. (September).

Danzon, Patricia M. (1992) "Hidden Overhead Costs: Is Canada's System Really Less Expensinve?" *Health Affairs*. (spring):21-43.

Diamond, Peter A. and Jerry A. Hausman (1984). "Individual Retirement and Savings Behavior," *Journal of Public Economics* 23 (February/March):81-114.

Easterlin, R. (1980). *Birth and Fortune: The Impact of Numbers or Personal Welfare*. Basic Books. New York.

Edmonston, Barry and Jeffrey S. Passel (1991a). "The Future Immigrant Population of the United States," Population Studies Center, Discussion Paper Series. Washington, D.C.: The Urban Institute.

Edmonston, Barry and Jeffrey S. Passel (1991b). "Population Projections for U.S. Racial/Ethnic Groups by Generation," Paper presented at the annual meeting of the American Statistical Association, Atlanta, Georgia (August 19-22).

Edmonston, Barry, Jeffrey S. Passel, and Frank D. Bean (1990). "Perceptions and Estimates of Undocumented Migration to the United States," in Frank D. Bean, Barry Edmonston, and Jeffrey S. Passel (editors), *Undocumented Migration to the United States: IRCA and the Experience of the 1980s*. Washington, D.C.: The Urban Institute Press:11-32.

Employee Benefit Research Institute (1990). "International Benefits, Part Two-Retirement Income," *EBRI Issue Brief* (October).

Employee Benefit Research Institute (1990). "Employer Spending on Benefits Exceeds $500 Billion in 1989." *Employee Benefit Notes*: (December) 11-12.

Employee Benefit Research Institute (1989). "Employer-plan Coverage, Participation, and Benefit Entitlement...." *EBRI Issue Brief*, no. 94 (September).

Enterline, P.E. (1961). "Causes of Death Responsible for Recent Increases in Sex Mortality Differentials in the United States." *Milbank Memorial Fund Quarterly.* Vol 39(1):312-28.

Ernst & Young (1991). "Accounting for Postretirement Benefits."

Feldman, J.J. (1983). "Work Ability of the Aged Under Conditions of Improving Mortality." *Milbank Memorial Fund Quarterly/Health and Society.* 61: 430-444.

Feldman, J.J. (1991). "Has Increased Longevity Increased Potential Worklife?" In *Retirement and Public Policy--the Book,* A.H. Munnell (editor). Washington, DC: National Academy of Social Insurance.

Feldstein, Martin S. (1980). "International Differences in Social Security and Saving." *Journal of Public Economics,* vol. 82, no. 5:905-26.

Feldstein, Martin S. (1974) "Social Security, Induced Retirement, and Aggregate Capital Accumulation," *Journal of Political Economy* 82:905-26.

Fields, G.S. and O.S. Mitchell (1984). *Retirement, Pensions, and Social Security.* Cambridge, Mass.: MIT Press.

Financial Accounting Standards Board (1990). *Statement of Financial Accounting Standards No. 106 - Employers' Accounting for Postretirement Benefits Other Than Pensions.* Norwalk, CT (December).

Flaim, P. O. (1979). "The Effect of Demographic Changes on the Nation's Unemployment Rate." *Monthly Labor Review.* (March):13-23.

Flaim, P. O. and H. N. Fullerton, Jr. (1978). "Labor Force Projections to 1990: Three Possible Paths." *Monthly Labor Review* (December):25-35.

Foster, Howard. 1990. *Employee Benefits in Europe and USA.* London: Longman Group UK Ltd.

Freeman, R.B. (1979). "The Effect of Demographic Factors on Age-Earnings Profiles." *Journal of Human Resources* 14:289-318.

Fries, J.F. (1980). "Aging, Natural Death and the Compression of Morbidity," *New England Journal of Medicine* 303:130-135.

Fries, J.F. (1989). "The compression of morbidity: Near or far?" *Milbank Memorial Fund Quarterly/Health and Society.* 67:208-232.

Fries, J.F. (1991). "The Workspan and the Compression of Morbidity." In *Retirement and Public Policy--the Book,* A.H. Munnell (editor). Washington, DC: National Academy of Social Insurance.

Fries, J. F. (Forthcoming). "Medical Perspectives on Successful Aging." In S.R. Johansson ed., *Aging and Dying: Perspectives on the Limits to Human Longevity.* Berekeley University of California Press.

Fu Associates, Ltd. (1991). "Health Insurance Microdata Base: Preliminary Design Report." Preliminary report prepared for Health Care Financing Administration, BOA# 500-90-0010, Task Order 0003 (March 11).

Fuguitt, G.V. and D.L. Brown (1990). "Residential Preferences and Population Redistribution, 1972- 1988." *Demography.* Vol 27(4):589-600.

Fullerton, H. N., Jr. (1982). "How Accurate Were Projections of the 1980 Labor Force?" *Monthly Labor Review* 105:15-21.

Fullerton, H. N., Jr. (1985). "The 1995 Labor Force: BLS' Latest Projections." *Monthly Labor Review* 108:17-25.

Fullerton, H. N., Jr. (1987). "Labor Force Projections, 1986 to 2000." *Monthly Labor Review* 110:19-29.

Fullerton, H.N., Jr. (1988). "An Evaluation of Labor Force Projections to 1985." *Monthly Labor Review*. 111:7-17.

Fullerton, H. N., Jr. (1989). "New Labor Force Projections, Spanning 1988 to 2000." *Monthly Labor Review* 112:3-12.

Fullerton, H.N., Jr. and J. Tschetter (1983). "The 1995 Labor Force: A Second Look." *Monthly Labor Review* 106:3-10.

Furer, Burkhard and Maria Lang (1990). "Benefits in the German Democratic Republic," *Benefit and Compensation International*:2-7.

Gibson, R.C. (1986). "Outlook for the Black Family." In *Our aging society: Paradox and promise*, A. Pifer and L. Bronte (editors). New York, N.Y.: W.W. Norton & Company.

Goldin, C. (1990). *Understanding the Gender Gap*. Oxford: Oxford University Press.

Gordon, Margaret (1988). *Social Security Policies in Industrial Countries*. Cambridge: Cambridge University Press.

Greenwich Research Associates Inc. (1980). *Large Corporate Pension Funds 1980 Report to Participants*. Greenwich CT

Greenwich Research Associates Inc. (1984). *Report to Participants on Large Corporate Pensions, 1984*. Greenwich, CT

Gruenberg, E.M. (1977). "The Failures of Success," *Milbank Memorial Fund Quarterly* 55:3-34.

Grummer-Strawn, L. and T.J. Espenshade (1991). "Evaluating the Accuracy of U.S. Population Projection Models." Presented to the annual meetings of the Population Association of America. Washington, D.C. (March 21-23).

Guralnik, J.M. (1991). Comment. In *Retirement and Public Policy--the Book*, A.H. Munnell (editor). Washington, DC: National Academy of Social Insurance.

Gustman, Alan L. and Thomas L. Steinmeier (1984). "Partial Retirement and the Analysis of Retirement Behavior." *Industrial and Labor Relations Review* 37 (April):403-415.

Gustman, Alan L. and Thomas L. Steinmeier (1989). *The Stampede toward Defined Contribution Pension Plans: Fact or Fiction?* Cambridge, Mass: National Bureau of Economic Research. Working Paper no. 3086.

Gustman, Alan L. and Thomas L. Steinmeier (1991). "Changing the Social Security Rules for Work After 65." *Industrial and Labor Relations Review*. 44 pp.

Haanes-Olsen, Leif (1989). "Worldwide Trends and Developments in Social Security, 1985-87," *Social Security Bulletin*, No. 2:14-26.

Hambor, John C. (1987). "Economic Policy, Integenerational Equity and the Social Security Trust Fund Buildup." *Social Security Bulletin*. (October):1987:1318.

Harootyan, R.A. (1991). *Aging in the 21st Century: The Quiet Revolution*. Washington, D.C.: American Association of Retired Persons, New Roles in Society Program.

Hay Huggins Company, Inc. (1990). "Pension Plan Expense Study." Report Prepared for the Pension Benefit Guaranty Corporation (September).

Hayflick, L. (1965). "The Limited *in vitro* Lifeline of Human Diploid Cell Strains." *Experimental Research*. Vol 37:614-36.

Health Care Financing Administration (1990). Calculated by Schieber based on data published in the *Annual Report of the Board of Trustees of the Federal Supplementary Medical Insurance Trust Funds*. Baltimore, Md: Health Care Financing Administration:28.

Heller, Peter, Richard Hemming, and Peter Kohnert. 1986. *Aging and Social Expenditures in the Major Industrial Countries, 1980-2025*, Washington: International Monetary Fund.

Hill, Michael (1990). *Social Security in Britain*, Aldershot, England: Elgar Publishing Limited.

Hilts, Philip J. (1991). "Corporate Chiefs See Need for U.S. Health-Care Action." *New York Times* (8 April):D1, D4.

Himes, C., S.H. Preston and G. Condran (1990). "A Comparison of Old Age Mortality Patterns in Low Mortality Countries, 1950-85." Presented to annual meetings of the Population Association of American. Toronto (March 1-3).

Hobcraft, J., J. Menken, and S. Preston (1982). "Age, Period, and Cohort Analysis in Demography: A Review." *Population Index*. Vol 48(1):4-43.

Hoem, J. (1990). "Social Policy and Recent Fertility Change in Sweden." *Population and Development Review*. Vol 16(4):735-48.

Horioka, Charles J. (1989). "Why is Japan's Private Saving Rate So High?" In Ryuzo Sato and Takashi Negishi, eds., *Developments in Japanese Economics* Tokyo: Academic Press:145-78.

Horlick, Max (1980). *Private Pension Plans in West Germany and France*. Washington: Social Security Administration.

Howland, M. and G.E. Peterson (1988). "Labor Market Conditions and the Reemployment of Displaced Workers." *Industrial and Labor Relations Review*. (October):109-122.

Hurd, Michael D. and Michael J. Boskin (1984). "The Effect of Social Security on Retirements in the 1970s." *The Quarterly Journal of Economics*, (November):767-790.

Hutchens, R.M. (1986). "Delayed Payment Contracts and a Firm's Propensity to Hire Older Workers." *Journal of Labor Economics*. (October):439-457.

Hutchens, R.M. (1988). "Do Job Opportunities Decline with Age?" *Industrial and Labor Relations Review*. (October):89-99.

Iams, H. M. and J. L. McCoy (1991). "Predictors of Mortality Among Newly Retired Workers." *Social Security Bulletin* 54:2-11.

Ioannides, Yannis M. (1989). "Dynamics of the Composition of Household Asset Portfolios and the Life Cycle," mimeo (October).

Ippolito, R. (1986). *Pensions, Economics, and Public Policy*. Homewood, IL: Dow-Jones Irwin, Pension Research Council.

Ippolito, R. (1990). "Toward Explaining Earlier Retirement after 1970." *Industrial and Labor Relations Review* 43 (July):556-569.

Ippolito, Richard A. (1991). "Pension Plan Choice, 1979-1987: Clarifications and Extensions. " Unpublished manuscript.

Johansson, S.R. (Forthcoming). "Introduction." In S.R. Johansson, ed. *Aging and Dying: Perspectives on the Limits to Human Longevity*. University of California Press. Berkeley.

Johnston, W.B. and A.H. Packer (1987). *Workforce 2000*. Indianapolis, In.: The Hudson Institute.

Kane, R.L., D.M. Radosevich and J.W. Vaupel (1990). Compression of morbidity: Issues and irrelevancies. In *Improving the Health of Older People: A World View*, R.L. Kane, J.G. Evans and D. Macfadyen. New York, N.Y.: Oxford University Press.

Kaplan, G. (1991). "Epidemiologic Observations on the Compression of Morbidity: Evidence from the Alameda County Study," *Journal of Aging and Health* 3:155-171.

King, Mervyn A. and Louis Dicks-Mireaux (1982). "Asset Holdings and the Life-Cycle," *Economic Journal* 92 (June):247-67.

Kingson, Eric R. (1982). "The Health of Very Early Retirees." *Social Security Bulletin* (September):3-9.

Kotlikoff, Laurence J. (1989). "The Economic Impact of the Demographic Transition - Problems and Prospects," mimeo.

Kotlikoff, Laurence J., and David A. Wise (1989). *The Wage Carrot and the Pension Stick*. Kalamazoo, Mich.: W.E. Upjohn Institute for Employment Research.

Kotlikoff, Laurence J., and Lawrence H. Summers (1981). "The Role of Intergenerational Transfers in Capital Accumulation," *Journal of Political Economy* 89.

Kovar, M.G. and G.S. Poe (1985). *National Center for Health Statistics: The National Health Interview Survey Design, 1973-84, and Procedures, 1975-83. Vital and Health Statistics*. Series 1, No.18, DHHS Pub. No.(PHS) 85-1320. Washington, D.C., U.S. Government Printing Office.

Kramer, M. (1980). "The rising pandemic of mental disorders and associated chronic diseases and disabilities. *Acta Psychiatrica Scandinavica* 285:382-397.

Kutscher, R.E. (1987). "Overview and Implications of the Projections to 2000." *Monthly Labor Review* 110:3-9.

Kutscher, R. E. (1989). "Projections Summary and Emerging Issues." *Monthly Labor Review* 112:66-74.

LaRue, A., L. Bank, L. Jarvik, and M. Hetland (1979). "Health in old age: How do Physicians' Ratings and Self-ratings Compare?" *Journal of Gerontology*, 34:687-691.

Laurene Graig (1991). *Health of Nations*. Washington, D.C.: The Wyatt Company.

Lavecky, John (1900). Review: Insurance: Its Potential Role in the Provision of Medical Care for Over Age 60; Institute of Actuaries, *Students News Letter*, United Kingdom.

Lazear, E.P. (1988). "Adjusting to an Aging Labor Force." NBER Working Paper No. 2802 (December).

Lee, R. and L. Carter (1990). "Modeling and Forecasting U.S. Mortality." Paper presented to the annual meeting of the Population Association of America. Toronto.

Leonesio, M. (1990). "The Effects of the Social Security Earnings Test on the Labor Market Activity of Older Americans: A Review of the Evidence" *Social Security Bulletin* 53 (May):2-21.

Lesthaeghe, R. (1983). "A Century of Demographic and Cultural Change in Western Europe: An Explanation of Underlying Dimensions." *Population and Development Review.* Vol 9(3):411-35.

Levine, P.B. and O.S. Mitchell (1988). "The Baby Boom's Legacy: Relative Wages in the Twenty-first Century," *American Economic Review* (May):63-66.

Levy, F. (1987). *Dollars and Dreams: The Changing American Income Distribution.* New York: Russell Sage Foundation.

Long, John F. (1987). "The Accuracy of Population Projection Methods at the U.S. Census Bureau," Paper presented at the April 1987 annual meetings of the Population Association of America.

Long, L. and D. DeAre (1988). "U.S. Popuation Redistribution: A Perspective on the Nonmetropolition Turnaround." *Population and Development Review.* Vol 14(3):433-50.

Louis Harris and Associates, Inc. (1990). For Metropolitan Life Insurance Company. *Trade-offs & Choices: Health Policy Questions for the 1990s.* New York: Louis Harris and Associates, Inc.

Lumsdaine, R., J.H. Stock, and D. Wise (1990). "Efficient Windows and Labor Force Reduction." NBER Working Paper 3369 (May).

Luzadis, R. and O.S. Mitchell (1991). "Explaining Pension Dynamics," *Journal of Human Resources* (Fall):679-703.

Mankiw, N. Gregory and David N. Weil (1989). "The Baby Boom, the Baby Bust and the Housing Market," *Regional Science and Urban Economics* 19 (May):235-258.

Manton, K. (1990). "New Biotechnologies and the Limits to Life Expectancy." In W. Lutz, ed., *Future Demographic Trends in Europe and North America.* New York. Academic Press:97-115.

Manton, K. (1991). "Limits to Life Expectancy in the U.S.: A Conceptual and Methodological Critique and Review of Recent Data." Presented to the annual meetings of the Population Association of America. Washington, D.C. (March 21-23).

Manton, K., M. Woodbury, and E. Stallard (Forthcoming). "Estimating the Limits to Life Expectancy: Modeling Mortality from Epidemiological and Medical Data." In S.R. Johansson ed., *Aging and Dying: Perspectives on the Limits to Human Longevity.* Berkeley: University of California Press.

Manton, K.G. (1982). "Changing Concepts of Morbidity and Mortality in the Elderly Population," *Milbank Memorial Fund Quarterly/Health and Society* 60: 183-244.

Masoro, E.J., M.S. Katz, and C.A. McMahan (1989). "Rapid Communication. Evidence for the Glycation Hypothesis of Aging from the Food-restricted Rodent Model." *Journal of Gerontology: Biological Sciences* 44:20-22.

Mathers, C.D. (1990). "Disability-free and Handicap-free Life Expectancy in Australia," *Australia Institute of Health: Health Differentials Series No.1.*

McDaniel, A. (1990). *The African-American Population Up to the Year 2012.* Final Report to the Rockefeller Foundation. Prepared at the University of Pennsylvania, Philadelphia.

McKusick, David (1988). "Long Term Trend Factor in Valuation of Retiree Medical Care," Society of Actuaries Health Section News (October). Actuarial Research Corporation.

McMillan, H.M. and J. B. Baesel (1990). "The Macroeconomic Impact of the Baby Boom Generation." *Journal of Macroeconomics.* (Spring):167-195.

McNaught, William, Michael C. Barth, and Peter H. Henderson (1991). "Older Americans: Willing and Able to Work." In Alicia H. Munnell (editor), *Retirement and Public Policy.* Dubuque, IA: Kendall/Hunt Publishing Co.:101-114.

Mincer, J. (1984). "Inter-country Comparisons of Labor Force Trends and of Related Developments: An Overview." National Bureau of Economic Research Working Paper No. 1438. Cambridge, MA.

Mirkin, Barry Alan (1987). "Early Retirement as a Labor Force Policy," *Monthly Labor Review* (March):19-33.

Mitchell, O. S., P. B. Levine, and S. Pozzebon (1988). "Retirement Differences by Industry and Occupation." *Journal of Gerontology* (August):545-551.

Mitchell, O.S. (1991a). "Pensions Reflect Employer and Employee Preferences." *In Retirement and Public Policy.* A. Munnell. ed. Washington, D.C.: National Academy of Social Insurance.

Mitchell, O.S. (1991b). "The Effect of Mandatory Benefits Packages." *In Research in Labor Economics.* L. Bassi, D. Crawford, R. Ehrenberg, eds. Greenwich, Ct: JAI Press:297-320.

Mitchell, O.S. (1991). "Social Security Reforms and Poverty in Dual-Earner Couples" *Journal of Population Economics.*

Mitchell, O.S. (Forthcoming) "Trends in Pension Formulas" In *Trends in Pensions 1991.* J. Turner and D. Beller, eds.

Mitchell, O.S. and G.S. Fields (1985). "Rewards for Continued Work" In *Horizontal Equity, Uncertainty, and the Economics of Wellbeing.* M. David and T. Smeeding, eds. Chicago: University of Chicago Press.

Mitchell, O.S. and R. Luzadis (1988). "Changes in Pension Incentives Through Time." *Industrial and Labor Relations Review* 42 (October):100-108.

Modigliani, Franco (1970). "The Life Cycle Hypothesis of Saving and Inter-Country Differences in the Saving Ratio." In W.A. Eltig et al., eds. *Induction, Growth and Trade, Essays in Honour of Sir Roy Harrod.* London: Clarendon Press.

Modigliani, Franco and A. Sterling (1983). "Determinants of Private Saving
    with Special Reference to the Role of Social Security - Cross-Country
    Tests." In F. Modigliani and R. Henning, eds., *The Determinants of
    National Saving and Wealth* New York: St. Martins Press:24-55.

Moffitt, R. (1987). "Life-Cycle Labor Supply and Social Security: A Time
    Series Analysis" In *Work, Health and Income Among the Elderly*. G.
    Burtless, ed. Washington, D.C.: The Brookings Institution.

Moffitt, Robert A. (1984). "Trends in Social Security Wealth by Cohort." In
    Marilyn Moon ed. *Economic Transfers in the United States*. Chicago, IL:
    The University of Chicago Press:327-347.

Moynihan, The Honorable Daniel Patrick (1990). "Why We Called for a
    Surplus." *The Washington Post* (March 7):A-25.

Moynihan, The Honorable Daniel Patrick (1990). "To My Social Security
    Critics." *New York Times* (February 9): A-31, and "It's a Matter of Trust,
    Rosty," *The Washington Post* (March 22):A-23.

Mutschler, P. (1986). "How Golden a Handshake?" *Compensation and Benefits
    Management Review* 2 (Summer):277-283.

Myers, Robert J. (1990). Statement to the Subcommittee on Retirement Income
    and Employment, Select Committee on Aging, House of Representatives
    (February 28):3.

National Research Council (1989). *AIDS: Sexual Behavior and Intravenous
    Drug Use*. National Academy Press. Washington, D.C.

O'Connell, M. and C. Rogers (1983). "Assessing Cohort Birth Expectations
    Data from the Current Population Survey, 1971-81." *Demography*. Vol
    20(3):369-84.

Office of National Cost Estimates, HCFA (1990). "National Health Expendi-
    tures, 1988." *Health Care Financing Review* 11, No. 4 (Summer):24.

Office of the Actuary (1990). Division of National Cost Estimate, Office of the
    Actuary, Health Care Financing Administration.

Olshansky, S.J., B.A. Carnes, and C. Cassel. 1990. "In Search of Methuselah:
    Estimating the Upper Limits to Human Longevity." *Science*. Vol 250(No-
    vember 2):634-40.

Organization of Economic Cooperation and Development (1988). *Reforming
    Public Pensions*. Paris: OECD.

Packard, Michael D. and Virginia P. Reno (1989). "A Look at Very Early
    Retirees," *Social Security Bulletin* (March):16-29.

Parsons, D. (1980). "The Decline in Male Labor Force Participation," *Journal of
    Political Economy* 88:117-34.

Pauly, Mark, et al. (1991) "A Plan for Responsible National Health Insurance."
    Health Affairs (Spring):5-25.

Petertil, Jeffrey (1990). "Challenging the Profession: Measurement of Retiree
    Medical Liabilities." Society of Actuaries Health Section News (January).

Piascentini, J. and T. Cerino (1990). *EBRI Databook on Employee Benefits*.
    Washington, D.C: Employee Benefit Research Institute.

Podgursky, M.and P. Swaim (1987). "Job Displacement and Earnings Loss: Evidence from the Displaced Worker Survey." *Industrial and Labor Relations Review* (October):17-29.

Popenoe, D. (1990). "Family Decline in America." Manuscript, Department of Sociology, Rutgers University.

Population Reference Bureau (1990). *Population Today.* Vol 18(12). Washington, D.C.

Poterba, J. and L. Summers (1987). "Public Policy Implications of Declining Old-Age Mortality" In *Work, Health, and Income Among the Elderly.* G. Burtless, ed. Washington, D.C.: The Brookings Institution:19-51.

Preston, Sameul H. (1970). "An International Comparison of Excessive Adult Mortality." *Population Studies.* Vol 24(1):5-20.

Preston, Samuel H. (1984). "Children and the Elderly: Divergent Paths for America's Dependents." *Demography.* Vol 21(4):435-56.

Preston, Samuel H. (1986a). "The Decline of Fertility in Non-European Industrialized Countries." *Population and Development Review.* Vol 12 Supplement:26-47.

Preston, Samuel H. (1986b). "Changing Values and Falling Birth Rates." *Population and Development Review.* Vol 12 Supplement:176-95.

Preston, Samuel H. and M. Haines (1991a). *Fatal Years: Child Mortality in Late Nineteenth Century America.* Princeton University Press. Princeton, N.J.

Preston, Samuel H. (1991b). "Demographic Change in the United States, 1970-2050," Paper prepared for Conference on "Demography and Retirement: The 21st Century." Sponsored by the Pension Research Council, University of Pennsylvania (May 9-10).

Puidak, Peter (1987). "Developments in the Equalization of Treatment of Men and Women Under Social Security in the Federal Republic of Germany," *Social Security Bulletin,* No. 2:49-52.

Quinn, Joseph F., Richard V. Burkhauser, and D. Myers (1990). *Passing the Torch: The Influence of Economic Incentives on Work and Retirement.* Kalamazoo, MI: Upjohn.

Quinn, Joseph F. and Richard V. Burkhauser (1990). "Retirement Plans and Preferences of Older American Workers," Boston College, mimeo (October).

Ranade, N. K. (1990). "Pension Plan Concepts Can Be Used To Design An Effective Retiree Health Plan" In *Journal of Compensation and Benefits.* 5:211-215.

Ransom, R. and R. Sutch (1986). "The Labor of Older Americans: Retirement of Men on and off the Job" *Journal of Economic History* 46 (March):1-30.

Reinhardt, Dr. Uwe (1991). "Recent Trends in Cost and Utilization." Health Care Symposium. Issues for Insurers. Princeton University.

Rejda, G. (1982). *Economic and Social Security.* New York: Wiley and Sons.

Riley, J.C. (1990). "The Risk of Being Sick: Morbidity Trends in Four Countries," *Population and Development Review* 16:403-432.

Riley, M.W. (1990). "Aging in the twenty-first century." Boettner Lecture, 1990. Bryn Mawr, Pennsylvania: Boettner Research Institute.

Rivlin, Alice M. and Joshua M. Wiener (1987). *Reforming Long-Term Care.* Washington, D.C.: The Brookings Institution:26-27.

Robertson, A. Haeworth (1990). "1989 Trustees Report on Social Security's Financial Health: Good News for the Elderly, Bad News For the Young." *Benefits Quarterly* (First Quarter):1-5.

Rogers, A., R.G. Rogers, and A. Belanger (1990). "Longer Life but Worsening Health? Measurement and Dynamics," *The Gerontologist,* 30:640-649.

Rosa, Jean Jacques, ed. (1982). *The World Crisis in Social Security.* San Francisco: Institute for Contemporary Studies.

Rose, Michael (Forthcoming). "An Evolutionary Perspective on the Outer Limit of the Human Lifespan." In S.R. Johansson, ed., *Aging and Dying: Perspectives on the Limits to Human Longevity.* Berkeley: University of California Press.

Ruhm, Christopher J. (1990a). "Bridge Jobs and Partial Retirement." *Journal of Labor Economics* (October):482-501.

Ruhm, Christopher J. (1991). "Career Employment and Job Shopping." *Industrial Relations* (Spring):193-208.

Ruhm, Christopher J. (1990b). "Career Jobs, Bridge Employment, and Retirement." In Peter B. Doeringer. ed., *Bridges to Retirement.* Ithaca, NY: ILR Press:92-107.

Russell, L. B. (1982) *The Baby Boom Generation and the Economy.* Washington, DC: Brookings Studies in Social Economics.

Ryder, N.B. (1986). "The History of Cohort Fertility in the United States." *Population and Development Review.* Vol 12(4):617-44.

Sammartino, F. (1987). "The Effect of Health on Retirement," *Social Security Bulletin* 50 (February):31-47.

Schieber, Sylvester J. (1990). "Accumulating Social Security Trust Funds: Money In Trust or Violation of Trust?" *Tax Notes* (July 2):88.

Schlesinger, Arthur M., Jr. (1959). *The Age of Roosevelt,* Vol. 2, *The Coming of the New Deal.* Boston, Mass.: Houghton Mifflin Co.:309-310.

Schmaehl, Winfried (1989). "The Public Old Age Pension System in Germany," in Korea Development Institute ed., *Policy Issues in Social Security.*

Schneider, E.L. and J. Guralnick (1987). "The Compression of Morbidity: A Dream Which May Come True, Someday," *Gerontologica Perspecta* 1:8-14.

Schneider, Edward L. and Jack M. Guralnik (1990). "The Aging of America, Impact on Health Care Costs." *Journal of the American Medical Association* (May 2) 263, no. 17:2337.

Schreitmueller, Richard G. (1988). "The Federal Employees' Retirement System Act of 1986" *Transactions, Society of Actuaries* 40:543-610.

Schultz, Charles L. (1990). "Setting Long-Run Deficit Reduction Targets: The Economics and Politics of Budget Design." In Henry J. Aaron, ed. *Social Security and the Budget: Proceedings of the First Conference of the National Academy of Social Insurance.* New York: University Press of America:18.

Select Committee on Children, Youth and Families, U.S. House of Representatives (1989). *U.S. Children and Their Families: Current Conditions and Recent Trends, 1989.* 101st Congress, 1st session. Washington, D.C.:GPO.

Shapiro, D. and S.H. Sandell (1987). "The Reduced Pay of Older Job Losers: Age Discrimination and Other Explanations." In *The Problem Isn't Age: Work and Older Americans.* S. H. Sandell, ed. New York: Praeger.

Sheiner, Louise and David Weil (1990). "The Housing Wealth of the Aged," mimeo, Harvard University (August).

Sheppard, H.L. (1977). "Factors Associated with Early Withdrawal from the Labor Force." In *Men in the pre-retirement years*, S. L. Wolfbein, ed. Philadelphia, Pennsylvania: Temple University Press.

Shorrocks, Anthony (1982). "The Portfolio Composition of Asset Holdings in the United Kingdom," *Economic Journal* 92 (June):268-84.

Simanis, Joseph (1990). "National Expenditures on Social Security and Health in Selected Countries," *Social Security Bulletin*, No. 1:12-16.

Social Security Administration (1990) *1990 Annual Report of the Board of Trustees of the Federal Old-Age and Survivors Insurance and Disability Insurance Trust Funds.* Baltiomre, Md: Social Security Administration:62.

Social Security Administration (1989). *Social Security Bulletin, Annual Statistical Supplement 1981*:195, and the *Social Security Bulletin, Annual Statistical Supplement:181. Baltimore Md: Social Security Administration.*

Social Security Advisory Council on Social Security (1991). "Social Security Technical Panel Report to the 1991 Advisory Council on Social Security":vii. Ibid.:8, 38.

Social Security Advisory Council on Social Security (1991). "Report on Medicare Projections by the Health Technical Panel to the 1991 Advisory Council on Social Security":64

Spencer, Gregory (1986). *Projections of the Hispanic Population: 1983 to 2080.* Current Population Reports, Series P-25, No. 995. Washington, D.C.: U.S. Government Printing Office.

Spencer, Gregory (1989). *Projections of the Population of the United States, by Age, Sex, and Race: 1988 to 2080.* Current Population Reports, Series P-25, No. 1018. Washington, D.C.: U.S. Government Printing Office.

Stoto, M. (1983). "The Accuracy of Population Projection."*Journal of the American Statistical Association.* Vol 78(381):13-20.

Takeuchi, J.S. (Forthcoming). *The Quiet Revolution: Improved Health and Longer Life in the Twenty-first Century.* Washington, D.C.: American Association of Retired Persons, New Roles in Society Program.

Thompson, Lawrence H. (1983). "The Social Security Reform Debate." Journal of *Economic Literature* Vol. XXI (December):1425-1467.

Todaro, M.P. and L. Maruszko (1987). "Illegal Migration and U.S. Immigration Reform." *Population and Development Review.* Vol 13(1):101-14.

Trustees, Federal Old Age and Survivors Insurance and Disability Insurance Trust Funds (1989). *1989 Annual Report of the Federal Old-Age and Survivors Insurance and Disability Insurance Trust Funds.* 101st Congress, 1st Session. House Ways and Means Committee. Washington, D.C.:U.S. G.P.O.

Trustees, Federal Old Age and Survivors Insurance and Disability Insurance Trust Funds (1990). *1990 Annual Report of the Federal Old-Age and Survivors Insurance and Disability Insurance Trust Funds.* 101st Congress, 2nd Session. House Ways and Means Committee. Washington, D.C.: U.S. G.P.O.

Turner, J. and D. Beller, Eds. (1990). *Trends in Pensions 1990.* Pension and Welfare Benefit Agency, US Department of Labor. Washington, D.C.: U.S. G.P.O.

Turner, John A. and Daniel J. Beller (1989). *Trends in Pensions.* U. S. Department of Labor, Pension and Welfare Benefits Administration. Washington, D.C.: U.S. G.P.O.

Turner, John and Lorna Daily (1991). *Pension Policy: An International Perspective.* Washington: U.S. Government Printing Office.

U.S. Bureau of the Census (1957). *Illustrative Projections of the Populations fo the Population of the United States, by Age and Sex, 1960 to 1980.* Current Population Reports Series P-25, No 187. Washington, D.C.: G.P.O.

U.S. Bureau of the Census (1988). *Statistical Abstract of the United States, 1990.* Washington, D.C.: G.P.O.

U. S. Bureau of the Census (1989). *Projections of the Population of the United States, by Age, Sex, and Race: 1988 to 2080,* Current Population Reports, Series P-25, No. 1018. Washington, DC: U.S. Government Printing Office.

U.S. Bureau of the Census (1990a). *Statistical Abstract of the United States, 1990.* Washington, D.C.: G.P.O.

U.S. Bureau of the Census (1990b.) *U.S. Population Estimates, by Age, Race, and Hispanic Origin: 1989.* Current Population Reports Series P-25, No 1059. Washington, D.C.: G.P.O.

U.S. Bureau of the Census (1990c). *Projections of the Population of States by Age, Sex, and Race: 1989 to 2010.* Current Population Reports Series P-25, No 1053. Washington, D.C.: G.P.O.

U.S. Department of Commerce (1987). *Fixed Reproducible Tangible Wealth in the United States, 1925-85.* Washington: U.S. Government Printing Office.

U.S. Department of Commerce, Bureau of Economic Analysis (1985). *BEA Regional Projections.*

U.S. Department of Health, Education, and Welfare (1975). *Health Interview Survey Procedure 1957-1974, Vital and Health Statistics.* Series 1. No. 11. DHEW Pub. No. (HRA) 75-1311. Rockville, Md.: National Center for Health Statistics.

U.S. Department of Health and Human Services, Social Security Administration (1989). *Fast Facts & Figures about Social Security.* Washington, D.C.: Office of Policy, Office of Research and Statistics.

U.S. Department of Health and Human Services, Social Security Administration (1983). "Economic Projections for OASDI Cost Estimates, 1983: Actuarial Study No. 90."

U.S. Department of Labor, Bureau of Labor Statistics (1990). *Employment in Perspective: Women in the Labor Force.* Report No 80, Washington, D.C.: G.P.O.

U.S. Department of Labor, Bureau of Labor Statistics (Various Years). *Employee Benefits in Medium and Large Firms.* Washington DC: U.S. Government Printing Office.

U.S. Department of Labor, Bureau of Labor Statistics (1991). *Employment and Earnings* (January).

U.S. National Center for Health Statistics (1990). *Monthly Vital Statistics Report.* Vol 39(4). Public Health Service. Washington, D.C.

U.S. National Center for Health Statistics (1991a). *Vital Statistics of the United States, 1988 Life Tables.* Public Health Service. Washington, D.C.

U.S. National Center for Health Statistics (1991b). *Monthly Vital Statistics Report.* Vol 39(12). Public Health Service. Washington, D.C.

U.S. President (1991). *Economic Report of the President.* Washington, DC: United States Government Printing Office.

U.S. Social Security Administration (1989). *Social Security Area Population Projections. 1989.* Actuarial Study No 105. Social Security Administration. Washington, D.C.

U.S. Social Security Administration (1991). *Social Security Programs Throughout the World - 1990,* Washington: U.S. Government Printing Office.

Uchitelle, Louis (1990). "Company-Financed Pensions Are Failing to Fulfill Promise." *New York Times* (29 May):A1, D5.

Vaupel, J. (1991). "Prospects for Longer Life Expectancy." Presented to the annual meetings of the Population Association of America. Washington, D.C. (March 21-23)

Venti, Steven, and David Wise (1990)."But They Don't Want to Reduce Housing Equity" in David Wise, ed., *Issues in the Economics of Aging.* Chicago: University of Chicago Press.

Verbrugge, L.M. (1984). "Longer Life but Worsening Health?: Trends in Health and Mortality of Middle-aged and Older Persons," *Milbank Memorial Fund Quarterly/Health and Society* 62:475-519.

Verbrugge, L.M. (1989). "Recent, Present, and Future Health of American Adults," in *Annual Review of Public Health.* Vol. 10. L. Breslow, J.E. Fielding, and L.B. Lave, eds.. Palo Alto, CA: Annual Reviews Inc.

Verbrugge, L.M. (1991). Comment. *In Retirement and Public Policy--The Book,* A.H. Munnell, ed. Washington, DC: National Academy of Social Insurance.

Waldo, Daniel R. (1989). *Measurements of Medical Care Inflation.* Healthcare Symposium. American Hospital Association and Society of Actuaries.

Waldron, Ingrid (1986). "The Contribution of Smoking to Sex Differences in Mortality." *Public Health Reports*. Vol 101(2):163-73.

Warshawsky, Mark J. (1991). "The Uncertain Promise of Retiree Health Benefits: An Evaluation of Corporate Obligations, Charts and Tables." Presentation at the American Enterprise Institute (April 9).

Welch, F. (1979). "Effects of Cohort Size on Earnings: The Baby Boom's 'Financial Bust'." *Journal of Political Economy* (October):S65-97.

Westoff, C. (1990). "The Return to Replacement Fertility: A Magnetic Force?" In W. Lutz, ed., *Future Demographic Trends in Europe and North America*. New York. Academic Press:227-33.

Whelpton, P.M. (1947). *Forecasts of the Population of the United States, 1945-75.* U.S. Bureau of the Census, Washington, D.C.: G.P.O.

Wilkins, R., and O.B. Adams (1983). "Health Expectancy in Canada, Late 1970's: Demographic, Regional, and Social Dimensions," *American Journal of Public Health*. 73:1073-1080.

Wilson, R. and T. Drury (1984). "Interpreting Trends in Illness and Disability: Health Statistics and Health Status," *Annual Review of Public Health 5*.

Wolfe, B. and R. Haveman (1990). "Trends in the Prevalence of Work Disability from 1962 to 1984, and their Correlates," *The Milbank Quarterly* 68:53-80.

The Wyatt Company (1990). *1990 Benefits Report*. Brussels: The Wyatt Company.

Ycas, M. A. (1987a). "Recent Trends in Health Near Age of Retirement: New Findings from the Health Interview Survey." *Social Security Bulletin* 50:5-30.

Ycas, M.A. (1987b). "Are the Eighties Different?: Continuity and Change in the Health of Older Persons," *Proceedings of the 1987 Public Health Conference on Records and Statistics*. DHHS Pub. No. (PHS) 88-1214. Hyattsville, Md: National Center for Health Statistics.

Zweekhorst, Kees (1990). "Developments in Private Pensions in the Netherlands," in John Turner and Lorna Dailey, *Pension Policy: An International Perspective*, Washington: U.S. G.P.O.

Index

Contributors

EMILY S. ANDREWS currently is a senior economist with Fu Associates, a Washington, DC based consulting firm. Previously Emily was an associate professor of labor and industrial relations at the Labor Research Center of the University of Rhode Island (URI) and a fellow of the Employee Benefit Research Institute (EBRI). Prior to her academic appointment at URI, she served as EBRI's research director. Dr. Andrews held policy research positions at the Social Security Administration, the Labor Department, and the President's Commission on Pension Policy. Her publications include 'Pension Policy and Small Employers: At What Price Coverage?' and 'The Changing Profile of Pensions in America.' She holds a Ph.D. in economics from the University of Pennsylvania.

G. LAWRENCE ATKINS is the Director of Employee Benefits Policy in the Washington, DC office of the New York law firm of Winthrop, Stimson, Putnam and Roberts. Previously, Mr. Atkins served for eight years as a staff member of the U.S. Senate Special Committee on Aging, where he was most recently Minority Staff Director with policy responsibilities primarily in health, employee benefits, and income security issues. Mr. Atkins has earned a Ph.D. in Social Welfare from the Heller School at Brandeis University. He also holds an M.S. from the University of Louisville and an M.A. from the University of Kentucky. He completed his undergraduate work at Kenyon College.

ALAN J. AUERBACH is Professor of Economics and Law at the University of Pennsylvania. He previously taught at Harvard University, and during the academic year 1982-3 visited Yale as the Irving Fisher Research Professor. Dr. Auerbach is a Research Associate of the National Bureau of Economic Research, where he has directed the Bureau's Project on Mergers and Acquisitions. Dr. Auerbach has published numerous articles in scholarly economics and law journals. He was awarded the David A. Wells Prize for his 1983 book, *The Taxation of Capital Income,* coedited (with Martin Feldstein) the two volume Handbook of Public Economics, is coauthor of the recent book, *Dynamic Fiscal*

Policy, and editor of two recent books, *Mergers and Acquisitions and Corporate Takeovers.* Dr. Auerbach holds a B.A. from Yale University and a Ph.D. from Harvard University.

DWIGHT K. BARTLETT III, is currently Visiting Executive Professor, Department of Insurance and Risk Management and Associate Director, Pension Research Council at the Wharton School. He previously was Senior Vice President and Chief Actuary, Monumental Life Insurance Company, Baltimore, Chief Actuary, Social Security Administration (1979- 1981) and most recently President, Mutual of America Life Insurance Company. Dwight, a past president of the Society of Actuaries, is a graduate of Harvard College and did his graduate work at The Johns Hopkins University. He has spoken and written extensively on employee benefit and insurance topics.

FRANCISCO R. BAYO presently is Deputy Chief Actuary, Social Security Administration. He also serves as Actuarial Consultant to the International Labor Office and to the PanAmerican Health Organization. He holds the B.S. degree from the University of Puerto Rico in mathematics and physics and the M.S. degree from the University of Michigan in actuarial sciences. He also has done postgraduate work in statistics at George Washington University and is a Senior Executive graduate of the Federal Executive Institute. He is an Associate of the Society of Actuaries and a member of the American Academy of Actuaries, the National Academy of Social Insurance, and the World Future Society.

JOHN H. BIGGS was elected president and chief operating officers of TIAA-CREF effective February 1, 1989. Prior to his election, Mr. Biggs had served as a CREF Trustee since 1983. In 1977 Mr. Biggs became vice chancellor for administration and finance at Washington University in St. Louis. He was named president and CEO of Centerre Trust Company, St. Louis, in 1985, and three years later, he assumed the additional title of chairman of Centerre Trust. Mr. Biggs is a Fellow of the Society of Actuaries and a member of the American Economic Association. He is a trustee of Washington University and the Danforth Foundation. Mr. Biggs also serves as a director for the National Bureau of Economic Research, McDonnell Douglas Corporation, Ralston Purina Co., and the Life Insurance Council of New York. Mr. Biggs earned the A.B. degree in classics from Harvard University and a Ph.D. in economics from Washington University, St. Louis.

CHRISTOPHER M. BONE is assistant vice president and consulting actuary with Actuarial Sciences Associates, a subsidiary of AT&T which provides consulting services to large employer plans. As an Alumni Distinguished Scholar, Mr. Bone earned a Bachelor's degree in mathematics from Michigan State University. He is a Fellow of the Society of Actuaries, an Enrolled Actuary under ERISA, and a Member of the American Academy of Actuaries.

ROBERT L. CLARK has been on the faculty of North Carolina State University since 1975. On July 1, 1990, Dr. Clark was appointed Interim Head of the Division of Economics and Business. Concurrently, he serves as Senior Fellow at the Center for the Study of Aging and Human Development at Duke University and as Senior Research Fellow at the Center for Demographic Studies at Duke University. Dr. Clark is a member of the American Economic Association, the Gerontological Society of America, and the International Union for Scientific Study of Population. This summer he was elected to the National Academy of Social Insurance. Dr. Clark earned a B.A. from Millsaps College and M.A. and Ph.D. degrees from Duke University.

EILEEN M. CRIMMINS holds an M.A. and a Ph.D. in Demography from the University of Pennsylvania. She has held professional positions at the University of Illinois, Rutgers University, and the California Institute of Technology. Currently she is Associate Professor of Gerontology and Sociology at the Andrus Gerontology Center at the University of Southern California. Her recent research has been on trends and differentials in the health of the older population.

PATRICIA M. DANZON has been Professor of Health Care Systems and Insurance at The Wharton School of the University of Pennsylvania since 1985. Her degrees include B.A. First Class (Politics, Philosophy and Economics), Oxford University, England, 1968 and Ph.D. (Economics), University of Chicago, 1973. Previously she was Visiting Professor of Business Economics at the University of Chicago, 1988-1989; Associate Professor at the Center for Health Policy and Institute of Policy Sciences of Duke University, 1984-1985; Senior Research Fellow at the Hoover Institution of Stanford University, 1980-1984; and Research Economist at The Rand Corporation, 1974-1980.

BARRY EDMONSTON has been in demographic and statistical research since 1974. He joined the staff of The Urban Institute in 1989. At present, he is a Senior Research Associate in The Urban Institute's Population Studies Program, focussing on demographic research and statistical consulting. From 1977 to 1988, Dr. Edmonston was Assistant Professor and Associate Professor at the International Population Program, Cornell University. While at Cornell University, Dr. Edmonston directed the International Population Program during 1980-81, and co-organized and headed the Graduate Field of Epidemiology.

STEPHEN C. GOSS came to the Social Security Administration in 1973 after graduating from the University of Pennsylvania with a BA in mathematics and economics and a MS in mathematics from the University of Virginia. He is a member of the Society of Actuaries as well as the Society's Social Insurance Committee. Mr. Goss has worked in the Office of the Actuary throughout his career on issues related to both the Social Security and Medicare programs. He currently heads up a group within the Office responsible for developing economic and demographic projections and assumptions related to estimates of the financial status of these programs.

DOMINIQUE G. INGEGNERI is a Ph.D. candidate in sociology at the University of Southern California. She is a trainee on a National Institute on Aging supported multidisciplinary training grant. Her research interests include the health of the older population.

ERIC R. KINGSON is an Associate Professor of Social Policy at the Boston College Graduate School of Social Work. Previously, he taught at the University of Maryland at Baltimore, was director of the Emerging Issues Program of the Gerontological Society of America and was a member of the staff of the National Commission on Social Security Reform. Prior to receiving his doctorate in social policy from Brandeis University in 1979, his work involved him in the planning and administration of social services.

LAURENCE J. KOTLIKOFF is Professor of Economics at Boston University and a Research Associate of the National Bureau of Economic Research. He received his B.A. in Economics from the University of Pennsylvania in 1973 and Ph.D. in Economics from Harvard University in 1977. From 1977 through 1983 he served on the faculties of economics of the University of California, Los Angeles and Yale University. In 1981-82 Professor Kotlikoff was a Senior Economist with the President's Council of Economic Advisers. Professor Kotlikoff has served as a consultant to the International Monetary Fund, the World Bank, the Organization for Economic Cooperation and Development, the Swedish Ministry of Finance, the Bank of Italy, and several U.S. government agencies.

PHILLIP B. LEVINE recently completed his Ph.D. in Economics at Princeton University and will be accepting a position in the fall as assistant professor at Wellesley College. His research interests include analyses of unemployment and unemployment insurance, women in the labor market, and the effects of demographic change in labor markets. Dr. Levine received his B.S. and M.S. in Industrial and Labor Relations at Cornell University. He has also received an M.A. in Economics from Princeton University.

OLIVIA S. MITCHELL is a Professor of Labor Economics at Cornell University's Industrial and Labor Relations School. She specializes in labor economics, evaluation analysis, and public finance. Mitchell also directs the Labor Force Demographics Program for the Cornell/ILR Institute for Labor Market Policies, works with the ILR/Cornell Center for Advanced Human Resource Studies, and is Associate Editor of the Industrial and Labor Relations Review. She is concurrently a member of the National Academy of Social Insurance and a Research Associate at the National Bureau of Economic Research. Mitchell hold the B.S. degree (1974) in economics from Harvard University, and M.A. (1976) and Ph.d. (1978) degrees in economics from the University of Wisconsin-Madison.

ALICIA H. MUNNELL is Senior Vice President and Director of Research for the Federal Reserve Bank of Boston. In addition to her responsibilities as Director, Ms. Munnell conducts research in the areas of tax policy, social security, and public and private pensions. Ms. Munnell is co-founder and served as the first president of the National Academy of Social Insurance. She is a member of the Institute of Medicine, the National Academy of Public Administration, the Pension Research Council of the Wharton School of Finance and Commerce, the Economic Policy Institute's Research Advisory Board, and the Pension Rights Center's Board of Directors. Ms. Munnell received her doctorate in economics from Harvard University in 1973 and joined the Boston Fed shortly thereafter.

ROBERT J. MYERS is an Actuarial Consultant to various Congressional Committees, the Federal Judiciary, and several foreign countries. He was Chief Actuary for the Social Security Administration during 1947-1970, Deputy Commissioner of Social Security in 1981- 1982, Executive Director of the National Commission on Social Security Reform in 1982- 1983, and Chairman of the Commission on Railroad Retirement Reform in 1988-1990. He is a consultant on Social Security to William M. Mercer, Inc., the National Association of Life Underwriters, and the American Association of Retired Persons. He is a past President of the Society of Actuaries and of the American Academy of Actuaries. He received LL.D. degrees from Muhlenberg College and Lehigh University and an M.S. degree from the University of Iowa.

SAMUEL H. PRESTON is Chair of the Sociology Department at the University of Pennsylvania and former Director of the Population Studies Center. His research has focused on formal demography and on mortality trends and determinants. He is past-President of the Population Association of America and member of the National Academy of Sciences, where he chairs the Committee on Population. Dr. Preston received a B.A. from Amherst College and a Ph.D. from Princeton University.

JOSEPH F. QUINN is a professor of economics and chair of the economics department at Boston College. He received his undergraduate education at Amherst College and his doctorate from M.I.T. He has been a visiting professor at the Institute for Research on Poverty in Madison, the Graduate School of Public Policy at Berkeley, and the Department of Economics at the University of New South Wales in Sydney. His research focuses primarily on the economics of aging, with emphases on the economic status of the elderly and the determinants of individual retirement decision.

ANNA M. RAPPAPORT is a Managing Director of William M. Mercer, Inc. She has a broad background in pension and benefits consulting, corporate research, and life insurance company management. She has taught graduate and undergraduate courses at the College of Insurance in New York, spoken at many professional meetings, and appeared in numerous seminars for Mercer clients.

Ms. Rappaport was a recipient of the ACME award for Literary Excellence in 1987. She is a graduate of the University of Chicago with a Masters of Business Administration degree. She is a Fellow the Society of Actuaries, a member of the American Academy of Actuaries and an Enrolled Actuary. She previously served as Vice President of the Society of Actuaries.

SYLVESTER J. SCHIEBER is the Director of The Wyatt Company's Research and Information Center in Washington, DC. He received a Ph.D. in economics from the University of Notre Dame in 1974. During his professional career he has specialized in the analysis of public and private retirement policy and health policy issues. Prior to joining The Wyatt Company in 1983, he served as the first Research Director of the Employee Benefit Research Institute in Washington, DC. Before that, he served as the Deputy Director, Office of Policy Analysis, Social Security Administration, and Deputy Research Director, Universal Social Security Coverage Study, Department of Health and Human Services.

MARC M. TWINNEY, JR. is the Manager of the Pension Department of the Ford Motor Company. Its pension fund liabilities exceed $16 billion. He holds the B.A. degree in Mathematics from Yale University, the M.B.A. degree in Finance from Harvard Business School, and is a Fellow of the Society of Actuaries. He is a member of the Conference of Actuaries in Public Practice, an Enrolled Actuary, a member and former board member of the American Academy of Actuaries, and a member of the Pension Research Council of the Wharton School. He has also been previously employed as a consultant by Hewitt Associates, Milliman and Robertson, and Hansen Consulting Actuaries.